Narrow Road to
the Deep North

Narrow Road
to the Deep North

A JOURNEY
INTO THE INTERIOR
OF ALASKA

BY KATHERINE MCNAMARA

MERCURY HOUSE
SAN FRANCISCO

Published in the United States by Mercury House, San Francisco, California, a nonprofit publishing company devoted to the free exchange of ideas and guided by a dedication to literary values. Mercury House and colophon are registered trademarks of Mercury House, Incorporated. Please visit our website at http://www.mercuryhouse.org.

United States Constitution, First Amendment: Congress shall make no law respecting an establishment of religion, or prohibiting the free exercise thereof; or abridging the freedom of speech, or of the press; or the right of the people peaceably to assemble, and to petition the Government for a redress of grievances.

Author photograph page 291 by Lucy Gray. Cover art by Jo Going.
Designed and typeset by Thomas Christensen. Proofread by Laura Harger. Additional editorial and production work by K. Janene-Nelson. Printed on acid-free paper and manufactured in the United States of America by Sheridan Books, Chelsea, Michigan.

Excerpts from this book have appeared in the following publications: *The Threepenny Review; The American Voice; Archipelago;* and *The Sacred Place/Witnessing the Holy in the Physical World,* edited by W. Scott Olsen and Scott Cairns (University of Utah Press). The stories by Peter Kalifornsky, translated by Katherine McNamara, appeared in: *Alaska Quarterly Review; New Voices in Native American Literary Criticism,* edited by Arnold Krupat (Smithsonian Institution Press); and *Northern Folktales,* edited by Howard Norman (Pantheon).

Additional permissions acknowledgments appear on page 292.

Library of Congress Cataloging-in-Publication Data:
McNamara, Katherine, 1946–
    Narrow road to the deep north : a journey into the interior of Alaska /
    by Katherine McNamara.
        p. cm.
    ISBN 1-56279-122-2 (pbk. : alk. paper)
        1. Athapascan Indians. 2. Alaska—Description and travel. 3. McNamara, Katherine, 1946–   4. Poets, American—20th century—Biography.
    5. Teachers—Alaska—Biography. I. Title.

E99.A86 M377 2001
917.9804′51—dc21

                                                                00-053699

To Lee Goerner

1947–1995

Days and months are travelers of eternity. So are the years that pass by. Those who steer a boat across the sea, or drive a horse over the earth till they succumb to the weight of years, spend every minute of their lives traveling. There are a great number of ancients, too, who died on the road. I myself have been tempted for a long time by the cloud-moving wind— filled with a strong desire to wander.

—Bashō, *The Narrow Road to the Deep North*

There are no uncivilized peoples; there are only different civilizations.

—Marcel Mauss

Contents

Author's Note

THIS BOOK IS a work of nonfiction set in Alaska between 1976, when the Alaska Pipeline boom was near its peak, and 1989, the year the world changed historically and, with it, our historical consciousness. The people, places, and events in it are real, and are described as they occurred; the names of towns (Anchorage, Fairbanks, McGrath) and rivers (the Yukon, the Kuskokwim, the Tanana, the Koyukuk) are as they appear on maps; but the names of most persons and all villages have been altered for the sake of what remains of their privacy. The late Peter Kalifornsky, the Dena'ina Athabaskan writer, is portrayed as himself. I drew upon certain conventions of fiction, and also of ethnography, reportage, memoir, and travel writing, though the work is meant as none of these: it is, somewhat after the fashion of the Japanese poet-diarist Bashō, the story of another kind of journey. The narrator, a version of myself as I was then, is a traveler drawn into the Alaskan bush, where she lived and worked as an itinerant poet, and where she learned a way to see the country.

Narrow Road
to the Deep North

Opening

ONE WINTER I was visiting in a small village on the edge of southwest Alaska. This was during a month of short days, sharp with cold, and iron-black, starry nights. For a companionable supper I was walking from the school, where I was lodged, to the teachers' house. The trail I followed lay to one side of the village, a community of families in thirty or so houses, with caches and outhouses, built low to the ground. Here and there oil lamps glowed through small-paned windows. The dogs had been fed, and were quiet; a light wind carried away the mumble of the generator. There was no sound but the *hough* of my breath and squeak of my boots on the snow. The village slipped behind my right shoulder; the blackness grew denser. From the heavens, the Great Bear pointed down to a spot not far off. Orion, the Hunter, strode along his own path. I lifted my hand in salute and in measure. Where it reached the height of my shoulder, the land ended: from there Orion rose. My hand arc'd above my head: so much of the sky he filled. Between us stood nothing taller than I. The village, turned in on itself, rested at my back. I was not from that place, only passing through; but just then I also was part of it. I walked on, watching Orion, my heart rising. The cold, its abstracting touch, braced the uncovered part of my face. I was walking beside Orion. The space between us was not empty, and through it I cleared a path that fitted my body exactly.

In my mind's eye I see that night again; now I see myself also. I see a human who is in proportion to the trail. I see the small village the trail is part of: the tundra they all sit upon: the great circle of the horizon: the vast inverted bowl of the night sky: and Orion, the Hunter. Orion is walking, endlessly, as he has done since he made his own trail. The village is the house of the body of people who have belonged to this place since their distant beginning. I am passing between school and teachers' house, buildings recently made, inhabited by people who come from the Outside and who, sooner or later, leave. Only for that moment am I there. Around my body the stars turn in their epic cycles; the people move surely in their seasonal rounds; the uneasy teachers sit, for a while, at the edge of town; and I live in that moment with Orion.

That is how I see, too, what follows in this book: in proportion. Here are these great and lesser cycles in their brief and recurring coincidences; here are the people and animals and spirits of that place; here are those who pass by at a tangent; here is a trail on which all converge for a moment. I am a human in proportion to that hard and beautiful night. All around me are the unending, lively, powerful beings of a full world whose story I have entered for a while.

Once I listened as a well-respected woman, an elder and, it was said, a woman of power, addressed a group of young women. "Long time ago, they told us stories," she said, "so we could learn how to become people." I will tell you what was told to me, and I will tell you what I saw there, at that time.

Part I

According to
Our Nature

It is a matter of transitions, you see;
the changing, the becoming must be cared for
closely.

—Leslie Marmon Silko, *Ceremony*

Something We
Do Not Know

I WANTED to learn this: how I could
tell a story and tell truth. These two virtues seemed, in my life, to be at odds
with one another. I did not believe they ought to be at odds, however, and
went looking for what else I needed to know.

But traveling has its own fascinations, and I loved them: the few small cases
you fit your belongings into, the curious people and the knowing people who
talk to you, the people who become your friends, cities and mountains, places
where the air is so pure you can no longer be sure what you are seeing. From
Paris, where my worldly education had begun, I went to Alaska. January 1976:
a cold winter. I thought Alaska would be a snow-covered, silent land.

o

ANCHORAGE IS a random city with a literal name. During the beginning of
this century it was assembled as a port and supply depot for the laying of the
Alaska Railroad, on a site where Turnagain Arm meets Cook Inlet. The inlet
was named for James Cook, the English explorer who sailed into the North
Pacific late in the eighteenth century: his ships carried him as far as the Arm,
where the mud flats and powerful bore tide of that shallow body turned them
back toward deep water. I arrived in Anchorage during the last days of the
trans-Alaska pipeline boom, just before the young middle-class professionals of my generation landed up there in number.

Anchorage liked to pretend it was a frontier city, but it was a raw town.
Ice-eyed men conducted their business in the bars over strong liquor or
strong coffee. Large, handsome women worked construction, waited on tables, danced naked in saloons not far from downtown. The notables who had
a say in public affairs ended their day in the Signature Room of the Westward
Hotel, where folk just in from the bush—some Native people were included
by then—mixed with the hiking-booted crowd from town. Oil men met at
the Petroleum Club or at the Captain Cook, the hotel built by Walter Hickel,
a land developer who had become governor, then Nixon's Interior Secretary.
Lawyers took the offices on K and L Streets that had prime views of the water
and mountains.

The downtown was small. Not all the streets were paved. Now and then,
moose ventured into people's backyards and even on to the Park Strip in the
center of the city. From the window of the liquor store on Fourth and D, in
the heart of the business district, a square red sign warned, with a wink and
a leer: NO WHORES ALLOWED.

Two hundred fifty miles northwest rose Denali, the tallest mountain in

North America. Like a sentinel or guardian he stood above the Alaska Range. He was not always visible to the city. When he appeared in the brief, crystalline light, people turned toward him for a moment and said his name gladly to one another, as if they needed his presence to counter the vastness and indifference of the land, and were grateful for it.

In the obituaries the average age of the dead was less than thirty. Someone said to me, "If you live up here for more than five years you're almost sure to lose someone: to an airplane crash, or the elements."

I was young enough and curious enough to think I could live by my wits. Life in the north was immediate, intense; physical in a way I had never lived before. People seemed exuberant at being so far from the Lower Forty-Eight, as they called the nation. They moved with the robust, sly, immigrant sense that Alaskans, because of oil money and optimism and energy, had a chance to start America again, and make something of her the right way.

Though they were strongly suspicious of it, the people were not yet separate from their government. They argued and discussed fundamental questions in their public life, and it was true that those questions drew out the deep conflicts that existed among themselves—boomers vs. conservationists, urban settlers vs. the bush, fundamentalist Christians vs. gays, Alaskans vs. the Texas oil men, to begin with—but they never called these class differences, for they did not yet separate themselves by income and education, and most of them made their living with their hands. In their public meetings they talked about whether, and how, to develop the state's renewable resources, because the oil and its money were not going to last forever; they knew that the oil consortium was important to the state's economy, though not many of them worried about the true extent of its power; they spoke in public, if uneasily, about the serious matter of land rights for Alaska Native people, who were not accepted as separate tribes; they argued about how the state and federal governments ought, or ought not, to supervise land and game management.

Anyone could have his say, and did. People called up the governor if they had something to tell him, and his wife might answer the phone; or they knocked on the door of the mansion in Juneau and talked to him directly. People knew one another by their first names. They didn't bend their necks to anyone, and took an American, self-defensive, pride in their individuality. The people who lived through a winter in Alaska, who decided to stick it out, were all in it together; and a newcomer, a Cheechako, an Outsider, had a chance to prove himself.

Sociology is not a story. You had to spend time, more than you thought, to learn what really went into a story. At a conference on the matter of justice in the bush, the attorney general of the state warned that popular notions about life in the rural areas were pipe dreams; that most folks in Alaska were afraid of the violence in their towns.

I wrote that last item in my notebook the first year, when I lived in Anchorage. I was twenty-nine and from the East, had been educated in history and the liberal arts, had lived abroad, and was traveling alone.

◐

HE WAS A MAN of the West, large-boned, watchful without appearing to be so, reticent about himself, eloquent about literature. He had worked both with his hands and with a cultivated mind. We talked about poetry. He taught me how to shoot a rifle and gave me a key to his excellent library. We became friends as, often, an older man and a younger woman do when they can open their minds, not their beds, to each other, and keep something unspoken between them.

He was not a drinking man, except for an occasional beer, and I drank hardly at all, but we often met in the Signature Room at the end of the day. He knew everyone but was careful whom he drank with, and he always picked up the bar tab. People who admired him thought he was generous, a big man who offered hospitality and gave them room to move in; but they were only half-right about him.

We drank coffee and talked about books, or about Alaska. Alaska filled all conversations, it grounded every subject. "This isn't the real Alaska," he would say. "Out in the bush there's something we don't know. You ought to go out there."

The question he always circled back to was this: You've stopped running, this is the last frontier, there is no place left to go: how do you live here, with respect for the land? Human and natural ecology were his themes, but he was of several minds about their connection.

One afternoon he had to run an errand and asked if I wanted to go along. He strode up Fourth Avenue, crossed D Street, and stopped at an army and navy store; poked through the bins until he found what he needed, and paid for it; and, unexpectedly, turned uptown again, toward the pawnshops and the Montana Club and the other down-and-outer bars. I had learned early not to ask him questions, to wait and see what would happen and figure out the situation for myself.

Some drunks were propped against the buildings and some drunks staggered on the sidewalk. Most of them were Native men. Even drunk they were graceful, balanced by some inner sense of gravity, like sailors on the deck of a boat in a heavy swell. He walked among them, a man who knew how to move without giving offense, but who could rely on his strength. I assumed he knew what he was doing and walked beside him, self-contained.

I don't recall if we went into the Montana Club; but we stopped at a bar like it and sat down at a table. I believe he ordered a beer for each of us and paid for them. We were the only white people in the place. Steadily, I kept my eyes on him: I couldn't see much more than shapes in the smoky, dreary shadows. One or two men muttered something hostile; the other drinkers left us alone. He made an ordinary remark to me, quietly, as if we were conversing.

A young man, half-shot, slid into the next chair and said loudly: "Hey, man, good to see you!" They shook hands and exchanged news. The young man was a little bleary, a little excessive, a little too grateful to be recognized. The big man sounded pleased to see him again, though his face gave nothing, neither pleasure nor pity, away.

The big man had lived for a time in a Yup'ik village along the coast of Bristol Bay, where he had been a teacher and, during summers, a commercial fisherman. Afterward, he had taught Native students in college, and took it as his duty to remain a friend to them long after they left the program. The young man called him a friend, effusively. The big man bent his head, as if to avoid hearing himself praised. He introduced the young man to me, and we said we were glad to meet one another. The young man explained (twice) what he was doing in Anchorage. The big man listened to him and at the end wished him well at it. He paused; the young man paused. With a slight shift in tone, yet still sounding cordial, the big man said we had to be going. The young man caught the tone instantly, closed down his effusiveness, and said good-bye. The big man left the change on the table.

As we walked toward his car, I said nothing. I had never known, and haven't known since, a man who could compel others with such courtesy, yet so completely, as he had done. He had the strength to face what he saw, without flinching; he spent time and energy trying to alter it to what might be better. His was the benevolence of the man who was in a position to act, in measure, with respect; but he wouldn't drink with the young man in the bar, and he paid the bill; and so the issue between them was something else, something deeper, that had settled into resentment and fury all but masked by the drinking and the polite exchange. The issue was power: who got to be the biggest man: but it was complicated, too, because of history, and there was always going to be an imbalance.

At that moment the social contract felt thin and tenuous. I could not tell what civility meant; and his steady, long-range gaze was disconcerting. A certain demeanor was required, a poker face, because he had just set me a test I thought was cruel to everyone caught in it, and I still had not passed it; and, half-annoyed but quite serious, I knew I had to pass it.

The people in the bars and on the streets seemed unhappy and far from home, and I did not know what, besides history, had brought them there. I didn't know about their lives or their homes. They had families somewhere. At last, deliberately, I said something low key: "Hard life," perhaps. I said I had seen drunks before, in the coal-mining valley I came from, where the main street of one town had fifty-two bars on it.

He gave me a hard, comradely hug; I came up short of his shoulder. "You're a good man, McNamara," he said.

Out on an Edge

THREE GIRLS whispering, their heads bent together: a white man has stopped to take a picture of them. This is the second day of Fur Rendezvous and many people have cameras. Instantly the eyes of one girl widen, and she murmurs to her friends. Delicately, she turns her back to the man and, swiftly, raises her hood. She is clothed in a parka so beautiful it draws stares. It is made of Arctic ground squirrel skins, with trim of wolverine and wolf tips and inlays of pieced calfskin. Her motion has revealed an inlay, chaste and simple, of black fur and white, on the back. The hood mantles her; its full ruff (her head is turned slightly) is wolf and wolverine.

The man takes his photograph. The three girls, laughing behind their hands, never looking at him, move away. The crowd ebbs and swirls festively along the street. The incident has taken less than a minute; the parka has vanished. This was my first glimpse of the bush.

◦

A WINTER AND a summer passed. One day in August 1978 I walked around the corner to say hello to a neighbor, a lawyer trying to reconcile his worldly ambition to ecological necessity. He was going out to inspect water-treatment plants in Yup'ik Eskimo villages along the Kuskokwim River; his client was a Yup'ik environmental group. They were going to sue the Public Health Service, which had installed the plants, and he was gathering evidence of malfunction. He asked if I wanted to go along. Yes, I said, and went out to buy a rubber raincoat and a fishing rod.

The chance came casually, as happenstance, an unexpected opening. The bush seemed still to be Indian Territory, though no one called it that; rather, a wary unease moved around beneath the surface of the city. Educated people felt it and could not quite define their discomfort, and it irritated them, it made them feel guilty, or nervous; later, it made them angry. They called the bush the Real Alaska, the Great Land, the Great Weather, a pristine wilderness, or they called it a place waiting to be developed, but something they could not come to grips with made them awkward about Alaska Natives. Their voices turned bright when they talked to a Native person, or softened to a mournful tone, or sounded faintly embarrassed, as if at their own good fortune. I could not place the sound then, but recognize it now: denial of emotion, memory suppressed, an unacknowledged disaster distorts the voice.

Their suspicion of newcomers, too, was on the rise. Though they were still warm to visitors, it was in the manner of their life to examine strangers, to find out what they wanted. During the oil boom, they had learned how quickly strangers bring changes they themselves could not manage. Now the boom was entering a decline. The wounds it had inflicted were visible on people's darkening faces. I watched them and developed a fretful, historical inhibition about the bush; it seemed to me whites were not welcome there, it was not our country. In the end, I decided to go only by invitation, a resolve that answered an uncertain conscience but limited my possibilities. I never had much money.

The lawyer and I flew out to the port of Bethel, on the Kuskokwim delta, where he had hired a guide and his boat. The two men laid in supplies, and we shoved off from the dock. For ten days we traveled up the long, brown Kuskokwim, the river flashing in the sun, coiling and uncoiling around its bends. We fished, and picked berries along cutbanks; at night we camped on sandbanks or a narrow shore. Beyond the immense river the tundra seemed to be without limit. It encircled us, and was inescapable.

One day we landed at another of the small Yup'ik villages that, intermittently, appeared along the banks. The guide, bored with us, went looking for a gambling game; the lawyer set out to find the mayor. I walked up from the beach. I was feeling aimless, a little shy, but also interested in being left on my own. I came upon a boardwalk, worn and silvered with age, and followed it through the high summer grass up the hill. It led to a gathering of log houses, small and weathered, with clotheslines strung from eave to eave. It was washing day. Every clothesline sagged: here hung a dozen softly faded flannel workshirts, there, twenty-nine pairs of jeans; over there, like birds on a wire, socks and socks and socks.

Around a corner trooped a crowd of children. They stopped short amid their giggles and stared at me. Their eyes sparkled in their sooty faces, their black hair shone in the sun.

"Hello."

"Hello." "Hello." They smiled back and in polite, husky voices, asked who I was, and how I had come to appear in their village. They said they had just been let out of Bible School. They introduced themselves, one by one, and told me how much they liked the songs they learned there.

I hardly understood what they said, but understood *them*. They spoke an English I had never heard before, atonal, without adjectives or adverbs, direct and clean. Their voices were sonorous, reedy as oboes. Their speech made a kind of aleatory music.

In a moment, hand in hand, the children and I were singing about Jacob's Ladder and dancing up the boardwalk.

I was not prepared for this. The sweet reality of it had nothing to do with what I may have supposed was there: the discordance knocked the sense out of me; my heart cracked open.

I MOVED SOUTH, to the end of the Kenai Peninsula, a rugged, sparsely settled area, though the Kenai was not the bush. People called it the city's play-
ground. On the weekends caravans of motor homes cruised down its lone
highway. But I came upon an isolated cabin outside of Homer, the nearest
town, and the owner, a real-estate agent, let me have it over the winter for fifty
dollars a month. A track led from the highway back to the property; whoever
went there walked in, or skied. The cabin stood about twenty yards from the
edge of a bluff, looking out to where Kachemak Bay met Cook Inlet. On fine
days the volcano on Augustine Island was visible, far down the water.

The cabin was wired for electricity and had a good stove, but no water,
unless I could locate the old springhouse. I packed in water in five-gallon jugs.
Down in the town lived people I had come to know; one of them, a woman
whose house had plumbing, let me shower there, and gave me dinner and conversation afterward.

I settled in, learning to live by fire. For a charm against the darkness, for
the autumn equinox had passed, I tacked broadsides on the walls and built
bookshelves, and the interior music of printed words silently filled the room.

That was a funny cabin, warm and tight when the stove was lit. A hard,
unsociable man, long gone from the area, or dead, had built it, and had built
it well. He was a nudist at home. Before the highway was paved he used to
deliver mail around the Peninsula: I found his old Jeep, rusted, gutted, buried
in weeds and snow. It was told how he had a Mexican mail-order wife, but
she had rarely been seen in Homer. No one knew, anymore, what had happened to them.

The stove burned coal. Veins of lignite seamed the face of the bluff. The
man who built the cabin used to winch himself over the edge and gouge the
coal out; now, erosion caused it to crumble onto the beach. Periodically, the
group of friends and I went down to the beach for a coaling party. One of
the men had a pick-up truck and, agreeably, delivered loads of brown coal to
our doors. I had an axe, also, and was just dexterous enough with it (I thought
wryly) to be able to chop kindling. On very cold mornings I chopped kindling inside, by the door.

I liked to tramp around the bluff looking for signs of habitation. One afternoon, I set off to find the old springhouse, and spent a peaceful hour
climbing around the hill back of the cabin. The snow was crusty and dented.
I was following moose sign. A cow moose lived on the bluff; now and then
she followed my ski track, not having to break trail for herself. Her trail led
lightly, disturbing little, through the arm-like branches of a willow thicket. I
went crashing through the willows: "old woman's wood" it was called, easy
to gather, light to carry.

I came out near the edge of the bluff, beside a windlass frame; it must have
been the one the man had used to winch himself down the face of the cliff.
I sat on the frame and looked out through binoculars over the blue bay. It was
tanner crab season. Even under magnification the boats were tiny: twelve

crabbers, rolling in the waves. The waves seemed not to move, but lay like coarse watercolor paper washed azure and marine blue. Clusters of black dots danced before my eyes: ducks, parties of fifteen and twenty, bobbing, visiting, riding comfortably on that sparkle.

Out of the bay moved a long tanker, its bow wave curling off the hull. It ran straight and true from my left to right, waves tossing aft, driving inexorably toward a path of sunshine so bright on the water I could not bear to look at it. The ship steaming into the glimmering sea disappeared for the minutes it took to cross over into the calmer water beyond. I swung the glasses toward Mount Augustine.

It was clear back there, except for a slender line of fog about halfway up the cone of the volcano. For the first time I saw the drilling rig, out in the inlet. The mountain on the horizon dwarfed it: it was only a small spot in the ocean; but it was big enough to catch my eye without the glasses, easily as big, on that scale, as all twelve of the rolling fishing boats. I considered its weight in a sentence: amid the ocean, the impermeable mountains, the open sky, *drilling rig* sounded lovely. There were the twelve boats, hauling in crabs; and there was the single rig, pounding through the floor of the inlet. What was the real relation between them, there in those nursery beds of crab and shrimp, treacherous waters full of halibut, salmon, seals, whales: what did that rig, sitting like a water strider, mean to the living ocean? It was pumping, pumping, pumping, pumping the black residue of ancient beings. The beautiful blue bay: a mirage above the deep black oil springs. New lives for old.

o

WHEN NEW SNOW fell on the bluff, the light was milky, with a faint tinge of gray. Unable to see the edge of the cliff, I lost the senses of distance and time. I walked out behind the house and watched the quiet snow fuzz the ridgeline. The yellow window of the cabin cheered me. Any tiny signs of settlement were pleasing then. I found I wanted the sound of other human voices.

Down in the town was a cafe where I liked to sit and write and listen to the daily chat. The morning was still fresh, and the coffee wasn't too bad.

A pair of long-haired workmen, drifters with the season, sat at the next table talking loudly about the gruesome things people found in food. "Woo! Imagine stickin' yer fork in the salad and bringin' it up with a big ol' potato bug stuck to it, his legs kickin'." There was the guy who fell in the Campbell Soup pot, or the one who found a thumb in the hot dog package.

The waitress, whose face was young and open, asked me what I was writing and was pleased and excited when I told her, a short story.

The drifters were going strong. "... Nigs," said one. "Saw a bunch in the Porpoise Room the other night. Couldn't get over it."

The young waitress, her face still, refilled my cup.

The man laughed, *Haw, haw,* to his buddy. The White People's Party put out phony five-dollar bills, he said: "Inside, it's a boat ticket to Africa." He had dropped one "by mistake" on the bar floor next to one of Them. Watched the fella eye it, then bend quick and pick it up, look inside. Tear it up in disgust.

"Love to see that. Works every time."

There were lots of Them in Anchorage. The drifters discussed where They came from as if Their presence were an invasion.

○

A STORM BLEW IN. That night, a friend who wrote for the local paper and I went to the movies. When we came out of the theater, everything had stopped: wind, snow, noise. The stars were enormous. We drove toward his house, parked, and skied in along the lake. Behind us another storm was moving in, rubbing out the stars, swathing the sky. In the morning, the snow lay thick and baffling on the house and yard.

The storm sat tight upon the bay. The wind was whiplike. The waves, gray-green and as urgent as sex, pounded on the riprapped shore. The storm was a fog taking up all the old, clear air into it. Everything had changed shape: the outlines of wooded ridges and the roof-tops were dark strokes, India ink on hand-laid paper.

Four-wheel-drive vehicles and skiers got around most easily. In the cafe the morning crowd grinned and said, "Some storm, eh!" They compared it to the big storm of '54, or last year, when it had rained all the time.

The day before the storm hit, Homer had had its first official stick-up. A man from Kenai had pulled a gun on a woman in one of the liquor stores. The woman had looked at the gun and said, "You've got to be kidding." Her husband, who was behind the counter, had said, "No, I don't think he is," and handed over the money.

A customer was talking to a waitress about it. Her voice twanged above the easy-going hubbub. "Homer's getting bad," she was saying. "Used to be you could leave your house open. The only thing was that guy who used to break in to the drugstore. Marvin What's-his-name. You know where he is now? In jail over in Kodiak. I did three days for drunk driving over there. Three days is automatic now. Used to be only two. You go in at noon on one day and get out two days later. You know what he did? Raped a woman and stole her purse—"

The waitress, middle-aged and graying, interrupted knowledgeably: "He's a heroin addict, you know."

"He is? Well, you know: they let him off on the rape charge. His wife had a new baby and he was showing so much progress. I worked with her in the cannery. Kinda slow you know, but nice—You know, I wanted to get my hair done tomorrow, but I didn't make an appointment."

○

I STAYED IN TOWN for most of the week, until the sky cleared, and then went back out to the bluff. One evening I climbed into my sleeping bag with a book. I was beginning to drowse when there came a tiny stir, a scrabbling, a brisk, efficient chewing sound. I burrowed deeper and left the light on all night.

In the morning I found specks of droppings near the wood chips inside the door. I checked the canisters of flour and Irish oatmeal, and the bread-bag, but none of them had been touched.

It may be a vole, the reporter suggested, when I asked him what he knew about rodents: They live in the fields, but in winter they like a warm place, and creep into cabins. I had never lived with an animal before. A house mouse lives with me now, I thought, smiling to myself.

But I couldn't say we lived with one another, really: it went on its rounds, invisible to me, making small whisking, comforting sounds; on my part, I wished it well and didn't get in the way.

I stayed well into the winter and wrote. Poetry was coming, and I wanted to be alone with it for a while.

o

THE RADIANT CHILDREN. I wanted to hear their laughing speech again. In their mouths lived another music, an English spoken at the farthest reaches of its home. As though the first word had been sounded in them: stripped clean of all that was not needed. Surrounded by silence.

I had loved the work of the tongue, the formation of shaped sound; the play of talk, the ardor of discussion; the construction of an idea through ar-gument: the youthful seizing of the world with thought. All this I had to learn to leave behind.

In the cabin, I worked slowly, word by word, training my body to accept silence.

Day by day, life proceeded. Experimentally, I began to call myself a poet. I accepted as true and interesting the condition that I did not know what words meant—*cold*, for instance, or *heart*. I called myself a poet; I wanted to go to the bush. I speak of two unities: a land; a consciousness. Different kinds of unities, forming at vastly different paces; going to touch each other.

o

AN INVITATION CAME from a new school district up in the Interior, in Athabaskan country, to teach poetry to Native children. I was asked to spend a month traveling among four villages along the Yukon River. I would get around by bush plane. The handful of teachers out there would look for me after freeze-up.

I knew next to nothing about the children. What did *Athabaskan* mean? The most I could say was, another way of living than mine.

It was not easy finding information about Athabaskans. The word, used as their name, referred also to the large group of closely related languages they spoke, which were related further to Navajo and Apache, Southern Athabaskan tongues. The Athabaskans were composed of many small tribes of Indians—neither Eskimos nor Aleuts—living in villages scattered throughout the great forests of the Interior from south-central Alaska north to the Brooks Range and east all the way into Canada. In Anchorage they tended to cluster in low-rent apartments and trailer courts away from the center of town. No white people I knew had lived in Athabaskan country; few had traveled there. On the whole, the sense conveyed of them was their "shyness," their "reclusiveness," their Otherness. They were seldom mentioned in the newspapers. A museum exhibit called them, oddly, the "Strangers of the North."

One person who had been to their country was the big man who had opened his library to me. His enthusiasm for the history of North American Indians was large. His shelves held excellent volumes containing the accounts of men who had lived through the loss of their old way of life and the forced coming of the new, and those of men who had witnessed it, and who had made it happen. The big man, patient with the untested newcomer he had befriended, advised: Read everything, but don't make up your mind yet. Wait and see. When you're out there, observe everything.

After freeze-up I flew out to the Yukon villages. When I recall the journey I can envision nothing; what became memory came later. A few notes surface: *This is magical country, the pulse quickens. The mighty river, frozen and immobile. Rolling hills covered in birch and willow, as far as the eye can see from the plane. Here and there a handful of cabins scattered against a hillside, ribbons of smoke rising from the chimneys. At ground level the forests are mysterious, full of invisible animals. The children are gravely welcoming. A new face is welcomed by them, if it doesn't scowl.*

In fact I observed nothing. The notes contain no descriptions of people, no glimpses of animals: only clichés, a reference to mystery, and an early insight into what children had to face. Whatever I had seen can be called neither accidental nor essential: it was all sensation, merely one thing after another, and I knew nothing about what it meant. Not one person or thing I can think of made me want to go back.

But—how to describe this, so long afterward?—I wanted to go back. I did not know what I had seen; but I had seen something. In those Athabaskan forests I had felt a cold slow shiver. I had recognized a presence that I could not name. Something waited for me; it lay below the level of words. I wanted to know. Silently, I promised: *Whatever happens I will see through to the end.* I was going to be required to learn patience, to observe carefully, and remain alert. This knowledge was inexplicable, intuitive, a movement in the heart.

○

IN ANCHORAGE, I used to go down to the edge of Cook Inlet to watch the sun set. In winter, the sun barely cleared the horizon; it set in midafternoon.

The tide rolled in along the mud flats, shifting small boulders of black ice that lay scattered along the water line. I used stand and stare across the inlet at the mountains. Susitna, a dormant volcano called the Sleeping Lady, rose from the water. Behind her a wall of peaks, dense and remote, lined the far shore: the Alaska Range, marching up the Alaska Peninsula, north to Denali. The low winter sun shone pink on their snowy flanks.

What kind of world lay behind them? Who were the people whose home they guarded? What were the animals of that country? I was a stranger to the North, and felt it acutely; and nothing I knew offered a hint of the reality that lay far beyond myself.

A story like this is filled with what is called coincidence, or accident, or luck; but that agency, that form of convergence, could be also described this way: You long for something, and you are given to find what matches it.

It looked as if I could make some minimal kind of living. A man at the state arts council arranged a residency in a Dena'ina village located about two hundred miles across water and mountains from Anchorage, behind the Range on the Alaska Peninsula and accessible only by bush plane. The Dena'ina, I was told, were a loosely federated group of small, Athabaskan groups who lived around Cook Inlet, from the foothills of the Alaska Range to the mouth of the Susitna River, and on down the Kenai Peninsula. They were "salt-water people," beluga whale-eaters.

The village I was going to visit, however, was in the area called the Kijik country, which lay inland behind the Alaska Range. In the old days, it was said, the Dena'ina who lived along the inlet used to walk across those icy mountains to visit their neighbors back in the Kijik country.

In the old orthographic convention the Dena'ina were named the Tenaina or the Tanaina. In a volume of physical anthropology, in a quotation taken from an American report about them, I came upon a glimpse of those old people. In 1891, a party of explorers led by one Alfred B. Schanz had traveled up the Nushagak River into the land of the Tenaina. Their expedition was the "first documented exploration" of the country north of Bristol Bay in the "American period." The Tenaina were among the hundreds of small clan-and-family-based tribes of Athabaskans; they were the southernmost of those tribes in Alaska.

Whatever else he may have been, Schanz was a good reporter. His journey had been sponsored by *Frank Leslie's Illustrated Newspaper.* For the paper he reported the following:

On that memorable Sunday (February 15, 1891 . . .) we wearily trudged over the ice in search of inhabitants, for, through days of delay caused by snow-storms and blizzards, we were sadly reduced in supplies both for ourselves and our dogs; in fact a number of the latter had already starved to death. Clark and I had no idea of the kind of people we would find but naturally supposed that they would be outposts of the coast Eskimos. When eventually, by a strange piece of good fortune, we were discovered by a native who had been looking after his traps and rushed to meet him, we found a handsome, well-built, athletic-looking young fellow, with fine, velvety black eyes and a laughing, rosy-cheeked, reddish-brown complexion. He was extremely vivacious, gesticulated a great deal, and addressed us with wonderful volubility in a strange language. None of our party could understand a word of his tongue, although I recognized a strong resemblance in the language to that spoken by the Tanana Indians, a language akin to Tanaina.

I was surprised most, however, by the fact that our new friend contrasted very favorably with our Eskimo. His dress consisted of a curious but sensible combination of jeans and furs, and looked clean and neat. With his lively disposition he did not spend much time in palaver after he found that we could not understand him, but started off on a graceful run ahead of our dogs evidently to show us the way to his village. Sure enough a brisk dash of a couple of miles over smooth ice, a short turn into the mouth of a river, and a helter-skelter climb up a low bank brought us into the very middle of a typical Alaskan Indian village. It was indeed a surprise, and I almost imagined that I had been miraculously transferred to the shaman's village on the Yukon. A score or more of fine-looking young men, with their inborn native courtesy, bade us welcome, at the same time, like children, examining our persons, or clothing, and our sledges and weapons with the greatest curiosity. It took us only a few minutes to ascertain that the chief of the village knew a few words of Eskimo and a few of Russian, so that with the aid of considerable pantomime we managed to make ourselves approximately understood.

The headman of the village wore cowhide top boots and a blue swallow-tailed coat with brass buttons, probably many years ago the dress uniform of some Russian officer. A number of others who received us also had one or two articles of civilized raiment. The houses and fish caches were neatly built of hewn logs and planks, the houses having windows made of tanned skins of mountain sheep intestines. The whole village bore an air of respectability and cleanliness almost startling to one accustomed to the filth of Eskimo huts. This impression was further advanced when, upon entering the chief's house, we found it floored with carefully hewn planks and heated by an old-fashioned Russian box stove with four holes for cooking. The chief had also built himself a bunk for sleeping, a table and several benches. Soon the teakettle was singing on the little stove, and before long we were stimulating ourselves with an infusion of fragrant tea, which the chief personally had served in some fancy china cups, of the possession of which he seemed very vain. His squaw also laid before us some excellent dried salmon, very clean and of a delicious flavor. All these surprising circumstances contributed much to our astonishment. We afterwards learned that these Indians had been accustomed to secure articles of

civilized comfort and luxury through intertribal commerce from the trading posts on Cook Inlet. The chief himself had repeatedly visited posts on
the inlet, having even gone as far as the store on Kinik Bay.[1]

I needed to know how to act among the people I was about to visit. If we
learn manners by instruction and observation, then my only source was
Schanz's account, for at least he had written about human beings. But that
had been a century ago. What had replaced people, in the writings then current, were two related tropes: things, and an idea.

Archaeologists and physical anthropologists, whose site research had been
done between the 1930s and the 1960s, were, by official consensus, considered
the closest observers of Native peoples. They had published monographs
that were catalogs of material goods, things the indigenous people had made
and abandoned, or buried.

In their schema, native Alaskan tribes were best defined by weapons and
tools, clothing and household goods—things—made from animal skins,
bones, wood, stones: local materials. These things, collected and classified
into a hierarchy of complexity of technique (a particularly American fasci-
nation), they then defined as "Native material culture." Next, they classified
these "cultures"—meaning the various Eskimo and Indian tribes—into a
parallel hierarchy, of authenticity, defined as adherence to "traditional" "material culture." In genuine sorrow they agreed that the Alaskan peoples had
lost these (attributed) traditions. They agreed that Athabaskans, Eskimos,
and Aleuts had "forgotten" how to live off the land, as they used to know
how to do, and now lived in diminished ways. These scholars called the Native people, those who remained, who had guided and taught them, "informants." Cornelius Osgood, in his *Ethnography of the Tenaina*, was so moved by their
reduced state that he wrote:

> Of native arts little or nothing has survived. Many of the younger Tanaina
> have even lost much of the traditional forest lore, *so commonly thought of as the
> essence of Indian heritage.*
>   ... Economically, it might be said that the Tanaina had a capitalistic so-
> ciety, with a peculiarly emphasized prestige mechanism, the giving away of
> wealth according to a ritualized social pattern, the potlatch. They were
> overwhelmed by a more developed capitalism and one in which prestige
> centered not so much in the distribution of wealth as in its acquisition.
> The Tanaina radicals, accepting the new system, made short work of the
> property-distributing conservatives, but only to find themselves at the bot-
> tom of the scale of the new order, against which their aboriginal training
> provided little with which to compete.... Culturally speaking, the real
> Tanaina are dead or dying. There are no more cremation fires. The relatives
> of the deceased stand beside an open grave watching the interment of the
> loved one. Tragic is the watch they keep on a father who has seen the last

of his children. It is not a personal thing, it is the end of a nation. Behind their sobs is the recognition of defeat. In their desperation they love each other so.[2] [emphasis added]

These Tenaina were the people—the Dena'ina—whom I was going to visit. Their suffering was bitter. History had spoken harshly to them, and Osgood—it seemed—had written their obituary.

It is well to remember that academic studies are composed in a private language, following specialized rubrics and agendas that are most easily accessible to those instructed in their intricacies. But ideas and categories are easily cut loose from their intellectual moorings. They float away on the jetsam-thick tide of public opinion and private interests. The always-astonishing idea that Alaska Natives could be classified by their *things* had lost its specialized, academic sense and been transformed into a kind of idea about "culture." Somehow this "idea" had passed into the common talk of Alaskan public life and become an axiom, repeated and unquestioned, that "Alaska Natives have lost their culture." An insidious idea; for if a people have lost their culture, and if you are stronger than they are and want what is left to them, that is, their land, then their claim to it is made tenuous, and you can move in as you like.

❂

THE PARIS I had left was the city of Barthes, Lacan, Lévi-Strauss, Foucault, of Jakobson and the émigré Prague school of linguists, torturing syntax; city of airy, brilliant conversations of those brilliant, troubling men. I had been among the crowds at lectures given by Lacan and Foucault. Studious, dazzled, not convinced. I had interviewed great anthropologists, Lévi-Strauss, Dumont, Soustelle. The library of Marcel Mauss, housed in the Musée de l'Homme, was open to me; Mauss, student of religions, ethnologist of tribal peoples, remarkable for never having to leave Paris to understand the nature of human societies. I had become interested in his teacher, the great but ignored Meillet, philologist of non-Indo-European languages. I had read Mauss's beautiful studies of Oceanic religions.

Read: but not very closely. I lost interest in my unfledged academic career. Paris was convincing itself, insistently, that narrative had ended, that the intention of the writer should be ignored. Literature had become the Text: texture, textile, cloth cut to fit the fashion. Clever ideas, that I couldn't assimilate. (But why did they write those airless novels; and why did their theories, gorgeous as fireworks, separate words from things?) I hadn't enough experience—enough life—to say why I thought this. And, my thoughts about Mauss and Meillet were not quite formed, but already were contrary to fashion.

But in Alaska, having read Europeans, and assessed their (problematic) loyalties to their own civilizations, their monotheistic religions, I recalled the intricate connections between their social sciences, anthropology especially, and European colonialism. And I could not help thinking the American scholars were disconnected from any historical or social consciousness at all.

Every year more Americans came north. The federal and state governments were expanding. An international consortium of oil companies dominated the state's economy. The new Native corporations, organized under the authority of the recent Land Claims Settlement Act, were in the process of re-acquiring areas of their homelands; these lands covered an enormous area of the state. Life was "changing": everyone's life was changing; even Alfred B. Schanz had noticed it, eighty years before. Alaskan Native peoples long since had learned from the outside world, as it touched them, and had adapted their knowledge to local use. Their real tradition, if we could have but noticed, was the close study of all that appeared in their world.

It would have been difficult not to notice that the new social scientists took jobs in government or industry, or at the state university. What of their "objectivity"? In their work they rarely attempted serious critical analysis of the economic and political status quo, nor did they question, at least not publicly, the current methods of analysis.[3] Perhaps this should not have been a surprise.

Drawing upon the growing number of professional studies, Alaskan civic leaders—among them the big man—declared that the Native peoples were no longer hunters and gatherers, and insisted that Natives, like the drunken men I saw on the street, were being absorbed into what was called, euphemistically, the "cash economy."

What could it mean, that whole peoples, nations, had "lost their culture"? How had so many people "forgotten" their skills in the forests? It seemed that impersonal forces—acquisitive capitalism, migration—were responsible. But, what had happened to all their land? They didn't live on reservations. Had their government and laws been set aside? If Indians couldn't hunt anymore, why was that; were they no longer Indians? Were there any "true" Dena'ina left? Who said so, and on what authority?

○

IN 1974 PETER BROOK had established his acting company in Paris, in a stained and peeling warehouse, the Bouffes du Nord. By some great luck I saw his first production, the great version of *The Trojan Women* devised by André Serban and Elizabeth Swados. In that grim, bare space I stood uncomfortably among the audience—there were no seats; it was theater-in-the-round, around us—as Greek soldiers marched through us to the walls of Troy. How can I evoke that astonishing experience? Swarms of actors shouting, whispering, singing, mourning in babel-languages: harsh consonants of warriors taking women as prizes; the sibilance of snaked-draped Helen, the trophy recovered; Hecuba's piercing cries as her young grandson, horror-struck Andromache's little boy, is thrown from the precipice, as a nameless Weaver throws her shuttle, a curved knife, across the warp of her loom and into herself. Evocation of the theater as sacred space filled with bodies and language: garble, mimicry, onomatopoeia; derangement of the senses. We the audience lived during those hours as near as the Chorus to the terrifying drama of war enacted by gods and humans. We felt ourselves suffering, and mourning; and felt that emotion shaped by its performance. I shudder, recalling it; it was my first experience of performance as art, as composed representation, an art representing complex emotional truth in a semblance of time and space. I shivered and wept at something real; but what was it? What was the emotional truth I had recognized? I was young, and did not know.

Overcome, I had fled—home—to the New World, away from the Europe of wars and decadent civilization; outward, into the immense space of America.

I put the anthropological studies aside. Underneath their professional jargon they encouraged in their reader an idea about Indians. They told a story whose plot was death and inevitable loss; I had left that plot behind. I needed to know about living people: what they ate, wore, thought, said; what they hoped for; what they dreamed; who their children were: I was going to be giving poetry to their children. I wanted a writer's shock of experience, a recognition of complexity, a real account of what it was like out there.

I put some books of poetry in a bag, extra clothes in my canvas pack, and drove up to Anchorage.

○

I PULLED INTO the gas station in Sterling and went into the cafe for a cup of coffee. A sign above the door advertised SQUAW CANDY FOR SALE. It meant alder-smoked salmon was available.

A middle-aged white man sat at the table. He looked like a local, a man with faded eyes and drab clothes who blended into the dim light. He had kind eyes, in fact, though I didn't see them at first. He asked if I was a bill collector.

"No," I said.

Pause.

"A real estate agent?"

"No." Pause. "Are you asking what I do, or are you hiding out?"

He smiled. "A little of both, I guess. Are you married?"

"No," I said.

"Would you like to be?"

"No."

"Well, that's my pass."

I poured my coffee from the Bunn machine, smiled to remove any threat, and told him I was a writer.

He began to talk. He told, as people always did, about his life. The man was avid for a listener: his face grew younger as he spoke. He said he was new in Sterling; he had come over from near McCarthy, looking for a job. He said something about being married, then qualified it, and I knew he meant he was living with a Native woman. Behind him stood a young man who looked Athabaskan, and he said, "My stepson. We don't look alike, do we?"

Cautiously I said: "Well, his hair's longer," and smiled again.

He relaxed a little, and I did, too. I didn't want him to be ashamed of the woman: I felt fierce about this.

He shook his head and talked quickly, as if he needed to explain and did not have much time.

The woman was Athabaskan; she came from the Ahtna region, by Copper River. He said, "The stories she tells! If you could only hear the way she tells them. Things that are gone now, things from her childhood that we'll never see. I can't tell it the way she can, you should hear her. Oh, she's tough and she's ornery as the devil, but I wouldn't trade her for anyone. Our kids, though, they hardly know the old life."

His eyes blurred. "The kids in school let them know," he said, "they call them 'Indians.' They don't know what the kids mean." His voice almost caught.

I looked away until he had control of himself, then said, softly, "People have had to go through so much. At least they don't get their mouths taped anymore when they speak their language."

His wife came in then. She was a tiny woman. At once his gaze flattened and withdrew, and he turned to her. They went off together.

I recognized the protocol for avoiding a jealous scene: the man, animated, talking to me and then, later, passing me in the parking lot with no sign of recognition.

The Mouse Mother

THE MAIL PLANE had made a bumpy landing on a lane of gravel scraped across the brow of a hill. A hard wind was blowing across frozen, rutted ground. There was no snow. I stood still, elated, and braced my back against the wind, to see where I had landed. The whole northern quarter was mountains, wild and serene, as immanent, as formal, as a Chinese landscape painting. Down the western meridian ran a line of spruce-covered hills. East of the airstrip, at the foot of a long slope, lay a long, narrow, frozen lake whose surface was dull as the clouded sky. The settlement on its shore was called Village Below, a contraction in English of its Dena'ina name, which described intricately the geography of the lake, and yet, I was told, meant something like, Small Lake Below a Bigger Lake. The latter was a beautiful lake near the ancestral village, unseen from here, in the wild northern mountains.

Across the gray ice the land swept back and upward into a saddleback pass. Beyond the pass glimmered white peaks, a thrilling glimpse of the Alaska Range, barely visible against the sky. As far as I could see was land so fresh it seemed newly made. I thought: This is the center of the world.

The plane took off. The agent loaded my gear on his cargo sled and said, kindly, that he would leave it at the teachers' house. If I followed the road down the hill through the village I would come to the school. I thanked him, hefted my bookbag, and started walking.

Outlying log houses came into sight, weather-worn, roofs sagging. The village was clusters of newer, board-sided houses arranged along a road. It was early afternoon. No one was visible. The air was silent; sharply so, as though something listened. A faint throbbing rose through my boot soles from under the road. I was too excited, and shivered; and my steps fell more lightly.

o

THE PUBLIC SCHOOL was a pair of dented house trailers propped on skids on a bare lot in the center of the village. A new building, under construction since summer, remained unfinished, and four teachers and forty-odd students were making do with these battered shelters. In the beginning I went from school to the teacher's house and back again. I was learning the names and faces of students. They, in turn, studied me. My first impressions dissolved in that artificial life and were replaced by new ones; and these, too, dissolved and were replaced.

In school I caught little sense of the village itself. I wanted to meet parents, face to face. I boarded with one of the secondary school teachers, Nancy Sigurd, who rented a house trailer on the lake side of the main road. One evening after dinner on the second or third day, she said she had to visit someone in the village and asked if I wanted to go along. People didn't mind if strangers came to their homes? No, she said, they like visitors.

By flashlight we found our way to the end of the road and stopped at a small log house. Mike Fitka's, she said, and knocked on the inside door. Inside, a man stood up from his worn chair to greet us. He looked sturdy, yet weary and hard-used by weather; he was like his house. Nancy introduced me. We sat down at the kitchen table, and his wife quietly set out tea cups. Nancy chatted with her, brightly, as though the woman couldn't hear, and soon she went away into another room. Nancy smiled and waited for Mike Fitka to speak.

He asked her simply for the chance of learning. He wanted to discover his reading level, and then to take home-study courses for a general equivalency degree. With his work, he said, he had no time for classes. He made a living as a fisherman and mechanic, and he believed he was a clear-thinking man, yet he felt held back in his job opportunities because he had only gone through grade school.

He brought out a gilt-edged dictionary and showed it to us. He consulted it when he wrote letters, he explained, so that people would not think him uneducated, and ignore him. He apologized: Maybe he should not bring up the possibility of GED classes so often; but it seemed that the squeaky wheel got the grease, and that it was necessary to keep requesting what he needed. His wife had not even been to grade school, he added, and he thought it would be good for her to be able to read the newspapers, she would enjoy that. Besides, he said, it is every citizen's right, or so he was told, to have a high school education.

It was clear that he did not wish to be thought rude by insisting, but his desire was fair, and his determination seemed firm.

His son sat at the table under the light of the hissing Coleman lantern, pretending to devour a book; but he never turned a page. He listened intently as his father spoke. He was one of the eight students who were going out the following month on a school trip to New York and Washington.

The next day, the principal told me that Mike Fitka had asked for the GED courses before, and had not come to class. The teachers, he said, used to hold "adult night" every week; no one came, or very few people did.

"I'm all burned out from setting up programs and not having them work," he said, not crossly. He had nothing more to say.

What did the earnest man, who consulted his dictionary so as not to be thought ignorant, desire to learn? He talked of home study; the principal talked of classes. What did school do for people in the bush? Were they embarrassed to go there? Why, I wondered, did so many adults not read or write?

IN ORDINARY WAYS the high-school students were like teenagers anywhere: the cliques and their leaders, the lines of authority and conformity, the shifting pull-and-resistance between teachers and students were obvious. Their courses were the same as those taught, but out of context, in any mediocre public high school. Reading levels were low; student writings, dull. These children had apparently read almost no literature, certainly no poetry except "haiku." Even their handwriting was childish. Yet in class they seemed to me bright and alert. For what were they being prepared? Where was the pleasure of learning found?

The library was pitiful. I had brought my own, both books and pages copied, and from these I read aloud to the students; no better way to transmit the stuff of poetry. Ted Hughes, John Haines, John Clare; Howard Norman's delicate translations of stories of the Swampy Cree; "The Bear" by Galway Kinnell. Lovely versions of Netsilik Eskimo songs, translated by the ethnomusicologist Tom Johnson. I read poems to them by Native American writers: Leslie Silko, Simon Ortiz, Joy Harjo. Good, necessary, not sufficient; the readings did not engage my students: something else distracted them.

High school classes met in one of the trailers. The room was chaotic: books had been dumped on shelves, boots and skates scattered against the wall, things piled and piled up without order. Grease blocked the sink and water wouldn't drain. Through the walls the generator hummed, low and everlasting. The teacher had gone off to drink coffee. The students were composing. I sat by the window and wrote in my notebook, and pretended to ignore the giggles and cellophane-rattling as they opened candy wrappers, and the skitter and swish of pencils crossing out and erasing. If I raised my head, sun poured into my left eye.

After class, a girl named Karen approached and asked, diffidently, if I wanted to read her paper. Of course, I said. Now? Yes.

I sat down and read a finely thought-out, lyrical essay on freedom. She had described the sunny day in loving detail; then described how it felt to be cooped up in darkness, in school all day, like a caged bird.

Like a caged bird. I looked at her face. It was pretty, intelligent, still unformed, a teenaged face; in her eyes was knowledge that made her resistant, but also petulant. She knew, was beginning to know, how to write, to compose and to think: but this school, I guessed, was not going to do enough for her, when she needed an education. In her theme flashed a spirit that ought to be protected from rote obedience and the limits of the narrow curriculum, from its dulling effect on the mind. She was fighting it in her own way, the only way she had; she was going to face trouble because of that.

The imagination is so strong, and is so terribly fragile, easily wounded, quickly put to sleep. Yeats cautioned that we must take care with the young: Only encourage, he said, encourage the young poets. The young, who need all that poetry can give them: a truth, spoken and unbreakable; the sound of a clear voice; astonishments of language formed and informed by its content;

the rigor of that form. They need its beauty. They can, themselves, make poems: *poiētēs,* from the Greek, means "maker." They love to make, and they want to make their poems well. They would see what poets had made; they would listen to what they themselves had made. I would say, and keep saying, yes to them.

The wind, an east wind, tore at the trailer. Out on the lake, the ice melted, froze, melted: flashing sheet-ice, green water riffling in the wind. It was only the surface forming and reforming; beneath it, the ice was solid, and went deep.

○

THE OLD LADIES liked to go ice fishing. They sat out on the lake, each one beside her ice hole, bundled in down parkas and leggings, stolid as boulders against the snow. Near darkness, they drove their snowmachines home, packing buckets of forty or fifty grayling on the sleighs behind them. Janet Alexey, who taught in the preschool, told me she never had that kind of luck. Once she had fished with her auntie out of the same ice hole, and her auntie had pulled in all the fish. She laughed at herself and marveled, "Those old ladies. They must be talking to those fish." The old women were out on the ice every day when the grayling were running. They stuck spruce bushes in their fishing holes to keep them open overnight. A small copse of spruce bushes had sprung up on the ice.

Afterward, I made a poem about the old ladies on the ice. An Aleut man, hearing it in Kodiak, suggested, "They must have learned about the spruce bushes from the muskrats." I read the poem in Bethel and told the audience what the Aleut man had thought. Bethel is on the tundra; the horizon is a great circle, and there are no trees in sight for hundreds of miles. A Yup'ik man murmured, surprised, "That's how they learned it!"

A poem carries layers of knowledge within itself, and leaves knowledge in its wake. On the level of the literal, I discovered, what I recorded in my poems had to be exact: people took their truth that way.

○

ONE DAY THE eighth- and ninth-grade students decided not to write. Something had made them miserable and uncertain, and it was not easy teasing the cause of it out of them. Their last class had been world history; the teacher had set them to writing on a theme of medieval warfare, a sort of "I was there" composition, familiar old task for prodding student imaginations. But the children had had no sense of how to comply. They tried to explain their difficulty. Finally, diffidently, someone asked me: "What does 'jousting' mean?" At once the trouble was plain: they could not picture a world they did not know. To have "made it up" was for them, I gathered, more than a little like lying; but because it had been asked of them, and they had been unsuccessful at it, the assignment also had left them feeling flattened and defenseless. So I recounted an Arthurian story, the marvelous scene from *The Once and Future King* where Pellinore and Sir Ector gallop at each other in friendly ongoing enmity. I described the boy Wart in the forest glade watching those determined knights take up arms: their heavy straw-stuffed armor, their clumsiness, the clang of steel against steel; their Percheron-sized battle-horses, their thunderous hoofs causing the ground to shake. The children knew about horses from photos and television; several had actually seen horses in Anchorage. The boys knew about swords from comic books. They all laughed at the tale, said it helped to be able to picture what the words meant, and went on with their day. And I was left wondering why the assignment had been made, and made to be so troublesome.

○

NANCY SIGURD was an outdoorswoman, having grown up in Minnesota, where the winters were cold. She decided to organize an ice-fishing party. She had a gleam in her eye. F would come too, she added casually.

F was handsome and well-spoken. When he laughed, his eyes flashed. Every day he had come to visit Nancy and flirt with me. I didn't encourage him; he wasn't old enough, and he wasn't serious; my life was elsewhere. I wanted to go ice fishing, I told her firmly, and borrowed her extra snow suit.

Not long after dawn four snowmachines stopped in front of Nancy's trailer. Janet Alexey and her cousin Aggie had come with George Gavril, his cousin Joseph Gavril, and F.

"This might be a short trip. Looks like snow," George Gavril said. The immense sky was heavy with clouds. Nancy and I stowed our gear on the sleigh and climbed onto the seats behind Janet and George, and we all set off down the lake toward a river narrows.

The ride was swift but chilling, the land gray and dull, without noticeable feature. For what seemed a long time we went downriver. At last, we pulled up along the bank, where Nancy Sigurd said there was a fish camp. "They always keep the ice holes open," Janet Alexey remarked. We stamped our feet and thumped our arms to get warm, then everyone set about their tasks. Janet showed me how to fish. She tied a small hook and a length of line to a hand-length piece of willow, then baited the hook with salmon eggs.

I looked down the ice hole into the dim, gelid water. Another world must have existed there: bottom plants waving slowly in the current; stringy clumps of fish eggs, amniotic fish-nurseries; moving shadows of the wary winter fish.

It was cold and the sky was darkening again. No one had had any luck. "We should go," Aggie said.

Seven chilled fishermen traveled back upriver, until George, who drove the forward machine, led us into a sheltered place. At once, F climbed a good-sized spruce and cut a few boughs. He made a small fire. Aggie hung the *chainik*, a carbonized tea kettle such as people carried when they traveled, from a green stick over the flame. Soon the water boiled. She threw in handfuls of coffee to brew. The others brought out smoked salmon strips, pilot bread, and cookies and passed them around. The young men held their salmon strips over the flames until the skin crisped and oil dripped from the meat. For a little while, we sat and talked with the ease that came with food and fire.

As we were packing up, F glanced at the small black smudge of ash on the snow, then back at the spruce he had climbed for fuel. "Anyone who comes here will know the story of this fire," he said, "just by looking at the hole in the tree."

The land was filled with such stories. They piled up in the village around door sills and in the corners of steambaths, and rolled down the hill to the lake; they swam in currents and drained off into the streams. They trotted up the ridges and over the mountains. They baited hooks and pulled up fish; they were carried under the pads of dogs loping down the trails, and as cargo on sleighs. Every tree, every rock, the vast fields of snow, the mountains in the distance, the frozen river and the life beneath the ice; all these, I knew in an instant, were part of a great web of stories, told and retold among these people who belonged to this country. The land was not empty or without feature, nor was the sky oppressive: they were alive with history, told and retold. I was the one who could not see or hear.

○

A YOUNG POET is shy; she is like an actor who assumes a new role with confidence and trepidation. In the beginning I picked up an actor's mask, the persona of Poet, and set it over my own face. I believed it would conceal my ordinary-self, and allow words to be spoken through me, my voice their instrument, their reed in the wind. To put it another way, the poet-mask was a cover, and was a gesture of respect offered in return for hospitality. But I was so young, so new at wearing it, that the mask often slipped to one side, and my voice cracked, my own face showed through and embarrassed me.

From the poet Gary Snyder I had learned an old gambling game that used to be played among tribes of the northwest coast of America. Snyder taught the game to young poets-in-training; he had learned it in part, I think, from old Indian men. In his version it was played as a contest between two sides. One side, six or eight persons, held a small deer bone: the leader hid the bone in one hand, the other side tried to guess which hand. In the old way, the players had laid elaborate bets, gamblers' stakes, on their guess. As we had played it, the game was an intense, elegant mental combat, the stakes were words for winning. On either side we searched for and concealed clues, any hint given by the eyes. To raise the pressure, and harden our concentration, each side sang a chant of its own making. We meant to sing our opponents down.

Mine was the voice that carried us. From a source unknown I made a rhythmic, intimate chant, a cradle song, meant to arouse an unbreakable emotion and hold off the other side. Caught in the moment, we played intensely,

as if we were still children. We were not children: we were young adults learning to give voice, and our singing had no consequence, except this, for me: in
the body, the first knowing of the tensile strength of the breath-line of the
song.

I asked F if he knew the game. His voice lost its teasing tone, and he replied seriously, almost defensively, that it was a good game, of historical im-
port. He had seen older men play: they called it *chin lahe.* By their rules, a man
held two bones, one marked and one unmarked, one in each hand, thus com-
plicating the bet and raising the stakes.

I asked him to show me how the old men played. It would be a good game
for my classes, as they could devise their own songs; but I did not wish to
upset the old people by introducing another tribe's way of playing. F said in
that case he would find out what some older people thought.

The next day he brought me a bundle in a brown paper bag. He had whittled a set of gambling sticks, a dozen fat willow twigs, each about sixteen
inches long, to use as betting markers, and had fashioned a pair of bone-like
pieces for hiding. He would not use real bone, he said, implying that bone
should not be used for fun. Half the sticks were tied with strips of red flannel;
one of the willow-bones was marked with a blackened stripe. A man named
Joe Gavril, who was, in their way, F's older brother, knew how to play the gambling game: I could ask him to show me how to do it.

I hardly knew the Gavrils, although they lived near Nancy Sigurd's trailer.
Joe was among the village leaders. He was not a talkative man; people spoke
highly of him for this. I had met him only once. His wife, Natalia, cooked
for the school; she, too, was quiet, and I had not seen her often. Janet Alexey,
who taught in the preschool, was her sister. Since the ice-fishing trip, their
eldest son, Joseph, usually came with F when he stopped by Nancy's house.
Determined to do things correctly, I knocked on their door.

Natalia smiled and offered me the place at the kitchen table where guests
sat. We drank tea. I chatted with her, awkwardly, then brought up the subject
of the game. Joe came to the table and sat. I showed him the willow sticks,
and explained why I wanted to learn. He looked at the sticks, knowing my
reason already, nodded, and said little.

Having begun, I went on: Would he show me how to hold the bones?
Would he sing a song?

He looked down at the table, where the sticks lay, and picked up the false
bones, which were only little pieces of wood. He put the marked piece in one
hand, the unmarked piece in the other, and placed one hand behind his back
and the other in front. You just guessed which hand held the marked bone
and which hand didn't, he said, and you bet on your guess. It wasn't much of
a game, he said. He didn't know any songs, he said.

I sat for a while, then thanked him and gathered up the sticks. Despite F's
help, I had intruded on something, but I had no idea what it could be.

There was an art of speaking in Village Below. Adults did not welcome questions, not even from young people. It might have been Janet Alexey who explained the difficulty to me: Joe had been raised in the old, strict manner of courtesy and indirection. A direct question required an answer, it was an imposition; but out of their deep respect for personal autonomy, one Dena'ina could never tell another what to do. In a situation such as I had made, the man questioned would have to speak evasively, politely, to avoid refusing to answer. He must not insult his questioner; but he could not allow himself to be imposed upon.

"They're really old-fashioned," she said. "We encourage the school kids to ask them about the old days, because they have to learn, and there's no other way to do it. Some of the old people don't mind these questions too much. But they never give much detail! They say questions mix things up, and they want to tell us about the old days in their own way."

Among them, silence carried weight. It was heavy with feeling and will.

She laughed, then looked at me quickly, then looked out the window. "No matter what F said, Joe doesn't know you. He wouldn't say anything."

Their world was made on many levels. I could enter it only gradually, only through hints and sidelong glances, riddles posed and answered. Not for years did I know this: the gambling game touched on power. It evoked the struggle between life and death. No man played it lightly, no women seemed to play, no young person would dare to play. I should be careful, people hinted. I should stop playing with children.

In Dena'ina, the word for play describes formless motion, activity without purpose or end. The word combines with another word and becomes, "He can form a spirit power." From this comes the word for shaman, *el'egen:* the one who "took the form" allowing him to send his spirit out of his body and into an animal helper. That helper was his master's watcher. Shamans watched each other, using their familiars, and so doing, worked to protect their own people from harm; for, in the old Dena'ina world, in the world of spirits, good and evil existed. The shaman was the guard of his people. Much later, when I was being told about such things, it was said that he "took so much pride in believing, in a religious way," that he reduced himself to suffering, "he sacrificed to receive power." His life was one of ritual; with formal acts, acts of ceremony, he made offerings to ask the spirits for help. The game *chin lahe,* I understood, itself verged on ritual. From play, from formlessness, comes potent form.

o

THE ANNUAL winter carnival was held in early March that year. School had closed for the holiday. Relatives arrived on the mail plane from town, and people from neighboring villages piled into the houses of their old friends. The carnival committee organized snowshoe races and ski races, the men's and women's dogsled races, games of chance, children's games; the competitions were open to all, villagers and visitors. At the end, the committee put on an awards dinner. The young men wanted to serve turkey, because it was expensive and would redeem their honor. The last time the village had played host, someone had embezzled the funds for the dinner, and spaghetti had been served instead.

The women's dogsled race was two days of twenty-five-mile heats. A woman, hawk-like, fierce of eye, twice as old as the other competitors, won both heats. She drove a team of five old-fashioned big dogs, dogs so mean that four men had to grab their harnesses to hold them still.

"Get out the way! Mad dog!" she shouted.

Janet and I, growing colder by the minute, were watching the first teams come in. "Did you ever race?" I asked.

"Sure," she said. "Once."

She had raced the first time she had driven dogs, during an earlier winter carnival. Her brothers had been teasing her. She decided to show them what she was made of. For a long time she had watched the drivers. She borrowed a team and drove it to the starting line. She stood on the rails and shouted at the dogs.

"My brothers said, 'Swear at them, they'll run better,'" she said, and added, dryly, "You're not supposed to do that inside city limits."

Her team pulled out. She clung to the uprights, and tried not to ride stiffly on the rails, which extend about a yard from the back of the sled. A few miles from the end she fell. She was dragged, but managed to pull herself back on to the sled, and crossed the finish line with the dogs. She was kneeling on the rails; the sled bolts were jammed so deep into her knees that she bled into the wood. She rolled up her jeans and showed me the scars.

After carnival the racing season slowed down. There were ten teams, whose drivers dreamed of racing professionally. On Saturdays they ran practice races. I wanted to know what it was like to drive dogs, and Nancy Sigurd, like a sturdy cheerleader, took me up on it. She talked to Janet's brother, who had a good sleigh. His partner had a team. Smiling, they offered me their outfit for the next race. Were they serious? I asked Nancy. Try it, she urged.

I bought a huge bag of dog food as a gift, and the partner drove up with all seven of his dogs. Janet offered no advice, but I heard her tell Nancy that five dogs would have been enough.

The ground was nearly bare. We raced on iced ruts in the frozen dirt. Good dogs love to run, but they can't respect a weak or inept driver; I was thrown, and had to be carried back to the village in someone else's sled basket.

I knew then why seven dogs had been too many. I laughed anyway, and went to the dance that night.

That winter, the village held dances again. People were pleased that no one was drinking, and everyone came to the hall. In that big room the light was dim. Chairs had been set along the walls. The band was four middle-aged men with slicked-back hair, who played accordion, bass, and acoustic guitars. Virgil, the bass player, had new teeth. He looked like Chuck Berry. He sang "Johnny B. Goode" like Chuck Berry, until the last chord, when his instrument went flat. Little children, teenagers, old people danced together; they danced polkas, one-steps, two-steps, schottisches, and a knee-bouncing jitterbug. Couples moved around the floor briskly, in a big circle. As each number ended, the gentlemen said, "Thank you," and bowed slightly to the ladies. Everyone applauded.

I sat out the polkas and schottisches. An old lady called me over to her. "I love you," she said. "You love to dance. I have a twenty-one-year-old grandson who is very nice."

I thanked her politely and told her I didn't think I was looking for a young man.

In the intermission, while people rested in the shadows, an old man, Blind Anton, played harmonica and sang Dena'ina songs. His voice was low and warm and rich.

Late in the night, my shoulder began to ache. F, who had remained nearby, watching me, touched it gently and said, "You did all right."

For a long time afterward, the shoulder ached. The boys had played a hard joke, and I hadn't been ready for it; but I had learned my own lesson on the trail. It was not only about driving dogs. For a little while I had felt their desire, and they, for a few moments, had answered mine. I had loved those moments of exuberance and balance, of shifting my weight on the rails, holding steady on the back frame, with all my strength dancing with the sled. I wanted those moments back; I wanted them to stretch into time. What I wanted was the strength of mind they summoned from me.

○

I WAS GOING to leave soon; I was going to fly north, into the Interior, to work in another district. But the world beyond Village Below had vanished. In the brilliant daylight F and I watched each other. At night, in the empty schoolroom, I sat at the desk. He circled me. I arched my neck, I lifted my chin: he circled, stalking me, making no sound. I made no sound.

○

THE CLASS was the second, third, and fourth grades: about fifteen children. A boy, ten years old, was watching me carefully from the sides of his eyes. "You write fast!"

"A lot of practice," I confided. He was surprised that I could put lines of words on the blackboard so quickly.

"Your turn," I said: the children were going to write their own poems. The teacher and I listened to the littlest ones and wrote down their pretty lines, and then read to them what they had made with words.

The boy nibbled on a pencil, wrote a word, erased a hole in the paper, looked out the window, wrote a phrase, tore up the paper; said, "I don't think I'll write a story now."

"Tell it to me," I suggested.

"Tell it? I can't tell a story. You should talk to my dad and uncles, they know how to tell."

"Really? No stories? What about when you're trapping and you see a 'rabies' fox?"

"Oh, yeah." He was quiet for a moment. "Put down THE RABIES FOX," he commanded, and a sure-footed story marched out of him. "Once upon a time, I was setting my traps ..."

He was a changed boy. He used his hands, eyes, whole body: eyes moved, intent, until they saw the fox, the trees, the set. Hands made the set, body moved to run from the fox.

Do you remember learning to write? Your small hand: the first, wobbly *A*. The tongue caught between the teeth, the nose hovering above the paper, the fingers squeezing the pencil. You cover the page with marks, until your mother cries, "You've written an *A!*" You are very proud, but you don't know what you've done until she shows it to you. Then you try to make your body do that praiseworthy thing again.

The boy said he couldn't make the pencil go fast enough. I asked him what he liked to do instead, and he said that after school he ran a snare line with his dad.

Tying and setting snares was precise work. His fingers, his eyes, his muscles, his mind surely worked well for it; his attention was finely tuned. It was required of a boy, if he ran a snare line, to notice what was going on along the line, and what was going on around him as he moved or kept still. He had to look closely, and he had to stand back and take in everything at once. He had to be alert.

Writing asked nearly the opposite of him. He had to sit still in an awkward position; he had to learn to do this. He had to focus his eyes on a near point. He had to ignore the noise and movement around him in order to concentrate on the paper; he had to let his hand, his wrist move in a certain way, his two fingers and thumb hold the pen in balance. He had to push the pen quickly and accurately enough to catch the words on the page as they passed through his mind. This was quite a lot for any child to do; I could almost remember that struggle.

I, like that boy, had had to learn—at first—to shut out the world. I knew the reward of it to be my liberation. But, what might writing, that cramped act, be like for active people, who came to it new? They were suspicious of writers, that is, teachers and anthropologists and government workers, who interfered in their lives; they were wary of books, which told wrong things about them. They knew the world with stories and their bodies. Being told they had to sit and write might feel to them something like punishment.

○

IRINA DEMETROV was one of the first Native certified teachers in the state. She came from the village, and had known her students from their birth. Her class, the last I was to see, was different from the classes of the other teachers. Her students, who were the junior high, were not talkative, not restless. Irina did not speak loudly to them or give them orders: rather, a current of internal agreement passed between her and them. I sensed it; and didn't know how to enter their relationship. What would delight them? I asked Irina if she thought they would like to write down an old story.

I assured her I wasn't trying to collect stories, which was frowned upon, but to let them write what they knew best.

"They know *sukdu*," she said. "The old stories about the animals. You get along well with them. It's unusual, you haven't been here long. I think it would be all right to ask them. If they want to, they'll tell you."

Warmed by her praise, I brought up the subject of *sukdu* with the kids. The room buzzed with eager voices:

"Yeah, sure! Just cruise around the village, everyone tells stories."

"I can't tell good stories, let Pete Junior tell one."

"My dad tells good stories."

"My uncle should come in here!"

"Remember that tea party when the old men came to visit?" Old men from neighboring villages had gathered to tell stories to each other. The kids laughed out loud with pleasure.

They took a while to decide which story to tell, and who could tell it best, and who could be the class scribe. They agreed on the story and scribe, and chose a reserved girl, tall and slender as a flower, to be the teller. She stood still for a moment, to collect herself.

"A lazy boy poured boiling water on a little mouse." She spoke without effort. The children groaned and then were silent, losing themselves in the story of the boy who hurt a mouse-baby. Her voice drew them closer to her. Now and then she paused to recall a detail, and another child supplied it, and the story carried her on.

A boy was lazy and careless. Everyone else was putting up the winter supply, but he was only playing. He poured boiling water on a tiny mouse, even though he had been told to respect the animals. Soon afterward, his relatives discovered that the animals were not coming around their country. The hunters could not find food, and the people were going hungry.

The boy was very hungry. He went into the woods to look around. He found a mouse hole. Then he heard a woman's voice say, "Turn three times with the sun." He turned three times and, all at once, found himself inside a shelter.

A mouse mother was waiting for him. She showed the boy her baby, whose skin was badly burned. Her baby was the tiny mouse he had harmed. "Your people are starving," she said to him, "because you were so careless."

He was ashamed. "I was not doing what I should have been doing, and I hurt your baby because I was mean," he said.

The mouse mother took pity on him. She fed him and sent him home. On his way back, he came upon animals who would be food for his relatives. They did not have to starve anymore. From then on, the boy was kind to everything that lived, and worked hard alongside his people.

o

THE STORY OF the mouse mother was the first *sukdu* I heard told in Alaska. I did not follow it easily; but over time I listened to many stories, and my ear grew sensitive. In the years following, the Dena'ina writer Peter Kalifornsky taught me that the old stories came from the First Beginning, When the Animals Were Talking. They were given to the Dreamers, the men of power who fasted and prayed to dream for the truth. These stories had been "laid before the people, like a road to follow," to guide them through life. He told me many such *sukdu*, as he had written them. They were stories for adults.4

This story of the mouse mother and her baby was told as a child's story. With intricate detail, the girl-teller imitated the voices of the boy and the mouse mother. She described the boy's journey and the mouse hole. The children sighed at the end of her telling.

The story was about the obligation to help your relatives, and about how the animals could withhold themselves because of the harm caused them and then give kindness when the debt to them had been paid; it was about learning to do what was right and admitting what you did wrong. It was about respecting even the tiny animals, the mouse mother and her baby.

o

F IS WALKING ME home in the moonlight. We pass into shadow, and the world changes: it changes, it becomes another time and place, a dream-time. I struggle not to lose my head. I'm not a young girl, this isn't magic. The world is real, and elsewhere, and I belong there; and this moment will change again. He will change. Love is no longer the question: his beauty holds me by the bowels. His face in sleep is an archaic mask; awake, he shines. He is tough and slender and beautiful. I would risk a lot for that beauty.

"Come back when you're finished traveling," he says. "Live with me."

The House and
the Road

THERE IS A little stir when I walk
down the road. "You came back!" a child exclaims. I ask a boy to run and find
F, and walk on, to Natalia and Joe's house. F is there.

o

FREEDOM AND NECESSITY, and their convoluted relationship, have long been
philosophers' themes. In human shapes they have tormented whole nations
of ordinary people. But in those years, in America, what was Necessity to me?
I went to school in the sixties: years of war, civil rights, economic expansion;
large movement, an eruption of event. In the seventies I became a young
woman who wanted to see the world. In the most ordinary way, wasn't I free?
It was, it seemed possible to travel in any direction, with no restriction but
the limit of my curiosity, and (perhaps) my very small bank account. "What
if?" I could ask myself, and reply, "Why not?" And these were not trivial
questions; hope and desire fueled them, excitement and curiosity were their
motor. They grew, I think now, from an American assumption of easy movement into what was presumed to be open space; and if I might well by then
have questioned that national assumption, I had no reason to question my
unexplored desire. "Necessity" was a European idea of limit and exigency
that my parents' parents' parents had come to America to evade. They had replaced their old-world Necessity with the larger, indeterminate idea of Possibility, choosing an imagined idea of what might be over the actual restriction of what is. Doing it, tossing their hat over the fence and climbing after
it, they must have felt their past fall away from them.

To ask, and to accept, *what is* is called realism. It offers a guide to living;
but to say *It might be* offers you possibility, the chance of new experience. The
latter thought widens your mind, in two directions. It suggests that you might
do something different, unexpected, something new; equally, it speaks to you
of the proportions of the world: it reminds you that something besides what
you already know, or believe in, or have been encouraged to think, might also,
already, exist. It proposes, or ought to propose, that that possible something
might be as real as your own what is. It does not suggest, however, that that
something might not be available to you—it promises, richly and slyly, that
you will have much to discover.

And so, removed from its source, I contemplate the idea of Necessity: not
in opposition to Freedom, but in intimate relationship with Possibility. I lift

these ideas and set them down, gently, in another place; I carry them back into memory, to a small Athabaskan village. What happened there followed from the moment when two human beings, a young woman and a young man, came face to face with one another. What I am writing is not a story of their love, which was a private matter, but of their dance between Possibility and Necessity.

o

I PICKED UP my canvas pack and we walked across the road, to a creaky, wooden, two-storey house once owned by F's mother, uninhabited since her death. Cold running water, a few sticks of furniture, candles and Coleman lamps for light, a wood stove for heat were the comforts it offered.

The two of us could hardly bear to look at one another. His face was transfigured, as if all he had dreamed of, but never dared count upon, had come to him. He spoke aloud, not to me but to the empty room, as if it were not empty. He was going to restore the house, he promised, down to the knicknacks on the shelves. His mother had done it that way. He was going to keep her memory alive. He spoke as if to her.

Once, sounding like a lost boy, he had called himself an orphan. His mother was not many years dead; but his father had gone away when F was still a child, the youngest of the family. During the first winter without him they had lived in a wall tent. They had often been cold, and often had gone to bed hungry. When his mother, wanting to find work, went away to town, she had left her children with various aunts and uncles. He was the only one of them who had returned to the village to live.

He wanted a man's life, to have a wife and children of his own; he wanted to work for something besides himself. He cared for the old ways, what he knew of them. He spoke of his ignorance, his need to learn; he spoke of wanting to live the good Native life. Deep in his longing was his great frustration. He dreamed, he felt himself wanting; he believed he could stave off the change threatening everything he knew.

I was silent. *I might have a child. I might have a daughter. She will be part of both our worlds, and will become the best of us.* The voice in the mind, my skeptical friend, replied to itself, amazed: *You never wanted a child.* What strange new world was this? What was I becoming? *Where is my mother, where are my sisters?* All that I knew and remembered and loved had suddenly gone far away, become an indefinable past. F knew nothing of the life I had come from, nothing of where I had been. Nor did he care that I was older. He, too, had no close family in the village, and I was glad of that. We will make our life for ourselves.

I had come to him, I can see now, because I, too, believed in the old ways. I imagined they were as I had read in books. I believed they were rich with song. That I might not find them in this house crossed my mind, and was forgotten.

○

ACROSS THE ROAD lived the Gavrils, Joe, Natalia, and their five children. When F's mother left, Joe and Natalia had taken him in and had brought him up with their own, and, like a true son, all deference and entreaty, he still called Natalia Mom.

I came to admire her, but I never knew her well. She was in her late thirties, I suppose, eight or nine years older than I was. Her demeanor was modest, even, as I assumed then, shy. She had married young and, I am certain, was thought to have married well. Her graying husband, a good deal older than she, came from a well-to-do family and could provide amply for her and the children. She had maintained her position. She cooked for the school, in order to put money away for her daughters to go to college. She was also the health aide for the village, always on call. Steadily, she bandaged the wounded and consoled the bereft. Behind her glasses her eyes were calm; I never saw them look tranquil.

Joe, her husband, was tall and high-shouldered, although he was beginning to stoop. F called him "Ala," Older Brother, a title of respect; he was F's mother's sister's son. He was a man of influence whose family was of high rank. He spoke with good sense, people agreed; though he rarely spoke in public. The council always consulted him. He carried an important name: his father, Gavril, had been the old chief, a strong man who had taken his people through important decisions, who was remembered with sadness in the confusion that had followed his passing.

Their house sat on the lakeshore side of the road, near the center of the village, where traditionally the chief and council had lived. Joe's aged sister lived next door with her daughter, Olga. Olga also had married well: her husband, who came from the Kenai Peninsula, was the postmaster. Their joint property, Joe and his sister's, had belonged to their father, Gavril, the old chief. The Gavrils had two caches, a boat and a snowmachine, a well-built steambath, and a small light plant, useful, as the village had no communal power plant; the school had brought in its own generator. Their wood-sided dwelling, one of the first built with grants from the Bureau of Indian Affairs, had three bedrooms and indoor plumbing; but for some reason, in snow country, its roof had no eaves. People joked pointedly that a Californian must have been the architect. F had stayed with them during the past few winters, as his mother's house was not warm.

Because of me, I saw, they had new hopes for F, and if they doubted we would do well, in their kindness they concealed their doubt. More often than I realized, F went to Joe for advice. Natalia never interfered, but when I needed to learn, she explained protocols or habits of good sense. I did not know how to live there; that is, I didn't know what to do. I was a child, new to the village: like any child, I was expected to learn by watching.

❂

THE HOUSE STOOD at almost the very center of the village. Downstairs, where we entertained visitors, a casement window looked out on the road. F pushed the kitchen table against the window, where it belonged, he said, so he could sit and watch people pass by.

The traffic on the road was the signal of the village mood. The tilt of a head, the shrug of a shoulder drew a map of emotion to be read at a glance. There went a grandmother, walking briskly toward the post office; when the mail came, she was always first in line. That tiny, energetic woman had borne twenty-three children. Where were all her children? She lived with her son and his family; but most of her children had gone to the city. She made good money in the summers cooking for construction crews. The girl with her, dragging her feet, was Karen, who had written the lyrical essay about freedom. Her family was proud of its pure blood and did not care for *gasht'anas*, white people. Her father didn't want her to become a teacher, as Irina Demetrov had done. Irina was her sister-in-law.

The store was open. That meant the mail had arrived and been sorted. An old couple walked slowly, going to do their small shopping. He was blind, the singer at the dance, and her eyes were growing milky. Janet Alexey went into the village office; she had been elected to the city council. A bunch of little kids were running home from school, and two sixth-grade girls turned to knock at my door.

In a moment the road had cleared. A man who lived alone at the far end came along, walking stiffly. He had been drinking, and he liked to fight when he drank. People knew better than to say anything to him. They stayed out of his way till he returned to his senses.

Upstairs, I lived in another realm. The house looked out on the sky, the lake, the saddleback pass across the water. The pass was called Ghost Mountain. During the last, great battle with the Aleuts, traditional enemies of the Dena'ina, many fighters had died on its slopes. The bodies had never been properly buried. No one went there now. If someone wanted medicine, people whispered, he could go there; they meant: if he wanted shamanic power.

During those first weeks, I dreamed I talked to a bear, or she talked to me. I was in the woods; silently I called "Bear!" She came and I rode on her back: she indulged me, as an amused adult plays kindly with a child. I held my breath, and woke up ...

Under the long window I fixed up a writing desk. When my books arrived I arranged them in Blazo boxes, sturdy wooden crates left over from the days before Coleman lanterns and oil stoves came in. The mornings were quiet; I was alone. In my aerie, in solitude, I read and worked.

❂

GRADUALLY THE outer rhythm of the days settled over me. Late in the morning, after people had drunk their first coffee, well after the children had been sent to school, the rounds of visiting began. It must have been Natalia who let me know that visiting was necessary. People liked to know what others—strangers like myself, I understood her to mean—were up to. Used to their habits, they fussed and worried when their routine was disturbed.

Ceremoniously, the old people called upon the friends and relatives of their own age. Women dutifully visited their elders, then went to their close friends, usually their sisters, where they gossiped and looked after one another's toddling children. The lively children: they ran in and out of their aunties' houses as their own. They were given hard candy and soft words by their grandmas and grandpas. After school, the teenaged girls went home to take care of them, and clean house.

That was the hour when the dandy young men liked to visit the unmarried teachers. There were three unmarried teachers: Nancy, Jane Canelo, and Ricardo Arias. During the lonely cold months, a warmth between Rick and Janet Alexey had sparked and flared, and died as the end of the school term approached. When Ricardo left for the summer Janet took it hard, and visited Natalia, her older sister, more often than usual.

The third teacher, Jane Canelo, was a solitary. I felt some sympathy for her because of it, for the lack of privacy could be difficult to bear, but her manner was brusque and she never offered coffee or tea. She was unfriendly to me; she had liked F a great deal, Nancy Sigurd whispered, and was jealous. When F confessed that he didn't care for her because of her manners, I asked why he bothered to visit her.

"We always pass by," he said, surprised I had to ask. "What if something happened to her, and we didn't know it? Who would help her out? We're responsible for her."

The weeks moved industriously, smoothly, toward their Saturday night, the time of the family steambath. Some of the older people, whose children cut wood for them, liked to steam daily; but Natalia's family fired up their bath at the end of the week. The bath followed an order of protocol. By late afternoon the older boys had split wood and carried water. They stoked the fire in a barrel stove that sat balanced upon large rocks inside the steam room and filled wash tubs with water; they left pails of water in the unheated dressing room and swept the floor. The smaller children ate supper early and went into the bath, usually with an older sister, while the adults ate their evening meal.

At mealtime I never heard the word *please*. Like everyone, F said: "I'll eat now." I thought him rude, and asked why he demanded food. "When I was a boy," he said evenly—it was the first time I saw him angry—"I had to eat at white people's tables. They always wanted you to say 'please.' No human being ever begs for food at my table."

Natalia set out cooked food, or left it on the stove within reach, even when everyone was satisfied. No food, especially never food from the land, was begrudged to anyone in the house; but no one overate. Too many people remembered hunger.

After supper, and after the younger ones had finished, the older boys and young men, including F, went in to steam. They took enough time to make the girls fidget. Then, they stoked the fire and refilled the tubs. Then Natalia's daughters and her sister Janet went in, and I went in with them.

In the shadows the only light came from the reddened stove and the gleam of a kerosene lamp. We scrubbed and rinsed, washed our hair, chatted about the day, as the heat built up against our skin. Their voices were quiet, confident. They talked about rock music, trips to town, boyfriends. They pitied a young man who was courting a well-off widow: every day, he did chores for her parents; but they thought she was not going to accept him. When it was very cold outside, they joked about a trick the boys liked to play, capping the chimney. The smoke backed down into the bath and drove the women, wrapped in towels, into the snow. The boys pointed and hooted, and laughed themselves silly. Any strange sound coming from the roof made the girls jump. Natalia's high-spirited second daughter planned a fine payback, just in case.

After the heat had built up, Janet would dash water against the stove. She warned me to breathe through a wet cloth so that my throat and lungs would not be seared, and to wrap my hair against the drying heat. Sweating away the grime of the week, I endured the steam with nearly fainting pleasure, until it drove me out the low door. In the small dressing room, in the dry, silent cold, I watched vapor rise off my flushed skin and frost the log walls.

After us, the older people went in. There were no elders in the household, so the last round was for the married couple. Natalia and Joe retired discreetly. Janet and Marya, the eldest daughter, grinned at each other, and the children went out to find their friends.

In the relaxing time afterward, people often came to the door. F's aunties came now and then to gather around the kitchen table. They drank tea, and talked and laughed, and watched the passers-by. They especially liked to tell jokes. They laughed at how human pretensions could be so easily upset by a small accident. Once, when the whole village went out ice skating, a self-important man who paraded his dignity at the wrong moment had fallen down in front of everybody. For days, the aunties laughed about it, with malice and real enjoyment.

Their anecdotes came casually, one following another. They talked to each other, it seemed to me, and I sat and listened, often puzzled, sometimes bored; but I began to remember what I heard, and put things together until I got the point: they were teaching me. Names, place-names, dates poured out, and I was expected to remember them. Endlessly, they talked about their relatives, and traced their family trees. "You're how old?" they said to me, polite but surprised: "And you have no children?"

A sorrowful auntie counseled me, "Kathy, we women have to wait a long time to get what we want. Look at me, I wanted twelve children. I only had five."

○

THE VILLAGE MOVED around two principal families, the Gavrils and the Dementys. Joe was a Gavril; Natalia's mother was, on her father's side, a Dementy. The two families shared a single ancestor, Dementii Gavril, so baptized by the Russian priests. In the nineteenth century, in a government census made when people spoke Dena'ina and Russian but little English, the man's two sons had each taken, or been given, one of the father's names as his own last name. Each brother had proceeded to establish a family. Across the generations the two families had become distinct. Some intermarriage had occurred, but it had not often been permitted. The rules of the Orthodox church were strict, more so than in Western Christianity, and very different from the old rules of polygamy.

Because of these rules, the unmarried men had a difficult time finding wives. Most of the young women were their relatives; they had to look elsewhere to marry. F, explaining this to me, said that white wives would strengthen the family lines, and also offer the young men better opportunities for making a living. "New blood," he called it.

The aunties said, when I asked, that clan connections still existed, and told me, though scantily, how F was related. Old people kept track of the clanlines; but the younger people, they were sure, had mostly forgotten them.

Natalia took me aside and told me about F's mother's family, who were Joe's mother's family also. Originally they were called Constantinov. They came from farther north, from the Stony River and the hills around Hungry Village. They had gradually moved south into the lake area, to marry and to find better hunting country. One old couple had remained in Hungry; until their recent deaths, they had run the family there. They were called *Chida* and *Chada*, Grandmother and Grandfather. Their children, who had inherited their stamina and their strong minds, were aging now, but still living. The old couple had lived for nearly a century.

From a cupboard Natalia brought out a black-framed photograph of Chada and Chida, and a framed copy of their marriage certificate. The photograph looked as if it had been copied from a faded daguerreotype. I could barely make out the faces. The man and the woman were small people, as I remember them, dressed in turn-of-the-century clothing, wearing expressions of calm, humane curiosity. They seemed to me both aged and ageless.

The marriage certificate was a photocopy of the original document, inscribed by hand in Cyrillic and roman scripts. It was a record of their proper names. Natalia asked me to repeat their names aloud, and to remember them, because they had been changed by the Americans, who could not pronounce them.

For clarity, I drew lines of an elaborate family tree. And as I graphed the Dementys and Gavrils, my father's clannish family came to mind. The hard-headed way my grandmother had ruled them until her death—her sons, the eldest always taking precedence, the younger ones (except the priest) ex-pected to defer. Men and boys going to their offices and private schools, be-coming active in civic life; going to their taverns (as Native men still went), as to the men's house; the daughters, married, sturdy, raising the children at home, in their own domain. The pattern repeated, until my generation—part of my generation—broke it. My valley had been settled by immigrants. I had grown up among second- and third-generation working-class families: Irish, Italian, Lithuanian, Polish, Slovak, Welsh. Until my generation, the families had stayed close together, dominated by the frail old grandmother who spoke broken English or the robust grandfather who had earned his manhood in the coal mines. How separate those groups of families had thought them-selves from each other, in their local, communal, old-country personalities: and how different, they would have thought, from the Gavrils and the Dementys.

But in my valley, those family relationships had been as intricate and un-varying as they were in Village Below. Every family was revered by its mem-bers. "We take care of our own" was their pride. In my distant valley, people had known who they were, and who they belonged to, and where they all be-longed. Every family had marked for life the bride from another neighbor-hood, the husband from a different religion. Reluctantly and proudly, they had given up their children to form new families. In the round of life, they could never escape the double burden of belonging and not-belonging. They had never dreamed of going anywhere else, and were surprised when their children left home in the sixties, went to universities, and wanted to live a different kind of life than theirs.

What I am thinking about is piety: religious devotion to and reverence for God, devotion to and reverence for parents and family: from Middle English *piete*, meaning "mercy, pity," from Old French, from Latin *pietas*, *pietās*, mean-ing "dutiful conduct," from *pius*, "dutiful." I came from a once beautiful Pennsylvania valley raked over by deep-mining coal barons, themselves long since gone with their riches, leaving the culm banks and hard need for mak-ing a living to us, who remained; and even the miners were not the people I came from: mine was the kind of family made up of doctor, priest, business-man, lawyer, and the dutiful wives who stayed home with the children: the kind that anchor, or did anchor, the small-town middle classes to property and propriety.

In the valley I had felt the pull of family and known the safety of belong-ing and of knowing that I belonged; and of knowing that I did not belong there, where habit and hard times offered women small hope of adventure or a life of the mind.

The auntie who had longed to have twelve children whispered that her husband, when he drank, beat her. "He call me 'ignorant old Eskimo,'" she wept. "I don't come from here." In its own way, this, too, was my valley.

Another six or eight extended families, each with its own well-drawn lineage, had standing in the village. Among them relations were socially correct, in an old-fashioned manner, but they seemed, to me at least, not cordial. F, who was very sensitive to rank, told me that the better families lived in the center of town, and the smaller families and the poorer people lived at the end of the road.

He knew this because he had grown up with it. He was proud of where his mother's house stood. His description was similar to the earliest layout of Dena'ina villages, described in the old stories, which had recorded such matters. The stories said that in those days, *barabarees,* the half-buried sod-and-skin-covered dwellings, had been laid out around an oval, with a road drawn through the long axis, which became the road we traveled on daily. In the center of the oval (where the school and village hall were now) had been the meeting place or courtyard. Around it, in order of precedence, had been the sod houses of the chief and the rich men. The poorer families, the dependents, and the slaves had had to live in shelters at the edge of the village.

I knew those families slightly, through their children, but did not pass much time among them. The friends I made were connected in some way to F. There was something about those people, a light in the eye, that drew me to them.

o

THE WEATHER-WORN church was Russian Orthodox and had an iron bell. On Sunday mornings its hollow *clang, clang, clang* woke the village with a grumble. F ignored its summons. People were hypocrites, he said. They cursed and gambled and talked about each other, and then they turned around and went to church. He sinned; he would never pretend he didn't. His disgust was a believer's. He was a man who longed for purity.

In church the men sat on one side of the aisle, the women on the other. They sang fervently in Slavonic, the men deep-voiced, the women high-pitched, in the Russian liturgical style. The mayor, who was also the IRA chief, was the first deacon, and read the Scripture. F, Janet, Joseph, Aggie, all said he was stupid; but older people were warier in their estimate. Although he was a Dementy, he was not very old to have that much authority. There was a faint tinge of—of what? Some secret hovered around him.

The priest visited rarely; occasionally on a feast day, to say Mass. People said, sorrowfully and bitterly, that he did not come because they had once committed a wrong. It was told that in 1796, someone in the area—they would not name the village—had killed a Russian priest. The priest had blue eyes, F told me. When he stared at people, as they thought he did, his blue eyes had frightened them. He had instructed the chief that having two wives, as was the custom of rich men, was immoral. The chief had been forced to choose. ("How could he choose one over the other?" F said, appalled. "Just let one go, just like that?") He would put up with no more of the priest's interference.

The martyred priest had been Father Juvenaly, the first Russian saint in the New World. He and a party of travelers, I read, were taking the children of some converts to Kodiak, to go to school, when their parents changed their minds and, with others, caught up with the priest's group. His party was allowed to go on only if Juvenaly stayed behind. Something happened then: he may have angered or frightened them. They speared him. Again and again he struggled to his feet, exhorting them not to lose their faith. They killed him.

It is easy to imagine the priest's devotion; and to imagine the monster he must have appeared to them. The chief must have been furious at being given orders—it was unthinkable for a high-ranking man to be given orders—and the people angry and fearful at what was unknown to them. How sad they must have seemed to him. He was as brave as they were.

There were other stories told about the martyr. A university scholar, himself a Russian priest, proposed that Father Juvenaly had in fact been assassinated in a certain Yup'ik village in the Nushagak River drainage, southwest of Village Below. According to a credible source, their descendants even now guarded their old beliefs in shamanism and the power of the animals. They taught their young people how to treat the animals properly, as creatures with souls whose purpose was to feed humans. Lately, they had been running catch-and-release sport fishermen off their land. They said the fishermen insulted the spirits of the fish by using them for play. This, in turn, endangered the supply of fish for the village, as the fish, offended at being ill-used, began to withdraw. I thought: They are facing down newer powers by calling to the old.

Later, an Athabaskan man, himself a poet and traveler, offered me an interesting speculation about Father Juvenaly's death. This observant man had been traveling for years in the bush. He had learned, or been told, that by the late eighteenth century, Siberian shamans wore ivory amulets carved in the shape of the Russian cross. In western Alaska, there had always been strong connections between the Siberians and the Bering Straits Yup'iks, although their shamans had been extremely wary of one another's power. Russian soldiers, traders, and priests had already established bases in Alaska. By the time of Father Juvenaly's mission, the rivalry between shamans had grown fierce and war-like. The poet surmised that Father Juvenaly, traveling in Yup'ik country (or, while still living among the Dena'ina), and no doubt wearing his cross, his badge of holy office, may have been taken for a Siberian shaman, and killed because of it.

o

THE PEOPLE HAD LIVED in the village for more than five generations. They had moved around their country hunting game and fish, settling by season into their hunting and fishing camps. They had worked hard, and they liked to play games afterward. Their love of gambling had not altered: avid old ladies played bingo, and everyone enjoyed cribbage. F, when he had money, was part of a group that played all-night poker. They gathered in a house up the road, where smoke, laughter, and an air of dissipation hung over them till dawn. The old ladies clicked their tongues, although Joe Gavril's aged sister sometimes played cards herself. The gambling desire was strong in F.

One of the players was George Gavril, Joe's nephew, whose mother also liked to gamble. He often came to visit us. He was a few years older than F and they had spent a year together in college. Subtly, they were intense rivals. George had been involved with a young woman, an anthropologist or linguist who had done fieldwork in the village, and he was still carrying the torch. Though he mourned his lost love, he also missed the prestige of having a white girlfriend. Now their positions, his and F's, had changed abruptly, and in F's too-casual welcome sounded a note of triumph.

George came to visit us because of the tortuous workings of masculine competition; but he also missed a sort of intellectual life. He liked to tell me about his childhood, even to lecture about it, and I liked to listen to him. His memories, when he told them without sounding didactic, were like the adventures of long-ago children in books, but they were real, and he told them happily.

When he was a boy the whole village had packed up and gone over the mountain to hunt. In winter, the caribou herd that foraged the Alaska Peninsula used to pass north of the village, above the Point. The herd was immense. The animals crossed the lake: *click-click, click-click, click-click* went their hooves, tapping, tapping on the ice. At once the whole village arose, hitched up the dog teams, and drove out to follow the animals. It was a wonderful time for a child: "If only you could have seen it!" Team after team driving out of the village, up the ice toward the mountains, teams of ten, twelve, fifteen big dogs!

He laughed: Old-fashioned work dogs, not these little runty race dogs! Women and children bundled in the sled baskets, covered with furs. Men in furs and skin boots riding the sled rails ...

I could almost see it; I tried to see it. I had never seen caribou. I had never heard the click of their hooves on the ice, or the snort of their breathing.

My own past seemed far away, insubstantial. No one asked where I came from, or where I had been; and, if they had, I would not have known what to tell them. I misplaced my sense of event, of time passing, and all became continuous time: turning by seasons, by memory. It was right; it was healing; but it was not mine. I wondered how I would find words to fit there; I wondered if I had a story for that old place.

o

IN ALL THE TALK of family, only F had told me about his other relatives. His father's father was white, he thought, and his mother's father was an Irishman who, during Prohibition, had been the biggest rum runner, with the fastest boat, in Bristol Bay. F was proud of him. His name was known.

F called himself half-white and all Native. He was Native because his mother was Native, and because he had been brought up in the village, and because he had lived among his relatives, in the same way they lived. He had never been to the East Coast, although as a student he had once gone to Europe. He cared not at all for city life, but he tried to like the idea of it, for my sake. He wanted Native children: they could have a good life in the village. I wanted a peaceful home for them. It never occurred to me that we could not raise them well in both worlds.

Nothing was clear. Neither of us knew what to do.

A silent picture came to me, of myself sitting at the table, smiling, listening, for the briefest moment; then, blink! I was gone, with no trace left behind. Who would come after me? I believed in love, then tried to believe in love; I was determined it would cross distance, and time.

As a young woman, much younger than I was now, my mother had moved to another part of the country to make her life with my father. I flew down to the regional town to talk to her; the store had the only telephone in the area. In a patchy call, put through on the rare day when my mother was out, I tried to explain to my father what I wanted. He had never heard of Athabaskans; but the Irish grandfather in F's past made him laugh with some relief. I thought he was laughing. He said, "How will this affect your writing?" and, "Do you ever pray?" and, "I wish your mother were here."

They Cover Up
Too Much

AN OLD WOMAN came into the school and told a story in her native language. She spoke a tongue intricate in its sounds. I could not follow it, nor follow her story: I followed her voice. It was soft and harsh, quiet and dramatic, warning of danger, fearful, dark, girlish. It carried the emotions of the story and she used it like a wind instrument.

The story was about the Aleut wars, she told the children, in her English. Aleuts had come to the village to fight. A mother, not losing her head, told her daughter to hide in the fish pit. (The people dug pits where they buried salmon to ferment over a winter; old people especially liked this food.) The girl stayed for a long time in the pit, hidden among the stinking fish, crying, afraid—the storyteller let her voice sound like the little girl. At last she heard only silence, and climbed out. Above ground, nearly everyone was dead; the rest were gone.

No one should laugh at how they used to bury fish, the storyteller advised the children: the little girl had been saved by the pit her mother had dug.

I had seen that old woman race dogs, shouting, "Mad dog! Get out the way!" and seen her win, and knew she was made of stern stuff. She came from the Stony River country, from Hungry Village: her parents were Chida and Chada. She was F's great-aunt, through his mother. He avoided her; he feared her a little. There was an air about her: the way she walked, as though in time to an older, slower beat; the light in her eyes, of a part held in reserve and still free.

I knocked at her door.

"Come."

I lifted the latch and entered. The light was dim. She was sitting on the floor, near an oil lamp. sewing caribou-skin boots. I did not speak, but nodded hello. She rose and motioned toward a chair by the table. She took the simmering kettle from the stove and poured a cup of water, and set it before me. I took a tea bag from the box, and waited. She sat down and dipped a tea bag into her own cup. I introduced myself.

As my visits became regular, she looked pleased to see me, and that look encouraged me to keep going back to see her. She knew I had taken a shine to her grandchildren, and that I was a writer of some sort. She confessed she did not read, except for the Bible, and then only the Old Testament, because she liked the stories. "Their families are like ours," she said with satisfaction.

In quick, evocative sketches, she told me about her Stony River life. When she was young, her father had taken her hunting. She had only brothers near her age, and, she grinned, she was "wild." Her mama had scolded her: she shouldn't play like a boy, with her own bow and her own spear; but her father said, "Let her go." Her mother and her grandmother tried to show her how to make birchbark baskets, but she hadn't learned the art well, and now, she admitted, she wished she had. She had watched her grandma sew: stuck her head right over her grandma's fingers, till her grandma told her to sit down and watch! But she couldn't see well that way. You have to go close, to be able to see.

Her face was like a hawk's: quick, fierce, proud, dark. When she announced her name, she said it proudly and expected you to listen to her; and you listened.

○

I WAS WATCHING for the plane when the old woman stopped at my door. I was going up to Hungry, where her relatives lived, to read poetry in the school. She brought a letter for me to deliver to her niece, and stayed to gossip for a while. She sat on the chair as if it were the floor, which she preferred, with her legs drawn up under her.

I had had a letter from my brother, who was heartbroken over a young woman. She nodded sympathetically, and said her younger son, also, had broken up with a young woman. The girl was from another tribe, up on the Yukon. She had left him and returned to her people. "It's good," the old woman said, meaning, good they had parted: "She wouldn't have no baby."

Young women who refused to have children caused the old ladies to wonder. Natalia told me of a woman who had had one child and decided not to have more, it was "too much trouble." Natalia said she had never heard anyone say that before.

"Life used to be different," the old woman said, "not like now."

When she was a young girl, a man had wanted to marry her. Her mother had agreed to it. "I thought I stay there. Then my mama give me away. I didn't know men. Not like now—we didn't know." A young girl's grief, inconsolable, shaded her voice.

She was sent to Village Below, to stay with her married sister, who had four little ones of her own. On the first day, the younger sister, who was about thirteen, comforted herself by playing with the babies. The older sister cooked for them. That night, they made up the beads. She was to sleep with her new husband, she was told; but she cried too much about it, and would not go to him. On the second day, again, she played with the babies. The man stayed away from her.

"I did not know how to be woman. I held my doll and picked berries, it was lots of fun!" She grimaced suddenly. "What a life. Now it's all work."

The man stayed away from her for a long time; when he came back, he tried to take her with him. She cried endlessly. Finally, he went away, and didn't return.

When she was grown, she had married her present husband, who was now crippled with rheumatism. He slept on a bed in a dark corner, and sometimes he cried out in pain. Her mouth tightened when that happened.

From the first, the couple had lived in the house of his mother, who later passed away. She had longed for her own home, but her husband had kept them living in that same house, darkened by woodsmoke and age. She had run away from him many times. Now she was eligible for a BIA house, a brighter, roomier place, she thought, to be built on her own property. She wanted that house. She was impatient to move away from the dead woman's house.

"I got my own rig, he got his. I want to hunt, I hunt. Got my own boat, he got his." She told me her two boys knew how to sew, to cut fish; and she could do men's work. She liked to stay alone and work hard. She did not drink or smoke.

"Have your own rig," she advised me, "your own sled, your boat, .30-.30. You wouldn't depend on your husband."

o

SHE HANDED ME an official envelope with her name written on it. The dentist might come to stay with her, she said proudly. He traveled to the villages for the Public Health Service, and was due for a visit. She liked that dentist. One time, she had to go to Anchorage, to the Native hospital. She had gone up to where patients waited for the doctor, where they told her it would be three days before she could get in. She had just turned to leave, when the doctor spotted her and told her to come into his office. He sat her down and poured coffee for her. He told her she would have to wait only a few minutes.

The dentist came into the room. He said to her, "Stay with me."

The doctor said, "No, she'll stay with us."

They argued over her. (She smiled.) She went to the dentist's house. All day his wife stayed with her, fed her tea, drove her around Anchorage, so that she saw the whole city.

"They don't even let me put my coat on myself!" she said happily. "Before I go to bed they tell me to have cup of tea, to have ice cream, like I'm little girl. They take such good care of me, nobody ever treat me that good. I go outside and I cry because they treat me so good."

At the end of the day, the dentist had thought to ask, "Would you like to take a walk? I bet you miss walking in the brush." They drove out to where she could take a walk in the brush.

She was drinking her *chai* before bed. The phone rang: someone wanted to talk to her. "'You answer,' I tell him. 'Tell 'em I'm not here, I already go to bed.'"

The caller was her cousin and friend, Helen Foma, with whom she went ice fishing: Helen kept a house in Anchorage. She had heard the old woman's voice in the background, and demanded that she come to the phone. The old woman laughed and said, "I tell her I never say that. She tell me, 'Come stay with me, I come get you.' I tell her I'm tired, I'm in my pajamas. She tell me, 'You be ready.'"

Helen took her home and they slept in the same bed and laughed and talked before they went to sleep. "The husband has to go away. We stay in the same bed, same covers. We're talking and laughing and he yell at us: 'Be quiet goddammit!'"

She wore a singular expression when she told me such things. Her face was softened and made innocent by kindness and friendship. She would have been a girl of great beauty, for her mouth and her eyes were still very fine. When she recalled good times, they were all of times with women; but the story of her betrothal remained in my mind: her mother had given her away, to be a wife. She gave me no sign she had any reason to trust and admire a man, or even to like him. I didn't know about men, she had said; not like now: we didn't know.

She asked me about my mother, and compared their ages. My mother was then in her fifties, and the old woman was only a few years older; I had assumed she was near eighty. My mother, I told her, was pretty, in the way Rosalyn Carter, the president's wife, was pretty.

She looked dismayed, and touched the beautiful skein of wrinkles on her face. "Look at me, look at my face. I'm old woman! I tell young girls, Don't work so hard. Look at me: I work too hard."

Her hair was still black, long and dramatic (my mother colored her hair), and I praised it one day to Natalia. She laughed. "You know how she takes steambath every day?" "Yes." "Grecian Formula."

○

WHEN THE SUMMER CAME, I walked down to her fish camp. When she took the back trail, I followed her, imitating her walk: placing one step in front of another, weighing on the balls of my feet, with my toes turned slightly inward. Walking so, I was balanced and efficient in the woods. One day I took the back trail to her camp and arrived just as she was carrying spruce logs, about ten inches thick, about five feet long, up the bank, to be bucked up for firewood. She tramped uphill hefting her load, as strong and graceful as a young man.

"Watch out," she commanded, as I lifted a log to my shoulder. "Don't hurt yourself."

In July, during the salmon runs, I helped her drag washtubs full of split fish up the bank, and watched her as she cut and stripped fish all day. It was quiet in her camp. She worked alone at the fish table, while her grandchildren played within earshot near the smokehouse. Fish camp was her place; she

talked more readily there. She remembered stories her father told her and described how he taught her to hunt with spear and bow; recounted a recent
murder that had been covered up; told me small things about the animals.
Someone had given her a seal skin to tan. She had worked on it for days and
was growing impatient with it: it was much tougher than moose skin; she
wondered how those Eskimo women did it. She showed me how to scrape
skins with a stone and how, unless you balanced yourself, your wrists and your
back suffered as you squatted while you worked.

She confided that she watched people who were drinking. "They think
I'm spying on them. But I'm not spying!" she said vigorously. "I watch. Maybe
they need help. I take care of them."

One day she asked if I wanted to learn to cut fish. I said I was ready. I put
on rubber boots, and a green plastic garbage bag cut like a poncho, and tied
a string around my waist.

"Come closer," she invited. "Watch how we do it."

Swiftly, steadily, she headed and gutted a salmon. The head went into the
fish box, a mesh pen sunk off the bank. Heads were good to eat, after they
ripened and floated. People peeled them and ate the cartilaginous nose; or,
for a rich soup, boiled them fresh, with salmon roe and some wild onion. She
pulled out the guts in a single piece and tossed them to the shrieking gulls
who wheeled above the water. She saved the eggs for bait or soup. The fish
was headed, gutted, and split down the backbone, with economy of movement. She sliced off the belly fin to dry, as a treat for her dogs.

"No waste at all," she said.

She cut one or two more fish, then handed me a knife:

"See what you can do."

Without my glasses I couldn't cut neatly. She joked I was as bad as the missionary women, her old friends, who had not been able to cut fish right in ten
years of trying. She showed me that every cut had its reason, and guided my
knife. After two or three tries, she said politely that I had not done so badly,
though she was impatient when I kept slicing off the belly fin from the wrong
direction. She let me cut as many fish as I liked, now and then looking sharply
at my hands and touching them. I worked steadily; and fell into a revery of
sky, water, light, fish, wave-slap, gull cries. Her dogs barked as a boat came
around the bend.

The afternoon grew longer. She suggested I stop before I grew tired. I
washed off my half of the bark-covered table, scrubbed the knife and the rubber gloves she had loaned me, and put down freshly scythed grass underneath.
The bark held the fish in place; the fresh grass went underfoot to keep the
platform clean. I walked back up to the village along the shore of the lake.
She was still cutting fish when I passed around the bend.

◊

ONE AFTERNOON she took me to drink *chai* with her sister, under a wall tent in fish camp; and there she let me listen to her language, a glottal tongue, issuing from deep in the throat and chest, rich in imagery and precise in its descriptions of the world's constant motion. The two sisters spoke softly together. I sat in the muted green light, discreetly watching their faces. In school, the old woman of the fierce eye had told her story in Dena'ina. I had not heard the language spoken again. It was not used when white people were present: it was said this was a courtesy, so that no stranger would think people were talking about him; but also, I think, it was meant to keep their language private.

A Dena'ina word represents a thing in its every movement, even to its negation. I am thinking of *mitni*, the lovely word for water, that is composed of two parts joined to make a new meaning. First is *mit:* what water does: it flows; then *ni*, which represents "island," or the shape of a point. Concisely, the word means: "It gets there, to the point, the tip"; but its whole image is of motion: motion stopped, motion resumed. This is the meaning of water: It moves, it flows, until it touches the point of an island, and divides and flows around the island, then rejoins itself, and continues.[5]

The poetics of this language are—can I understand this in English?—literally figurative. I think of the word for "one's father," *betuk'da*. Drawn from its source, it means: "He's got his face in the water" and "He's fishing with hook and line." Enchanted, I took this to mean, "He's pulling his mirror image out of the water." The conception of father contained in this figure goes deeper than its calm picture, however. One's father is not necessarily one's sire: he is the one, rather, who performs a certain act of the mind: who draws from the water the form of his wish for the child: who imagines who the child will become.

The logic of Dena'ina resides in its poetics: that is, the precise, associative way that the things of the world are connected to one another is revealed within the structure of its image-words. In this, Dena'ina seems to me similar to Chinese, or to Chinese poetry, as I understand it. In a Chinese poem, the radicals, the roots of an ideogram, in their immediacy represent (and so, link) picture-sound-thing that become, in the moment of beauty drawn by the calligrapher's hand, image-idea. In the Chinese poem, the world is drawn from its own image; but drawn as the particular face it shows that poet: drawn, in answer to the poet's longing, through the poet's educated, intuitive eye.

In Chinese poetry, the world is actively described and represented, not transformed, in the linked imagery of the poet. In a similar way, with great intensity, the Dena'ina picture-idea words mime, or copy, their world. They copy the world of relations: they do not name its beings in any fixed or static sense (although Dena'ina has a rich vocabulary of what we call nouns), so much as they represent its, and their, motion.

The names of animals always describe how they move; or, onomatopoetically, catch the sound of an animal's call, and enclose it. They are composed, or composite, words—perhaps not "words," not nouns and verbs as English

knows them. They are built from stems, with strings of qualifiers, or modi-
fiers, added on, to indicate their particularity of mood, voice, kind of motion, time, gender (which is not masculine/feminine/neuter, so much as
classification according to shape or position or some other essential quality),
and spatial relationship to other objects or persons. And the stems and
qualifiers also correspond, in their turn, to what exists in the world. Because
of this intricate system of association, the story of an animal is often given,
like a riddle, in his name.

Dena'ina describes its world microscopically. It attends to the small details. And yet the details are, I must understand, the outward sign: for everything has an inner and outer face.

An old man told me, wistfully, "In my own language I can say so much
with one word, that I cannot say in English." Athabaskans are said to be terse,
as they often are, men especially, when they speak in public, or to strangers.
They hold verbal compression to be a mark of knowledge and facility with
language, akin to the riddler's art.

○

A FEW DAYS LATER, the old woman complained to me that an anthropologist had come to her in fish camp, with a tape recorder. She had told the anthropologist to find me, to help translate from her village English; but the
anthropologist had not understood her, or had not found me. The old
woman was annoyed. She had been putting up her winter supply, and could
not be bothered—"She wants me to tell her story. I'm cutting fish!"—but
finally had talked into the tape recorder. The anthropologist had recorded a
story and flown away that afternoon.[6]

F did not think much of my visiting her so often. She was old-fashioned,
he warned, not like his mother at all. I should stay away from her.

Natalia's son, Joseph, told me that when he was a boy, he thought the old
woman was a witch; but when he was ten, he had got tired of being afraid,
and had gone to visit her, and they had drunk tea together until he put away
his fear.

○

THE VOICE OF the old woman began to sing in my ear: immediate, urgent, in
steady rhythm. I heard her most clearly then, away from the fleshy reality of
salmon hung on the drying racks, when I had stood at the table, cutting precisely into the bellies of fish as their eggs slipped onto the bark; when I had
listened, watched, strained to watch, to move: away from the laying on my
body of her summer dance of cutting fish.

I wrote versions of what she had told me—the death of a sister, driving
dogs in the moonlight, loons in the morning—laying them on the paper as
if they were like poems, breaking the lines where she took a breath, as in the
breath-line of a song. I wanted the voice in my ear to stop. As she had moved

my hand-holding-knife-to-fish, she had moved me also with her cadence, moved my body, until I had to write.

I was using my body—my ears, listening; my fingers, writing—to carry her into written language. But as I did this, my own speech, even its rhythm, was changing, to adapt to what I heard; I did not wonder if this was a risky move. It seemed to be necessary, and was good for learning to live in her country.

OLD WOMAN SCRAPING SKIN

Skin

All day yesterday I scraped
till my wrists hurt.
Somebody gave me this sealskin.
Five times I soaked it
and scraped it.
My son helps. He's good at scraping,
strong. He can sew—his brother, too—
and knit. My grandchildren knit,
young children! I teach them.

But I'm tired of teaching.
Let their father do it now. He can
take them trapping, teach them
how to live. How to hunt.

Now twist the skin: see, softens it
a little. Last night I twisted
and twisted. Marks all over my hand:
See? on the knuckles.
I wonder how those Eskimo women
do it. Moose is softer.

Yesterday, I sat here scraping
all day. No one visits me
in fish camp; I work on the skin.
Those tourists stand and stare.
I hide quick behind this bush.
Haven't they ever seen an old woman
scraping skin?

Crow

One time
a crow began bothering my fish.
That crow came at them and
came at them.
I chased him.
He came back.
Chulyin. Chulyin.

I shot him.

I never told anybody.

In her tongue, which is one of four Dena'ina
Athabaskan languages, *chulyin* is Raven, who is
always called Crow. He is spiritually powerful,
and very tricky. She risked his retaliation.

Fear

One night in fall time—
you know how the dark is then—
I came down to fish camp
to watch bear.

My girlfriend came.
She brought her husband.
We climbed up on the old tin cache
in Olga's camp.

The cache starts to rattle.
I say to my girlfriend,
"Why have you brought him?
I've got a gun, I can shoot.
He's got nothing
to be afraid of."

Watching

People think I'm nosy,
but I'm not nosy.
I know who drinks,
I watch,
then I take care of them.

They were all surprised when Ken Junior
stabbed his brother-in-law.
I wasn't.
One time last year
he came to my house.
His eyes were strange.
Later they found a man dead
in his own house.

They covered it up,
but I know:
Ken Junior did away with him.
He was always
a murderer.

Death

When the plane crashed
I didn't think anything of it.
I got on my Sno-go and went up there.
I came to where there was somebody
on the ice.
I looked, Oh—
it was my sister.
She had cut her head,
long cut, lots of blood.
Somebody was holding her,
my son,
blood was dripping on his gloves.
I told him: Get away!
She don't need you now!
Change your gloves!
I felt nothing.
She bled lots.
Before she went she said,
Mama.
Mama.
Mama.
Then she went.
I jumped on my Sno-go
and went home.
I threw that Sno-go down there.
I went inside and
changed my socks.
I felt nothing,
nothing.
I went back up.
My own sister.
They took them to Anchorage.
Her son-in-law went on the plane:
he bled and bled. Died.

I went home.
Then I went crazy.

Grandchildren

Look at those kids, my grandchildren.
Their mom never tells them what to do!
I have to watch them.
They help me sometimes.
When I pack fish up from the beach
to the smokehouse, they pack fish too.
They can build a good fire.

I have to look after them all the time,
keep them home.
Keep them away from village kids.
Those kids smoke.

I'm always hollering at them.
They're like chulyin.

Sometimes I remember myself
when I was young.
I was terrible!
But I don't tell them.

"Smoke" means marijuana.

Dogs

My grandchildren still play with dolls.
People used to say,
If a girl played with dolls
she would have lots of children.

I never played with dolls.
I had bow and arrows, spear.
I played with my brothers,
I went hunting with my daddy.

Even now, I have my own gear,
Luke has his. I have my own boat,
own traps, own .30-.30.
I go when I want to.

One time I went with my daddy
to Swift River for silver salmon.
We speared fish.
Then we went over to mouth of the Stony,
then down to the Mulchatna:
lots of country to cover.
We traveled with dogs.
I love going with dogs.
You come into new country, you stop,
look around, see where you are.

It's good traveling by moonlight.
Trees are bright
and dogs go fast over the snow.
In open space, they slow down.
But in timber
how they fly!

Murder

For two days the dogs were barking.
The year before last this happened.

I set bread to rise on the oven.
I had time,
so I went out my door
to go to fish camp.
I wasn't going to lock up:
then I heard a voice
right behind me. I turned.
It was Ken Junior
and Johnny Kay.
They scared me. Their faces
looked awful, their eyes
were big and their mouths—
their lips, you know:
were dry,
dry.
I asked them, What do you want!
Ken Junior said:
You're going to fight fire next year?
We're making a list.
I knew it was too early for that.
I went back inside,
locked the padlock.
They went away then.

I wanted to go to fish camp
but I was scared.
I saw three boys working in the next yard.
I went to them
and said, You watch me
go down the trail.
If I holler, you come quick!
They said, All right.
What are you afraid of?
Nothing, I told them. Black bear.

...

One day passed, then another day.
I said to Luke, Have you seen Wassily?
He had not come past in all that time.
I went to pick berries.
I picked berries a little while,
not too long, and then
I went to cut fish.
But when I got to fish camp
no one was there. My house was locked,
my son's house was locked,
there was no key.
I put down my berries—
I only had a little bit—
and ran back up the trail.
Everyone was at Wassily's house.
He died, they said. No one went in.

When the trooper came
I went into the house right behind him.
I held his coat. I was a little scared,
but I wanted to see for myself.
It looked like they had thrown him down.
His leg was over the bed,
his hands were stretched out.
Ken Junior was standing there.
His face looked terrible.
The trooper looked at him,
moved the hands.
He said to me,
Looks like a heart attack, doesn't it?
I said, Oh dear.
That's all I said.

. . .

Later I asked him,
Where's the head trooper?
Juneau, he told me.
Oh, I said.

His face looked flat.
You couldn't see his nose,
eyes, mouth: nothing.
The trooper put one bag on him;
zipped it up.
Put another bag on him,
zipped that one up.
When the body came back to the village
they kept the box closed.

I can never forget
Ken Junior's face. It looked
as if he did something.

They cover up too much.

Morning

The lake
was flat calm
and so quiet:
I saw
eight loon.

Visitors

IN JUNE THERE WERE mornings of slender, silvery rain, when the sky, the lake, the tin roofs rhymed. I rose at six to fire up the stove and fix breakfast. I liked the crackle of drywood catching fire; but F intended to put in an oil stove before freeze-up: the wood stove was a twenty-four-hour job, and he disliked sawing logs. That season he had a job on the construction crew at the new school; he left the house by seven, and I had the morning to myself. I walked across the road and down the slope past the outhouse, to the beach where wild peas and wild onion grew. Terns and swallows crisscrossed the sky like jet contrails, and fine droplets pricked the water, the only evidence of the rain: that, and the net-like mist on my hair. Three boats rested on the lake, as still as their reflections. One was bright blue with a red stripe, and had a tent in the bow. "I haven't seen that in a long time," F had said, pleased: "a tent in the bow."

The small motors were silent so early in the day. *Tzik'istla*, the thrush, called, called, called. The twitter of mud swallows nesting under the eaves of houses filled the air as they fed their hungry young ones. In less hectic times, it was said, people used to stay in tents outside the village in the springtime, to listen to the songbirds. Village Below used to be a birch forest. George Gavril told me that not many years before, they could hardly see the houses for the trees; but they had needed a road, and new houses, and the trees had fallen.

The first mechanical sounds of the day came from a plane flying up the lake. From then until the last, late hour of light, planes of all sizes flew in and out, carrying mail and supplies, freighting material for the new school. Soon after the first plane landed, Joe's niece, Olga, who lived across the road, dragged her gas-powered wringer washer into the yard; and the quiet dissolved under the throb and hum of motors.

By early afternoon the sun had burned off the mist. A small breeze sifted the wild grasses around the house, leaving me restless. I had washed clothes, carrying pails of water from an outside faucet, and was hanging them on the clothesline to dry. The line sagged. A cut alder-sapling lay in the grass. I lifted it to use as a clothes pole and saw, with a child's eyes, a memory: tall, weathered, notched poles, clotheslines of sheets lifting in the breeze ... Every spring when I was small and we still lived on the street where my father had grown up, Irish ladies in their brick houses had taken down the lace curtains and, by hand, washed away the winter's coal-grime. Patiently they had hooked the curtains onto tenters and set them out in the back yards to bleach in the sun. Behind them, sheets billowed on the lines.

White butterflies ruffled about in the long grass. The ghostly women hovered, drawing me back among them, as, faintly sickened, I hung up pair after pair of jeans.

A girl came chasing a butterfly through the yard and caught it delicately between her hands. She was the lovely teller of the story of the mouse mother whose baby was harmed by a careless boy. We found a Mason jar to house her catch, and she went off to pick the small yellow flowers that nourish butterflies.

She came back with her flowers. In the jar, the butterfly sat with folded wings. She looked at it and said thoughtfully, "I suppose I should let it go. I know what it means to be caged." And released it.

○

TWO BOYS WERE RUNNING down the road trying to lift off their bird-kites, but the wind had died. Natalia's youngest brother, who was the same age as her youngest child, Lizzie, ambled behind them, hands in his pockets, as usual.

Children were loved, and if they were not any more emotionally secure than children elsewhere, with parents so often dying or going away and leaving them, there was always a hug for the little ones, a grown-up to hold a baby, a man to swing a toddler into the air. All the old ladies still called F their baby.

Children were treated with courtesy; and I was treated with courtesy. But unlike most adults, I sought out the company of children, who were ingenuous and candid and taught me much about the little matters of daily life. My status in the village was not quite defined, for I did not occupy a conventional position for whites, being neither anthropologist nor linguist nor government agent nor teacher nor oil developer. I seemed to be treated as a young bride, though I was neither very young nor a bride; and thus found myself in a role I had not expected to play. I had been an independent young woman moving easily through the larger world; here, I discovered, I could do very little on my own. All around me were the things I should have known, and did not know: how to keep house, and how to cook as the people preferred; where to fetch fresh water, and where to dump the wastebucket; how to wash clothes in a gas-powered machine, bathe in a tin basin, crimp the copper joining on a kerosene bottle; how to preserve berries, cut fish, can moosemeat, keep mold off the smoked salmon. In its intricate details, the village was unto itself. The workings of its hearts lay deep, and were not apparent to me; my own heart was most baffling of all. In their circuitous manner the aunties, Natalia, the old woman of the fierce eye, each let me know that, whoever I thought I was, in the village I was not that person. I diverted myself, then, by looking through a child's eyes, as though learning everything anew, without preconceptions; yet, with my own eyes.

When I allowed myself to feel easier, when I ceased to worry about losing myself in contradictions, a younger person—Janet, perhaps, or Aggie—would come and say, "Well, the old people see that you want to learn, so come to fish camp," or "Come pick berries with us." Adjusting to this life was a slow process, an internal tide of uncertainty ebbing and flowing.

○

F SELDOM SPLIT enough wood for the stove. I didn't mind the job, enjoying the heft of the axe and its elegance as a simple machine, but was not adept at it. Anyone could see it, I worked in the front yard. Billy Alexey, who was F's hunting partner, and a man named Gurrie, were out for a stroll and stopped to watch.

"You'll stand there till I do it, won't you?" I said, amused.

They nodded. Billy sat down on the broken-down snowmachine parked near the woodpile.

"Better help her," he said to Gurrie, who lived alone. Gurrie picked up the axe and swung it easily through an upended spruce log. He showed me how to lever the weight of the axe more efficiently, and how to whittle rooster-tail shavings for tinder, and they walked on.

I carried an armload of split logs inside and dumped them into the box by the stove. It was always dirty around that stove, with chips and bits of bark and the greasy ash of burned spruce. Over the years, layers of dust from the road had been ground into the wood floor. The aunties never failed to notice the condition of the house. "It's very clean," they would say kindly, with the slightest edge to their voices. But it wasn't clean. I couldn't carry enough water to make it clean.

I was trying to make it neater, when Lizzie opened the door. She was a lively girl, almost twelve, with all the confidence of a loved child. I had sprinkled a little water and was sweeping the floor, pushing the broom away from myself. Lizzie chattered as she watched me closely, and I caught surprise in her face.

"This is how you do it." She took the broom and brushed it in smaller, precise movements across the grain of the wood, toward herself. Though the dust rose, it was an exact copy of the way her mother did it.

○

RESIGNED, I closed my book. Lizzie said, "What if you had a different-colored pencil for every day of the week?"

"What if," I speculated. "What would you have: for Monday?"

Her shoulders slumped. "Black. If I was sleepy."

"What if you weren't sleepy?"

"Brown."

"Tuesday?"

She held up a yellow lead pencil. "Just a lead pencil ..."

"Wednesday is blue! That's how I feel Wednesdays, just blue."

"You mean, you feel kind of let down?"

"No, that's the color."

"Thursday?"

"Red. No, orange, almost happy." Pause. "Friday is red." She smiled.

"Saturday?"

She considered, then grinned: her dimples appeared. "One of those pens that has all different colors."

"Okay: Sunday."

"I don't work on Sunday. A broken lead pencil."

◊

LIZZIE HIKED up the stairs two at a time and stepped into my study, breathless. Her friend Alexa crowded in behind her. They settled on the bed and chattered about everything, until I finished typing.

"You should be in a play," I teased them. "You should both be in a play called *Arsenic and Old Lace*." I told them the story: two sweet, tough-minded old ladies who poison their boarders.

Lizzie laughed, delighted, and immediately described her costume, invented a cane, then hobbled across the floor, a perfect old lady on the stage.

◊

MARYA WAS washing dishes. That was what high school girls did: wash dishes, and take care of the little ones. They seemed to do nothing but chores. There were standard divisions of labor, "women's" and "men's." F and I argued about this. He was not about to be shaken. He would never do his own laundry, for instance, and could not consider washing a dish.

Natalia said sympathetically, "Marya hates those eternal dishes. Janet and Aggie and them are the girls she looks up to. They're interested in education. In what goes on around them besides village gossip." Marya was her eldest daughter; in autumn she would be a senior.

The high school was inadequate. Marya knew it, and her sister Sally knew it, and they had talked about it to me. Marya hoped to go to college in California, and her parents were for it, but she doubted she would meet all the entry requirements. Other students also wanted to go to college. It was all too likely they would be blocked by the school, or be discouraged because college was difficult in ways they were not prepared to face. They would have to be strong and clear-minded: college was hard; it was, by its nature, meant to change people, to educate them for a literate, complex world. Beyond the intense, normal stresses that freshmen always had to undergo, however, college would be harder for the youngsters from the village.

Joe had been working at the school site so that the family could get ahead for the winter. He and Natalia had put money aside for Marya.

If people agreed to it, I thought I might run for school committee in the next election. It would be a delicate matter; people assumed that whites tried to assume positions of leadership. I must be patient. Parents, having had hard experience with formal education, were intimidated by the experts, found their opinions ignored, and grew cautious, or angry.

F said, "You have something we need: knowledge."

Joseph could have gone to college. He was observant and thoughtful; he always had a book in his hands.

"Why doesn't he go, then?" I asked.

"I tell him all the time he should go. But you know how people are around here. He's afraid to stand out."

Because of their schooling, inadequate as it was, there was promise for the girls and young women; but the young men were withering. There was nothing for them to do.

F had hated school. That was why he worked so hard, he said. At home he was restless. He sat and looked out the window, his eyes always moving, fingers drumming. He jumped up, ran out, darted into this or that house.

○

LATER THAT SUMMER a visitor was lost in the river, below the fish camps. He was a tough, beefy man from Oklahoma who had come out to supervise the building of the new school. That year high schools were under construction in every village in the bush. A recent legal settlement had instructed the state to educate Native students at home. For generations Native students had been sent away to boarding school or a mission school, usually outside Alaska. This had meant that—for those who received schooling; many youngsters did not—their formative teenaged years were spent away from the village. Traditionally, this would have been the time for their instruction in history, language, myth, their training in the art and ceremony of the hunt. They would have learned to live off the land. They would have been formed by their elders. Instead, following the old government regulation, they had had to go away to dormitory school. Generations of Native people had grown up without parental guidance during their crucial years; it followed that, as parents themselves, they had no experience with teenaged children at home. Perhaps this was why, in part, so many adults were not literate; and why so many boys and young men no longer knew how to hunt. Certainly it had to do with why the young men were restless, at loose ends.

People were waiting to see whether the new school would be good for the village. The men had strong opinions about the construction practices they were told to follow. They were building on the hilly muskeg at the lower end of the village. The site stood in the bed of an underground stream that flowed from the upper slope. They doubted the drainpipes they had laid could divert the summer snowmelt without eroding the hill around the schoolyard, and thought the pipes would freeze in winter. They could see, they said among themselves, that the Outside architect had not understood the demands of subarctic winters.

The supervisor spoke for the management of the construction company. He had agreed to hire union members from the village as laborers, but he had brought in his own workers to run the heavy equipment. Some older men, including Joe Gavril, were bothered by the disparity. They told the supervisor that they had been trained on the pipeline to use heavy equipment, and that they belonged to the right union. Nothing changed. Their mood grew heavier. The supervisor asked F, who was nearly the youngest among them, to boss the Native crew.

The idea of giving orders to the older men, especially to Joe, shocked F. He raged about the unfairness of the job. He shouted at me that all of the workers were building the school to be used by the village, but the Native crew was always below the white crew. He told the supervisor that he would be boss of the whole crew, or no crew at all. The supervisor said that that was too bad for F, and chose an older man instead. Publicly, F accepted the choice; privately, he nursed his hurt and said bitterly that everyone knew the man's whole family was lazy. The man took the job. Joseph told me he had done it unwillingly, only to prevent an open dispute.

Before breakup, F had warned me that construction wages would bring liquor into the village. The bootleggers would do well. After payday, the voices of young men and married men were raised in the night. Some had gone that way before, those who had worked on the pipeline, or in the commercial fishing fleets, or on construction crews in town. With pity and dread I looked into the begging eyes of a father who wanted whiskey and tried to keep himself from asking for it. The Vietnam veteran had to be tied down when he drank.

"We wondered what you'd think of the drinking," Janet said.

I had grown up with drinking. In my valley, men of the older generations, working and professional men, taught their sons early how to drink. Alcohol was their social oil, easing them, allowing them to talk to each other; or, in harder situations, blunting their emotions, helping them disguise, thus endure, their intense feelings. It was an Irish malady, but not exclusively: men from different backgrounds followed their own liquid styles. Drink was their tradition, and although families did suffer its ravages, the social fabric was not rent. I myself hardly drank; not that I wouldn't have enjoyed it. But I could have conveyed none of this to Janet. That milieu was too distant, indescribable. I did not realize then that nearly all the men I would come to know in Alaska, including educated men, professors and bureaucrats, those who wanted to do some good in the world, or do something important, would drink, hard and regularly. Was this their tradition also? They seemed lonelier when they drank; they blustered and pretended they were not helpless. They would not weep, not even to their women friends.

On the nights when bootleggers grew rich, everything changed on the road. People staggered from house to house, some silent, some muttering. Aggie was helping her father home through the twilight but she couldn't manage to hold him up by herself. I took his other arm, and we stumbled up the path to her house. She put him to bed, and came out to walk me back. In the shadows we ran into three men. Among them was the mayor, whom Aggie despised.

"Where the hell you're going, beautiful," one of them slurred.

It isn't bad, I told myself, my mind recording facts. Aggie muttered: "Challenge them. Keep cool, don't hesitate." No such thing as a harmless drunk. You can't predict what he will do. I felt too old to be angry: I laughed.

I locked up the house; but the voices would not die down. I remained upstairs, among my books. When, afterward, I read Michael Herr's *Dispatches*, his account of the war that poisoned my generation, I recognized where I had been: in its shadow. Out of the blasphemous mouths of his soldiers came the same profane, horror-struck language of those men in the village. They, too, were former soldiers, warriors turned construction workers, numbed veterans of the inhuman pipeline. In the village they were home but not home; they would never come home from the war.

In midsummer the sun did not touch the horizon till well after midnight. The deepest part of the night was twilight. The twilight moved and slipped around the voices, as if it were thick with shades. The metaphysical smell of death seeped into my room. I was always sick to my stomach then.

◊

DOWNSTAIRS, F ranted at Joseph and Billy.

"My grandma said, Learn the white man's ways. They're going to make a fucking park out of this place! I grew up hunting. I went out whenever I wanted. No one tells me I can't hunt.

"They gave me a slice of land. Fuck! This all was our land, we were the first people in this country. Fuck. I should have been a fucking graduate in the law of Indian heritage. I've read this fucking state constitution so many times I could probably recite it to you.

"I'll never live on a fucking reservation, man, they might was well come after me, 'cause I'll stand here with my rifle, and they better not try to take my life unless they don't mind losing theirs. I'll never live on a fucking reservation!"

Joseph and Billy, their voices dulled, muttered, "Yeah, right on," until F fell asleep in his sprung-seat armchair.

◊

THE WHITE CREW had gone into town for a long weekend. The supervisor stayed in the village. On Saturday afternoon he went boating with some people whose family he had done favors for, a young couple, and Nick Demetrov, whose brother was married to Irina, the teacher. Nick drove the boat, which was his father's. There was a bottle.

Later we learned how the accident happened. Nick, drunk, had begun to drive in circles. The supervisor sat near him, in the midsection of the boat. The young husband wanted to take the tiller, and he and the supervisor stood up to exchange places. It was rough going just then, and they both tumbled overboard. All the wife could see was red water. Somehow she pulled her husband into the boat and managed to drive home. Nick had all but passed out.

Someone came running for Natalia to bandage the mutilated man. After the shock wore off, after he was medevac'd to the hospital, people looked around for the supervisor. F asked the dazed wife where he was. Startled, she remembered that he had fallen into the river.

"He's still down there," she said.

Everyone thought she meant he had climbed ashore, or was down at the portage landing. She meant, He is in the water.

For weeks the village waited for the body to surface. Men in boats scanned the river for another hazard. Faces showed the strain. The dogs howled, inexplicably.

One afternoon, a man took his family on an outing downriver, and quickly brought them back. The body, caught on a snag, had risen, far below where the fish camps stood. A party of men formed, F and Joseph among them; and they went down to recover the corpse.

The two of them sat at the table and were unable to stop themselves talking. Joseph had touched the body. He said: "The skin was tough, but there was no rigor mortis." He sounded very young. He said: "The face was bloated and covered with green-brown algae, like an old, dead fish." He said: "There wasn't much blood left."

That night F slept at Joe and Natalia's house, as he used to do, and had bad dreams. The next night, F and Joseph slept like brothers, at our house.

The boat was to be burned. Nick Demetrov's father had not intended to do it; but people had begun to talk, and no one would go in the boat with his family. After the decision was announced, F grew calmer.

The day of the burning, the Demetrovs, father and son, towed the boat to fish camp. The father had built the boat; it was ten years old and still the best one in the village, broad enough in the beam to weather the lake winds, yet fast in the water. He had borrowed a blunt-prowed river boat from the husband of the old woman of the fierce eye, and a forty-five–horse motor from another man. As they passed my window, Nick and his father, the father was driving. Nick sat away from him; his back was bent. They turned beyond the Point. The wake of the two boats fanned out behind them.

Time passed. Gray smoke rose and blew downriver, toward where the body had risen, away from the village. The road was empty. The air was quiet.

A while later, the thin buzz of a motor traveled up from the lake to my study. I looked out the window. In the boat sat Nick's father, alone.

o

JOSEPH ASKED ME if I was going to write about the accident. I wrote a kind of dirge, and gave it to him.

> . . . .
> Not even that God turned His back
> on this visitor,
> but that he slipped
> through the net of kinship and drowned
> because no one could attend to him.

He nodded. "That's it."

I breathed out. I had put the death in its own place, and could sleep quietly again, for a while.

o

IN THE INTERVAL between the accident and the recovery of the body, a well-loved old man, who in his day had been known as a good hunter, was accused by the game warden of poaching a moose.

Notices of a meeting appeared on the doors of the post office, store, village office, and the hall. On the appointed afternoon, boat after boat drove up from the fish camps. Representatives from every family filed into the village hall, where folding chairs had been set back to form a circle, and took their places. The old man accused of poaching, whom everyone called Uncle Peter, and Tassie, his wife, sat among their own people. He was F's uncle; F and I sat near them. No one spoke.

The heavy door was pushed open, scraping the floor loudly. For a moment, sunlight flared through the doorway. The mayor stepped into the room; behind him came a stocky man wearing aviator glasses and the heavy uniform of the state fish and game enforcement service. The two men entered the empty central space, and it became a courtroom. Nervously, the mayor made a short introduction, and sat down. The officer, who was stationed in the regional town, spoke into the charged silence. "There's been a crime committed." The scene was turning into a bad movie, only no one laughed. He took off his glasses, folded them, put them in his pocket, and glanced around the room; he was nervous and sweating. Faces remained immobile. Eyes were held steady, but off his eyes.

"It's my job to see that justice is done. Now, we don't know each other. And that's too bad, though I've been down in Big Lake for most of this year. I heard a lot about you people, though. They call the young guys 'cowboys.'" He chuckled heavily. "But they don't mean any harm by it. I'll admit it, I've been a little afraid to come up here."

Oho! the air responded.

"... but I want to make up for that now, get to know you people. See if we can't work together to protect our fish and game."

No one moved; no one spoke. Faintly, the drone of a plane engine drifted in through the window, then the piping laughter of children playing in the old schoolyard and the sleepy sigh of a breeze in the tall grass.

"Now, there's been some illegal activity going on, some poaching, and we have the evidence for it," he went on. His eyes still moved too quickly around the room. "This fine elder has been accused of illegal possession of game meat. But he says he did not kill the moose out of season. He tells us that someone found the meat and gave him some of it, and that's what we found in his cache.

"Now, it's been said, and I surely do believe it, that an elder would not lie. So I believe this man. I'm taking his word, and we're not going to prosecute him, though we had to confiscate the meat. We're going to take his word for it. I want you folks to understand that, and I want to ask you to help me with keeping this sort of thing from happening again in the future. If you have any questions, I'd be glad to answer 'em."

At *not going to prosecute*, the taut circle of people eased slightly, and Tassie cried out. Uncle Peter slumped back in his chair.

After a few moments, a council member asked what kind of evidence the fish and game people had found.

The officer answered easily, switching to technical jargon as if to a natural tongue, to explain how a piece of moose horn picked up near the carcass had been matched to the horn found in the old man's cache.

"How they found that horn in the brushes?" another man asked.

From the air, the officer explained: he had been flying, and spotted a dead moose. When he located the animal on the ground, he found that it had been shot, and most of it left to rot.

For the first time, faces showed emotion. Heads shook, *No.* A feeling of sick disgust flowed around the room.

A middle-aged man stood up. He was known as a good speaker before white people, because he was talkative. Carefully, he explained that a Native person would not have left the moose to rot.

"It's not our way to kill an animal for nothing," he said. "Not our way to leave it. This elder would never do this terrible thing. He is respected as a hunter. This proves he is not guilty."

The fish and game officer nodded politely at the spokesman. He suggested that maybe some wild young men had been out drinking and shot the moose by mistake.

Faces stiffened and replied motionlessly, *Not our people.* Somewhere in the room was a slight uneasiness.

Smoothly, the spokesman suggested that maybe the fish and game officer could explain the hunting laws once again to the people, especially the part about moose season and illegal hunting.

"We want to cooperate to do what's right," he said. "Maybe us older people can try to keep our younger men in better order. You know how young men are sometimes. Sometimes they get a little enthusiastic and don't pay enough attention to the calendar. Let us know the rules. Then we can keep an eye out.

"We're pleased to meet you," he went on. "Took a while. We like to know who is our fish and game cop. We like to know who we're dealing with. You could visit us more often. You could let us know what your plane looks like. It's what color? You have a number on the wing? We could look out for it and welcome you here. We need to have information to help us do this hunting the right way."

The fish and game officer thanked the spokesman, the mayor, and all the good people for being cooperative and law-abiding. He promised, now that the ice was broken and he could see that this was a peaceable village, that he would be back to visit more often, and hoped to make many friends.

A small group gathered around the old man and his wife. He was speaking now in his own defense, slowed by a stammer. F touched his sleeve and went to the door. One or two of the men who worked as hunting guides spoke to the officer. Everyone else quietly left the hall.

That night I heard expressions of relief around the table, mixed with anger and a never-ending disbelief that *gasht'anas* would try to tell the animals when they could be hunted.

Fishing Is for
Women: We
Are Hunters

BEFORE THE RED SALMON came up
the river to spawn, the women began to move down to fish camp, and by the
sunny days of mid-July they were in place for the great job of putting up the
winter supply.

Below the village the lake narrowed into a river that was the red-salmon
route. For days, a long shadow moved through the limestone water. Above it,
along the high banks, sat the fish camps, which were called by the name of
their oldest mother: Mary's, Tassie's, Natalia's, Ruth's, down the east side;
Vera's, Helen's, Olga's, down the west.

The camps were built in the tall grass where birches and alders had been
cleared, enough to make room for one or two small cabins of log or rough-
cut lumber, or a wall tent. Nearby stood the smokehouse, as tall as a two-
storey building, made of spruce poles or rough board and roofed with
flattened oil drums. The outhouse was set back in the brush, where overgrown
paths led around to the other camps or off to a favorite swimming pond; a
cleared space, a yard, led down to the water's edge. There, cutting tables were
set up near willow fish racks, called *entasie*, and the bone racks for dog food.
Fish boxes made of chicken wire and lumber were sunk into the shallows.

The work was hard; but the days were long enough for anyone to find time
to pick wildflowers, or to sit on the bank, drinking tea and enjoying the
beauty of the season. Life slowed down to a hum of peace, calm, and light.
Couples could find time and place to be alone.

In Natalia's camp, Lizzie and her cousins showed me where they caught
the fat brook trout that lived in the creeks, and where they liked to swim with
the other kids, and where they picked berries with their grandma. Their
grandmother, Agrafena, who had given the camp over to Natalia (it was the
same camp where I had been taken ice fishing, months before), had brought
up ten children there. Every summer, when the time came to move, she had
settled the smaller ones in the boat, charged the older ones to look after them,
and rowed them safely down the lake. She had boiled diapers while she cut
fish; and disapproved, discreetly, of how young women complained now,
when they had fewer children, and boxes of Pampers. "We didn't mind then,"
she said gently.

Lizzie, that summer, was radiant, about to come into her womanhood, and she alternated between the energy of girlhood and the first proud modesty of her time. She liked to come down to the cutting table and watch us: Janet, her favorite auntie, guiding me; me, trying to cut fish.

Janet, who doted on Lizzie, gave her a small trout for practice. She worked away while Janet and I cut dog salmon, until, with a flourish, she held up a piece of the rainbow: a poor, tattered fillet. Overhead, the terns wheeled and screamed. She threw down her knife, cross. "Those birds! They don't have to keep looking at me." She looked down at the little fish. "Poor fish, having me to learn on him."

Late in the day, Joseph drove me up to the village, following an off-shore channel. Beneath us, as far as I could see into the green-brown, vertiginous depths, swam masses of spawning, dying red salmon, uncountable numbers surging against the current. Life.

◊

DURING THE WARM SEASON, husbands and sons came down to set and check nets, sometimes to cut fish. At night they went back to the village, particularly if they worked on the construction crew; or they left town to join the commercial fishing fleets, or were called up for fire-fighting crews. F always slept at home; he refused to go down to camp, even on the weekends. "Fishing is for women," he said. "We are hunters."

Joe Gavril stayed in the village while he worked at the school construction site. Joseph, however, went back and forth to camp. He was unemployed, because his hair was too long for construction work. His father, an Army veteran with a crewcut and a belief in hard work, strongly advised his son to cut his hair and get a job.

Joseph, who was tall and broad-shouldered like his father, but whose hair fell, gloriously, halfway down his back, would fold his arms across his chest and narrow his eyes into an imposing, unsmiling squint. I could never tell whether he was amused or angry. He tied a bandana around his head and looked rather like a movie Indian and yet indomitable. He would say nothing.

The argument between father and son went on for half the summer. Even F urged Joseph to cut his hair and end the dispute.

In the end, Joseph gave in. But Joseph had wit, and he made his point, and it silenced his father and his friend. He flew into Anchorage, went straight to the beauty salon at Nordstrom's, a frilly pink shop where his sisters went, and had his beautiful hair cut short and permed, like a woman's.

◊

THE TWO SONS of the old woman of the fierce eye stayed in camp to assist their mother. One of them had a wife and two children, who also stayed in camp. The sons set and checked their mother's net.

The old woman's daughter-in-law, who was called Lily, asked me if I wanted to go with them to pick the nets. Four of us, Lily, her husband, her father-in-law, and I, set off in their long, blunt-prowed river craft. Her father-in-law, a semi-invalid during the cold months, took pride in working despite his rheumatism. Their set-net site was an eddy not far above camp.

The salmon were graceful when they were still firm and silver. They hung in the meshes, shining, jerking slightly, riffling the water. The men hauled the nets, one after the other, into the boat. With small bill-hooks they pulled away the mesh from the gills and loosened the fish. The old man's gnarled hands somehow were nimble, and he showed me how to work the hook. Salmon flopped into the boat until they rose nearly to the gunwales and the nets were empty.

Back at the camp I helped Lily carry the fish to the waterbox, to keep them fresh. The old woman, who always worked alone, would gut and strip them later. It was a back-breaking job, carrying fish.

"You work too hard," Lily said gently.

"I don't mind."

I was free to stop but knew she would keep working. She grinned—she wasn't pretty, but her grin lit up her face in sweet gaiety—and suggested we walk over to the next camp, where her father spent the summer.

I hardly knew her family. They lived near the far end of the village, near the new school site. Her father was a widower; he had never remarried and still put up his own winter supply. People spoke well of how he used the knife and about the number of fish he could prepare in a day.

In the camp, some people were cutting fish and some were hanging fish on the racks. A few people lounged on the bank, drinking tea. Their spare movements, their relaxed voices, were as calm as the air. Lily brought us two cups of hot tea, and sat down beside me on the grass. The scene was like a summer day in the provinces, in a Russian novel of the nineteenth century.

A bent old man hobbled on crutches into the warmth of the sunlight. I had seen him before, in his son's house: he sat in the corner, near the stove. Someone had whispered to me that he was the wisest man in the village. He wore a Greek fisherman's cap and a baggy rust-black overcoat. His face was smooth, the ephemeral gone from it; his lips curved downward with age and, even so, seemed to smile. He had no teeth. A young man guided him to a wooden chair near the bank. Infinitely slowly, he lowered himself toward the seat. Gradually, the coat settled around his shoulders.

Near Lily and me lay an infant in a blanket-lined box, kicking busily, waving its tiny arms, babbling to itself. The old man, in his silence, might have been thought deaf, but he heard the infant's contented noises. He turned his face and then, by degrees, his body, toward the sound, and in his old, thin voice, as though now he had seen all he could hope for, cried joyfully, "Baby! Baby!"

o

THAT NIGHT, someone in a drunken fit emptied the fish box. Lily said to me, "All I could think of was you carrying those fish. All your work, for nothing!"

o

THE WOMEN, who could set nets and pick them, preferred to cut fish. Red salmon, food for humans, not the dogs, was sliced in one of several ways, depending on how it would be used. "Dog" salmon, an inferior variety, was cut according to a different pattern. Each wife had evolved her own way of cutting, learned from her mother and apparent to the practiced eye. She followed her own recipe for putting up the fish, its ingredients as varied as the eddy where the net had been set, the quality of the fish caught, the proportions of salt to water in the brine, the cut of the salmon, and the time allowed for brining, drying, and smoking.

Having been brined, having dried for a day or two, the cut fish were hung in the smokehouses over an alderwood smudge. I loved to go in and look up at the racks of dripping salmon. The water-silver skins turned gold; the once-red flesh deepened, to red-gold; the oil and smoking wood smelled darker and deeper than peat. Sunlight, filtered through narrow spaces between the shed poles, turned gilt and copper. The smoke swirled upward, as incense. Alchemy, their curing. Those strips of fish meant food for the winter; no starvation.

Natalia showed me how to use a pressure cooker, and how to jar fish, and from their catch I put up a small winter supply for F and me. Wild onion grew around the camp. I asked if she had ever seasoned the fish with it. No, she said, but it might be worth trying.

We cooked a few extra jars of salmon with onion. Billy Alexey, her brother, tested a batch. "Good," he said; Natalia ought to cook more fish that way. I was pleased, and a little proud—I wasn't sure I could taste the difference—and am amused at myself for it, and smile at the memory of their kindness. Was I learning to be domestic, by the grace of wild food? Soon the berries were going to be ripe; now that I knew how to preserve food, I could make jam also.

o

A SMALL ROOM opened off the main room. We never used it; it smelled of damp. Two narrow iron beds had been pushed against opposite walls as if to divide the space in half, and at the foot of each bed stood a dresser, its top covered with dust. A few Blazo boxes did for night tables and, nailed up on the walls, for shelves; a corner was curtained off as a closet. Otherwise, the room was empty.

Empty, but somehow cluttered. Debris had drifted up against the furniture: a pair of shoe pacs, part of a snowmachine suit, two or three pairs of heavy gloves, all with holes in them. A yellowed, dog-eared Western novel lay crushed between a bed and its dresser; a few old bills had slipped down behind it and were wedged against the wall. The names on the bills were smudged—not bills, but bank statements, corporate-earnings statements; tattered messages from secular powers sent to what brief sojourners? Those whom a sudden event had called away: fishing had opened, or they had gone out to winter camp, and would be back. Or, they would not; but would go on to another house almost like this, also shabby, soon to be abandoned. The messages would never reach them. I piled the papers and shoved them into a drawer. We were going to sleep in this dim, small room. His brothers were coming to visit, and would have the rest of the house to themselves.

○

I DID NOT GO UP to the graves until after the brothers left. The path up the hill promised quiet. As I climbed, the path turned parallel to the ridge behind the village; beyond the ridge, beyond the rosy hills, the sun set, never visible from below. I saw his mother's grave first. The Russian cross was raw plywood, but the wooden fence around it was painted white, and plastic flowers had been placed on the mound.

F still agonized over her death, his eyes wide and grieving. She had collapsed in fish camp and died in his arms. His body had felt the tremor of her spirit passing, thrilling him, shocking him. He blamed himself, because he had given her so much grief. I saw a picture of her taken late in her life. She had died at fifty; in the photograph she looked much older; she looked worn out.

Thrush song rose up from all around the hill. Mosquitoes hummed. Where did people find the faith to go on?

According to Joseph, her children had found half a lid of marijuana among her things. She had been one of the first adults to smoke grass in the village. She was pretty cool, he said.

Athabaskans put their graves on a high place above a lake or a river. They used to leave their dead on platforms, elevated, so that the spirit could see sky and water. The bereaved still burned food near the graves, to feed the spirits; people did not like to speak of this. "We carry our dead with us for a long time," Janet had said. They came back in dreams, to give advice, to sing a song, to take the dreamer on a journey. Their spirits passed into the younger generations, as their names did, and were greeted again with pleasure. Who had told me this? Natalia? Joseph? F, when he was drinking?

What would you think of me, woman? Would you have wanted someone different for your son?

F's older brothers had gone bad. Ace was a hustler, his bright eye fixed on the shadiest main chance. F seemed to think he was successful; he half-admired Ace, half-wanted to fight him. Lou was next, a pale imitation of the suave thug that Ace was. Inspecting me, he had said, insolent, warning me: "You must be a fine person, you are sleeping in my mother's bed."

Ace was a bootlegger. When he and Lou had the money for it, they dealt cocaine. The three brothers had worked on the pipeline; everyone in the camp had used cocaine. During the war, Anchorage had been a major entry point of drugs from southeast Asia, and the drug trade had remained steady and lucrative. F had come off the line with five thousand dollars, and had spent it on coke. A man he knew in Anchorage had put him up for a few weeks: F had gathered his stash, poured it out on a mirror, set the mirror on the coffee table, and invited visitors to help themselves. He and his buddy had had many visitors; then the coke was gone.

"It was too much money anyway," he said. "I gave it away."

He had been defensive, worried that I would leave him. He was right to worry, I nearly did go, but he swore he was clean. It was good to give away what you didn't need, he believed; but then he was left with almost nothing.

People seemed to have been buried in the order in which they died, the first-gone lying nearer the village, the crosses climbing the hillside from there.

It came to me that his mother did not bless my presence in that old place. She knew that I would have to leave; it was only a matter of time.

o

I STOOD IN THE CENTER of the small room, almost not seeing what was there. Visqueen still bound the window against the distant winter; filtered light touched yellow and green surfaces but hardly disturbed the shadows. A little dust stirred. I stood still for a long time.

In this room their grandmother had lived, had sickened and been bed-ridden, and, at a hundred and fifteen years, had died. Never once had she spoken her husband's language. Her husband had been the Irish bootlegger with the fastest boat in Bristol Bay.

I leaned into one space, not the other; toward one bed, the one we used, not the other. Which was the mother's, which the grandmother's? How those women must have hated whites.

For some reason, we had slept on the bed farthest from the window. It was an old-fashioned window, older than the others in the house, its panes hand-cut. They were seven inches by nine, old-timer's panes, people said. Someone had carried the glass all the way from Bristol Bay, whence it had come by boat from Seattle.

That night I woke up and saw nothing. Uneasily, I stretched out a hand and touched the wall. F slept beside me; there was hardly room to move. As I turned toward the window, he turned with me in his sleep, and muttered. The light seeping through the Visqueen was as faint as vapor on a frosty morning. For a long time I lay thinking about the coming of the darkness.

o

A HUGE ORANGE MOON hung in the east, over the mountains, after a red sunset. Twilight had settled on the land. Peace was there. Fish jumped in the water; red, red fish hung on the racks; alder smoke drifted along the banks. The season was nearly over. I had pitched a tent in the old woman's fish camp.

F sang to me. How complicated his spirit was. He had been drinking all night and into the day. He had breathed hard and stomped about, and then begun to relax, or fall back on the alcohol in his veins; and he began to sing a song. He stopped, and looked quickly, shyly, at me. "Ain't I a good song maker-upper?" Surprised, I said yes, and then he sang again.

He sang to me that he was scared to be loved. He could not say the words, but they had come out easily in his song. He said he made up songs all day. He closed his eyes and rocked himself into his song and made the hurt go away, or at least made it stand at bay.

"I wish I could stay a kid!" he had cried, "I wish I never had to grow up!"

In a hard voice, as if he had accepted a hard decision, he had said: "The old ways are gone. People have to learn to live the new way."

He was fighting, desperately, to make something of himself; that meant making money: "When money talks, nobody walks." Was he talking to me, or to himself? He was thinking of opening a liquor store.

Very quietly I told him I wouldn't live with a man who sold liquor.

He continued to reveal, to unravel, himself. Bad examples like his brothers kept him going: he saw in them what he did not want to become. The pressure built up; he needed to drink, to release it; but the drink did not work, and then he talked, and then he was exhausted. Music was the key; he needed music. He had so much music in him.

He stopped speaking. His gaze turned inward; then: "I've seen death."

Panic had risen in his voice. I sat still, breathing steadily, allowing myself to feel nothing, and willed him to remain sane.

Before his mother's death, he had seen something—a wall of the house had dissolved before his eyes, a curtain of fire flared up ... His eyes rolled in his head. I remained still.

"I have a strong heart," he said loudly. He was talking to the room, not me. He shouted: "My strong heart saved me!"

He grew calm, almost cold; and then, hopeful: "Maybe it was a drug flashback. That's all it was."

He knew I had been uneasy in the small room. "My grandmother drove you out of there," he said spitefully, and then: "You learn too fast. It scares us."

The orange moon rode in the sky. I was tired, and understood nothing; and knew that I was not going to be able to save him; and knew, finally, that I had another kind of work to do. If I were ever to have children, their father would have been F; but I was never going to have children, they were not my calling, and it had been a dream that I could stay in this heartrending country.

In the twilight I could see the village on the lake, easy to get to, and remote as a place could be.

◦

BY MID-AUGUST the light had begun to recede, the stars to reappear in the darkening sky. The mountains turned redder, the rose-brown color of caribou hides. The men began to talk about hunting. They sat on knolls outside the camps and watched the country through binoculars. The first caribou had come into sight. In a few weeks, before the rut began, the moose season was going to open. By that time the women would have closed down the camps and gone back to the village, and the children gone back to school. The nights would be dark again. The tang of snow would be in the air.

I did not know wild meat. This startled F. He was ready to go out for game. His hunting partner was Billy Alexey, Natalia's brother. She took care to reassure me that Billy knew the country well. The two men decided to go "up the mountain" to look for caribou. They departed just after dawn, walking in file, Billy in the lead, each carrying a .30-.30 on a sling, and salmon strips, tea, and a few shells in his pack. They expected to return that night, but they did not reappear. At last I went to bed, and dreamed.

I set off on the trail to find them. I left the village, and found myself in a pretty town that I recognized as a capital. The town was white: its buildings were white and well-made, and were built upon hills.

I entered a yard and saw a white house framed in white flowers. Leaning toward me, leaning diagonally across the frame of the dream-picture, was a white ladder, too fragile to climb. The whiteness about me was clean and fresh. These qualities moved and delighted me; but the green mountains were far away, and as I walked toward them they receded, and I got lost.

I floated through crowded places. They were pleasant, but, urgently, I knew I had to keep moving. Mist covered the mountain peaks. I was entirely lost.

I was on the ground again, walking up a gravel road. I passed a pillared, weather-beaten building. A sign above the door said Almond Oil, signifying a workshop for orphans. I understood that it was the old Sitka Native orphanage. I walked farther up the road. A girl stood barefoot on the bare grounds of the orphanage. Distantly, I became aware of her. She wore a faded wash-dress that was too small for her; she was old enough to sleep with a man. I walked past her, absorbed in the dilemma of my journey, wondering how, by what inexplicable means, I had lost my way; and with a start, saw that her face was black with fury, and the air around her as dark as a storm. She hissed at me: "Suffer!"

The strength of her hatred startled me. I turned and asked, "What did you say?" She stared at me with such malevolence that I woke up.[7]

◦

F ENTERED THE HOUSE just after dawn, weary, stained, peaceful. "Meat's in the cache," he said. He gestured toward the Gavrils' cache and, without undressing, fell into bed in the small room.

I went upstairs to the study. After several hours I heard him stir, and came down to greet him. I hardly knew what to say, and felt awkwardly formal, even shy. He walked out of the small room, tousled, stretching, looking happy and expectant. He sniffed the air.

"You're hungry?" I said, smiling. "Eggs?" We had reasonably fresh eggs.

His face went blank. His mouth set in a line. When he left, he pulled the door shut hard behind him; when he returned, he carried a piece of caribou, fresh and bloody. He lit the Coleman stove, took out a pan, and fried the meat. He sat down, and, using the butcher knife to slice off small hunks, ate with his hands. He put down the knife, and licked his fingers. He looked at me, his eyebrows raised, and said: "What did you do all morning?"

"Beg pardon?" I had never seen freshly dressed meat. The room smelled of drying blood, a smell so intense, so clotted with life and death, so real, that I knew I had been playing a part; and that, abruptly, the play was over.

He was maddened. "You want me to bring home meat, and cook it, too?"

"You want to write the poems?" In an instant I was impetuously, wildly furious.

"What were you brought up for?" He stared hard at me to remind me of my duty.

I stared back: "To be president!"

He looked at me, his mouth open. I wanted to weep at the pity of it, and I could say nothing, and felt the heat of anger drain from my body. How could I describe education, travel books, comfort, my father's faith in me? How could I tell him: Not to be a wife.

He tried to command: "We will share my half of the animal with my Older Brother. You, go out to the cache and put aside our piece of it."

"I don't know how to do that," I said simply, feeling absurd, and very sad. "I've never touched fresh meat. I don't know how to divide it, or know what our part is supposed to be."

He looked away. The play was over for him, also, but he had no choice: in disbelief, he had recognized his bad luck; now he had to swallow it. He left the house and went to the cache. Afterward, he said little, washed his hands and the knife, and went back to bed.

The unmendable differences between us had come into the open. They were so simple: fresh meat; the work of the hunter, and the hunter's wife; the hunter's wife who was no wife, who had her own work to do. He could not envision the possibility of it. He had wanted to live in the old way. By my act I had vowed, *I will not.*

I think now he was as much an actor as I was. I think our play was a melodrama; it was a tragedy; it was a prehistoric ritual. He played his role as the hunter, he performed its rite, but, to his horror—I think it was genuine, religious horror—I did not perform the answering rite. I did not complete the ceremony; and my refusal must have seemed to him like sacrilege.

I was shocked by this scene, and by its heart-wrenching meaning, and could not speak about it; and so, could not bring myself to ask Natalia how to use the meat . . .

❍

THE LAND WAS RICH with animals. Caribou, moose, bear, mountain sheep, small game, birds: all fed and clothed the people who lived there. In the streams, grayling, pike, whitefish, trout, and the red salmon abounded in their seasons. Sport hunters and fishermen from as far away as Germany and Japan were attracted by the plenty. The most experienced men worked as packers and guides at fly-in lodges on the lakeshore north of the village.

When the moose season opened, so did the lodges. Their float planes docked on the lake. More strangers appeared. The Dena'ina guides led parties of hunters into the back country: these were for the most part trophy hunters, who were willing to leave the meat to rot rather than pay to freight it out. The village, appalled, worked out a cooperative agreement with the owner of the nearest lodge. He consented to distribute the unused moose flesh to the people.

One day, the lodge owner drove his Jeep slowly down the road. Lizzie ran to tell me, "If you want meat, wait by your door."

Throughout the village, women stood by their doors. The lodge owner called first on the elders. He halted his vehicle before them, one by one. He was smiling. Haunches and ribs were loaded in the back seat. He sliced off a portion and, with hearty courtesy, presented it. With dignity, each woman accepted her piece, and went inside. He divided the rest of the meat among the remaining households.

I carried my small piece of roast into the house, lit the Coleman stove, and canned the meat in the pressure cooker. Now we had a small winter supply of moose. This was useful work.

For hours after the Jeep passed, the road lay nearly empty. The air was still, as if something held its breath. That day I knew nothing about the ceremony of the hunt, about the proper kill, about the prayers and gifts to thank the animal, about the songs of thanks, about returning its bones to the earth, so that a new animal would come back in them: but I knew that what had happened was not right. The women, all of them, had stood stiffly by their doors as they faced the lodgekeeper. No pleasure had shown in their faces; no thanks had been given. The distribution of meat had lacked grace, and was not smooth; it was a bitter necessity. In their bodies I had seen grief.

The meat, nonetheless, was food for the winter, and this way it did not go to waste.

❍

BILLY ALEXEY and his friend Gurrie, the man who had cut wood for me, told me about a hunt they had made a few years back. They had sighted a moose; but for most of the day it had stayed out of rifle range. They had followed it, as they saw where it was headed. The village had come into sight. The moose had stayed on its path!

"We followed it all that way," Billy said. "We had him in our sights by then. But he came into town. You know what he did then? He went straight up to the Mayor's house, and turned left, and trotted back toward the woods. So we had to let him go."

I enjoyed the story, and appreciated their sportsmanship. They seemed to be chuckling at themselves, and at the joke the moose had played on them. They grinned, I thought, when I said "sportsmanship." Billy said casually, "Yep, that's a good story, all right." Gurrie said nothing; he nudged Billy, and they drifted off.

What Are You
Going to Be
Like with Him?

THE DAYS OF SEPTEMBER were beautiful, each one more than those before it, though changeable—one moment diffused light, the next a rain shower. Steadily the air grew colder. The alders were golden on the ridges. The house was warm and dry; I was restless and decided to go walking.

One Saturday Lizzie and I set off for the woods. Up the wet trail we climbed, toward the mountain behind the village. I was glad to leave the press of other people, and breathe the fresh woody air. We walked nearly to the crest, then found a mossy stump to sit upon, and talked; or, Lizzie talked.

She described the cabin she meant to build. It was going to have a fireplace and a rocking chair to sit on; and she was going to raise horses, chickens, and goats; and she was going to dig a garden. She had picked out the site, a table below the cliffs at the end of the trail. She was full of questions: When you were a girl, what were your toys like? Did you have lots of toys? Did you have lots of friends? What kind of games did you play? What did the house you lived in look like? Did you like your sisters and brothers?

The day was rare: the walk up the mountain, Lizzie poised on the brink of young womanhood.

At home, F scolded me bitterly. Natalia had been extremely worried. I was irresponsible! Had I no sense, leaving the village without telling anyone, without taking a gun, without asking him, or Joseph, or Billy to come along with us? What did I think would happen if we had run into a bear? Bears were all over the woods at this time of year: no one left the village without protection.

○

I WAS THINKING about stories, not animals. In school they showed the children animated versions of animal stories told by native Alaskan tribes, though none of them was from Village Below. The films had been made to bring "Native materials" into the curriculum. In the village, however, the old people were particular about the *sukdu,* their oldest stories. They knew which stories were their own, and which belonged to other people. They were indifferent to the stories of other people; they thought the children should learn their own history and language.

I asked F what he thought of the cartoons shown in school. He shrugged.

"Well, take Smokey the Bear. I grew up with bears; they're all around here. I saw that bear walking around in his hat and little pants and carrying a shovel, and I just thought, 'Those Outside bears are different from ours.'"

A literal, particular quality of thought. A younger person, an English-speaker, as F was, who saw a creature called "bear" that was not like the bears he knew, accepted its difference. It was as if the words *bear* (the kind we see around here) and *bear* (running around in his short pants, Outside) were in parallel languages, not converging in their meaning. The Outside bear was amusing, but it did not affect him; it was a different kind of "bear," not his kind.

When the Dena'ina distinguished humans from animals, they said, in their tongue, Those who stand upright, and, Those on all fours. But *ggagga*, the word for brown bear (*Ursus horribilis*), was also the word they used when they spoke of any unspecified animal, or all of them. An old man could refer inclusively to the four-legged ones by calling them bear, employing a synechdoche (or, perhaps, a sort of inverted synechdoche), gathering them to the creature who is the biggest, the most powerful, of those beings. He would have supposed there was no animal larger than what he saw, and had studied, and had learned from his father and uncles. He would have known exactly what the word contained.

An old Dena'ina story says: "The bear knows you. What are you going to be like with him? If you hunt him with good faith, and clean, he will do the same to you. And if you leave him alone with good faith, he will stay out of your sight. You would have no problems with him."

This graceful lyric is about, among other things, etiquette. What are you going to be like with him?

o

HE WAS LYING ON THE FLOOR, his hands clasped behind his neck. He had just told me some event of the day, and we were both laughing. I stood up to take a glass from the table and, unthinking, was about to step across his long legs, when he rolled out of the way, in the same movement stood up, and shouted: "Never do that!"

Surprised at his anger—he was tense with it—I stepped back. He muttered, a sort of apology: "My mother told me you should never step over anybody." I thought, So damned proud—how dare you shout at me.

Something happens, an incident divides a man and a woman. Their house is warm. The night is black at the window. They are handsome people, there is an erotic charge between them and a love that often masks, and now less often overcomes, their differences. They have just been laughing; and then, their separate prides affronted, they face each other, glaring, at odds over a thoughtless movement.

At that moment they would not have known—it would not have occurred to either of them—that the word we use for forbidden behavior, *taboo*, comes from the Tongan word for "menses." In 1777, Captain Cook had brought the word back to England, where it passed into our language, to mean "consecrated; set apart; forbidden for use," especially "forbidden for use by women." Within that application lies the ancient Judeo-Christian connotation of womanhood as unclean, a near occasion of sin.

F's visceral reaction was my first—felt, not understood—demonstration of the power of women. He had sprung away from me, then been too angry for the occasion to justify. But he could not tell me why he was angry. He was too proud, too well trained in what could not be said, too fearful; and I did not know how little I knew, what I knew wrongly, and what I would learn, about what he feared. Moving so, I had touched a deeply rooted Athabaskan belief in the blood taboo. I had nearly violated a protocol of the hunting compact. The essence, the blood-trail, of a woman should not cross a man's body or touch his gear: her essence would come between the hunter and the animals.

Native peoples of the Pacific and Alaska freely mention their feeling of being related to each other. They know the world in similar ways; the similarity between them may exist even in etymological forms. For instance, *hutłaanee*, the Koyukon Athabaskan word for "taboo," used by women as a caution or to forbid behavior, is derived from the root *hutłaa*, meaning "menses." The derivation is similar in Iñupiaq, the language of the North Slope people; their word *agliganaq* refers to the laws of behavior toward the supernatural: the rules also applied to personal relations between men and women, and to their treatment of fur-bearing animals. The same connection exists in Yup'ik Eskimo, and in other Athabaskan tongues.[8]

These words for "forbidden" are used in the North as *taboo* is used in the Pacific, but not quite as it is used in English. From Native women I would learn the nature of the blood-taboo: they knew the monthly coming of their menses as their most powerful time. The blood contains a quality, a spirit, that heals and gives life. But the women did not know their blood as unclean, and the word for "taboo" is not a simple negative. It is about the enormous spiritual power of women and its implications for the men who were hunters.

As for that moment with F: I had nearly stepped over him in my strength, not my weakness or uncleanness. If my blood-trail had touched him improperly, had endangered or left him impaired: that was what a man knew, and how he must explain it to himself; it was necessarily his concern. What was known and believed by women, and by the women who taught some part of it to me, was rare, and was good for me to know.

Now, perhaps, I realize—I think, sometimes, that I do—why he spoke so often of women with contempt, mixed with fear. His mouth was foul—*bitch, cunt, whore*—and he was not alone in this, it was the habit of many young men, though not Joseph, whose courtesy was innate. I tasted copper when I heard those words, but he did not wish, or didn't dare, to speak to me that way. I wondered if this man thought he abased women, rather than himself. I was appalled and embarrassed for him, and embarrassed to be in his company; the feeling grew, even while I loved him. What loss, what loss and degradation, what fear.

He never spoke rudely of his mother, however. Like other young men, he spoke prayerfully of his mother. She had given him life. He revered her sacrifices for him, her mother-love. It was the work of mothers to sacrifice.

We did battle more and more often. He had a long way to go, I told myself fiercely, before he understood much about women. He expected me to keep his house: all he had to do was ask—tell me, really; he thought he could give me orders and have them obeyed.

What could women have done to him? What men did he turn to to learn about us, what father, what uncles, what older brothers?

I swore: Find me three old women who don't wish their life had been different! Find me three who think husbands are more than life's painful necessity. With what hopes could they have started their lives, and with what fears more than hopes?

○

TO MANAGE, I adapted my body to another protocol of decorum. Among Athabaskans, even the gaze was subject to a strict, although unspoken, rule. To look a person straight in the eye, as I did, was taken not as a mark of honesty or self-respect, but as an offensive act, and caused a small shock, as though an intruder had pulled back the veil of the soul. Out of politeness I imitated their oblique gaze, learning to keep my eyes averted or level, raising them no higher on another's face than the cheekbone. In school I did the same with the children, and they with me. I did not expect them to look at me directly: to demand it of them would have violated their privacy. I learned to gauge their interest by other signs. With time, this behavior became normal for me. Its graceful qualities were pleasing, and so its disadvantages were not apparent to me for some time.

Yet it was a difficult practice to master. In their glance the body's energy was diverted, turned aside or inward, so as not to intrude on intimate spaces. For people who lived so close to one another, it was a motion signifying self-control, not meekness; depending on the circumstances, it could be the sign of genuine humility, or of cold pride.

But, so often, the averted gaze of Native people had annoyed those who held authority over them. One often heard that children were referred to as "sullen," and "stupid," because they would not "level with" their teachers. One heard that adults were considered sly, or else submissive, because they would not look you in the eye. And yet, the decorum of the oblique gaze was widely practiced not only among Natives but many Asian peoples as well; one noticed it easily in photographs, for instance. Yet, as personal conduct it was easily overcome by the stare. Even the man of open countenance, who at home was taken as forthright and honest, a man of energy and vision, might easily, in the bush, be feared as the aggressor. That fear, surely, was rooted in history, as well as custom. Father Juvenaly, after all, had been martyred.

What, in such a situation, would anyone think of the woman?

Between peoples of weighted civilizations or, let us say, of different backgrounds, etiquette is a fraught question. It has been mediated by diplomacy and argued by war; each method follows its own protocol. Among ordinary people these differences may be accommodated with goodwill. But when action conveys meaning, how will a woman, traveling alone, be assessed? It always depends on the circumstances; she must always know what they are.

The men, except for a couple of young men—because of my bold glances?—were circumspect with me. When I was alone in the house no man would visit me, or visit any other woman, without his wife or a female relative along, and I could not walk in the road with any man but F without his hearing about it at once. He was jealous, and gossip wounded him.

Yet on occasion a man could speak more directly, without the necessary buffer of teasing. The rules, it seemed, were different for each sex and varied with age group and degree of kinship. For Outsiders, the rules covered different conditions; as for me, my position was not quite defined.

School was easier, because it was familiar. I chatted with the janitor as he straightened up the classrooms. He was probably in his early forties, but he looked fit, and he worked steadily. Among themselves the teachers said he had taken a vow to stay away from alcohol; that was why they preferred him, although officially he had been hired because it was his family's turn to hold the job. There were few regular jobs, and most of those were given out by the school; the school committee thought it fair to rotate them among families.

His name was Gabriel Ivan. When he was not much more than a boy and the village still followed the hunting way—this must have been the early 1950s—he had hunted caribou with his brothers. He was the youngest of them and so, in camp he had done the hard physical labor, carrying water, making fire. In the woods he had always run ahead of them on snowshoes, breaking trail for the sleighs.

"Before the white people came," he said, and notified me of his real point—why life had changed so much, and why he worked indoors now, and why he was so strong—"we camped. I broke trail for the dogs from six in the morning until six at night. I always won the snowshoe races at carnival."

When George Gavril came to visit, F was always at home. The two of them, neither one quite used to the change in their positions caused by me, sat stiffly in opposite parts of the room. They spoke to me, and, smiling, I listened to them; they competed with stories about how they had been trained as boys. George had written a term paper about games and play, and offered to show it to me. Earnestly, he explained: "Psychologists say that children learn by imitating their parents. That was our way. We always had education, but it was through games."

He described how boys had always played strenuous games to develop strength. They had danced to learn the movements they would need to survive when they hunted. "Even when they made toys," he said, "boys copied the men. It was how they learned. They made little copies of the tools and weapons and pretended to be men."

"I was one of the boys the old chief trained," F countered, jumping up, pacing. Old Gavril had raised several boys with his grandsons, in the log house that had stood where Joe and Natalia's house stood now. The boys were the first ones up in the mornings. They brewed their tea, ran barefoot through the snow to the outhouse—"Made us fast runners all right"—and brought fresh coffee to the old chief and his wife in their bed.

He boasted of a hero whose strength and courage were legendary among men. His eyes flashed when he told the story, and he laughed with joy at the hero's feats.

It began with a girl who lived with her parents. She had a baby boy. He had no father.

The grandparents took him as their own and began his training at once. In the bathhouse they tossed him back and forth over the fire, to toughen his skin. They threw sticks at him, then sharp stones, to teach him to move quickly.

The boy grew older. His grandfather began to hurl knives at him. The boy ducked, and learned quickly how to snatch knives from the air.

He became a young man. It was time for the final test. The grandfather sent him out on the trail. The young man knew then what he would hear: a whistling, the sound of an arrow in flight. Again and again the grandfather pulled his bow. Time after time the young man caught the arrow.

"You have learned to evade your enemy," said the grandfather.

"Yes," said the young man, and killed him.9

This man became a chief. One year he walked over the mountains to visit the people who lived by the inlet. They welcomed him with presents and gave him a fine kayak, a one-man skinboat, of his own. The men of the village took him down to the shore to let him try the skinboat. But he had not been trained on the salt tide; when the kayak rolled he nearly drowned. Back on shore, he laughed and showed no sign of anger at the trick.

That night the salt-water chief gave a feast in his honor. In return, he presented the chief with many gifts and compliments, and invited him to accompany him back to his village. Together they set off over the mountains.

The trails along the ledges were icy, the paths narrow. On a dangerous stretch the salt-water chief slipped and nearly fell into the canyon. He clung to the edge of the cliff by his fingers. Then he asked for help.

The inland hero urinated on his skin boots for traction and stepped across the chief's hands. He said: "I got out of your ocean. Now you get off my mountain."

Ah, how I loved F when he told that story. I loved him with a young woman's admiration for a warrior, I loved him for his pride, his arrogance, his defiance of enemies.

○

WINTER APPROACHED. I had to think practically. Was this the life men lived? It required endurance and skill. In a winter past, a son of the old woman of the fierce eye had been caught in a bear trap. He had walked home from his trap line, cradling his arm and shoulder clamped in the iron teeth. He had recovered, and still ran the line.

In many old Dena'ina stories, the hero has no father, making him an orphan and of low status. He makes his way on nerve and strength. A father was a man of responsibility and stature, who could afford to keep two wives and support a family. If he was a rich man, he could feed his dependents as well: the orphaned sons and daughters of a dead sister, perhaps, and the poor people—the lazy ones, or the unprotected women who were sexually available, or the slow of mind, who were his family's slaves. A father was a man who raised his son and saw to it that he was well trained by his uncles; a father was a man who wished, who willed, a son into existence, and provided for his mother.

In F's story of the fatherless hero—a man who killed his own grandfather; who with contempt triumphed over his opponent—I heard the law such men lived by: competition and revenge, the balance of nature. The man who caused shame or insult had to pay for it. The strong man got back his own.

But the nature of a story is complicated by its circumstances. The story a proud young man told a desired woman in front of a possible rival, might well have been his own story. In that case, who else could know it as he did? As winter approached I wondered at the hard, indomitable character of the hero, and how F would continue to meet his own tests, and how I would find the strength to live with his choices that, more and more often, were not mine.

○

THESE MEN had been warriors. They had trained themselves to endure hardship and pain. Long ago they had fought wars with the Aleuts, the tribes who lived farther south, who were, according to scholars, of Yup'ik stock and not "true" Aleuts. But the "passing of a century and a half has lost for cultural history the possibility of an adequate account of primitive warfare." Yet from memory or habit the Dena'ina persisted in calling these people "Aleuts," for they had long been enemies, and history, although it might be seen in a new light, was not forgotten. Ghost Mountain stood witness to the last great battle between them. It offered seekers the medicine power of struggle and death. But in the anthropologists' laments, if not in the talk of passionate young men, those days of war were gone . . .

I had written this paragraph, I wrestled with its sentimentality, and the meaning of an incident fell into place.

During winter carnival, crowds of visitors, including Aleuts, had come from all the villages in the area. F had strolled up the road, too casually, hands in his pockets. Two young men approached. They saw him, I observed—they couldn't help but see him, he was cock of the walk, he was looking for trouble—but they looked straight ahead. When they neared him, their shoulders straightened, their steps hinted at swagger. As they passed, F muttered something. For an instant the air contracted with shock, and then they walked on, the swagger drained out of them. F threw a brief but naked glance of contempt at their backs.

"What did you say?" I asked later, curious.

"Duch'ay."

"That means what?"

"Aleut."

Years afterward I was given a Dena'ina/English dictionary, and looked up *Duch'ay.*

Dutna; Duch'ay, the entry read: "Yup'ik Eskimos; Yup'ik woman."

I sorted through the usages. Eskimo, Aleut, the differences were academic. The point was: F had hurled his insult: "'Aleut' *woman.*"

0

ONE EVENING when I was alone in the house, an old man and his wife came to visit. I had seen them together but had never met them formally. He was the blind singer at the dance, whose voice had been rich with Dena'ina songs. He could no longer hunt or work: now he was known as a teller of stories. His wife was his guide.

I served them tea, and chatted politely. As I recall, they spoke of inconsequential matters, and after a pleasant visit the old man made motions to go. After he had put on his cap he handed me a manila envelope containing a cassette tape, and told me that I could use it. His wife helped him out the door and they walked off slowly into the dark.

0

I LISTENED to the tape. It was the blind man's voice. He spoke for some time in his language, then told a story in English, in the dialect his generation spoke. Line by line, I transcribed the English, then much later translated it into a more accessible written version.

0

"A TRUE STORY," he began:

A long time ago, before the white men came into this part of Alaska, before they brought their religion and beliefs, in the time when the people did not have what is called religion, they said there was a champion called Strongbone. This was up in the old village.

There were two sisters. One of them had a baby, but she had no husband.

The two of them raised the baby boy. In the mornings they washed him in rain water and tossed him back and forth over the pit-fire, which they used to have in the middle of the house, to warm him. They kept on, they kept on doing that.

They used to have birchbark cradle-baskets for their babies. The two sisters kept the baby in that cradle. They stuck knives through the side of the basket. When the baby moved, the knives cut his skin. They kept on, they kept on doing that.

The baby got bigger, he started running around outdoors. They made a bow and some arrows out of little sticks and taught him how to shoot. In those days they used to have wars, and they used to make war clubs out of horn, two or three feet long. The two sisters made a little club for the boy and tied it to his arm. They kept on doing that.

The boy grew into a man so tough no one could beat him. When they fought with the Aleuts—they had a lot of war then—sometimes he killed four hundred, five hundred people. When they came here for war, he killed them, just with his club. He never used arrows. They kept on making war for a long time.

The Aleuts had a champ, too. He was called Big Ears. He was a tough guy.

One day Strongbone and his partner were out hunting. They saw two Aleuts, hunters. The Aleuts started running. They caught one, and said: "Who's that with you?" The Aleut said, "That tough guy, he's Big Ears. He's the one."

Big Ears is running. That Indian champ runs after him. They keep on running, keep on. Strongbone's getting closer, closer, about fifty feet behind him. There's a swamp—that Aleut dove into it. The Indian watched, and saw him come up. He ran after him and came closer. The Aleut ducked again, the mud shook around him. He dove, the Indian dove, till they came to solid ground. When Big Ears came up for air, Strongbone was waiting for him.

The Indian champion grabbed him and pushed his face in the water.

"Your name's Big Ears?"

Big Ears nodded.

Strongbone killed him.

His partner held down the second Aleut hunter. They didn't kill him, but sent him home with a message. "Go back to your people," they told him. "Tell them Strongbone killed Big Ears. Tell them! Next time, let them send more men than this to fight me!"

So they sent him home, and went back to their village. Strongbone, Indian champ. They had one more war; then they quit fighting.

That Indian champ was getting old. He didn't get killed in the wars; he was about eighty years old. Some men said they were going hunting. He said, "I'll go with you. You might see brown bear."

"Go ahead," they told him. So he went with them. He was so old he didn't want to wear heavy clothes, no caribou or squirrel parka; he wore rabbit skin, a little parka. They went up the mountain. There they saw three brown bears, all three the same size. They went up close to them.

He told the men, "You fellas stay here, and watch me. I'm going over there." He didn't take his bow; he picked up a spear. He walked toward the first bear. He walked, he walked right up close, he started to run at that bear. The bear charged. Strongbone killed him.

He killed the second bear.

The third bear he only wounded. He jumped to the other side, and jabbed him again. Back and forth he jumped, jabbing, jabbing. The bear fell down, and he died.

The old man fell down. He was so old he was winded.

The other men came down and saw all of them lying there: three brown bears, one old man.

He rested. Then he said to them: "That's the way I wanted to do it. This is the last animal I'm going to kill. That's the way I wanted to do it. I wanted to listen to his voice, the bear. That's the way I wanted to do it."

The hunters came home. Not long afterward, he died. Strongbone died, of old age.

○

"THEY HAD WAR AROUND HERE," said the old blind storyteller. "They told us stories. This is a true story."[10]

○

WHAT SHOULD I DO with the story? Why had the blind man given it, with no warning and no instruction? It was an ambiguous gift, to which an obligation of some sort must be attached.

Yet at first it interested me hardly at all. His style was unadorned and rhythmic; he spoke in the idiom and accent of his generation. It was if he had wrestled it from the Dena'ina into his own form of English and had, at the same time, bent and shaped that limiting form until it was fitted to his meaning. And the form of the story puzzled me: the flat assertion of the opening, its terse setting of scene, which the old man's audience would have recognized at once; the abrupt jumps of the plot, its two climaxes, its flat resolution. I could not take in the strangeness of its details, and did not see its point. It sounded to me like a fragment; perhaps it was the ghost of an epic. Out of some obscurely felt obligation I typed it out in English, exactly as he had recorded it, and put it away in my notebook. Even on paper the story remained embedded in the old man's voice.

Why was his story so difficult to understand? There were two reasons, I think. One had to do with history; the other, literature.

The matter of history was probably simple, even obvious. According to the views then current, the "old way of life" was gone. The era of "primitive" warfare was said to be finished; according to historians, no reliable records of it now existed.[11] Archaeologists concentrated on gathering physical artifacts and few were interested in cultural anthropology. Linguists held that the Native languages were dying, and they recorded what remained for scholarly use. In the methodology of all disciplines, however, Native epistemologies and poetics were rarely studied except as artifacts, and had no standing as explanatory theories. And I myself had no contact with the university; I had put aside academic interests, which in any case had been more theoretical.

At the same time, the settlement of the Alaska Native land claims, in 1971, had already altered Alaskans' expectations. By federal law, a two-tiered structure of Native-owned corporations was now in place that held title to and managed the lands and funds distributed to Alaska Natives by the government. The legal complications of this structure perplexed ordinary Native people. In private, they feared that the lands restored to them were still under threat. In public life, those who spoke for them had reason, they must have thought, to play down memories of traditional warfare, even in its modern guises, if only to pull down from the air the arrow of the "primitive." It seemed from the outside to be in their best interest to work together. They were corporation people, businesslike men and women who clearly meant to show that they could manage the returned lands and run the corporations for the benefit of their people; they were not scholars. Indeed, in those years there were very few Alaska Native scholars, that is, those with university training, at work.

I wonder if the blind storyteller had known these things, or something like them, and known that the noise of public life muffled the truth of his story. What were his intentions? In that world of woe, to whom did his story matter?

The reason about literature is, for me, deeper and more complicated. Language is at the heart of the matter.

A poet once wrote, smiling, "I say 'I am in poetry' as I would say 'I am in love.'" Suppose that a tongue is like a heart, in that each in its way animates life. Now, suppose that cutting off language is like cutting out a tongue. Life—a kind of life; an energy—stops. Where does it go? The energy of the tongue: where does it go? What new form does it take?

Life—energy; the tongue; a language—does not end, even if it is cut off, or cut short. Language does not "die," but, rather, takes a new form, perhaps as the soul, according to Native beliefs, enters a new body. What happened to the old man's epic, I think, was this: he wished to carry over its energy—the quality that gave it meaning—into English. He was translating that "energy" into American English: but into a version so local and specialized, that few ears (and not mine) could hear it clearly. And so, the energy—the meaning—of the story was weakened.

To put it a different way: he spoke "broken English." For Americans, descendants of immigrants, this has long been a vexed subject. The play and clash of speech are part of one's early experience. The sounds fascinate a writer, endlessly. Her head is full of voices.

In Village Below, between the five generations then living my ear caught habits of use and accent as distinct as the faces of different families. Yet each voice (to my ear) belonged to that village and not any other. Something in their cadence or intonation identified them as clearly as a face did. Strangers who had passed through the country, and those who had stayed to father children and churches, also remained in the living tongue. The elders' voices echoed with Russian traders' words, British and Irish sailors' slang, American traders' bargaining lingo, the ornate rhetoric of earlier waves of American teachers. On feast days I listened to hymns sung in Church Slavonic.

But my ear was tuned to another music, and often, their talk sounded flat to me, or like static, as a language you are just learning can sometimes sound like noise. Words carried private meanings, or had only local referents. "He's going out," I would hear. A man was going to look for game farther north, around the big lake in the mountains, a direction and area indicated only by a quick tilt of the head. Everyone but me knew what the speaker meant. They surmised where the man was going, and why he was going there, without his having to say it.

They would say: "Maybe he'll find something." They spoke of the future conditionally, to allow for possibility, to avoid telling a lie. They used euphemisms for animals and nicknames for persons, for fear of hurt feelings, and for fear of bad luck. A word could be perfectly innocent, perfectly loaded. It was as dense as their word for bear; it was a parallel English, their synechdoche, that had been transplanted from Dena'ina and had grown into their tongue.

I found myself in a curious spot. Deeply, I loved my language, and missed speaking it; and I could not speak it. Here is where the irony, and the risk, lay: in having to simplify, as though I were speaking a foreign tongue. I was losing my language. The energy of my tongue was weakening. An exchange was taking place.

For, as I made the transcription, adding nothing of my own, I felt a shift in mind. The story had never been written; yet it existed in the world as surely as writing existed, but apart from writing. It spoke through the old man's voice, and through the voices of a long line of old men. It carried their authority.

Theirs was an old way of knowing. Theirs were minds formed in an animist logic, in an extra-Indo-European tongue. The Dena'ina were warriors, in their memory and deep-grained habit. They were, by livelihood, hunters. Men who went to jobs, women who taught school, the children in school who had spoken American as babies, F, who spoke only American: all of them had been formed by war and hunting; formed as the earliest humans had ever lived, in relationship with the animals who kept them alive.

Something existed in them, not always benign, embedded in the layers of their experience, that was separate, nearly shut off, from mine. Their tongue was part—was a counterpart—of human experience; using it, their stories had figured knowledge and feeling, belief and history; described human relations with the animals; recounted all life in that place.

It is an ancient fact of poetry that words are connected to things. The country was full of these *things*: material beings and objects, and non-material forms; humans, animals, plants, their spirits and relationships. They were enclosed in riddles and secrets, and disclosed themselves in Native languages. But surely their proper words existed in the great storehouses of our literary tongue; I merely did not know them yet. The work of poetry was to learn them—some few of them—and learn to use them, accurately.

This story's true.
Long time ago the people
live around here and up in Lake————
they call K————,
that's the place the old timers live in.
Them days, that's way before
white people came into Alaska,
there's no priests,
no religion, nothing,
the people don't believe nothing,
no religions.

They said
there used to be one guy
he's the champ,
the prizefighter,
that means that guy, his name's
[Tzonktpolyas], Strong-bone.
That man, first he born,
two ladies,
sisters,
one of 'em got the baby
without husband,
and they start raising him,
that baby there.

They used-to-be have the fire
right in middle of the house
them days, they didn't have no stove.
They put lots of wood on the fire there
and they take that baby,
they took his clothes off,
and when it's raining, morning-time,
they take him out and they wash him
out on the outdoors.
Soon as they bring him in there
by the fire in the middle,
then one guy stand on one side
and right across one guy stand the other side,
and they throw'm to one another
forth and back
inside the flame,
they make him warmed up.

They keep on, they keep on.

They used to have a basket
them days, the baby they keep
on the basket, the birchbark basket,
that they leave the baby on [in] there.
When they put him in the basket
they put knives on both sides
right next to his body
so when that baby move around,
sometimes cut his skin on the side.
They keep on, they keep on.

That baby's getting big
and he start running around outdoors.
They make him bow and arrows,
they teach hm how to shoot the arrows.
They make him little stick.
(Long time ago
they used to have a war.
Out of horn about three-feet
or two-feet long—the horn—
they use for club.)
They make one like that
out of little sticks
and they tie it on him, the side, and he
learn how to shoot the arrows.
And they keep on, they keep on.

After he grew up
that man there,
he's so tough
nobody can't beat hm.
Every time the Aleuts
they had a war with them,
he's the only person
sometimes he kill four hundred,
five hundred peoples.
All the guys make war
come up in here,
this the only one person,
he killed 'em, all of 'em,
with the clubs. He don't use

arrows, he use club.
They keep on, they keep on.

The Aleuts, they had champ.
His name's [Jilowan?],
that Aleut champ,
his name's Big-ears.
He's tough guy.
Once that Indian champ
and one guy with him,
they're out hunting.
They see two Aleuts, hunters.
Then as they see this,
they start running, though.
That other guy, they catch him,
they say, "Who's that with you?"
He said, "That tough guy,
Big-ears, he's the one."
Already that guy, he's running.
Then that Indian champ runs after him.
He ran after him,
keep on, keep on,
he's gettin' closer, closer.
About fifty feet right behind him
is a swamp, and that Aleut,
pretty soon he went down,
just like he dive in the water,
in the swamp. And he standing there,
he's watching him.
Pretty soon he come up.
Way over there he come out.
He start running, he keep on,
keep on.
He go right across and under
the ground again when he
was watchin', the ground was shakin'
when he was goin' under the ground.
Soon he start follow him,
follow him, pretty soon
he come out right in front of him,
he grab him.
He grab him, and he wash his face
in the water.

He ask him, "Your name's Jilowan?"
That Aleut said,
with his head he said, "Yeah."
Then he kill him.
He kill him, he went back to
his partner, and that other Aleut,
the one with Big-ears, he didn't kill him.
They told him, "You go back
your peoples, and you tell
your peoples Tzonktpolyas
kill Big-ears. You tell them.
You tell them no more Big-ears.
You tell them. So the next time,
more peoples got to come and fight me."
So they sent him home.
They came back to their village.
Strong-bone, Indian champ.

He keep on every time wars.
After that they had to fight once,
after he kill Aleut champ.
They had war once, then they quit
the war.

That Indian champ,
he's gettin' old.
He didn't get killed on [in] the war.
He's about eighty years old.
Some man [men] says to go out hunting.
He told them, "I'll go with you guys.
You guys might see brown bear."
They told him, "Go ahead."
So he went with them.
He was so old he don't want to wear
heavy clothes, like a caribou parkee,
or a squirrel parkee, he don't want to wear that,
he wear rabbit-skin parkee,
little short rabbit parkee,
light.
He went with them, and they went up the mountain.
They see three brown bears.
The brown bears all the same size,
big ones.

They went right up close.
He told them, "You fellas stay there
and watch me. I'll go over there."
He didn't take no bow and arrow,
nothing. He took spear.
He started walkin' toward the bear.
He walk, he walk right up close.
He start to run to that bear.
That bear, as soon as he see'm, he charge.
Soon as he charge him,
he kill the first one.
The second one he kill.
The last one, he poke him,
he jump right over and hit him on the other side,
he jump backward right over and hit him on
the other side.
The bear fall down, he die.
That man, he fall right down too.
He's so old, he's out of wind.
But them guys come down,
all the brown bears laying there, three of them,
and that Strong-bone, he laying there,
he's so old.
After he rest he told them,
"That's the way I want to do it,
this is my last animal I'm gonna kill.
That's the way I want to do it.
I want to listen to his voice,
the bear. That's the way
I want to do it."

After they come back,
not too long, he died.
He die of old age.
The story they used-to-be tell us,
long times
they had war around here.
They told us stories.
This is a true story.

Being Indian

I GLIMPSED THE ORDINARY trials of little boys. Billy Alexey was driving the town's garden tractor, towing oil drums on a trailer, the trailer piled with kids, who loved to ride on anything moving down the road. There was young Georgie running behind them, pulling a white dog by the collar. He jumped mightily onto the trailer and sat down, legs dangling off the edge, facing the dog, whom he was still pulling, and who was still resisting him. The dog triumphed. Thump: down sat Georgie in the road. Up he scrambled as the other kids giggled, scooped up the dog, who was half as big as he was, and set off in a clumsy run after the slow-rolling trailer.

The teenagers were showing stress in spectacular ways. One night a bunch of them had ripped up the missionaries' garden. Flo and Doris had lived in the village for ten years and bothered no one, except on Sundays, when their loudspeaker blared hymns and disturbed hangovers. The teenagers had torn out lettuces and cabbages and dumped them on the trail to the fish camp of the old woman of the fierce eye. She had always befriended Flo and Doris. Then, someone had stretched a rope across the road, neck-high, so that anyone dashing along on a three-wheeler might have been garroted. They also had thrown toilet paper around the construction workers' shack.

F was furious. He fired Karen the essay writer, who had been helping me in the house, calling her an "irresponsible kid"—he found out that she had been one of the ringleaders—and stopped talking to William, who was staying with Natalia and Joe while his parents were away. William was another of the leaders. I thought he was a pretty good kid.

Mike Fitka dropped by in the evening, to talk things over. Lately there had been a good deal of annoying vandalism: machinery tinkered with, the new school marked up with graffiti. Mike Fitka was a reflective man. The mischief hurt him, although he did not want to think badly of the youngsters. He said, "If only they could realize what harm they do."

The teenagers didn't seem to know the cost of their actions. What was to be done about them? They were restless. That was a restless town; there was always a nervous coming-and-going. The young men talked about going out to the woods, or flying into Anchorage, anything for a break, because life in the village quickly grew too intense. One of them remarked that in the old days, when they went out to spring camp and summer camp, tensions had not built up so easily.

The town council took no action. Few people could constrain their children. F's solution was "a big stick." I wondered what sort of authority restless teenagers would respect.

○

IT WAS FULLY AUTUMN. Yellow leaves were falling. Clouds sat low on the mountains. The sun swung south; we lost daylight rapidly. The world was closing in on us. I developed a cough and a stuffed head, slept fitfully, grew cranky. Natalia stopped by with a packet of tablets. Legally, I was not supposed to be her patient, but instead of thanking her I said, sourly, that medicine would never cure a cold.

"Listen to what I told you," she replied crisply. Something snapped in my ears. "This will give you relief."

I could also try Indian tea, she suggested. If you steeped the needles of the Hudson's Bay tea plant in boiling water, they made a sort of tonic. She gave me a handful of the leaves. They smelled faintly like turpentine. The bushes grew thick in damp areas; I could look for them and pick them easily.

It struck me then that all summer she had been telling me little things about plants. She liked to use plant remedies, most often those made with parts of the spruce tree: bark, bast, needles, pitch. These were good for stanching wounds, making tonic or tea, and for other uses. I asked her about the spruce and the Hudson's Bay plant, and she gave me a keen look.

"Maybe you'd like to study plants and Indian medicine," she said. "You could come around with me."

A day or so later, she invited me to watch while she checked on the progress of a wound. An older man, Joe's cousin, had cut himself badly with an axe. She showed me how she had sewn and wrapped the wound. It was black with spruce pitch and was healing well.

Her offer was appealing, but I held back and, carefully, she did not insist.

○

I SEE HOW THE OPENING, the becoming, was working its will on the young woman I was. My point of view had shifted to the stand-point of the village, as if to the center of the world, as if from inside a glass bowl.

The body, becoming assimilated. In the house the only mirror was a small, tarnished face-glass, hung in a dim corner. My dark hair and green eyes were shadows, my pale skin was ghostly; my beauty had become ghostly. F, Lizzie, Janet, Joseph were beautiful also, but sunlit. I looked into their faces as though into mirrors. They moved gracefully as dancers, with the disciplined, confident ease of people at home. I moved alongside them, never as graceful, but placing my body in imitation of theirs, as I had let the old woman of the fierce eye place my hands on knife and salmon. This was the inversion of self-absorption; rather, the self had been absorbed.

The mind, being lost. Within weeks, even days, of one another, three curious events had occurred:

The dream of ladders. This dream had been as vivid as a film; as mysterious and disturbing as Bergman's, when as a student one had watched his films; and inscrutable: the films, at least, had been subtitled. In the dream, the whiteness of the ladders had been lovely, but the face of the orphan girl was black with hate. "Suffer!" she had hissed. I made myself ignore her.

The visit of the blind storyteller. He had given me his story; but I could not take in its strangeness, and did not see its point. Yet, accepting it had placed me under obligation: to the old man; to the story, itself . . .

Natalia's summons. Often, Catholic girls and women will feel they have received a calling to become a nun; they take that feeling seriously, testing it until its meaning is clear. The call is not often genuine; when it is, it is insistent. Not wholly dissimilar is the calling of poets to their work: the voice in the inner ear, or merely the word, or an inner music. And those who hear the call answer it until they learn, painfully, whether it is genuine, or false.

Natalia's offer to teach me plant medicine was a call. That was the gentlest sort of culture shock, and the most disturbing, because I wished to say yes. To ease the suffering of fellow humans was a humane profession. Her way of knowing was ancient, and honorable. I watched her dress the man's wound, and was fascinated. At that moment, I stood poised before a long road. If I had stepped onto it, I could never have come back.

o

YET, AS THE SEASON TURNED, I grew short-tempered, sharp. Our life, F's and mine, was flickering, flickering. I thought, How bare this house is, and how poor the life in it; my mind has gone stale. From Anchorage arrived an unexpected invitation, and I accepted at once.

In town, I stared at fast cars. More traffic lights. Men wearing jackets and ties under their parkas, women in dresses and high heels instead of corduroys and boots. Anchorage was changing. It resembled a city. Housing developments had spread like lichen over the lower slopes of the mountains south of town. Condominiums were for sale. Capital construction had rearranged the downtown: more tourism, more business to be enticed North. A "fern bar" advertised the first dress code: NO BUSH CLOTHES, DESIGNER JEANS ONLY. In the air was the glitter of a new kind of money, and the eyes of young professionals gleamed. "Welcome to Los Anchorage," said a sardonic cabdriver.

I had my parka cleaned, and bought a new pair of Levi's.

A conference for women writers had been organized, the first of its kind, and I had been asked to participate. I had brought some new work to read, about the old woman of the fierce eye, and was nervous because it was unconventional. I looked forward to seeing friends.

The theme was Common Ground. As if we could look beyond the history of that land, beyond its other, darkened histories; as if people could meet in common, without guile, as though their conflicting communal pasts had no volume or dimension or sting. As though we were new, and could begin again. We buzzed with vitality, the voices of young women doing real work, discovering themselves at work.

On the second day we were addressed by a well-known writer whose essays about women and nature, and their intimate, mutual connection, had taken her into the forefront of feminist theory. She spoke about the crimes committed against women in Alaska. The incidence of rape and abuse of women and children was the highest in the nation. How, she demanded, could we be so casual about the violence around us? On her journey north she had stopped off in Haines. Late in the afternoon, wanting to walk in the forest, she had set off from the outskirts of town. Men had watched her leave. They are always watching us, she said forcefully, and reminded us that rape is about power, not sex.

The audience was quiet. The person on my left was a dogsled racer. She, too, shifted in her seat, and we looked at one another. "Bears," she murmured. "Feeding time." Naturally, people had been watching: they had thought the woman was reckless, or stupid, to go out in the woods without a gun. They were looking out for the visitor.

The racer, who was confident, articulate, and remarkably handsome, stood up. "I ran the Iditarod last year. It's a thousand-mile dogsled race," she said. "You want to know what I worried about most? Crossing Norton Sound I was so cold I was afraid my legs would double up on me, and I wouldn't be able to push the sled. I know what the cold can do to me. I don't worry too much about men."

We were superior to our visitor; we knew (we believed) something she did not know. We were too enamored of our strength to allow ourselves to name what surrounded us: to say out loud that we lived in a place laden with menace. The absence of threat was why we were so happy, even giddy, at the conference. We felt normal again, we were away from the threat; and we refused to say this was true. We were willful, arrogant, insouciant, and badly wrong; but I am not sorry for it, for we loved that land and our physical competence on it, and it was good and right for us to love it. How rarely can we know our ease of movement that way.

But we turned away from what, as writers, we should have faced directly, because we wanted to believe that we were safe, because we couldn't bear to say we that we were not.

○

I KEPT A CAR in Anchorage. When F flew to town to join me, we decided to drive to Homer, on the tip of the Kenai Peninsula. Once I had spent a winter there, in a cabin on a bluff overlooking the water; it seemed a long time ago. For hours we wound through mountains and across the flats, until along the coast, at last, we caught sight of Cook Inlet sparkling in the sun and, across the water, the mysterious volcanic peaks of the Alaska Range. It was a beautiful journey; the marvel of it lay in the facts of a road not too badly heaved by permafrost, and an engine functioning without a hitch.

In Homer I looked up two old friends, the woman who used to give me a hot shower, supper, and good company, and a man who had originally come North to write a novel. They knew each other well, and both of them wanted to meet F. The woman invited us all to her trailer for supper.

Nothing about the evening was out of the ordinary, and everything was altered. I see F as he appeared that night, in that room. He sits like a dandy in his chair, one leg crossed over the other precisely at the knee, one hand resting on his thigh. His elegant body is still, his brown face is composed. His clear eyes watch the three of us entertain one another.

The woman, the man, and I are telling each other our recent adventures. The man has spent the summer fishing for crab in the storm-tossed Bering Sea. He has grown a mustache and wears a handsome air of assurance, and he tells us he is writing fiction again. The woman has found a new love, this time, she thinks, for real. She has grown softer in her body. She is at peace with herself.

I remember being aware that we liked one another. We were pleased for each success, the spirit of our generosity warmed the room. I remember being at ease, and noting how rarely it happened now. The man and I talked about the books we had been reading. We discussed our new work. The discussion went on; I lost myself in it, and was happy; until, gradually, insistently, a distant peal, a distress call, an angry buzz, began to sound in the back of my head. Resolutely, I ignored it. This is my time, my place, my stubborn self replied; and I swam back into the absorbing pleasure of talk. F remained still. I didn't look at him.

I told them about my summer in Village Below. It was a partial lie: those months had not been as idyllic as I made them out to be; but, silently, I offered the romance of my tale to F as a gift, and he, silently, accepted it. I told them how I had learned to cut salmon; and as I talked, knew how silly it must sound to him. He sat among white faces: I wondered if he was uncomfortable. At home, the link between his body and his country was palpable and visible; he was grounded in his land, and the land strengthened him. In this small room, he had lost his substance. I felt a small shock, a terrible kind of culture shock: he was ineffable. The long history he carried in himself was unknown here, and so, here, it had no resonance, no meaning; and he betrayed none of it to these people whom he did not know. He was poised, but I was aware of his displacement. *I* was aware of it. He gave no sign.

Subtly, the woman drew him into the conversation. He spoke gracefully and charmed them with his manner. The man and the woman were interested in all he had to say. They are like so many of us who come from Outside, I thought: curious, intelligent, ready to be friends, certain they can make their way in this immense land. They don't know who he is, or what, exactly, he comes from. They are kind to him, and beautifully polite. He can speak well, and so they treat him, almost, as an equal.

The next day we drove back to Anchorage; it was an uneventful trip, except when, at intervals, his anguish erupted in shouts. He asked tormented questions about the writer, the same questions over and over. Had he been my lover? Why did I want to see him again, then? He groaned at what he believed had happened between us, and at his own humiliation at having to meet the man. Wearily, I tried to reassure him: White people have different ways; he had misunderstood us.

The long afternoon was darkening. I was drawn tight with exhaustion, and drove silently. His suffering was awful, and pointless. The cry of his jealousy beat against the air like a drum.

The last leg of the trip took us along Turnagain Arm, on a narrow, winding road between the mountains and the edge of the water. Abruptly, his mood changed; he was quiet, intent. He said he would tell me a story; he said it was about being Indian.

One time, he and his brother Lou had driven down this very road, going to Kenai. There were some other guys with them. They were all doing cocaine.

Lou challenged him. They stopped beside a mountain, and Lou dared him to climb it. The mountain was a rock wall. Lou said he would be crazy if he tried it; but F took the challenge and went up the rock.

He loved this part of the story. Hand over hand he had climbed along a small ridge, then crawled up the face of the rock. He found minute footholds; his muscles had strained against the rock, and he loved the hurt. He had pulled himself up over the top and sat on the edge drinking a beer, watching the others move around far below.

He did not describe the descent. It was the moment of sitting on the edge, drinking a beer and watching them, that sounded peaceful in his telling; but it was the going up that had mattered to him.

He asked me to pull over to a turn-off, a flat place where the cliff receded about thirty feet from the road. The night was moonless. I left the headlights on and the motor running. His eyes were shining. He got out of the car, and came around to my side. "I have a surprise for you." He waved his arm toward the cliff. "This is the mountain. I climbed it," he cried, almost breathless with need, nearly weeping in his joy.

It was a rock face, with ledges and what looked in the headlights like handholds; it rose straight up about a hundred feet. I turned off the motor. He could not stay still: his leg jiggled, his fingers drummed on the door. He talked very fast. He wanted to tell me what it meant, being Indian.

"Here's what it really means: it's a challenge. I'm always competing, I'm always testing myself. At home, everything you do is a direct test to see who's the better man. I'm the best fighter, the toughest, the strongest. Ask Billy, ask anybody! Being Indian means pushing yourself as far as you can go."

The night was silent around us. There was no traffic on the road.

"I notice everything. I look at white men: what hand they lead with, what foot. Whether they walk on their toes, like fighters, or back on their heels— they're afraid to fight. I see how they check me out. I watch how their muscles move, if they're alert, how they sit. You always see me use my left hand with other Indians. I always use my left hand, in conversations and like that, because I fight with my right hand, and I don't want them to know it too soon. I'm quick, I'm as quick as Muhammad Ali: I can see anything coming!"

I looked at the rock and the water, rather than look at his exalted face. *He sees, analyzes, catalogues, concludes. His eyes are piercing. He senses instantly the smallest change in mood, inflection, attitude. He is wrong about what he thinks he saw in the* gasht'anas; *he is wrong, except that last night he knew, finally, that I don't belong to him, and he cannot understand why.* To the man and the woman he had looked elegant and graceful: I knew this; and knew that the thoughtful way he had talked about the village had intrigued them. They had no idea how closely he had studied them as they moved and spoke. They would have been startled by it. They might have pitied him (the woman would have pitied him) and been disturbed by what had been done to him. None of us could have imagined a warrior's life; we were wholly ignorant, and so we got him wrong. He was a warrior-hunter, taken out of time, out of place.

He had watched the writer closely, to see if he wanted to fight. He had expected the man would stand up in my presence and shout, "She's my woman."

I struggled with myself, with the unworthiness of my pity for him, and my respect for his integrity, and an ache, again, at the enormous distance between us. I spoke softly, and suggested we go on to Anchorage. He had wanted me to understand his climb, without his having to say it: he had wanted me to praise him, and exult with him over that small triumph, and I could not do it; but I wished not to wound him. I called softly, and he climbed back into the car and sat becalmed, almost sated.

I drove through the darkness. *I observe what is around me with longing and detachment. I record and reflect upon the world; while he is a naif, and feels through his senses all that is around him: because he knows it already. He is of it. He is made of his world; and his survival depends on the existence of everything that is part of it.*

This quality he embodied did not make his world peaceful, nor more peaceful than mine. Men fought and drank and the lives of women were hard and could be mean, children cried, and the gossip and bickering of families had become unbearable to me. I wondered when, in the long history of human community, men and women had been able to know peace, whatever peace might be. I doubted peace had ever lasted, or human societies would never have needed marriage, or government, or regulation, or education, to direct their passions.

When afterward I heard white people speak longingly of Indians and their harmony with the earth, I saw F as he was that night, in love with the challenge of his mountain. I saw his shining eyes, quick hands, his fleet-footed balance: his constant habit of studying the land: his love and jealousy of that worthy adversary, his nourisher. He was always a hunter, always a fighter; to save his life, he could not have been anything else. He confided to me that he still sang a prayer to the caribou before he shot.

o

THE DAY I RETURNED TO HIM was cold and bright. I was holding on behind the snowmachine driver, coming down from the airstrip, when I saw him walking slowly up the road to meet me. He looked young and thin, and his eyes were pained. He had been jumped the night before, and two of his ribs had been broken.

He refused to tell me why it had happened. Some young men, drinking, had come to the house and called him out. He had resisted, but they would not go away. A fight had broken out. In the end, to drive them off he had fired two rounds of his rifle into the ceiling.

He was holding out against the alcohol; he was staying alone in the house; he was trying to go straight.

Violence blew through the village like a narrow whirlwind roving across some huge, flat plain. It swirled in, tore up a few trees, and whisked off again. The people replanted or replaced the trees, and continued their daily work. The ones who lived near the downed trees might have had a little damage done to their roofs, spent a sleepless night listening to the wind. Later, it was something to talk about.

If what happened was horrible, or funny, it was told again and again, even at the same sitting: or else it would stick in the throat and chest. It had to be spat out. It had to be told.

o

YET THE DAYS were serene; and I was busy. I was helping the working members of the council, who now were Aggie, F, Billy Alexey, and Joe Gavril, to organize the haphazard council files. We spent long hours at it, for they faced an urgent land matter that was going to be decided by Congress within the next two years. The alarm had been set; the clock was ticking.

As a corollary to the land claims settlement act of 1971, a clause, known as "D2," required the president and the secretary of the interior to set aside a minimum of sixty million acres of land for wilderness protection. In those wilderness acres, immense national parks were going to be formed. One of those parks would be near Village Below.

North of the village, in the old Kijik country, was a beautiful, fjordlike lake set amid the wild mountains, the Bigger Lake in Village Below's Athabaskan name. The area was home to many kinds of animals and was renowned for its glorious scenery. Native and some non-Native families held property along the lake; an auntie of F's, his mother's sister, had a fine house there, where she lived with her adult sons. Men from Village Below hunted bear, moose, sheep, caribou in those mountains that had once evoked, for me, the mystery of a Chinese painting.

The federal government had selected that area as part of the new wilderness lands. It was going to be managed by the National Park Service. This meant the hunting lands of Village Below, their Kijik relatives, and their neighbors around the lake would be under federal direction. Furthermore, some of the federal land was most likely going to be open to sport hunting. But the classification—park, preserve, or wildlife refuge—had not yet been made. How those lands were classified was critical to the village. The people were assembling their defenses and putting them in order.

For some years, a ruthlessly fought battle over the national-interest lands had been waged between environmental groups, Native regional corporations, the village corporations, sport hunting lobbies, the National Rifle Association, the oil companies, tourist agencies, and concerned citizens. (That Outsiders—journalists, the Sierra Club, editorial writers, and so on; the oil companies portrayed themselves as "Alaskan" in their advertising— played the greater part in forming the government's judgment astonished Alaskans of all classes. They resented the hard fact that so many other people—who did not live there, who did not make a living by the work of their hands—had a say in their, Alaskans', destiny.)

In the villages, most people guessed that hunting and trapping were going to be, at best, sharply restricted, at worst, eliminated, by the law: because the government was going to limit their access to, and movement within, the park. It would include most of their old hunting lands and trap lines.

(They were correct, as it turned out. The final act, the Alaska National Interest Lands and Conservation Act, went harder for all Native hunting— "subsistence" hunting, as it was called—than people had been told it would. Effectively, it subordinated their freedom to hunt to the higher value placed on wilderness preservation.)

F, exhausted by the paperwork, considered resigning from the council. The responsibility was too heavy; the old people demanded too much from the young. "They use us up," he said bitterly. But he did not resign.

●

ICE! It was the event of the week. On Tuesday, Joe went out with an axe handle, and measured its thickness on the lake. That night was cold: the freeze deepened. The next morning came the grand event, the marking of the ice.

I was in the new school when the word flew around the classrooms. Kids jammed up at the too-small windows, and watched three men walk about on the lake, small black figures pacing evenly back and forth. They tested the depth along a long rectangle, then chopped holes and planted small spruce trees at its boundaries. Barely restrained, the kids leaned against the doors. At a word, they flew down the slippery hill and swirled onto the lake.

The ice was like glass. Every child in town had found a pair of skates. By nightfall, fathers had gotten out their sharpening stones. At the Gavrils', Joe sat by the stove filing the blades of Lizzie's skates. F honed young Gavril's, and recalled taking his own to a grindstone when he was a kid, to keep up with Billy. The house was full of quickness and happy memories.

○

DAYS OF FOG, RAIN. Ghost Mountain was gone in the gloom. Fog breathed on the frozen lake, and wrapped my window like a cocoon a moth. I wanted to drowse all winter, quilted and warm. Occasionally I awoke, drank tea, looked out: for a moment, the fog thinned, the mountain appeared; then it was hidden again, sleeping, like me.

The end of a dream woke me.

I had landed in the village with a plane full of refugees. The village was unrecognizable. The refugees were village people, returning home. They pushed forward. An agent, perhaps a federal marshal, waved a pistol and threatened them. Those poor people were desperately thirsty. He shouted at them: "Maintain order!" He was quick, intelligent, worn to the bone, and had all but gone over some mental edge. I managed to take his pistol away.

The plane lifted off and rose above the field. The field was thronged with bystanders. Dust rose everywhere. A young woman complained, loudly and crossly, that the plane had taken off without her. I thought she must have arrived with us. She had relatives in the village, but she did not live there. No one trusted her. Someone said, "It's bad she's back."

Now I stood before a warm and carpeted house, built where F's house used to be. How comfortable it looked! The lamps were lit and glowing; a family of Outsiders lived there. F, who knew them, ordered them to give me a place to stay. It seemed we were no longer together, and although he was courteous, F had no more time for me. He knew that all was finished, and that it had to be ended correctly. I stowed my gear in a bedroom, where there was a real bed.

The town was lit up by mercury-vapor lamps. Spread across the center, where the old chiefs had lived, was a large gym mat covered with people lying on their backs in neat rows. I could not see their faces, only their feet, which were placed carefully side by side. My heart ached. A young woman talked slowly and clearly to them, as if she were giving instructions. Someone explained to me, "These people are dying, but they don't know how to do it. They had to hire an expensive consultant, to show them how."

It was very hot. The young woman, who had come from Outside, offered to show a long-haired girl (her hair was cut like mine) how to tuck it up under a scarf, as the old women did. Tenderly, she wiped the foreheads of the dying people.

I stood on the airfield. The immense sky was empty. No more planes would come; we were sealed off, and the menace and confusion of the

Outside would never trouble us again. The air was beatifically quiet. My heart lifted, I was absolved of guilt for the disorder; then I understood that I could never leave. I woke with a tumbling sense of confusion, freedom, a gnawing in my stomach . . .

○

WE SETTLED ON A PLAN of staying in Anchorage for the winter. Freighting in enough oil to last the cold months was too expensive. I would leave first; F would join me a week later.

For three days it had rained and blown. F woke up, happy for a moment. He had dreamed of his mother: she was coming for him. Then his face turned dark, and he looked very frightened.

○

HE HAD NOT BEEN CHEERFUL, nor had I. The strain had been intense. I blamed myself for it; something inside me was dying. At night I lay in bed looking up at the ceiling, the ragged ceiling packed with fraying, blackened insulation that no one had ever finished covering up, and I heard his breathing, but not my own, and thought I would smother.

We argued, and retreated into hard positions: I, all mind; he, all body. Each of us would never see the other at her freest, his most glorious. He swore he would never take a woman to camp; and I: my mind could not work around him. He longed to persuade me: he had been a "nothing" until I came; now he was a "something," thanks to me.

In the night, he cried out, "I'll do anything."

○

Dear B.,

This house that was fine all summer is not fitted out for winter. The stove uses too much oil, gutters and dies, so we've been making do with jerry-rigged measures. I draw cold water in the dark and carry it into the Blazo-lit living space. The lake froze deep enough to skate on, and that has been our big excitement. Fur prices are up. Trapping fever has hit hard now. A boy snared a fox last night; this morning, everyone rattled their traps and set off up the mountain. You can get $175 for a big red fox, up to $500 for prime large lynx. Three lynx can buy you enough fuel for the winter. Besides, it's good for everyone to get out. If I were going to stay here, I would do the same.

The relationship with F is going to—end, I suppose; change, at any rate. I miss my freedom, though it's a lonely thing. It's harder for me to write honestly here. My worries and angers stand in the way. I feel trapped; and responsible; and miserable that our life isn't what I had (impossibly) hoped it would be. I can't divide myself: when I must put so much energy into this love, I have less of it for work; I mean, the energy you generate to keep a usable space around yourself. I've no hope of resolution. I don't want to be so damned independent and alone; but it seems to be necessary, for some reason I can't fathom.

I tell myself that I go on with this work in order to repay a debt. I owe life, because I'm unable to stay and form the usual lasting ties. If I remain—here, anywhere—I'm mired in their pain; how can I take on their lives? There is so much unhappiness. It seems the world is truly a vale of tears, as the prayer says it is, and in it, laughter equals courage. Yet, these people keep going, day after day.

Sometimes I miss the old hard intellectual edge. I'm growing less articulate. I discover that the beauty of living lies in perceiving the balance between pain and courage. What I love is the courage of these people with few alternatives, people for whom the limit—of tradition, of their boundaries, of few opportunities—is both relief and frustration. Their virtues are genuinely inspiring, deeply moving. I want to be like them; I don't want to; I can't. I have to fight my displaced nostalgia: honor still requires clear sight.

I keep talking around and around my heart-soreness. I'm getting ready to leave here for a long time, and it's like leaving the family hearth to go out into a wet night: hard getting out of the soft chair, though you know the whip of the weather brings its own invigorating chill.

○

SUNRISE WAS BRILLIANT, and opened into a lovely day to fly. It is a marvel of humans: those who move, those who belong to their place. One can try to do no harm; but the heart is more fragile than it is tough, I believe.

Gently, sorrowfully, firmly, Natalia had urged me to keep trying with F. "You two are good together," she had said. "We would do what we can to help you."

The old woman of the fierce eye had said, "It's hard saying good-bye to friends." Her face: its active, dark eyes: its well-shaped, strong mouth: its wrinkles. I had touched the faces, round-cheeked, rosy as peaches, of her grandchildren. Lily, their mother, had placed on the table a hand-sized sled she had whittled of birch with an axe blade. It was a fine sled! She had grinned and shaken her head: her father told her her hand was still too unsteady to carve.

Natalia's daughter Sally had said, "I'll send an order for jeans with you."

Lizzie had turned a somersault and said, "I'll send an order for YOU with you, and you'll have to send yourself back here."

I had packed my gear in boxes, and mailed them. I looked around the bare room, and stared out the window at the road, the lake, Ghost Mountain standing full in the sun across the ice: I had wanted to climb that mountain.

But the house had been my mountain, and, bowing to its unyielding spirit, I would leave it as bare as when I had entered; it was a grave house. His mother had tried her best to protect him. She may have won, for our lives were separating; but she could have done a better job for him, for he was full of me and all I had given him. Now he must do his part, which was to be tough and wise.

A last touch of myself remained. I had picked a bunch of dried grasses and beach peas: they stood in a little glass on the table. I took them back to where they had grown, and scattered them along the shore of the lake.

According to
Our Nature

THE BODY CHANGES: with it, perception; and so, language.

I went East to spend Christmas with family, then on to New York, Boston, Seattle, to see friends. In their company I strolled down those familiar streets. We drank European coffee and ate in good restaurants, we indulged ourselves in the good life of cities; but, fine as it was, as much as I loved it, I was already marked. I could not seem to walk in step: inwardly I limped, as after a badly set break has mended; as though some strong thing I could not name had taken me in its grip, and bent me, leaving a scar on the bone.

o

THE OLD WOMAN of the fierce eye, the blind storyteller, Joe Gavril, his niece Olga, his cousin who was badly cut by an axe: all are gone. Natalia lives as a widow. I've been told her eldest daughter, Marya, went to college, married, and lives in Anchorage, Lizzie is old enough to have finished college. The teacher Nancy Sigurd married a lodge owner and moved away. The big man left to teach the history of the American West in a state university. Most of the white people I knew have moved on.

According to the papers, the village looks quite different. It has become a staging area for entry into the great national park that covers the Dena'ina hunting land. Nearly everyone works for the park. Money flowed: new houses went up, with electricity and running water, and a road was built to connect to the regional town. During the boom, F's brothers promoted schemes to the village corporation; most people were wary of them. The boom collapsed, as it always does, leaving some of the people a little worse off, more of them a bit better off; all of them older, more experienced, probably cynical, perhaps wiser.

About six months after I left, I dreamed about them again. After a long time away, I returned. The village looked like a town in a twenty-first–century movie. An urgent message: Natalia had been taken to an institution, perhaps a hospital. I walked through its spacious grounds and came to a large, complicated, well-appointed building with a central staircase. Inside were Village people I had once known, very young ones who had grown up. I no longer recognized them!

I walked into a classroom and learned it was the room for a theater group. The youngsters bowed to me courteously, in the old Russian manner, then chattered with excitement. I saw Lizzie, and asked about her mother. She replied vaguely.

I searched for F. People were reluctant to talk: "He's not here, we don't know where he is." Gradually I understood; then it was whispered: "He's living with someone." Karen? I asked. "Yes," they said. I looked for a boy to carry a message. No one would do it.

I went into a meeting room full of Indians and asked if someone would find F. My informant—this word, like *Indians,* was in the dream—whispered that no one would leave the room before 5:30, and it was only 5:10. The Indians, seated on folding chairs, glanced at me sidelong, annoyed: now I saw that they were watching television. The program was *Dallas.*

I overheard news of Natalia; the details were cruel. She had been hurt emotionally and had retired to the institution to rest.

I passed an airline counter, modern and impersonal looking, lit by fluorescent lights. Young Native women were taking bookings. I joined the line, hoping to book a charter out for the next day; and was told, brusquely: *Be at the field when the plane lands, First come, first served, Seat fare paid in advance.* The Native regional corporation owned the company. Manners had changed. I was determined to finish what I had come to do and leave.

I entered another building, and stepped into a small, gracefully furnished music room. F appeared in the doorway, laughed falsely, greeted me too loudly. I was happy for him, I said coolly. I intended to leave as soon as I could get a seat on the plane. His smile disappeared, and he turned toward me in anguish: I was wrong, the woman was not Karen, but one I did not know; we had been apart a long time, after all. We held one another, weeping. Over his shoulder I spied a music stand, on which a rare folio lay open. On the recto sheet, in hand-set type, appeared three lines of poetry. I read: *The humanness of events.* The words were attributed to me. When had I written them? Where had they been hidden? Music was scrolled beneath the three lines. Who had made this beautiful book? Who had found it, and put it there?

With learned authority a bald man commented on F's "impassivity, characteristic of the Native." F's back was to him; he could not see F weeping on my shoulder. I lifted my head to stare at him. My eyes were red. I heard a voice say of the beautiful folio: Oratorio. I said: Who was given permission to use my words? I thought I owned them!

❖

I TOOK A JOB in McGrath, farther north in the Interior. F remained in Anchorage. He and I continued to see one another for a half-year; he flew to McGrath; we traveled Outside.

January 22, Anchorage
    Tomorrow I go to McGrath. F and I have spent too many days here with his family. We argued again this morning, after nights of interrupted

sleep, after days of arguments. Talking to him was about as effective as punching a pillow. His brothers love it that I have a car: Let's make a beer run! When I think of his hurt, smoky eyes I fear this is not over for me; but what I say to him doesn't sink in. I say the same things time and again, but the words seem to mean nothing.

January 27, McGrath

My anger evaporated before his desperate pleas: that the world I've opened to him not be closed off again.

I clashed with his brother Lou. Lou lectured me: "A man is a man," "A woman has her role," and so on, fatuous Lou being on his usual high. The terrible pressures on F; my anger at his family, and my real anger.

What weighs on my shoulders is drinking-memories: watching him go over the edge; seeing him sprawled on the steambath floor, or being carried upstairs. "You can't help but worry," said the old woman of the fierce eye. "It makes you sick."

I know less now than when I first came to Alaska. I would know more if I had not thrown myself so completely into it all.

March 7, Port Townsend, Washington

The Centrum Foundation has organized a conference called "The Power of Animals." I'm among friends; poets and writers, ecologists, naturalists have assembled from all quarters. F has come with me. He has the gift of poetry in him; he may hear something to make him catch fire.

The writer and translator Howard Norman sang us Cree songs. They were direct, clean, full of marvel. He told us about having spent seventeen hours translating at a trial: the Crees had brought suit against the governments of Québec and Canada. Québec wants to build an immense hydroelectric power station at Baie James and flood Cree land. After hours of Cree testimony, with Howard translating, the government called as witness an ecologist who had never been on that land. He certified it was fit only for flooding.

A Cree man with little English said, "But we call it the Garden." There was silence.

And among us, silence and weeping.

Thus we are: speechless in our astonishment at an incomprehensible lie.

March 8

H.N. tells us that in the Crees' Garden, the exchange of information is round, and that stories are round. Stories live in certain places: they gather at night and talk to one another. Every so often a story goes out and inhabits someone for a while. When a storyteller begins a story, it is not by saying, "I'm going to talk about moose." *About* removes him. He says, "I'll talk moose." The story comes out: it goes around: and he sucks it back in.

H.N. points out that when one culture moves in on another, the mythological animals are the first to go—he gives the example of Windigos. Is this because of the priests? Or, because of the failure of the imagination? Does the new culture think they "made up" the Windigos?

He talked about all the people who have no language now, neither Native nor English. I've heard the same thing said in Alaska. What can this mean? Can such a thing be true?

March 11, in transit

F and I stopped in Juneau, where I had some business to conduct. He kept marveling at the Animals conference, at the people he met, at how "open-minded" they were.

"Not in Alaska," he said. This is true. People refuse to hear what displeases them, or frightens them.

May 12, McGrath

F came to visit for a few days. We flew south to Hungry, where his mother's people live; it was his first visit there. His relatives were pleased to see him. He was appalled at McGrath: "The whites have all the goodies here."

I go through the anti-white anger with him often now. We've had two big fights about it lately. Now he's gone fishing in Bristol Bay, fishing a skiff. He has no license or berth on a boat: he was "double-crossed" by his backers, he said bitterly. He doesn't know what to do: for all his great heart, he can't follow through on his own impulse; then something goes wrong, while he depends on people who never come through for him. He is no judge of character. He thinks Lou and his wife are good people, because they never roll him when he is drunk.

And the drinking: he said that every day he needs alcohol, and this is making him despair.

What can I do for him? I have a helpless grief, and no answers at all. He clung to me. He talked about the alcohol; no denying it now. He loves the stuff, he said. He recalled with disgust how he had been last summer.

"What do I have to do," he cried, "become a Christian?"

Is there no other way? Who can help him? I mourn for him, and for us.

June 5

It's over with F. He smashed up the car, too.

The following January, I heard, F joined the Marines. About three years later he phoned me. He sounded well and happy, and had news: he had married a girl from Bristol Bay. He was working: he had a job with the corporation; they were developing some new plans. His wife was expecting a baby. It was not clear whether he had been a Marine.

After wrecking my car, he told me, he had had to appear in court. He had owned up to whatever fault he had been charged with; the judge had let him off with a light fine, impressed with his frankness, his having told the truth. F laughed painfully.

"I never lie to anyone," he said, "except myself."

o

IN THE VILLAGE, often, I had the fleet sense of something else, something barely visible through the interstices of language. Trying to see, I found a handful of words, and made a few poems that sounded accurate to me. That was all; yet what I saw in Village Below was less than what existed. My intuitions were good, my corporal memory clear; my understanding was still unformed. I had to learn to know what I had witnessed.

Billy Alexey and his friend Gurrie had told me a hunting story. They had followed a moose the whole day, until it entered the village! The animal trotted up the road, turned left at the mayor's house, and went back into the woods. They let it go.

At the time, I had admired the hunters' gallantry, their chivalry and humor, that let the nonchalant moose escape; and so, I had missed the point of the story.

The old people (I would learn) were always uneasy when a large animal came too close to a settlement. Animals prefer their own ranges, and normally stay within their boundaries. It was odd, strange, disturbing, that a moose walked up the road. It was known that an animal would not have strayed from befuddlement, any loss of its sense of direction: animals are too intelligent for that, having more, and sharper, senses than humans do. If an animal came near humans, someone might have called it. (Was this why their voices dropped when they mentioned the mayor?) No hunter would be foolish enough to interfere with a spirit call. Safety lay in maintaining respect, in staying out of the way.

My respect for those hunters became more complicated; my sentimentality dissolved. I had been notified. Alert to the signs, the two men had realized (and I should realize) the moose had come into the village for a serious purpose, other than their own need for food. A man of power lived there. The moose had gone to him.

o

IN THE COUNTRY of the Dena'ina four dialects were spoken. By its mother tongue, or dialect, each tribe identified itself. The tongue of the old woman of the fierce eye and the blind storyteller had been what linguists called the Inland dialect, which I heard spoken in the Kijik country. Across Cook Inlet, on the Kenai Peninsula, existed another, attenuated branch of Dena'ina still spoken and written by a remarkable old man, who was well known as an author and storyteller. His name was Peter Kalifornsky, after the ancestor who had accompanied Russian traders south to Fort Ross, California. When I came to know him, around the mid-nineteen-eighties, he was already the author of two collections; he was the first Dena'ina to write *sukdu*, the old stories from our parents' lips.

His repertoire of *sukdu* was much larger than these, I learned; for besides the animal tales, he knew intricate stories about belief, the power of the animals, cosmology, law, the training and curing of the body, and the inspiration and use of the mind in visions, dreaming, imagination, and making metaphor.

I had seen a story written by him in Dena'ina, which seemed to me full of meaning and implication, but which in translation was opaque. I went to Kenai to visit him, to ask if he would care to discuss this story with me.[12] He did wish to discuss it; indeed, he was delighted to talk about the "back story," or the meanings behind the stories. So began our long conversation in which he traced out the world of his ancestors, the old Dena'ina, through their stories. "The history of the human mind," he called them. But they were not simple, nor easy for me to understand, and his explanations of them took years.

He had drafted a new series of stories, on whose English versions we were collaborating. To introduce the section he called *History* he wrote a short piece, *"K'egh,"* which he translated with knowing humor as "Anthropology": *k'egh* means "about the whole thing." He might have called it his condensed history of the Dena'ina.

> It is a good thing to write in Dena'ina. The language will be preserved.
> The Dena'ina people have not been persuaded to give up their laws. They were one united people who made agreements with other chiefs.
> The Dena'ina are said to be competent in many things. They are strong-minded. They traveled by boat, and on overland trails they made caches. What they learned they taught to one another, by giving advice. They visited among themselves and told each other their ancient stories. They told of plant medicine and of good plants to eat. They listened to old stories and learned from them, and they handed on their stories and knowledge for the use of those who came after them. They wished to be the first to learn new things and to hand these on to their neighbors.
> They lived long lives in good health; they trusted one another; and they taught one another to avoid sickness.
> They did not depend on outside villages.

"'They did not depend on outside villages,'" said the old man. "People might read that and think, 'What kind of writer is this? What did he mean by that word?' In any history now, what is it like? They could be describing themselves as a powerful nation."

Nearly seventy years before, when he was a young boy, he had been sent to stay with his uncle, his mother's brother, in camp. His mother's people lived across Cook Inlet from the Kenai Peninsula, at the base of the Alaska Range. Every evening after a long day's work in the canneries, his uncle's relatives came to the camp to visit. The little boy was the last person of his generation to whom those people told stories in their own language.

"They said, 'This one will be our reserve,'" he recalled, shaking his head slightly. "They liked their steambath every day and so, I was steady on the axe." In the steambath and in the relaxing time afterward they had poured story after story into his ears.

He had spent three seasons with his uncle. When he returned to his father, on the Kenai, other old men had made time for the curious, growing boy, who had not followed the other boys to school. Then, in his sixties, after having had a hard life, he had learned to write his language, and had published several volumes of stories. Now he wished to pass on the intricate meanings webbed about his great circle of belief stories, the stories of law and regulation, stories from when the animals talked, and the histories. Because he knew he would not write it, and because I was very interested in what he had to say, I became his amanuensis.

"Dena'inas said the animals know exactly what you're thinking," he said. "I don't know how, but they say animals have your sense of mind. If you respect them they'll be there before you. They're on the dark side of the daylight, we're on the light side. When the daylight breaks, they're up there waiting for us: they can see what kind of person we are."

He had been studying and thinking about animals since the year he went to his uncle's camp. His stories about them are very old. They tell of the First Beginning, When the Animals Went in Pairs: the time when the animals separated and chose partners; when the animals—Porcupine and Beaver, Crow and Camprobber, Lynx and Wolverine—paired for friendship and mutual assistance; when the smaller animals like Porcupine and Beaver chose a larger animal like Moose as a protector.

Stories of the First Beginning came to the dreamers, men of power who dreamed for the truth, in order to help the humans live a better life: to learn how to be humans. The animals called the humans The People Who Sit Around the Campfire; they talked to the Campfire People, and understood their language.

I asked: "Does that mean that humans and animals can still talk to each other?"

"I can't say that they do. And, still, I can't say that they don't." He made scrupulous distinctions. He spoke of what he had learned for himself, and what he had learned from others; but experience, he reminded me, had to be examined and compared with what was known, and he would not say he knew truth. The test of truth is rigorous, and he was too careful to presume it.

"Same as the bear story I gave you," he said. "If you are hunting in bear country and you find his bedding, say, 'Great-grandfather, it's me,' and rub spittle on his bedding; then go. If you come near him, go upwind. He'll smell you and leave you alone. I can't say that's *true*, even though I've been through it myself."

More and more often in the work he touched on matters with which I was preoccupied, particularly matters of the spirit, and especially the spirits of animals. By then he knew me well enough that I felt I could venture a confidence. I asked him to help me understand an experience of my own.

Several summers ago, I told him, a woman who had become like a second mother to me and I were at her summer residence. We went hunting for mushrooms. We were in the woods later than usual, toward the end of the day, when the animals came out to feed. She was walking slowly, and I went ahead of her on the path. I came around a curve and saw a thick clump of the kind we liked very much. As I bent toward it, I smelled a powerful odor and, simultaneously, had this sense: that a slightly quizzical, interested, not unfriendly being was standing near me. I could not see it, but knew I had gone too close to its place. In my mind I responded, saying carefully that I had come there only for the mushrooms and was leaving now with no harmful intent.

We sat, silent. It is a very old Athabaskan belief that everything that exists has its own spirit, and that that spirit must be respected. Speaking of bear, brown bear, is a delicate matter. His name is attached to him, as words are attached to things; he demands respect and is referred to obliquely. Great-grandfather. Big Old Man. Speaking his name lightly might call him, if one were out in the woods. Athabaskan women followed a strict etiquette with him. I had watched women, and tried to act as they did.

At last the old man said, "The animals fear humans. But they have better smell and better ears than we do. And also, he can sense your mind, if you are a danger to him or not. So in the stories, as we go along, they talk to the animal. 'So, Big Old Man, I'm not for you.' That's been experienced. It's my feeling and my sense that I am in the woods for him; and also, that I stayed out of his way, and he out of my way."

Then he added, carefully, "But I don't *know* what makes that. It's my feeling or my sense that he received my mind contact. Maybe somebody in my place would put that for the truth. But I can't, even from my own experience. Because I still don't know the answer to it.

"What you told me, you experienced. Combine that with my experience. By looking at it that way, it has to be a better witness."

"But how do we know the truth, then?" I asked.

"This has been happening to a lot of people, but there's no real answer to it. Sometimes a person is getting into danger. You have that sense that something is watching you: is that a warning to protect yourself better, that you might have an accident with a wild animal? Say you'll be in a place where there is nobody or no animal, and all at once you have that funny feeling that somebody's watching you. Something's watching you. That eye penetrating you, sensing you. You may see it or you may not. Not only me: you have that experience. But I can't say it's true, even though you hear it from lots of people along the way."

"But you know you have had a feeling of something," I persisted. "You don't know what is out there to cause it?"

"No," he said. "You don't know what it is."

○

A FEW THINGS REMAIN from those days: a small, hand-carved sled, sitting on a bookshelf; under my desk, a paper bag with a dozen peeled willow sticks in it. Six have strips of red flannel tied to them. They are gambling sticks for the game that I had learned from a poet, the sticks that F, who sang a song to the caribou before he shot, had whittled.

From Peter Kalifornsky I learned the meaning of the game of *chin lahe*. Old men play it, he said, though not so often now. They sing an old refrain, a chant of four murmured syllables: *Di ya du hu*. This chant came to them from the First Beginning, before the time that Crow, the wily trickster, gave the Campfire People their first songs and stories. It was the rhythm that had kept them together as they worked, rhythm being the fundamental unifier of all social peoples, and, as the poetics of all languages reveal, the primal animator of their lyric arts. The old man sang the song, and showed me how he hid the bones in his hands so that no one should guess which bone was marked. He told me about *chin lahe* because one of his oldest stories, a story of belief, is called "Gambling Game."

> At one time, Dena'inas used to tell stories. In this story, two rich men met and said: "Let's play the gambling game."
>
> One of these young men was a shaman. The other man followed all of the traditional beliefs.
>
> The shaman began to win everything from the young believer. He took all his possessions, until all the young man had left were his wife and children.
>
> "What will you bet me?" the shaman asked him. There were his wife and children, three girls and a boy. He longed to keep them. But all his belongings were gone. "I will bet you your children against them," the shaman said. The young believer wished to keep his wife and his boy. He gave the shaman his three daughters. His wife and boy remained.
>
> "Against all your things and the three girls, bet me your wife and boy," the shaman said to him. Whom did he love more, his wife or the young boy? His wife, too, he gave the shaman.
>
> Then he bet the boy against all his belongings and his wife and girls. The shaman took the boy, too. The believer was left with nothing. The shaman had won all he owned, even his last gun.

The young man went out and walked far off. In the foothills, he found a ground squirrel caught in a trap he had set. It was chewed up; only a small skin lay there, for the animal had not returned to its reincarnation place. He picked it up and put it inside his shirt.

Far off he walked, until he came to a great shelter where there was life. From inside, someone spoke. "I heard you. Turn three times the way the sun goes round, and stoop down and come in."

It was spacious inside. A very big old lady sat there. "I am the Mother of the Animals," she said. "My husband is gone, but he will return to us."

Not long after, a giant man came in. "Hello," he said, "what happened that you came to meet me?"

The young man explained what the shaman had done to him. "The shaman took my wife, my girls, and even my last child, my boy. And somehow, I came here."

"Good," the giant said. "Well, rest, and I'll fix you up."

The young man rested. As he sat, the little skin inside his shirt began to move: and out it jumped! It once again formed itself into a ground squirrel and scampered across the floor.

"Yes, you have come to us with our child," said the giant. "I searched all over for my lost child. And the one who gambled with you, who played with you: he is a shaman, you say. Good. I, too, have power. I'll prepare you to go back to him."

Animal skins were piled in the house. He cut little pieces from each of them, and put them into a gut-bag. With them he put down feathers.

"You will return with this. When no one is looking, sprinkle the down on it. The skins will grow into a large number of animals. These you will bet."

Then he laid out three sets of gambling sticks and wrapped them in a bundle. "With this first set of gambling sticks, you will play with him, and both of you will win, back and forth. As you go on, he will increase his bet.

"When he thinks, 'I will take everything from him,' you will bounce down the second set of gambling sticks. They will spin three times, the way the sun goes round, and you will take back your belongings, your wife and girls, and the boy.

"Again the shaman will win something, and he will increase his bet, trying his power. You will bounce down the third set of gambling sticks. They will spin against the sun, and you will take everything from that shaman: his property, his children, and his wife.

"Then you will tell him: 'What I have done to you, you too did to me. I went out, and I went to the one they call K'luyesh. K'luyesh resupplied me, and gave me three sets of gambling sticks. With them I won everything back from you. Go to K'luyesh and tell him, Give me the gambling sticks.'"

Believer went back. Three times he gambled. He won everything from the shaman. Using the animal skins, K'luyesh blocked the shaman's power.

The shaman tried to transform his spirit, but he could not make it take the form of an animal. He failed in his power. And he went out, and there was no more word of him.

K'luyesh, searching for his lost child, the ground squirrel, had walked far above us across the sky. He left his footprints on the mountains; and then, disgusted that he could not find his son, he sat down hard on a summit and left the print of his hind end. His trail became the streak of light forming far above us, which we call the Milky Way.

The old man smiled. The Gambling Story was one of his two favorites; he liked to tell it, and to reflect on how deep it took us into a world not visible to us. There were times, and stories, when we went so deep it made his head spin, and he grew cautious; but now his voice was light: how the old Dena'ina recognized the guardian of the animals, the giant K'luyesh, pleased him. "K'luyesh: they say they can see his tracks in the sky on a clear night. His trail is the road he travels on, the Milky Way. They say that on top of the mountains they would see his footprints."

If you looked at a topographical map of the Alaska Range, you would see where K'luyesh's trail touched earth. You would see that the peaks and ridges are pocked with small lakes and cirques that look, in the cartographer's hand, like footprints, or like the kind left by a giant who has sat down in the snow.

But what I heard in the story was its ritual nature: the three-times turning, with the sun, and against it; the lost ground squirrel sought by its Father, and its rebirth in the Giants' shelter; K'luyesh's gambling sticks, sprinkled with down, to unloose their force; the shaman, who took everything from the hapless believer, and who lost it all to the Guardian's, K'luyesh's, greater power. I saw the shaman as greedy, implacable Death.

When the believer throws down his three sets of gambling sticks, and they turn sun-wise, counter-sun-wise, and back, they cause reversals: so the old man called them. Reversals are a corrective, both morally and ecologically: they curb excess, they restore balance to the world. Reversals cycle perpetually through Dena'ina stories. They are the cycle of all existence, and carry the weight of natural law. The old man saw them as fundamental. "These reversals are what's behind all the stories," he said. "As the world revolves, or the moon turns upside down in its cycles."

I asked why the story said three: three times turning, three rounds of gambling. (Was it a Christian variation on an archaic story?)

His answer went to the ancient heart of the matter. "To begin with, that shaman was in the wrong: using his power to do wrong against this person, through gambling. And for doing wrong, the same punishment he gave out came back on him. That meant the end of his shaman work: K'luyesh blocked him from transforming himself into an animal.

"When that second set spun the way the sun goes, that's for the right thing, on the good part. The third set he spun against the sun: that goes on the bad side. The shaman did the bad work, but that same bad form was reversed back on him.

"That 'three' seems to go in a cycle through all the stories," he pointed out. "Why three? In the 'Gambling Story,' it's a human life cycle: live, die, come back."[13]

F had loved to gamble; he was hardly alone in that. In the village, gambling had seemed to be in some people's blood, their zest for it was palpable, though the Christian ladies disapproved. Could it be shaman's work? I thought of my bag of willow sticks, and how fiercely, unknowingly, I had played with the poets; and how I had asked the children to play. "But then, is it wrong if I gamble," I asked, carefully, "but right if you do?"

"It has to be okay," he replied kindly. "You have to do your part for living, and I do my part. And it gets down to it: we're all gamblers for living. We take chances. Maybe that's why that gambling game story was laid out: to look behind it.

"Human life is a gamble. You have to go out and gamble, take chances, do things."

"But why is it a gambling story?" I persisted, knowing the answer already. (It is a game of poetic justice.)

"It's human life," he said.

○

I REREAD MY NOTEBOOKS; I recall old stories; I reflect on what passed in the Kijik country. Those people did not speak lightly: a stranger-child had to be shown how to live properly, or she might bring harm to them. They lived in a parlous state, in dangerous times. What should be kept unspoken; what told? What could be revealed to such a visitor? Was that visitor an enemy?

In time, the woman who became my second mother would explain to me their (and her own) obligation, and, implicitly, remind me of mine. "We have to treat people according to their nature," she would say.

"We don't tell you things for nothing," she would add.

Interlude:
Hungry, Holy

I was washing outside in the darkness,
the sky burning with rough stars,
and the starlight, salt on an axe blade.
The cold overflows the barrel.

The gate's locked,
the land's grim as its conscience.
I don't think they'll find new weaving,
finer than truth, anywhere.

Star-salt is melting in the barrel,
icy water is turning blacker,
death's growing purer, misfortune saltier,
the earth's moving nearer to truth and to dread.

—Osip Mandelstam,
tr. Clarence Brown and
W. S. Merwin

Endurance

For the past two days, a full moon has filled the sky. Yesterday it crept up quietly, round and pale, behind the hills across the river, about due east, before sunset. Today its rise was slow, stately, gliding in from the northeast. Its face was orange, and was luminous.

Long after dark, a fire roared and crackled against the tender, navy blue sky. Its flames chewed out an old lady's tinder-dry log house; it had been the oldest house in town. She used a hot plate, the wiring went bad; the inside walls were covered with cardboard and contact paper; she could save nothing.

The wind has been more westerly than north these past two days, and blowing; the fire was hard to control. Fortunately, it blew away from the unfinished house in the next lot, though a corner of the frame burned. The men organized a bucket brigade. Red-orange sparks shot out from the logs and whirled through the wind. Showers of sparks landed on the cold, dry snow and did not go out.

◦

THE INTERIOR is a literal place: it is the vast area of the northern forest within Alaska. Alaska is itself a literal name. Alashka. Aleyeska. The writing of the (Athabaskan) word varies in form, but in each form, it seems to mean Great Land. The literal is also metaphysical: *great* seems also to imply power of a holy kind. Athabaskan place names are descriptive, and can be so in a double way, limning the visible and the invisible. If a young man learned the complete name of a place—a certain hill, or a bend in the river, or a village—that name would describe the physical characteristics he needed to know to recognize the site; and it could also tell him something more.

For instance, on the west side of Cook Inlet there is a small place now known as Polly Creek. Its Dena'ina name, however, is very long: it marks where an ancient man of power called the Whale Hunter, also called Gashaq', killed a whale; an impressive feat, for the salt-water Dena'ina did not hunt whales, except for the small beluga that come into the mouths of rivers in early spring and shoal there, white as quartz on sand.

According to the story, this Believer, Gashaq', believed in the great unknown power whose euphemism is "little speck of dirt." He himself had power: not in the shamanic form, in which the spirit leaves the body and acts through an animal familiar, but a greater, direct form: he could make his word act by itself, and come true. According to the story, he killed his whale and called for a heavy wind, the wind came up and blew for a day, and the Believer told the people where to expect to find the dead animal. They waited in that place in their kayaks and bidarkas, and the whale floated in to them on the tide. The Dena'ina name of the place, then, is a long description, of the wind, the tide, the inlet, and how the people in their skinboats, the whale lashed to them, drifted ashore.[14] The place-name is the history of that awesome hunt. It belongs to the stories about the Whale Hunter; and the stories belong to the man who told them to me.

In English, many Alaskan place names are utilitarian, like the old gold-mining town of Flat, in the Iditarod area; but often, they are lovely and evocative. On the Kenai Peninsula is tiny Hope, on Resurrection Creek, where one spring I helped dig a garden.

The Interior is a literal reference to the areas of northern, or boreal, forest inside Alaska. The adjective *boreal*, however, is metaphorical and natural: that is, it is derived from Greek nature philosophy of the fifth century. But scholars of Greek religion remind us that Boreas was originally a divine figure, not simply a force of nature personified in language, who appeared in the era before the pantheon of the Greek poets: he was the North Wind. The Athenians prayed to him to destroy the Persian fleet menacing them.[15]

Even so, it is not Classical belief or convention that confers authority on the North of the New World. Rather, the North's power is immanent, and implicit, and has for long ages been so recognized and described on this continent. For example, an Apache woman told this to a gathering of Athabaskan speakers in Fairbanks: "A lot of our Apache medicine men still sing about the north where it is always white. White is the color associated with the direction north. The Big Dipper is used a lot in the songs. A lot of the medicine men call upon the power of the north in their songs and rituals."[16]

One manifestation of this power of the North may be what Koyukon Athabaskans call *sinh talaa'*, which seems to be the source of medicine power and which comes from the earth. Speaking of it, a Koyukon man told the anthropologist Richard K. Nelson: "The country knows. If you do wrong things to it, the whole country knows. It feels what's happening to it. I guess everything is connected together somehow, under the ground."[17]

From the Distant Time, as the Koyukon people call the beginning, the Interior has fed, clothed, and instructed people. It is the home of all the Alaskan Athabaskan tribes except the Dena'ina, who live farther south, and, as well, of inland Yup'ik Eskimos. The Interior is made of forests composed of spruce, birch, alder, aspen, cottonwood, willow; the tussocks of the muskeg; some areas of permafrost; and wild grasses, many kinds of berries, the Alpine flowers. Its major rivers are the mighty Yukon, the brown Kuskokwim, the Koyukuk of clear summer water, the twisting Tanana, and, near the Brooks Range, the Porcupine and the Chandalar.

To the Outside it has given up gold and furs in astonishing amounts, since the days of the earliest Russian traders. Having settled on isolated homesteads, or in villages, or in towns like McGrath and Galena, or in Fairbanks, on the Chena River, white people, and also those whom Athabaskans once called "black whitemen," live in numbers that are now greater than those of Natives.

When I left Village Below, I went north, into the Interior, to the town of McGrath, and spent two winters there. McGrath was the headquarters of a new school district, covering an area the size of Ohio, as they liked to say. About three thousand people lived in the district. I had given poetry in their schools; so, in a way, I returned. But why I returned to McGrath I couldn't say, exactly. I was coming to know people: there was some comfort in that. I needed a job, but that was accidental. Perhaps I was drawn by a quality of the light, or the lie of the land; perhaps by the half-buried memory of a presence in the forest. I learned endurance there, and was given an unexpected gift.

○

I PAUSE to remind myself of all I did not know about the animals. In the Interior I scarcely saw wild animals, except for their beautiful skins, and the way women used them. In Village Below I had glimpsed a small part of the enormous store of knowledge and belief by which people lived. I had eaten animals. I had heard old stories from the lips of respected tellers, and the more informal instruction adults give children. In the Interior I entered a country governed by the imagination, where the tracing out of animals-in-life is done.

I had never known animals, not even domestic animals, but at a distance. A deer might venture down from the mountains and pass through the backyard, delighting us; raccoons banged through garbage cans as we lay sleeping; on hot summer nights, the sweet pungent smell of skunk rolled into our noses. On country roads, dead animals—or, at night, the eyes of transfixed animals—appeared for a moment to us through car windows.

I read German fairy tales and Norse and Celtic myths, and encountered strange, otherworldly tellings infused with animal magic. As a young scholar I advanced to finely wrought studies of tribal religions, and came to recognize them as intricate mappings of the animate realm and complex protocols for living with immanent powers. It was as a young poet, however, that I turned back, intentionally, to the logic of myth, in which we travel on older streams of knowledge, born before writing and carried into writing. I turned to these works as I turned to poetry, as I traveled in the enormous country of the imagination that is distinct, but not separate, from the prosaic world; it is another, rich layer of the reality of the world, that contains rigorous forms of expression and comprehension.

Inspiration—in spirare—describes the act of blowing into, or breathing upon, as in, "To breathe life into." In one form, says the OED, it describes "a special immediate action of the Spirit of God (or of some divinity or supernatural being) upon the human mind or soul." Again, it refers to the infusion of "some thought or feeling into (a person, etc.) as if by breathing." Our Western poetic and religious traditions vibrate with the luminous writings of visionaries—St. John of the Cross, Hildegard of Bingen, Blake, Coleridge, Rilke—into whose ear was breathed the word of god, or God. It seems to me that between the imaginative forms of very different societies, such as this from which I come and the Athabaskan peoples among whom I lived, there do exist certain special places of communication; and that one of those mysterious places, a charged area through which I myself was nearly allowed to pass, is located within the poetic and religious phenomenon of the imagination that we call inspiration.

The old Dena'ina, also, believed that the breath was a mystery, and a holiness. Peter Kalifornsky described to me how they understood this mystery. In their old stories, he said, occur three riddles:

What is this story about? We cannot find out what is behind it.
The story lays a trail before us: we follow it to become human.
Something gives us what we breathe: what is it?

In his language, that awe-filled question, *Something gives us what we breathe: what is it?*, evokes the marvel of existence. Its words represent the motion of the act: going *toward* something. They indicate: "'Something we lost, and we've found it back.'" It is life, returning again and again to the sentient world: *life, death, coming back* is the cycle of existence, for humans and all other living beings. The motif of that eternal return is breath.

The old Dena'ina believed this: Everything that exists has its own spirit, its own life, and that life must be respected. They believed that truth occurred when the spirit, of a thing or being, touched one's mind, "like an electrical contact," and the mind formed an image of that contact. Peter Kalifornsky described how this happened: "Then, all at once, some inspiration, something like a picture, appears in the mind."

"They lived life by the imagination," he said: "the power of the mind." He said also: "People tried to live up to it in some way; and, in some way, it became a religion, became 'I believe.'"

The word he translated as "imagination" is *eynik' delnish*, a word composed (as his language was artfully, meaningfully, composed) of linked images. *Eynik'* is joined from "in-between" and "nose," to mean: *Something works on the mind invisibly, contacting it*; implying: *breathing into it. Delnish* is "It turns over," indicating the motion of turning side to side, regularly, cyclically, as the seasons turn. It is the same motion described in a lovely old story: how the mother bear, sleeping in her winter den, turns from side to side in midwinter, turning the world at solstice back toward the sun.

More intricately, *delnish* is related both to "nose," and to *dnelnish*, meaning *the pattern that we recognize*, the very pattern of the world laid out before the old Dena'ina and given to them in their stories.[18]

In their country and throughout the Interior, there still exist the makings of an intricate human consciousness similar to that which lives at the root of most ancient human communities: the stories of the animals, which are the oldest stories, the myths, of tribes. These come down from the time when humans and animals spoke together. In the North they are not called myths; that word, used carelessly, implies that the old stories are fanciful, a sort of fiction: but they are not; they are true, in the way myths are true: in their mimetic, associative logic, and in the precision with which they describe the other-than-human world. In the Interior, those old stories are woven into personal, practical knowledge of the visible relationships between humans and animals; and this interweaving forms the textures of the ordinary (as Malfa Ivanov called it), for so many of the persons who still live, physically and spiritually, by the rules of the game.

Along this line of thinking, a Koyukon woman once made two observations to me about the inner and outer faces of *what is.* The first was: "When men tell stories, they always look at the big things, while women pay attention to the small things around them." The second: "A spirit comes to a destitute person in a form he can recognize."

○

I WENT INTO THE INTERIOR to learn: I mean, to learn how to live. I longed to remain in that thrilling country. I wanted to learn from people who had always lived there, and try to learn in their way. Their old knowledge, it was said, was well founded and truthful, not new and transient. From them I would learn about various animals; but first I had to recognize what I already knew.

I knew, and sensed, that the animals were there, beyond my sight, yet entwined in the lives of humans. I knew, or imagined, or sensed, that when the animals were offended, they withdrew from humans, who needed them to live. But, looking back, I cannot tell exactly how or when I knew it, or what I knew of animals and humans, hunting and trapping, at any given moment. The accumulation of my knowledge was slow and circuitous, formed from brief conversations, or in small observations, or some experience of the body, and by intuition, and in dreams.

I had dreamed I talked to a bear, or that she talked to me. I was in the woods. Silently I called: "Bear!" She came and I rode on her back: she indulged me, as an amused adult plays kindly with a child. Desiring revelation, I held my breath, and woke up.

This was a dream I had inspired in myself: I had pictured my own wish. Ah, I desired to marry the country! I begged to hear its unspoken words, its town, its attitude, its nuance.

The real female bear, that is, her spirit, did not appear in my dream; the dream animal was only my longing. Because of what I learned afterward, I think this is an accurate description of the event. I must be precise about this, for I am reconstructing what I knew and did not know about the animals; and how I knew, and what I learned about them; and why I had to test everything: because there, where nothing was clear to me except the hard demands of physical life, I had to know what to believe.

I am describing a way of living *in-between,* along the borders of distinct worlds that were, within themselves, composed of relatives and allies, or themes and variations; and composed of strangers, or differences. I longed for reconciliation.

o

AN ANIMAL TRAVELS through this account. He is Wolverine, *Gulo luscus,* a mean, spiteful, greedy, far-ranging creature. He is trapped for his fur, not his meat. Among the Iñupiat and certain Athabaskan tribes, only married women wear his skin and claws, as a ruff on their parkas. A Koyukon woman described to me how the wolverine's spirit was known to be unfriendly to women, and how her own baby daughter had cried inconsolably when a wolverine skin was laid near her. The mother took the skin away, recognizing the reason for the tiny girl's distress, and she was content. A woman I knew well, whose husband trapped wolverine, told me it was the custom in their Catholic village to potlatch its spirit. The trapper and his wife performed the ceremony: they put a small piece of salmon or moosemeat in the dead animal's mouth, and set it on a blanket in the house in the place an honored guest would sit, and let it remain overnight, to thank it for having given itself to them.

A white man who had lived in the Interior for a long time, who spoke an Athabaskan language and observed the ways of his neighbors, recounted an incident to a group of listeners, including me, about Athabaskan protocol toward wolverine, and an occasion when it was thoughtlessly violated. "When the animal was taken, it had to be treated with respect or it would stay away," the man began. "Fur bearers should be left in the house overnight, offered hospitality; they should skin him and chop the carcass."

Several listeners nodded, and murmured agreement; this was correct.

"I remember there was a story I heard a piece of in Fairbanks. One of the game wardens a few years ago confiscated some contraband wolverines and so, as a favor, he flew over a village and dropped one, as he couldn't land. He thought he was doing them a favor, they could use it for ruffs or something. I guess people were pretty upset. You don't treat a wolverine that way."

"A whole wolverine?" asked a listener, incredulous.

"Yeah, I don't know, somebody'd shot it up or something, it was contraband. They were really mad in that village, the game warden treating the wolverine that way."

Small stories, anecdotes, behaviors revealed in parts of sentences: in their understated way, people passed information around, so that newcomers could learn to behave properly.

o

NOW I AM GOING FORWARD. I moved into the Interior, made my way, and left; but while I did this, another story was put into play. A white man trapped a wolverine, saved its tiny toe bones, and made them into jewelry.

◦

IN DENA'INA, "Wolverine" is *yes hughn'u.* The word refers to his skin, which is noteworthy in its coloration, and describes how he moves: he is a strong, powerful animal, shifting around inside his skin almost like a cat; he is "rough and tough," always on the move. "Today he's here, tomorrow he's up in Anchorage." People prefer to use euphemisms for animals, particularly the most powerful ones; his euphemism is *idashla,* Little Friend, but covertly it means, "Bad one for a friend." "It's like anything else," I was told: "Instead of using a bad word for him, they use a good one."

Words are powerful. The animal might be insulted, and reverse an epithet back upon the human who said it. Among Koyukon people he is considered so powerful, I was warned, that if a human out in the woods passes near even the bones of a wolverine and, inadvertently, says something that the animal's spirit takes as disrespect, that spirit might retaliate against him.

Richard K. Nelson, whose *Make Prayers to the Raven: A Koyukon View of the Northern Forest* was read closely in Koyukon villages, was taught about the complexity, and individuality, of beliefs in the spirits of animals. "Not all spirits are possessed of equal power," he wrote. "Some animal species have very potent spirits called *biyeega hoolaanh,* which are easily provoked and highly vindictive. These dangerous spirits can bring serious harm to anyone who offends them, taking away luck in hunting or trapping and sometimes causing illness, disability, or even death. Animals possessed of such spirits include the brown bear, black bear, wolverine, lynx, wolf, and otter. The beaver and marmot have similarly powerful spirits but are not so vengeful."

He quotes one of his teachers about the spirit and name of an animal: "The animal and its spirit are one in the same thing. When you name the animal you are also naming its spirit. That's why some animal names are *hutlaa-nee*—like the ones women shouldn't say—because calling the animal's name is like calling its spirit. Just like we don't say a person's name after they die ... it would be calling their spirit and could be dangerous for whoever did it."[19]

◦

WHILE I LIVED IN MCGRATH, I was given a gift. The man who had trapped the wolverine made the toe bones into jewelry. He made them to give to me. He receded from sight; I left the Interior. Several years later, things happened around those bones, small disturbances of the psyche, acts of the imagination, that led me to suspect a spirit was attached to them.

How I came to receive the gift, and to understand its nature, is at the heart of this long story; or, it is the thread that led me along my long, winding, narrow road. But it is not enough, I find, to describe that road. To write about the spirit in prose is nearly wrong for it: the experience lives more precisely within the domain of poetry, where its figuration is mighty, and nearly invisible to our ordinary eyes.

My gift of poetry was not big enough to tell the story of the animal's bones, and how I came to carry them, for surrounding it is a larger story of human and animal life, and in it I am like the blind poet singing in his corner to those he cannot see. I cannot write the text of my experience without setting the context in which it occurred; and when I reflect on how the gift came to me, I can see that nothing about it is straightforward.

Hungry, Holy

WHEN YOU ARE NEW to the country, your eyes are fresh; you cannot know yet how it fits together, as it does: that one thing develops out of another: everything is connected, and there are no accidents. The end carries you back to a new beginning; and so, I began again. Not long before breakup, I set off from Village Below on a month-long journey. That moment of departure leads me into a branching-off, back into a pocket of time.

I was going up to Hungry, to give poetry in the school; I had packed, and was watching for the plane. The old woman of the fierce eye came to give me a letter to carry to her sister, and we gossiped for a while, until I heard the plane approach. I said good-bye to her and ran to the field. Soon, we were aloft.

We crossed the Mulchatna (which was open, and it glinted like a knife blade), the Swift, the Stony River. After an hour and a half we touched down on the gravel landing strip of the mother village of Village Below, that they called Hungry. I walked down to the settlement.

Hungry, April 2

I had just arrived, and already there were smiling visitors to the one-room school where I was going to camp. People were looking me over. The two white men who teach here, who are married to women from Hungry, came to meet me. Bobby Foma is here, also: his mother is Helen, the old woman's closest friend; they haven't seen him here since he was a little boy. He has come to Hungry to look for a wife; and has told all of them about me and F, I suspect.

April 3

All day it was like visiting relatives: everyone laughed easily. Frank, one of the teachers, suggested yesterday that I go to Emma and Alec Ivan's cabin for breakfast every day; and this morning they fed me bountifully. Emma's brothers, Fyodor and Efrem, who are the old men here, drank coffee with me and taught me some Dena'ina words. I listened to the words: they no longer sounded strange; they were something I had been on the edge of, and was about to slide into.

"Don't be shy, make yourself at home. If you want caribou, you cook some," Alec said in welcome when I entered their cabin. I thanked him shyly.

They keep a small summer bird whose feet had been hurt: they fixed its feet, and now it stays with them and hops about the cabin. They had had a raven, a *chulyin*, who also lived with them. It copied them; it listened to the phonograph, and turned the pages of a comic book. Fyodor's face curled in laughter as he told me this: his whole face was made for smiling.

Now I'm sitting on a stump outside Marie's cabin, with Chris and his dump truck. Chris is Marie's little boy; her husband is Frank, the teacher, who has been here so long he mumbles when he talks to me, and blinks and looks away, as if the light is too bright. Marie is more forthright.

A moose skull with its rack is leaning, upside down, against the cabin. The cabin itself is old, made of heavy logs and banked earth, and is settling into the ground. This moose head, too, is old: the rack is bleached and pitted; the long lower jaw points to the sky. The lower teeth are pointed and sharp: the moose must have been only a few years old. They are like the mountains hereabout, saw-toothed and snow-covered.

The top of the skull is gone, and there are small lichens, dried now, at the end of winter, growing out of the cavity. The rack is like the trees that grow farther up the hillsides. This young moose is gradually turning into the muskeg, leaning against a house settling back into the earth.

April 4

I walked upriver on the ice to visit Alice Ivan, Marie's mother. The old woman of the fierce eye, in Village Below, is her sister. The old woman walks more proudly and is more sophisticated with strangers, but the resemblance between them, which lies in their bearing and the piercing intelligence in their faces, is strong.

Sixteen years ago, Alice left her husband, taking her children, all nine of them, with her. They once lived in Marie's small place: they must have slept on the floor. Her own place was fine, built high up on a bank about a mile from the village. It was quiet; the sound of the school generator was blocked by the hill. She was trying to fix the exhaust pipe on her old wringer washer. She said she gets up early and walks, then goes to work; the whole family is like that, F told me. Five of the children are still at home: Nick, William, Junior, Liz, and Rosalie.

When she left her husband, the boys helped her: they hauled wood and packed water and did the heavy work. They were pretty rough when they were growing up; she said they've settled down now, but they're messy— she just gets the house fixed up and they throw down their jackets and use up cups for tea. The girls have to keep things clean.

She pointed to the radio. "Him's my partner. That way I get all the news. I know if bush pilots land, I hear news all the way to Bethel. If I get bored, I change around."

I've gone to Emma's every day for breakfast. Alec, her husband, is a brother of Gabriel Ivan, the caretaker of the school in Village Below. His watchful silence is like his brother's. Emma's brother Efrem came in, and we talked, and I listened to the three of them speak Dena'ina. Efrem has been teaching me more words: I seem to pronounce them all right, but they have not been easy to remember. I liked sitting in the cabin with the tame summer bird hopping around; I drank boiled coffee.

Outside, people were cutting wood or heading off to the fishing lake by dogsled. The lake is called 6-o-6, Six-oh, for short, because somebody read the altitude marking on a map as the proper American name. Many big pike have been coming out of that water lately.

Fyodor was chipping his boat out of the ice on the bank. He said, "Be careful walking on the ice." Somehow, the talk came around to hunting. He said he used to walk out to hunt caribou and moose, so as not to be bothered with a team: the moose and caribou came right down to the hills across the river. Then he would go later with a team to get the meat. He and his wife had thirteen or fourteen children; nine are still living. Matryona is his wife.

But this is the merest surface, what I've written about this tiny village in the mountains, filled with the smell of woodsmoke and the barking of big dogs. I'll write of the texture of things: the bitterness of boiled coffee, and Efrem leaning like a piece of carved, cured wood against the back of a chair. Talking. Considering. Talking.

Emma was fixing pancakes as I walked in. The light in the cabin was dim and rich, between sepia and gold, full enough for me to pick out the cast-iron stove, coffee pot, kettle, old cast-iron griddle; beds along the walls, ancient armchairs with sagging seats. On the table, plates, the can of honey, sugar, butter, a frying pan full of bacon, salt, pepper, canned milk: food and hospitality. A couple of dishpans rested on the floor near the stove. The things were aged and used—cardboard boxes for insulation, Blazo cans for seats: always new uses for every item.

The skies have been gray since yesterday; the air is warm: snow's getting soft. I've made a friend of Christopher, Marie's son, who is four years old and responsible. He handles a knife well, and he loves to be tickled and cuddled. F is like that: his great need for affection, his real tenderness. In the same manner, George carries his nephew about, laughing and kissing him. Boys are not embarrassed to show love for youngsters: children are allowed to be who they are; they are guided, not forced. People say that they allow their kids a lot of freedom in their (relatively closed) environment, and its closeness will protect and teach them. Chris learned to use the knife well almost as soon as he could hold it, because he would always need to use it, and because his parents were not afraid to let him try.

But, I've seen, when they are caught up in the rictus of a larger, indifferent world; when they must face a disorder based upon strict control and external discipline, as happens in school, they feel caught between opposed rules. Teachers in the McGrath school, who have been around for decades, mutter that Native people don't discipline their kids; but I don't think that's accurate. The people allow their children to test their world, and that world to test them, because they have to be fit for it. I've seen this; and have been told how children are trained and advised. I think that the older white teachers believe that in public schools they are required to order their students around. The two men here are more sensible. I wonder if that is because they are part of the village now, and have learned its ways.

When I look at America from here, as if at a flat picture, from the outside—when, say, I remember how lovingly Italians, say, treat their children, or watch these Athabaskan boys hold the littler ones—I see how harshly we treat our children, how we constantly discipline them and tell them what to do, as if we don't like or trust them; and yet, at the same time, worried, careful parents try to protect and insulate them from their (dangerous) surroundings. "No, don't touch!" "Be careful, it might hurt you." "No." "No." "No." From here, I see how frightening is the frightened world Outside.

In public schools, Native parents have been saying, their children are treated badly. Even so, many of the kids learn to be good students and follow the rules of school. They have to do it; how would they manage otherwise, when they go away from here? They have to walk on a balance beam in their young lives: distress and uncertainty have led many of them to stumble, even to fall off. The rules, these constant, foreign rules, are hard on adults, too; liquor follows. The kids see everything, and are half-wise.

April 6

I ran up to Alice's yesterday. She told me how to tan a moose hide: you scrape the skin to get all the flesh and fat off; then wash it in detergent (Tide) a couple of times; then rub caribou grease and marrow in, to soften it; then twist it in your fist till it's soft; then let it dry. You can smoke it over rotten wood to color it.

She was wearing *istla,* the plain caribou-skin boots that her sister always wears in Village Below. I admire those boots: their plainness is handsome in its own right, utile, not arrogant with decoration.

Late breakfast at Emma's: I ate boiled dryfish. Alec didn't talk much. He is smaller than Gabriel, his brother, but has the same quality of stately movement and dignified silence. He told me how once he killed a caribou with a knife.

They hunted on foot, with knives. One time, they came to a spot where caribou crossed a frozen river. Under cover, the men and boys waited. He heard the drumming and click of the hooves on the ice. (He imitated the sound of the clicking.) He ran close to the herd and grabbed the horn of a bull: the bull tossed its head: Alec went flying. He crouched, and the bull charged. He grabbed the horn again and leaped to its back!

"He give me bad time," Alec said.

The caribou tossed its head, but Alec held tight: so tight—he was grinning as he told this—he broke off a tine. He took his long knife, and put it to the animal's throat.

As he described his hunt, he was reenacting the fight between the bull and himself. He threw his head back and forth, as the caribou had done, and his hand gripped the horn in the air. Every move was elegant, so practiced as to come from beyond conscious control: he was dancing. Nowhere was there slackened muscle; even reclining, his body was poised, as if the plumb line through the body fell true. At rest, he drew his legs close, his back leaning sideways and of a piece with his neck and shoulders, his neck supporting his head, to honor the line; his eyes seemed to drowse, and to see a place far away, as his memories replaced the vision of here and now.

One of the kids asked how you know if it's a poem, and when I was trying to figure out a short reply, the oldest girl, Sandy, who is quick on her feet, said, "Imagination and words."

April 7

When I walked in for breakfast, Emma was lying on her bed, and there was no cooking smell. The day was mild and clear: the boys must have gone after wood. Alec was still at school, cleaning up; and Efrem was outdoors or with his grandchildren. It was quiet and airy in the house. I poured myself a cup of coffee. "Oh. I forgot all about you," Emma explained. I said I wasn't hungry on a day like this.

Fearing it would be rude to leave, I sat in my chair for a while, and ate cold pancakes and honey. Bobby, her son, came back with the team, and left again. Alec came in, smiled, said, "Eat lots," as he always does. He sat in his chair.

Emma was nursing broken ribs. "I just want to stay in bed," she said. The cabin was quiet. Alec's eyes were shut and his mouth was open a little. He wore a green silk jacket with a map of Vietnam embroidered on the back. Somebody at the air base across the mountain must have brought it back with him and given, or sold, it to Alec; or a son-in-law went for a soldier in the war. Under that he wore a pink sleeveless sweater, and I saw his arms, lean and fit as a young man's.

Emma talked to me. Some people think she's crazy; if it's true, she makes awful sense in spite, or because, of it. She didn't mention her broken ribs. She talked about men. "I don't want no mens," she said. "They tell me, 'Get married to him'"—she nodded toward Alec—"but I say I don't want no mens. That man, what's his name?"—a missionary? I asked. She nodded.—"He tell me, 'Get license.'

"I say, 'What for I need license? Got enough license. Got trapping license. Got hunting license. Enough license. Don't bother me!'

"One man's enough. Before him, this doctor come. He say, 'Get married.' But what for? I don't want no mens. But he sleep with me. On my bed. I don't want him. I got my own blanket. He stay, he say, 'You want little girl, or little boy?' I tell him, 'Little girl.' I don't hide it. No point hiding it, everybody know.

"He go away, down States. Send me letter for while. Then, no more letter. He say he find other doctor to marry me.

"Pretty soon, my stomach grow"—she held up a fist—"and I feel it moving in there. I lay down, it stop. Pretty soon, three months go by,"—she held up two fists—"my stomach get bigger and bigger.

"I don't know what to do with baby. It's hard. It's hard.

"So I don't want no mens. They tell me, 'Marry him.'"—Alec, again—"down there,"—nodding toward the church—"but I keep saying no. They tell me, 'Stand next to him, and if you want to marry, say yes.' I keep saying no. I try to run right out the door. They bring me back. Finally I say yes.

"We been together now how many years? Long time. But I don't want no mens. Don't need no mens—leave me alone."

She was going to say more about the pregnancy. Her voice went away into the long-time-ago: it rose and grew soft, as if she were talking to a baby; her eyes saw another time.—Efrem came in then.

Alec had left. I wondered how often he had heard this terrible story, and how he felt about it. His movements are always gentle and precise. Had she ever cherished him for that; did the beauty of it ever make her stomach tighten? Did that remind her of the cost? But how had her ribs gotten broken?

So Efrem, and Bobby her son, and Bobby Foma came in with the sunshine. The bird started hopping around on the table; and Jennie, Efrem's whiny puppy, stirred and started chewing on my coat. And Emma was gone, lying back on the bed, gone back into silence, while the men and I ate boiled dryfish and drank our coffee. Efrem asked if I had slept well, and I asked about his grandchildren. Bobby, Emma's son, joshed Efrem about his no-good dog, *shishtoon* dog. The other Bobby, her nephew from Village Below, said he was hot from cutting wood and took off his bulky flight pants and parka.

A country-western song came on the radio, and from her bed Emma sang along, in a humming monotone, as if to herself.

> *I didn't mean to hurt you,*
> *When push comes to shove.*
> *I just wish that you were*
> *Someone I could love.*

April 8

I gave Emma some money for the week's breakfasts; she was surprised. She was lying down again. She said, "I just lay here and I make money." She gave me some tiny boots and mitts she had made from the skin of a king salmon and advised me, "You sell these."

No, no, I protested, I like these, I want to keep them to remember you by.

"You sell them," she insisted. "You sell, you remember: buy low, sell high."

April 9

Bobby Foma was in love. We were sitting on the wood pile talking; that is, he was talking. I inhaled the sweet fresh smell of birch and half-listened as he talked about Paula, Emma's sweet-faced daughter.

"I don't know what to do," Bobby moaned. "Maybe I should leave. Travel. Just leave forever, let her find another to take my place.

"I want to talk to Emma. She'll never agree. She'll start cussing me and I won't take that. That'll be the end of everything. I'll go away.

"I don't know what to do. What would you do if you were in my shoes?

"My life's all fucked up. I don't know the words to use with Emma.

"I never should have got involved with Paula. I want to marry her. But Emma. I don't know how I could get along with Emma.

"I should sell my house and my land and just take off. Travel. I'll never come back. Probably get involved with murderers down the States. Let her find another. She'd be better off without me."

April 11

Tom Charles, the other teacher, is married to Efrem's kind daughter, Mary. He told me about Emma and the supernatural. They say "super-natural" here, not "medicine"; sometimes, they say "superstition."

Tom doesn't quite say to me what he wants me to know. He alludes; he lets his face speak, and his hands. He has a particular gesture that means caution, astonishment, this-is-the-end-of-the-story, I-can't-speak-any-more: he puts his face between his hands, a child saying, "Oh dear."

This is what he told me about Emma:

He thinks she is schizophrenic, though the contrast between her calm and disturbed states is less violent now than it used to be. The story of her children's fathers varies—the major at the air base, the doctor from the States. Tom doubted it. The plot of the real story is this, he said:

Someone from downriver wanted to marry her; he wanted it for a long time. He was considered a bad man—this meant he had medicine, I understood—and Chida and Chada, her parents, who ran the village, said no. Emma refused him because of that. In anger and power he told her, "Whatever you're enjoying now will never be the same again."

Since then, Tom said, things never have been the same. The man cursed her; Tom wouldn't say it, but he believes it. I wonder if she may have been going to tell me about this, in her own way, as she lay in bed. Could she have cared for the man? Could his vengeful spite, grim oppression, lay so heavily on her spirit as to crack it? Often you hear older people speak of the need to be strong-minded, as the old-timers were, and how bad feelings are hurting people. I begin to understand: they mean this literally. Could cursing occur more often than I can comprehend, passions ripping lives apart?

Tom notices how the supernatural had great hold over the older people of Hungry: they are not far removed from the days of the shamans. He used that word; they don't say medicine men down here, as they do farther north. His father-in-law, Efrem, (he said) is a fine woodsman and (he intimated) knows about, or has, power. According to Tom, the shamans had come to use their powers tyrannically. People were afraid of them. Some people would not travel to another village without the company of a medicine man, to protect them from bad wishes on the part of the village they were going to visit.

He said also that the Ghost Dance came up here, "piecemeal." Efrem's ancestor (a parent? a grandparent?) had had a vision of the future of the Indians; Tom asked Mary's grandmother about it, before she died. He compared what the old woman told him, to Black Elk's vision; he took both visions very seriously.

The old person predicted, first, that Efrem's generation would turn to alcohol; then, the next generation would become like white men. Finally, something would happen, a disaster, that would cut people off from the Outside. People must lay things by, this old person had warned urgently, especially shells: shells they cannot make themselves; for the rest, it is a matter of relearning the old ways, to be able to survive off the land.

The old person had also foretold that the time after the disaster would not bring a return to the old ways. It would bring a new way of living.[20]

Tom and I talked elliptically about such power as the shamans and the visionaries had. We were careful, following normal practice, not to speak with unguarded tongues. (Does that mean I believe in the power? I don't know; I can't deny it exists, however, and might as well behave with respect. It seems to me no different, in that regard, than the Catholic pieties I grew up with.)

From our talk, I inferred that people believed—they felt—that if any one person acquired too much spiritual power, if he did too much, using his mind, as happened with the shamans, or with the man who cursed Emma, something in life would become overbalanced. About men and women, Tom implied that each had the duty—and might have power of some kind—to keep a balance among the strong, constant forces alive in the village, and in the country around it.

This was no abstract notion; it had to do with the finite space of a village, and how everyone moves through that space. Too much power concentrated in any one person, or in any place, creates a disturbance, distress.

Hungry times. Tom said that when people had known hunger, when the only eating was porcupine, they would hang a bag of bones in a tree. When things got to be at their worst, they would haul the bag down and boil the bones for soup.

As I write this, I reflect upon the astonishing country we live in. We are deluged with anthropologists' studies that count calories and protein available from the land: amazing numbers of calories per moose, astonishing numbers of grams of protein. Hunting, it seems, equals sustenance, defined in biological and economic terms, defined materially as raw consumption.

Our public discussions are full of these analogies. Many of the state anthropologists are trying to prove to the government that the Native peoples' hunting is central to their lives. (They are talking about human lives, but speak as if they were objects.) These researchers are disturbed, I can see, by the egregious way the whites have moved in. They don't want to be agents of that change. But surely they translate hunting into the wrong terms. Theirs is not "scientific evidence" (if such anthropology is ever "scientific"), as they represent it to be: it is a method of persuasion in the political arena, and they are advocates using trivial statistics and false analogies. And, because their premise is wrong, its effect is going to come back and hurt them. Not the anthropologists, who will always find refuge: it will hurt Native people. An expert will be found who will conclude that, since now there are stores in villages, people can substitute grocery calories for their food from the land, and still be properly nourished. Ergo, hunting can be curtailed by law, with "justification" supplied by science.

We must think well and accurately, truthfully, about life. Knud Rasmussen, who lived among the Iglulik, in Greenland, was taught by them that the purpose of the "old rules of life," which were based on experience and wisdom, was to avoid offending the souls of food animals, even though the animals had to be killed, since "food consists entirely of souls."

Surely Native people know and believe the same thing here. They are reverent of food from the land. Why is this belief—which also is closely observed knowledge—not considered valid? Is the ear of the government so deaf? Are the anthropologists such committed materialists, that they can find no form of argument that allows for belief in the supernatural? Desperately, they work to save the right of Native people to hunt on the wilderness lands the Federal government is going to manage; but I think they are doing it badly, and wrongly. Because of their practice of thinking by (false, wrong) analogies, what is sacred is going to be turned into an instrument wielded by ideologues.

o

AFTER HUNGRY, I flew north, up the Kuskokwim, first to a village even tinier
than Hungry, then to its related village, one a little larger, a little more
worldly. Again I camped in the school. I carried a small supply of fresh fruit
and vegetables, knowing what school food was like.

Dear KW,
    I doubt you would find this tiny village on the map. It's a pretty place:
a few log cabins, a small cemetery, a beautiful Russian church. In the early
part of this century, they say, a detachment of American cavalry set out
from (or toward) Fairbanks and, in winter, lost its way near here. The men
would have died, as they had all but used up their supplies, when the chief
of this tribe found them and wintered them over. Well before they came
upon those errant soldiers, the people knew strangers were in the area: a
hunter, having taken a bear, had opened its stomach and found a meat he
did not recognize. It turned out to be bacon.
    Now the village has been given a five-hundred-thousand-dollar, one-
room school for its six students. The pilot who brought me here cracked
that the building, because of its roof-shape, looks like a Pizza Hut. True.
    I have no sense yet of village life, since no one I knew has relatives here.
The teacher is away for the week I'm to stay. If you were here, you would
see chained dogs, woodpiles, a few old houses lined up along the road,
caches built up off the ground, steambaths sinking into the muskeg, kids
peeking around corners. You would smell fresh-cut spruce; hear quiet
voices, engines of prowling snowmachines.

I talked with a strange (to me), almost hermaphroditic person: a young
man with a woman's face and voice and very long, graceful hands and legs.
He told me his name was Theodore. He had a direct gaze and an acute
sense of humor: sort of loony, in fact. The "loony" poets write of, who
knows all. A holy person.

School doesn't begin until ten o'clock, so I sleep late. Today I'm going to
let them write little poems and translate them into Indian. That's how they
refer to their language, and to themselves, at least in front of me. They
speak a different Athabaskan than in Hungry, I hear differences in the
sounds. The older boys are learning to write it. I've been told Athabaskan
languages are very difficult to learn: Native speakers, I hear, tell white
scholars that their tongue takes a lifetime to master. They say that is one
reason old people are wise: *they know how to speak.*
    To know how to speak must be a high art. I've been reading *Riddle and
Poetry Handbook,* by Richard Dauenhauer,[21] a poet and translator and folk-
lorist, who's lived up here for decades. He's reworked a selection of old
Koyukon Athabaskan riddles, published in 1913 by Fr. Julius Jetté, a French

Jesuit who lived on the Koyukuk and Yukon Rivers. Jetté observed that, among the old Koyukon, people riddled with the return of light, after winter solstice. He wrote down the riddles in Koyukon, translated them literally, made free translations, explained what they meant, and commented on them. This must have been a superb piece of scholarship.

What strikes me about Jetté's riddles (or, Dauenhauer's versions of them) is this: they describe the world the riddler sees, but in a different way than I know it. I look around me, try to re-imagine what I see, and realize I have hardly seen it in the first place. For instant, this:

> Smoke-like
> it spreads out on the water:
> butchered salmon blood.

I've seen salmon blood in the water: I see it clearly now; I hadn't thought of it as smoke-like; but it is. Can't you smell the alder they burn to cure the salmon flesh? Can't you see the smoke drifting along the bank? Salmon blood in the water.

Yet, how coolly the image is expressed. In English, something is not there that I think must exist in Koyukon: it's as if another quality, a quality of mind, of perception and knowing, has not yet come across from that language to ours; that we haven't learned; that, perhaps, our language has not learned. These riddles are as difficult and complex as Chinese poems; and, the content of the riddlers' knowledge is highly specific. The content might be harder to understand than the structure is: to solve it, you must know the country already, as the riddlers do.

You write of teaching college students; you ask, "Why do I need to make them better people?" Behind your question I hear the deep responsibility that always weighs on you: the morality and discipline of committing your life to the word. In this country, I've found, words mean a great deal and carry enormous weight. Every person tells stories; even children know how good stories ought to go. Stories illuminate and preserve life. And because of that, everything has, is presumed to have, meaning. This is a charged world. It's true that village life is intense; it is because of this, I think: what happens is not aimless or random. When anything, any small thing at all, happens, its meaning is investigated and reflected upon for long hours afterward; and then the story that comes out of it is told and retold.

The words are a moral responsibility: that is why they must be exact. The endless struggle for precision. How long can we live this way?

K: I'm tired of metaphor. I'm tired of false metaphors. They mix categories, and convey false information.

Yet, riddles are metaphors; aren't they?

The Koyukon riddles aren't simple. They raise the hair on the back of my neck, in fact, even as I admire them. They contain a knowledge of this

world that goes deep into the heart of it, a knowledge I think we haven't
been privy to. Even the old English riddles seem to me more comprehen-
sible, viscerally more familiar, than these do.

Your admired Wm. Carlos Williams wrote: "No ideas but in things."
Are the words of this country, things?

"Follow your voice," I told the kids. The laugh that gleamed in Matthew's
eyes, and his discovery of a voice: here's the heart of poetry, there is no excess sound in it. Now it's snowing, and this place shuts in upon itself. This
is rolling country, wooded in birch and spruce. It is so quiet.

Theodore came to see me tonight. His voice is high and clear; but he is
twenty-nine. He is not languid: a luxurious word; rather, something about
his movement implies somnolence, there is no gathered force. Several times
he talked about being drunk, and once said he wished he were passed out,
as if that would be a release. "Everyone sits around," he said, "waiting for
welfare checks. I sit around ..."

Sometimes he watches me, as I bend my head into a book. I avert my
eyes, I don't want him to misconstrue a direct gaze. But I grow easier; I
think he will not misunderstand, and I'm interested in his observations.
He said he and Ben and Willie were coming to visit me last night, but the
boys were stoned, and he didn't want to be with them; he doesn't seem to
like smoking, nor their smoking. He has odd, small eyes that hide themselves, then shift suddenly toward mine. When I say certain things, he
shines his lamp on my face, as if to probe for truth. When I say I'm thirty-
one, his torch flashes. I look as young for my age as he does for his.

Our speech is intermittent. I read; he sits twirling gently in the teacher's
swivel chair. He mentions the time and the day, and I say how fast it's going.
He says, How slow. "Don't tell me how fast time goes." I smile, and he says,
"I'm kidding."

He gets up suddenly to go, lays a hand on my shoulder, and says, "I
wish you good night." It feels like a blessing, or a gesture of companion-
ship.

The snow blew all day, and it was quiet. No run for me; I went visiting.
These houses are long, dark, tiny, and old; there are only seven. Paulina
took me around. She is from the village I'll fly to next week. Her mother
teaches Indian in the school there; and her husband, Andrew, who is
Theodore's brother, writes their language and is teaching the students here
how to write it. She was kind enough to suggest what I hoped would happen: she would introduce me. I am too reticent to knock on the doors of
people I don't know; and am not certain if they expect it here, or if they
prefer to come to meet me. People are welcoming, however. I find that as
I feel less shy around them, they seem more open.

Their faces reminded me of old photographs of Athabaskans I saw at the university, taken in the early part of this century, when photography was new to them. They had never seen themselves mirrored before that. They look sideways; they avert their eyes before the eye of the camera. Their bodies are slightly tense, unsettled, those older people in the photographs. Someone has intruded on them, you think, bringing a new thing into their lives. They are willing to test (or, are they coerced into testing?) its effects. They are respectful of its existence, perhaps of its power.

The only children in school are boys, all from one family. Matthew is my favorite, a quick, smiling child, good with words. I love their soft voices, and my own answering softness.

We've been given a clear, white day, the first since I got here. The sun coming through the window is hot on my back. This morning I walked out the back door of the school and saw an enormous mountain filling most of the sky. Where did that come from!

Denali, someone said gently. The mountain is only about fifty miles from here.

Its presence is immense; holy. I am humbled, and lifted up, and happy.

The people here have always lived with this mountain. I can't speak of it.

Theodore has just come in. His face looks like a lynx's.

The mayor, who is about my age and is well thought of here and in McGrath, told me about Theodore: he is somewhat retarded and probably epileptic, from a childhood head injury. His uncle was playing with him. Something happened. His uncle committed suicide in remorse. Later, Theodore caught tuberculosis of the spine, and had to be operated on; he hunches from it. If he works hard or stays up late or gets excited, he has seizures.

Was Smerdyakov the epileptic like that? Dostoyevsky made him the most malicious of the Karamazov brothers, but without the force of their terrible father; but I discern no malice in this young man. People love him; I can see it. His own uncle died for the injury done him. He carries the awful burden of knowing too much.

o

CHARTERED PLANES arrived every day, when the visibility was good. On Saturday I was waiting on the field when the charter from McGrath landed. The teacher climbed out. The pilot unloaded his gear and boxes of supplies; the teacher and I introduced ourselves to each other, and immediately said, So long; I took his place on the passenger side of the plane; the pilot lifted off, and we flew to the next village.

Tuesday

Strong feelings are churning through this school. The teenagers are pent-up and restless. I had ten students today, and taught them the gambling stick game; they said no one played it here. They made songs and (at my suggestion) used sticks to make drumming sounds; but the songs and drumming turned raucous and disruptive. I asked Bernie, the teacher, not to interfere. The students were trying to shout down school and, probably, to test me. I let them make their noise and clap their sticks together, and only asked them to stop when the tumult grew loud enough to bother the junior high. They needed to shout out those feelings—to do something, I don't know what. Something is wrong here.

Wednesday

Last night at dinner, Julia, polite but firm, expressed her concern at the uproar I had set off in the high school. Her junior high class had been disturbed; this had, in turn, disturbed her. I told her (as I told Bernie, earlier) I thought the older students were strained and on edge. These weren't emotions fit to work in, so I tried to let the kids ease back from them. They're kids!

The teenagers in Bernie's class sit behind a wall of self-protection, but a higher, thicker wall than teens usually build. It has taken me two days of persuasion to get them to open up a little. In Julia's class, on the other hand, the students are still young enough to be fresh and direct. In both classes, the students are more open when the teachers are not present.

They fed me a good dinner. Fresh vegetables! Julia is a gracious hostess. She laid a tablecloth and used her pretty china. She and Bernie are married; this is, I think, their second year here. They come from the East, from comfortable backgrounds.—Correction: Julia is from the South. Calling her an Easterner would dismay her; anyhow, "back East" covers unknown, feared ground in the North. Both of them went to a good university, where they met, and are well traveled. I supposed I should have felt at ease with them; but I don't. Bernie is energetic, ambitious, a little loud for a village. He took a masters in education at the end of the Vietnam War, then found he didn't mind teaching but preferred running things. Julia is gently bred, a lady. They've brought a handsome Airedale with them, who is a curiosity to people here.

Their apartment is attached to the school. This is an old BIA compound, standard model, with the school and teachers' quarters joined to each other, separated from the village. Julia has unregimented their rooms with plants and quilts and embroidery. She's kindly given me a couch in the living room; no camping in classrooms this week: I'm sleeping on sheets.

At dinner they spoke respectfully of the school parent committee, but hedged when I asked about the students. From both of them a look, a tone in the voice, a hint of disillusionment; by dessert, grievance overcame hesitation. Last month, teenagers broke into their place, opened a locked cupboard, and took marijuana, whiskey, and incense. Two weeks later, they broke in again.

Julia is crushed by it: "We've tried to do so much for them! And we thought we were getting somewhere," she wailed. Bernie is trying to be tough, but feels he's been taken advantage of, and that hurts his pride.

The boy whom Bernie thinks was the ringleader works hard at his studies and is reasonably bright. (What would Natalia think if one of her sons broke into a teacher's house? How must these boys' mothers feel?) The teachers were robbed; it was an ugly, worrisome matter. But robbed of what? Whiskey, grass, incense—things teenagers like. Things the teachers, out of discretion and some unexpected measure of good sense, didn't share with students. Alcohol and marijuana are common, they're certainly legal, but people here can't afford them. Julia, with her fine sensibility, now sees life in the village as squalid and violent. Bernie knows, suddenly, shockingly, that he is powerless. They are beginning to realize they can survive here only if the village helps them. They are amazed and appalled at this fact. It undermines their sense of themselves.

The thefts are a warning. I'd say the boy and his friends were telling them not to bring those things into the village. This is their home. And then, the teachers didn't share what they had. Is this why the kids are so angry?

Last week, after Paulina took me around the village, we went back to her house. Andrew, her husband, offered me some smoke, and I accepted it. After a time, his voice blurry, he said, "You're better off than us Indians."

I tensed inside; but I must accept it. I have something he does not, though I think we don't see that "something" in the same light, or even agree on what it is. But I am better off. And he resents it, and sorrows over it; it was in his smoky voice. He didn't mean me—"You're better off"—since he doesn't know me. He meant, You white people, who don't belong here.

Julia and Bernie see themselves as good. They aren't among the exploiters: they're doing *good* for these people! As they are, in a way that shouldn't have to patronize the students, for these are well-educated, intelligent teachers, and the very good money they make is perhaps not their only motive for being here. Exploiters are bad people, their pride tells them, and they themselves are not bad people.

But they are foreign to the village, and, not thinking of the consequences, they have brought whiskey and marijuana into this place, and they've caused a large disturbance by their act. The children of the sixties are suddenly grown up, and have become bewildered adults. Now we wonder about ourselves: How did it happen?

❍

AT THE END OF THE WEEK I flew to McGrath. That easy-going town was loud and busy; it was commerce and bureaucracy, and pick-up trucks racing down gravel roads. I had been on the road for a month; I was tired.

It was my third or fourth visit. People had begun to recognize me; I knew some of them. Daylight lasted eighteen hours, mud replaced the melting snow. I checked in at the district office. I walked around town wearing high rubber boots, and said hello to acquaintances.

I stopped at the roadhouse for morning coffee. An old lady spoke to me without warning. "Eskimo," she said, slurring, "with three beers in me before noon."

She tilted her head and looked at me frankly.

"Who are you?" she asked. "You're beautiful. I like to tell the beautiful ones hello."

An ancient, bent lady hobbled past us and muttered, "Oh, you're just kidding, I know you," in a cracked voice. She moved fast for an old person. Her edge cut through the fog of the Eskimo lady with three beers in her. I was the visitor, too polite to question anyone.

About sunset, I walked down to the river. The northwest sky was transparent yellow, and would last the night. In the twilight the Kuskokwim was brown and smooth. Two days ago, the ice had gone out. The last floes swirled downriver, or caught on bits of drift; they were brittle and rotten, or were clear and sharp as mirrors. When they grazed each other they tinkled, like crystal.

Robins were back. All winter, ravens creaked and mumbled; the robins sang a sweeter song. The night air was fresh and clean. I was afraid; I was afraid, and I didn't know why. I could change nothing about this hard world.

○

TWO NIGHTS before I left town, I had dinner with Deborah Madison, an itinerant teacher who fed me whenever I passed through. When I arrived, she was saying good-bye to a young man I knew slightly, a boy really, from an old, dwindling McGrath family. He had just said something that made her laugh. For an aching moment he reminded me of F; his bearing, the pride and resilience in his young face. He said hello to me, and then he left.

Over supper she explained that he often came by to talk. He was full of troubles. He was quick and bright, but something had gone wrong for him, and he seemed to have no one to turn to. She suspected he didn't have much of future in McGrath.

"What can I do for him?" she asked, regretfully. "The men here won't help him, he's not their relative. I listen to him, it's all I can do."

She treated him like a younger brother, as in a way, he was. His older brother, who had once been Deborah's lover, was in the Bethel jail, for attempted rape. The woman he assaulted was the old lady in the roadhouse who said hello to the beautiful ones. She had been drinking now for three weeks. The young man was torn up with shame, and went to Deborah for solace. She didn't turn him away; but she treated him, carefully and precisely, like a younger brother.

o

MY LAST NIGHT in town. I sat in the bar with Deborah and drank one Coors, very slowly. A man came over and introduced himself. His name was Rocky Johnson, he was a famous dog musher; he looked like a man who was used to being famous locally. He asked what kind of work I did. I said I was a writer. He puffed up his chest and offered to tell me his life's story.

It was quite a story, he began. One year, he and John Hill went to Fairbanks. They had no money, so they robbed rubber machines in men's toilets. They took sixteen thousand dollars that year. They spent the money and were down to nothing. They went back to their old method, and raised three hundred (or maybe thousand) dollars; bought a new Buick sedan; and took off for Knoxville, Tennessee. Rocky worked the high steel there; John did something else. Then they headed out to Salt Lake. They sold the car for fifty-five dollars.

But the original title had been written wrong. They were hauled off to jail. The Utah troopers had to call the Fairbanks auto dealer. Apparently that settled the matter, and the two of them, Rocky and John, lit out, riding thumb, for Seattle. Then they came home.

I said nothing. In the cool fluorescent light my hands looked green.

Rocky revealed how he had come to follow his course in life: teacher threw him out of the schoolhouse when he was in the fifth grade. He was sixteen. He went trapping.

He said, "I know every lake, river, crick in this country. I was born here. Alaskans, they don't lie. You want to hear stories, you'll hear stories."

"They stretch those stories a little."

"A little," he agreed amiably. "But Alaskans don't lie."

I told him that, anyhow, I wasn't that kind of writer.

"What kind are you?" he asked.

"Poems," I said distinctly. "I write poems."

"A poem writer. Well. I'm gonna have to change my whole approach. Poems. I used to make poems, used to sing songs."

He liked being in the open country, he said, by himself.

"You start singing. You see a mountain over there, something makes you feel like singing.

"One time, I was going along singing, and I stopped by a house, someone I knew. The guy told me he heard the singing a long way off ."

Rocky looked embarrassed. I asked if he remembered any of his songs.

"Naw," he said, "they weren't worth shit."

○

ON THAT TRIP I came face to face with what I was afraid of, and met what would protect me. These things were the ancient war between men and women; the schools and American rule; metaphors, lies, curses, and riddles; the supernatural, and the fear with which it must be approached; writing and singing. All of them were clear in the mind, and all were confused in life; and not till the journey was finished did I know what would help, and what would harm me.

I was young, and I believed that people worked hard and did their best; I did not know how badly people could treat each other, or from what pain and fear and anger they would act. My innocence was complete, and willful: I was searching for the truth. What I saw, what I met, what aided me, were tied up in a bundle of stories that gathered around, often in some shabby disguise, waiting for me to listen.

The stories rested on the great land of the Interior, which spreads out below us. The air is clear: it is the ether, and it holds us aloft. In the distance we see a slight haze, breath made visible in cool weather. The lives of humans and animals fall away from us. We look down on small ponds, and braided rivers of copper-green, as they open to spring; we see lines of greeny-yellow willows along the banks; we see aspens and alders on the low hills fuzzy with reddish buds. We are flying south by southwest. The Alaska Range is on our left; its snow cover has turned light blue as the earth tilts, and the sun travels north, toward solstice.

The plane, a Piper 206, floats along the Range. Denali and Foraker, two tall brothers, shine, immense, holy, through the windshield. It is going to be a long run to where we're going. The pilot, who was born around here, switches to auto-pilot, and yawns.

It's not that he isn't awed, he apologizes. I know; we all are awed, all the time; but it's hard to concentrate on so much grandeur, and finally, it's sunny, and he is—bored. Flying is easy. He's going to take a nap.

Denali rises high on my left. Under the roar of the engine I can hear myself singing to the mountain.

Big one laa la la la
la la la la la

Part II

Into the Interior

Further on, ... we were to reach the frontier which
was to divide me from my native land for many years.
                              —Pablo Neruda, Nobel Lecture

Here it is much more difficult to trace the origin of the fear and ascertain
why it lasts so long, and [why] quite specific symbols arouse fear again and
again. Why, for example, many people of our generation have such a terrible fear of authority. When was this injected into them? Why can so
many people in our country only stand up for themselves against authority in fear?
                              —Christa Wolf,
                              tr. by Hilary Pilkington

A Man's Life

MCGRATH STOOD on boggy ground within a U-shaped bend in the Kuskokwim River across from the mouth of the Takotna; but it was an air town as much as a river town. When Pan American opened commercial routes across the bush after World War II, McGrath was a convenient passenger and refueling stop, where DC3s and DC4s touched down halfway to the Bering Sea coast. Until then, bush pilots, and before them steamboat captains, had ferried in the hordes of men and their tons of supplies, thousands of them headed for the nearby Iditarod gold fields: fields developed by big outfits like the Guggenheims, and small operators like my landlord, old Joe Devlin, and his boss who came from Europe, and many another adventurer looking for a strike at a rich vein.

When the gold petered out, McGrath became a transportation hub. The FAA built a regional station with an air traffic control tower, rare in the bush. A colony of single-engine planes, airy and fragile as winged, bent-legged insects, lined the long runway. By the time I arrived, three air taxi services ran charters and mail flights to the surrounding villages. In good weather, a small scheduled airline based in Anchorage flew a dozen or so passengers, three times a week, through daunting Rainy Pass; and on Tuesdays and Fridays, the dependable jets of Wein Airways brought them home safe over the mountains, along with tons of mail and freight. The jets now were the bush freighters; the town could never have survived on local resources.

About three hundred people, including children, lived in McGrath. Most of them seemed to turn up at the field when the jet landed. The passengers rarely were strangers; those who were were examined with skeptical though friendly curiosity. An interested newcomer strolling through the town, someone like me, who considered staying on, would call it calm and picturesque. Its roads were mostly unpaved and, in the mosquito-clouded summers, became skids of gravel and dust. Tall-spiked lupine grew prettily in its kitchen gardens, woods softened its house lots. Its downtown was a dozen weather-worn structures lined up on one side of the long runway. A wooden sidewalk ran parallel to them and kept pedestrians above the mud and snow.

The downtown commenced beside the river at the Alaska Commercial grocery, a prefabricated metal shed also housing a warehouse and liquor store. The burly storekeeper stocked an abundance of bush necessities: canned vegetables, sugar and tea, spatter-ware tin coffeepots, instant coffee, instant pancake mix and mashed potato buds, knobby cabbages and white-eyed potatoes, white bread, canned milk for coffee, pressure cookers, cookies, cupcakes, candy. In the late afternoons women came to do the family shopping; they were orderly but competitive gatherers, sorting through the root vegetables, checking the newest eggs for cracks. The AC, a bush-wide chain, also ran a check-cashing service at the liquor store, one of three liquor stores in town.

Next door was an outfitters supply shop, where working men gathered to sit, drink coffee, swap stories. When a man stepped outside, a machine-shop smell of oil and dust and cold metal cut the air before him; the hollow *thunk, thunk* of work boots on wood followed him as he walked away.

Where the wooden sidewalk ended the road turned into gravel and cinders. Set back on a weedy lot was a dark ramshackle pile connected to the town's generators, immense rumbling oil-burners. An intersection pointed toward the residential area. Across the road, in a field, slouched McGuire's saloon, a low-roofed, shabby place with a bleached-gray moose rack hung above the lintel. Some glad-looking people went in. A man came out, walking carefully. This daytime scene never varied. Next to McGuire's was a tallgrass lot where two dull-silver Airstream trailers sat on pads; then came the post office, which shared a trim log building with the Wein Airways terminal. Here, midfield on the runway, the jet rounded on its taxi and rolled to a halt. The steel-blade shriek of the engine drowned the town, as the ground crew hustled to unload containers of baggage and freight, and people milled around. The event was over in half an hour.

The post office stayed open for a few hours in the afternoons. Tuesdays and Fridays, jet days, were mail days. I would wait in line at the window, as eager as anyone; letters and packages were our fragile link to the outside, and the post office was, briefly, the center of town.

Farther down the runway were a couple of cottagelike offices, then the control tower. On the far side stood the FAA compound, the spit and image of every federal compound: set apart, tidy, squared off, subduing. The civil servants who worked there looked the same.

The long runway crossed a shorter landing strip before petering out in crumbling asphalt. Back in the brush you came upon a rifle and pistol range, where the high-school shooting team practiced, and the McGrath sporting club held turkey shoots. I broke in a .22 Remington lever-action rifle there. I had won a chainsaw in a raffle but had no use for it, and traded it for the rifle to the comptroller of the school district. I used to go shooting with him. He showed me how to handle a pistol. A photo from that time shows me standing, intent, knees bent slightly, hands gripping the pistol, sighting down the barrel toward an invisible target. I enjoyed shooting tin cans, but was no good at skeet. Toward the end of my time in McGrath, I would keep the rifle by the door, with a shell chambered.

Around the corner from the AC was the old river road, curving along a bend of the brown Kuskokwim. A little way up, Joe Devlin and his wife kept a roadhouse, where they ran a cafe and a bar and billiards room, and rented the few bare rooms in the back to travelers. Joe's wife, Margarety, was an ill-tempered woman; hard to say if it was only because of her bad rheumatism, though people gave her leeway because of it, and because they enjoyed the stories about her mean tongue. She was not a good cook, but she served an edible hamburger. School administrators, bureaucrats, and local businessmen met there every day for lunch.

That was the downtown. It had an old-time, engaging, sham-romantic feel to it, like a Saturday-afternoon Western movie set, except that the old wooden buildings and the lore behind them were not false fronts or tourist draws. People lived and worked in them. A dusty aura of gold and furs, steamboats and trading posts still hung in the air. The downtown looked as raw and possible as any frontier town must have looked. To my eye, McGrath was still on the frontier and, despite what I might find to say in its favor, it gave my heart no solace; it was a frontier town of American history.

Pioneer chronicles told a restless people that the frontier was a great, unbounded place, where men went to find freedom, solitude, and fur-bearing animals to trap and sell; where the Indians, whose country it was, had to be fought and killed, or pacified and moved: a place for soldiers, the killing policies not necessarily having been set by them, but carried out by them; where farms and small settlements could be hacked out and built up, if the pioneers worked hard and long and had enough good luck. They wanted a piece of land to call their own where they could live a life of sturdy self-reliance.

Any American child knows about the frontier. Mine was first a child's knowledge, all words and pictures, and no experience. The frontier was part of Eastern history. The child, curious and full of longing, had read wonderful tales. Daniel Boone leading wagon trains over the great Wilderness Road, and Daniel Boone moving west, deeper into the woods, whenever he smelled his neighbor's chimney smoke. Entrancing, the idea of going deeper and deeper into the unknown woods. How did he learn to survive—who taught him? I meant: how did he *know how* to move silently, to walk without leaving a trail? How did he *learn* to know animals?

I thought Indians must have taught him. I played being Indian and painted my face and chest, until the summer I had to wear a shirt, and made twig bows strung with butcher twine that in my mind were mighty bows; in summer camp, I pulled real bows, as heavy as I could handle. I knew the names of every nation west of the Mississippi, and most of those east. I read of the wars, the massacres, the suffering of women and children freezing, starving, dying of no buffalo.

Into the woods: become wild, or, in its original sense, savage: a man removed from (his) civilization.

The child grew up. Chronicles and narratives of mountain men, scouts, farmers, soldiers; the photographs of sod houses and farmers and farmers' empty-eyed wives; the movies (John Ford's, Howard Hawks's): these were not hard for a young woman to understand. Westward expansion was how one kind of people moved outward and overcame—asserted a God-given right to overcome—another. In the sixties, it was a formative idea, and all the while I lived in Alaska it framed American history for me. What does the idea mean, however, when your mental pictures of "the frontier" came from chronicles and movies; from fiction, and photos of people you never knew? The West, where frontier and wilderness are confounded, was, for such an Easterner, unimaginable in its scale and absence. Would you change your mind if you went there: if you experienced that distance, that ethereal light? What would happen if you brushed up against—what if you were part of—the implacable movement that desires to inhabit it? What is that movement composed of; who are its actors? Can it be enough to say, *They were individuals, like yourself?* What hard facts would you have to face, then? Which ones would you try to ignore?

Frontier, says the *OED,* comes from an Old French word for forehead; it grew in figuration to mean the front edge, the leading part, as in the forward line of an army, and as in the part of a country that *fronts* or *faces* another country; its marches. *Frontier* also means "boundary," the place a man crosses to enter another country. This is not the usual American meaning, except, I believe, among Native Americans; the tribes, even those called nomadic, among them the Alaskan tribes, have always been rigorously conscious of boundaries, their own and other tribes'. But the Alaska I lived in grew from the American idea. We were the Last Frontier, said Alaskans, thus claiming the place with that *we:* as if the frontier were the "wilderness," an open space, a freedom from social constraint. *North to the Future* said our license plates: as though our frontier were the unbounded future we crossed into, and our small, crowded, disappointing pasts could be left behind, Outside.

When the United States had its ever-expanding frontier, Americans (and not only Americans) went to it. They needed no passports for the right of passage. Who would have heard them say they had crossed the frontier; who, that they had reached the other side?

More than a century ago, Frederick Jackson Turner proposed to American historians that the frontier ended in 1890, when the last open lands were conquered and claimed under American law, and the first fences put up.[22] If Turner's thesis had been a useful definition of the American frontier, then it seemed to me its analogy was inevitably, in lore and law, the Alaskan frontier. And if that was so, as I saw it, then the Alaskan frontier was closed in 1980, when the last great boundaries, which overlaid and contradicted the old Native boundaries, were set in place by the passage of the Alaska National Interest Land and Conservation Act.

But I went to McGrath in 1978, and although some people could foresee some of what was going to happen, the boundaries were not quite closed. In the brief time they remained open, while the oil economy was still expanding, the town's life had the hum of regularity. People knew, more or less, what to expect across the seasons. In winter, the snow fell six or eight or ten feet deep. All perspective changed then. Cabins sunk to roof lines under their blanket, pencil lines of smoke rose from smudges of chimneys. In the brief light, trees were black sticks in the blinding snowfields. Tamped-down footpaths led up and down hillocks, wound under branches of alders and birches along the margins of yards and lots, and passed through willow thickets where no one had built yet. Snowmachines plowed their trails. Farther back in the woods you saw tracks of rabbits, foxes, mink, small birds. In the falltime, boys and their fathers hunted moose; in cold weather they went for birds: spruce hens, ptarmigan. They ran far-flung traplines.

The winters were times of closing in and closing down, when the line between in- and out-doors was rigorous, when, well-protected, we passed from one condition to the other. At winter solstice the sun turned back toward north. We knew it, but could not yet rejoice; the siege would not lift for two long months. We battened down, cranky and impatient. As the sun came back we felt it, and counted the minutes of its advance day by day, four more minutes, five, six, as it rose toward summer solstice. At last the returning light opened our shuttered faces. We looked around at ourselves, pale and squint-eyed, and saw how the long, cold darkness had hammered us.

Around the end of February, the Iditarod race passed through McGrath. Every day for nearly two weeks long teams of dogs whirled in, halted, and were tied up alongside the paths, chained in the snowy fields, staked in side yards and off the long runway close to the checkpoint near the FAA compound. Hospitable folk of the town race committee cooked bottomless pots of stew and brewed great urns of coffee for the exhausted mushers, who stopped for five minutes' warmth and pressed on, or crashed into a few hours' sleep. Their handlers and suppliers moved around like roadies, efficient, conscious of their glamour. Trappers sold them beaver carcasses for handsome prices, then they cached the meat along the trail for dog food. Every day opened on a new wave of mushers, their yelping dogs, handlers and trappers, packs of reporters in their new parkas, thrilled tourists trailing the progress of the race. Everyone crowded into the roadhouse bar or McGuire's saloon, shouting and singing, trading news and wild speculations, spending freely; the odd confidence man bounced a check in the bar. The town was heady with excitement and relief.

A woman showed up at the height of the fun, a fine-looking high-spirited sportswoman who had run the race, then retired to write children's books. I knew and liked her. We had met in Anchorage, when she had told a feminist writer about the real perils of crossing Norton Sound in the cold. We sat amid the noisy crowd in the roadhouse, toasting our fellow drinkers, barely able to hear ourselves speak. She leaned across the table. She was trying to persuade me to train for next year's run.

"You can do it!" she yelled over the din. "I've got the dogs, and I've got the equipment! You'll have to train hard, but you're strong enough! Of course women can do it! We've got stamina, and we're not kids! Hell, no—older mushers are tougher! They know how to pull for the long haul! Dogs are temperamental! You have to treat them like babies! Some of these bastards treat their dogs like shit! They push them too hard! The vets don't always see it! You have to let them rest! You have to watch them for sickness and sore feet! One thing's for sure! You end up carrying your dogs to Nome!" She grinned her skewed grin.

A different life, handling dogs: feed them, keep them healthy, train them, smell them, learn their idiosyncrasies, live with them, clean out their pens, work out, eat cold meat on the trail, sleep in the snow. Don't even think about money. You're not in bad shape; why not? "Do it," she shouted gaily. We ordered another round, and flirted with two dark-eyed men from a Spanish camera crew who had come North to film the race.

Two days later the Spaniards and their pilot were killed in a plane crash. My friend had left for Nome to greet the first team to cross the finish line. I rubbed the late-night remnants of smoke and noise out of my eyes. For a moment longer, I toyed with the idea of racing: it still sounded possible, I told myself, if I worked hard enough at it. If McGrath was on the frontier, it was, on the face of it, because of the sense of possibility that still crackled in the air.

○

AT BREAKUP the town turned to mud. Little kids ran straight to the puddles, shouting with glee in icy water up to their knees. During the second winter I had an office in an old trading post on the riverbank, not far from the roadhouse. That year the ice went out at the end of April, the earliest date in general memory, at about five o'clock in the afternoon. I was reading and keeping my eye on the river, but grew sleepy and stopped paying attention. The next thing I knew a boy skidded up on his bike, banged on the window, and yelled, "The ice is moving!"

The town was built on a peninsula inside a bend in the river. In some years the ice jammed along the banks so that the river flooded. An old man named Enos Chandler stood leaning on his stick. He nodded hello. I nodded back. We watched the river flow past. I asked him if he thought it would flood.

"Not this year," he replied. "We've had such warm weather lately that a good deal of snow atop the ice has melted. The water underneath has worn away more of it. Even where the ice jams up, I doubt it is more than about eighteen inches thick, and pretty rotten.

"People have always liked to see at least a threat of a flood," he went on, "to make things interesting. Now that we are growing so fast, and there is so much government, we could probably apply for federal aid if it floods, and grow faster." He shook his head, and recalled another flood.

"It was a peaceful flood," he said. "People went around by boat to the store, or to collect driftwood, and waited for the water to go down. Late one night I got out of bed to check on the situation and, looking into the moonlight, saw a canoe glide by, with a pair of lovers in it. I knew who they were, and knew they had left their respective spouses at home. I grinned to myself, and lowered the curtain." Amusement flickered in his pale eyes, and around his mouth. "A little while later, I got out of bed again, and opened the front door. Another boat floated by, with another couple in it: same story. I figured everything was calm, and went back to bed."

During summer the second great wave of transients crowded into town. In the Interior fire-fighting was an annual preoccupation, when the dry heat prepared tinder, and flames leaped and sped through the forests. At some moment the smoke blown from a distant fire darkened the sky: we tracked it like a storm moving in, wondering if the wind would shift. Over the CB radios we heard that villages were being evacuated. Twice I tasted ashes in the air, and smoky haze stung my eyes and lungs. Once it seemed to me that the ghosts of animals flew in the smoke. Later on, flying over a great burn, I saw it was the dark hide of some immense animal of the mind stretched across the ground to cure. But quickly the burns begin to recover, and turn pink and rose with fireweed. "It is called fireweed," wrote the botanist Ada White Sharples, "because it is usually the first plant to take possession of burned-over areas, quickly covering the blackened scars."

For the Bureau of Land Management, McGrath was a regional field base. Hundreds of crews from Native villages around the state were called up at a few minutes' notice. Outside the town was the permanent BLM camp, where thousands of firefighters, and hundreds of pilots, in rotation, camped in wall tents. During the light-filled days and twilit nights, the roar of plane and helicopter engines never ceased.

The town profited from these annual events, welcoming the diversion, and remained undisturbed.

○

AWAY FROM THE RIVER, in the heart of the residential area, McGrath was about to boom. A market for commercial space had opened; a bustle of movement stirred the dust. Native-owned village corporations, set up under the land claims settlement, invested in local, Native-owned enterprises. Non-profit agencies, offsprings of the corporations, offering health care and social services, used the town as a regional base. A consortium had built a two-storey professional building; houses and meeting halls were being converted into offices. The school district administration had spread across two buildings, and wanted another. A new school was in the works.

And the population was growing. As bureaucracies began to alter the seasonal-work patterns, a new kind of resident appeared, the people who managed the schools and offices, lived on a salary, followed a corporate calendar.

These new people came from small towns and the state colleges and universities of the West and Midwest. They needed homes and places in school for their children. Most of the houses near the downtown were small, neatly kept, often had gardens, but were old as well, and in short supply. The teachers, businesspeople, pilots, and young bureaucrats took out mortgages and built large, handsome, expensive, wooden houses on town land that had been newly platted for development.

McGrath needed, and had, an active religious life. Ministers of several fundamentalist faiths led ardent congregations. A pilot-priest flew in periodically on his rounds among the Catholics of the region. The Baha'is, kind people, formed their fellowship. The churches were composed of families whose values were order, modesty, decency. These people set the civic tone.

And so, this river-and-air town seemed to have achieved a successful mixture of people. There were the old-time white settlers, men and women who had come with the steamboats and the gold; and their younger successors, who had left town and farm for a more independent life. There were the established families of Native-and-white ancestry, often descended from Russian or European traders; and the younger Native people from the villages, who hoped they could at last be proud of their culture in public, and who looked for opportunity in the expanding economy. And there were the bureaucrats; among them was me.

The various groups followed their own habits without serious conflict. The town had a peaceful, law-abiding tradition, people said confidently. No murders had occurred within living memory. Drinking and domestic troubles were—properly, they thought—kept from public display. They had a habit of privacy and personal respect; and what went on in a man's house was held to be his own business.

o

FROM OLD JOE DEVLIN I rented one of the Airstream trailers: "the Cadillac of trailers," he pointed out helpfully, one of a pair he had brought in by barge to take advantage of the housing shortage. The new school district was a bounty for the few but growing number of landlords because it underwrote teachers' rents. At once all rents had risen to the limit the district would pay. I was not a teacher and did not get a rent subsidy; but Joe let me negotiate a reasonable price for the Airstream.

For my needs, the place was ample. The storage bins held my books. An oil furnace would keep it warm enough, and Joe had wired it for electricity. It had well water and plumbing. In the Interior running water was seldom standard. Sweet water was rare and precious. In most households, even in McGrath, people carried water from the river, or, in winter, cut blocks of ice to melt in tubs. Wells were expensive to drill, because they had to go deep; even then the water was hard and full of iron. People's hair and skin always smelled of rust.

Joe Devlin took care of his tenants, most of whom were young single women who taught school, or, like me, worked in the administration. He saw to my oil supply, checked the well, and reinsulated the skirting before winter set in upon us. In return, he liked a hot cup of tea and a chance to talk.

And so. "Joe," I asked the usual question: "how did you come to Alaska?"

"Well," he said, pleased, settling back. "I got out of the Army in 1934. I came back to San Francisco from Hawaii with no money, spent all the money on the ship playing cards. So I got to San Francisco and I thought I'd head north, heard about Alaska, thought I'd give it a try."

And, having begun, he went on.

"I fell in with a horse wrangler from Wyoming. He'd been horse-packing into some of those remote sites in Crater Lake, fire stations in Crater Lake National Forest. And he was on his way north, with twenty head of horses. He said to me, 'Why don't you team up with me?' So I did.

"We came to the town of Medford, Oregon, near Grants Pass. Little town, sort of like McGrath, people minded their own business, didn't care much about what you did. Well, we decided to winter there—lots of pasture back then, lots of open country. So we spent the winter there.

"Well, the spring of the year rolled around, and I decided to head north. Thumbed. Just outside of Portland there, I was standing by the side of the road and I saw this car weaving back and forth. I hailed it. The driver pulled over and asked, Where ye headed? Alaska, I said real casual.

"You know, I believe in fate. Can't explain it, it's just how things seem to work out. Turned out he was from Alaska: a contact, you know. Hop in, he said; so I did.

"He asked me if I knew how to work, and I said it was all I ever knew. He owned a mine, you see, and asked if I wanted to go to work for him. I said, Sure.

"He taken me north to Spokane; but he had family there, so he left me off, and he told me to look him up in Seattle, he was staying at the Frye Hotel.

"I went right through Seattle. I thought I'd head for the border, as I didn't have much money and I didn't want to lose time. But you had to have sufficient to guarantee your passage or they'd turn you back, especially as it was still cold at that time of the year. So, I headed back to Seattle.

"In Seattle I was walking down First Avenue—remember, this was 1934, and I didn't know a soul there—and somebody hails me. It was this fellow who'd picked me up outside of Portland. He asked me how I was, and I said I'd been up to the Canadian border and back already, because I had, and he asked why I hadn't looked him up. Well, you know: I figured he was just pulling my leg about a job, just kidding, you might say.

"He was one of those old-timers, not used to the traffic patterns and so on, and he asked me to drive him around Seattle. Some of the boys were out there at the university, old friends, and he wanted to visit. So I drove him around for a few days, and at the end of that time he offered to pay my fare.

Gave me forty dollars, and I could pay him back. I bought a steerage ticket. I was miserly with that forty dollars, steerage cost just that. I booked passage on a steamer.

"Got off at Seward, jumped a freighter, and landed in Anchorage. He given me a letter to McGee Airlines. They flew to Ophir in those days. I said I didn't have any money but I was going to work in the mines, and they said, That's all right, pay us when you can. That's how they did things in those days. Well, they taken me over there, and I went to work.

"But this man and I, we had a difference of opinion. Couldn't get along, you know what I mean: personality differences, you might say. I knew how to work, always had, but he wanted too much out of me. From the old country, you know. So, I rebelled.

"Eventually we came to agreement, and I bought him out. We mined that property for twenty-five, no, twenty-seven years, bought property contiguous to it, and worked that.

"That's how I got to Alaska. Not a common story, you might say, and that's why I say fate, luck, what have you, is important. Here was this man who picked me up outside of Portland, and look where it got me."

○

STORIES OF GOLD traveled happily around McGrath. People liked to tell about an old-timer up in Takotna, who used a one-pound nugget as a doorstop. Nugget jewelry—oversized rings, bracelets, earrings formed of tiny bits of gold—was popular among women; men wore wide nugget watchbands embedded with chunks of Alaska jade. Early one spring the school superintendent glowed with the notion of prospecting an old site out near Flat that (someone had confided to him) was ready to be exploited, if the necessary capital could be raised. He suggested I throw in with him: life was healthy in the open air, we would sluice for gold.

"You could become rich, you know," he said hopefully.

That March the air was warmer than usual. A light breeze softened the snow, dark patches of bare ground showed on the roads. With a consultant who had piloted down from Fairbanks, I walked over to the river to watch an old-time miner, a man named Don Tweed, carry his gear across the ice by Cat-train.

First the ice had to be tested. Grog Johnson, brother of Rocky and himself a famous musher, had driven his own D-7 Cat to the site, and was rearing and scraping his way over the bank. He stopped at the edge to hook his bulldozer to a five-thousand-gallon oil tank, mounted on skids; and, tentative, prepared to leap at the first sign of danger, drove his machine out onto the ice. A trapper named Mick Hannigan watched Grog Johnson with practiced interest. The ice, he told me, was twenty-nine inches thick: but the water was thirty feet deep in the channel.

Slowly the machine rumbled toward a sandbar on the other side of the river.

From out of the woods behind us roared Don Tweed in his D-9. At the edge of the bank he dropped the blade with a crash. (The D-7 was maybe twenty thousand pounds lighter, the consultant from Fairbanks remarked: a good test vehicle.) Don Tweed's adopted son, John, and John's friend Dave Frimmel moved in, to help the older man hook tow chains between three flat-bed skids. The skids carried his wanagan, a scraper, sluice boxes, and trappings. The boys were strong and lithe, and worked carefully and quickly. The machines dwarfed them. They pretended not to notice the cluster of high-school girls, who watched them, thrilled; then their task absorbed them, and they were no longer aware of anything but their work. They leaped about the machines as though born to them.

As his Cat idled, Don Tweed supervised them. He was a burly man with a watch cap glued to his head, and looked to be about sixty. He had made the Cat move as easily as the boys moved their own bodies.

They found a hairline crack. Grog drove back to our side, in order to drag Don Tweed's skids across the river. The men talked; pointed; walked out on the ice. The D-9 remained perched high on the bank. By the time we turned to go, they had decided to detach the blade and ferry it across the ice. Tweed had another D-9 waiting on the far bank.

The consultant from Fairbanks said you didn't see many Cat-trains these days. Federal regulations about land use prohibited them in many places; and they were expensive to run.

I turned to go and, over my shoulder, watched an improbable sight. The D-7 rolled on, dragging the three skids, one spaced precisely behind another, across the wide, frozen river, under an immense, brilliant sky. On the long runway, a relay of small planes lifted off, light as mosquitoes in the air. In the middle distance, the mountains, crisp and icy, shone. The train lumbered out toward the horizon; the huge noise of its engine faded; and the optical effects of light and distance condensed it to a line of toys.

o

"I'VE BEEN HERE thirty-four years," mused Joe Devlin. He was as small-framed as a cowboy, but looked fit, though his red hair had lately grown ashen. He had been stopping by more often. He held his mug of tea in gnarled hands.

"When I came here I didn't have any home ties. And over the years we've done pretty well. Of course, the price of gold being what it is now, we're going to pay more attention.

"Over the years, we've taken about a million dollars worth of gold out, and that was at thirty-five dollars an ounce. At these prices today, we'd be getting sixteen times that.

"But you know, I don't get very excited about the price. I never was struck by the gold fever, that is, I never lost the use of my logic about gold. I know it's in there, I know what's on the properties. On one of the properties, they made it pay, back in 1915, 1917, taking the material out with picks and shovels. There's a lot they overlooked then, and of course eventually you have to go deeper, which they couldn't do. That makes it just about right for machinery. Oh yes, I know it's there.

"But I wish we had a place like this"—he gestured at the walls of my little metal home—"over in the mining camp. It isn't practical to haul a thing like this out there. One summer the wife and I stayed out for four months, never saw a single face. That was no way to treat anybody. Next year, I told her, we'll give this up, close down the property; and I'll go to work for the Air Force."

But he had kept trying. Early one spring, while the rivers were still frozen, he drove an ancient D-7 Cat he had rebuilt out to the property. (He screwed up his mouth when he recalled the event.) First thing, he said, he broke through a small lake and had to walk back to town, to find someone who could drag the Cat out of the water. Not an easy matter, he said crisply, but there were still a couple of old-time miners around, with heavy equipment.

In that season the sun rose higher, and the days grew longer, in no time at all. A week passed; it had warmed up appreciably, and he set out once again on the Cat, dragging a sledge with a wanagan.

(I had seen that Cat, the sledge, and the wanagan on top of the sledge, parked outside the roadhouse in midwinter. The wanagan was a frame shelter, built like a tiny house; a stovepipe stuck out of the roof, and smoke was rising straight up from the chimney, as Joe worked inside. Maybe he was finally insulating it. A Coleman lantern glowed like a jack-o'lantern at the window.)

Joe made a day's progress. That night, the temperature dropped to minus thirty-five. He was caught in the open, with no shelter—the wanagan wasn't warm enough—and only peanut-butter sandwiches to eat. When he got back to town, the hamburgers Margarety served looked mighty good to him.

"The property was marginal anyway," he concluded philosophically, "and you might say we were barely getting out of it what we were putting in. So I could make more, working for the government.

"But I like the life. Been here forty-four years and, as I say, I had no home-ties when I came here to the country. It grows on you. You get stuck, you might say.

"I like being independent. It's not the money. At our age, we have everything a couple like us could want, so it isn't as if we needed more. But I like the chance to do what I want, and be independent. It's a man's life out here, I suppose you could say."

○

I HEARD ANOTHER Iditarod gold story. A Native woman who lived in a Yukon village on the western side of the district suffered from rheumatoid arthritis, for which she received injections of gold. Her doctor had given her a standing prescription. When she was in Anchorage, if she needed a shot she went to the Alaska Native Hospital.

One day she was assisted by a nurse she barely knew, a white woman who told her crossly that gold was too expensive to be injecting it into someone every time she asked for it.

The Native woman was of course given her shot; but her ear had caught a certain tone, and soon she had the nurse talking about herself and her unhappiness. It happened that the nurse's husband had the same disease, "poor man, and couldn't afford the shots himself. And here she was so upset," this lady said to me: "Imagine, a Native woman getting gold shots, free!

"I laughed to myself," she finished lightly. "Here they came right into our own country to get gold; they exploited us and took our land; and now we can have gold when we need it, to save our lives." She laughed and laughed. "And you know what my husband says to me? He says, 'I wonder whether that stuff comes out when you piss. Imagine how much you've pissed away.'"

What Things Do
in Our Country

WE WERE SITTING near the river on a
pile of logs in the sun. She was making something intricate with her hands.
A man she had known for a long time walked by looking for her husband,
and she spoke fondly of him to me. He called out a playfully gruff hello. She
answered with a teasing laugh, a deep, female, middle-aged laugh, so that he
should feel admired by an old friend who was also a woman. It was quick, but
seemed unhurried and luxurious. After he passed, she sighed for him. "His
young wife is in the hospital waiting to go into labor, and he's very worried.
He'll feel responsible if anything goes wrong."

"Our men are strong," she added, thoughtfully. "We give each other
strength, we pass it on to each other."

How often I've seen it, I thought, in public places, airports especially. Men
and women are sitting, waiting, slumped back to back in those fixed plastic
chairs. A woman, smoking, says something to a companion; her hair is caught
up in a fine, beaded comb. Behind her, his plastic chair facing the opposite
direction, a friend recognizes her voice. Worn out (I feel) by the demands of
too much travel to too many government meetings, they speak to each other,
letting the murmur of their voices ease their weariness. They tip their heads
back and for a few seconds rest lightly against one another.

We continued to sit by the river, a young woman and her second mother,
in the graceful mixture of intimacy and distance that shaped their friendship.
A young woman living alone in that country was in a complicated position;
and in time, I realized that she was watching over me. "I had to protect you,
and teach you, as my daughter," she explained. She was the woman who used
gold for medicine. I will call her Malfa Ivanov; it is the name she gave me to
use in this account.

I had gone to work for the school district; and if privately I called myself
a poet, outwardly I became something else. Among my duties was the job of
persuading the state university to provide educational services to adults in the
villages of our district. The Fairbanks campus ran a teacher-training program
for "rural," particularly Native, students. Based in regional centers throughout the bush, the program was designed for the benefit of the widespread
group of bright, activist people, in those years usually women, who wished
to earn a useful college degree but could not leave their families or village.
For a decade the program been the principal route by which Natives had gotten their degrees. It had taken heavy criticism from traditional academics, the
state department of education, and the teachers' union, and yet it had been

proven sound. There were still not many Native teachers in bush schools, however, and none from the Iditarod area. For years the university had promised to set up such a training center in our district; but, for obscure reasons, had put off doing it.

By the time I finished, the district had won what it wanted, although only after the unpleasant and thoroughly commonplace intrigues, arguments, alliances formed and dissolved—all the tiresome small workings of academic power politics. The struggle was worth its cost, however, to me at least, for through it I came to know Malfa.

She lived with her husband in winter camp near the village called In the Shelter of the Hill, on the Yukon River. They made a good living from the barge and hauling business they had built together, and in winter he trapped. They had four children of their own, and had fostered others, who had grown and formed new families; and they had close friends and relatives along the rivers, the Yukon, the Koyukuk, the Kuskokwim, the Tanana. During the sixties, when the War on Poverty had helped raise political consciousness in the bush, a group of Yukon elders had trained Malfa as a speaker, teaching her debate and argumentation. Now, having taught her children at home, she wanted to go to college. She was in her late forties.

Someone directed her to me while I was still marking out my new position, learning my way around the district. Of our first meeting I recall trying not to stare at her soft, alert face, particularly her eyes, but wanting to look at her nonetheless; and, more clearly, becoming aware of an active mind delighting in its own movement, wanting more. Her manner was decorous, her gaze oblique: shy, I thought, mistakenly (I didn't realize that deference did not mean meekness), and I felt shy and earnest in response. She was my senior by fifteen years, and my only claim to authority was the accident of position; but I had access to some of what she needed and was determined to help her get it.

(Within another year she would begin her studies at the state university. Later she would take an advanced degree at Harvard. She would teach social science for several years in the high school in Shelter, and work at devising a civics curriculum for bush schools based in the Alaska Native Land Claims Settlement Act. When the political climate shifted and the district decided to ignore her curriculum proposals, she went on to consult with and advise various districts around the state, became a noted speaker, and contributed articles about Native education to Canadian and American journals.)

We continued to meet, although not often at first. She seldom came to McGrath; generally, I flew to Shelter, where I had business with the high school. Slowly, our attachment grew. Now it seems to me we've always known one another, but I think our real friendship began at the moment our positions became reversed.

"Poor little boy," she was saying, naming a child in the Shelter school. "It was spring. The swans were flying back to us. A teenaged girl was watching for them at the window. 'Swans!' All the students jumped up and rushed out to the schoolyard to watch the birds pass. Their dark hair shone in the sun; so black, like ravens' wings. Only that little boy, who was white, you know, his mother was a teacher here—he couldn't see those swans: he didn't know where to look.

"I thought and thought about him. We liked him, my husband and I, and I thought, If we could take him back to our camp for a month, we would teach him where to look to see the swans. Our children always know where to look, because we teach them. Only that little boy didn't know."

Teach me, I asked silently.

Afterward, I reminded her about that moment when we were new to one another. "You wanted to know," she replied. "I thought for a long time about that. What you needed to learn. What to tell you. Finally I realized: I told you, 'Pay attention to what's ordinary.'"

By ordinary she meant the things I might overlook. One day when I was at her house, she turned on the television; by then, in the early eighties, bush households received television via satellite transmission. We watched a performance by Yup'ik dancers and drummers from a village downriver. She was studying their language; it was related to Aleut, her mother's tongue.

Yup'ik drums are bladder skins scraped thin, stretched over great hoops of steamed birch and attached by sinew to a short handle. With one hand the drummer holds the drum; with the other he holds the stick, a slightly curved willow wand, and strikes the drum with it.

Those old men held drums made of green plastic garbage bags stretched over hoop-frames. Skin drums were difficult and expensive to make, explained one old man to the camera: for everyday use, plastic did just as well.

"Look what it does," Malfa said, deeply stirred by their cadence. "That plastic—it's the drum; but not just the drum, it's the sound. And it's the sound: but not just the sound, it's the effect. The lowly thing, the ordinary thing: the sound it produces, what it does to our hearts. It holds off the Mighty."

And so, I kept my eyes open; but for years, whenever I asked her *why* and *how* and *what:* when I said, *I think that,* and *I saw this:* just when I thought I *knew:* she would nod, look at me patiently, and advise: "Pay attention to what things do in our country, not what they're called in yours."

○

IN MY HABIT of watching her, in my absorption into the country's movement, I scarcely considered why she had chosen me. I don't know why she had, merely that it did not seem unlikely. I think we must have been so hungry for one another. Even so, I remind myself that hearts are various, and that people have reasons of their own for accepting a stranger in their midst.

An acquaintance of mine, an anthropologist, had done her field work on an island in the South Pacific that had been a Dutch colony. She had boarded with a family of distinguished lineage who, she hoped, would serve as her guides into their culture. Some years later, we sat in her garden in Virginia, telling each other travel stories. She described her relationship to the family and how it had continued even across great distances, and mentioned that she planned to do some research in the Dutch archives on their behalf. We talked aimlessly. Neither of us had anything to prove. The yard was sun-dappled. Cicadas hummed. Idly, she remarked that she had been staying with the family for a while, weeks, or a couple of months, but nothing had happened. She was beginning to worry, as she had gone there to observe rituals and ceremonies, and had seen none, and was losing precious time. Suddenly the father, who was head of the extended family, accepted her. His acceptance opened the way to her entry into the life of the village, which in fact was highly ritualized. From that time people spoke to her willingly and showed her whatever she wanted to see.

What happened, I asked. Why had he accepted her?

"He had a dream," she said, somewhat embarrassed. It seemed that an honored ancestor had come to the father, and had spoken of her, the visitor, with approval. He had reported his dream to his family and village, she said, and from then on, people had opened everything to her. The event still puzzled her.

I was certain that his dream was the fact that had justified all that followed, the key to their mutual experience, to her having been allowed inside the life of that family and their community, and so I asked if she had mentioned the dream in her dissertation. She had not, she said; she herself had felt it was meaningful, but it had not fit the conventions of the dissertation. A dream was considered a subjective matter, not fact.

A chasm opens at any moment between different ways of knowing, each with its method of explanation; and if often, in our society, this chasm is greatest between artist and academic, equally, it can exist between societies. Had the dream not been knowledge for the father? It had authorized him to bring her, a foreign woman and a guest, into the life of his family, living and dead. A scholar who had been treated as an honored guest, I thought, would have been obligated by two standards of learning, her own and her host's, to acknowledge the dream. It was an element of his logic, it had not been secret, and he had been her teacher. Surely, it should have been respected, in those terms at least, and been part of her scholarly report.

She had taken her degree at an important American department, with cultural anthropologists who followed the trends of French thought, which gave primacy to Indo-European logic and linguistics, in essence translating non-Western patterns into Structuralist and post-Structuralist frameworks. From my point of view, the question was about how we know things across cultures. I pressed her. With finality, she said the dream and its logic weren't credible to her professors, and she had wanted to get her degree.

The question of credibility is fundamental, for it asks: On whose authority is knowledge advanced? And, further, begs: What, then, is the nature of knowledge? I accepted the dream as a vital, poetic fact, a valid conveyer of messages that could be interpreted and understood across several layers of context.

My acquaintance also remarked that, while she stayed with the family, her dreams had been vivid, thrilling; and in their content, unlike anything she dreamed at home.

o

GRADUALLY, I understood that Malfa was watching over me. An important woman in Shelter had invited me to dinner to meet her son, visiting from the city. I admired the woman but had no intention of meeting her son. I explained my dilemma to Malfa.

"You're wishing for someone?" she inquired, delicately. I told her enough about F to explain why I wanted to be alone.

She offered to adopt me. "I'll screen your suitors," she laughed. "I'll make them work for me. They'll have to show me what they're made of!"

o

F TELEPHONED from time to time; in the end, he always asked for money. I could no longer remember his beauty, only that he had been beautiful. I sent money; then, stopped sending it.

In the village, where nothing had been hidden, a great deal had not been spoken. The power of alcohol was undeniable, but I had not grasped the intensity of its seduction. I described to Malfa the strength of his dependence: how he had feared its domination; how his visions had terrified him; how he had cried out that only his strong heart would save him. He had dreamed his mother was coming for him and, for a blinding moment, had been happy; and then had feared he was going to die.

Malfa looked serious, and asked carefully, "Does he know he can refuse it?"

A small hope stirred.

After a considered silence, she said, "In the late sixties, all our adolescents were sent away to boarding schools; but some of the students were allowed to remain in Alaska. They could attend public school in the cities. They boarded in group homes, and, usually, Native parents were in charge. My husband and I lived in Anchorage then, and I was on the parent committee of one of the group homes. Do you know who is Mrs. Reliance?"

Mrs. Reliance was a respected Koyukon woman whose late grandfather had been a medicine man; the fact still carried weight, although now Native people dared only whisper the word *medicine*. They feared ridicule; they feared retaliation from the priests, and also from disturbed spirits. Yet, Malfa's husband had family in her village and their ties to Mrs. Reliance were close. Mrs. Reliance spoke often in public about the necessities of education and, equally, learning the old stories. She had been brought up in her grandparents' camp, where they had taught her to work but had not allowed her to go to the village school. Longing to know how to write, she had taught herself in the day's odd hours, by copying by firelight the labels from tin cans. Using the backs of the labels for paper, she had written out her grandparents' first grocery list.

Malfa said: "The school happened to have a psychologist on staff. The psychologist was an Indian woman, fortunately. I say that because that meant she knew us. She was Outside Indian, though, and some of our customs are different.

"One day she came to me, and asked about a boy who was having difficulty. He showed his trouble by withdrawing from the other teenagers. He hunched himself down in his shoulders. He was miserably alone, and no one could reach him. 'He should have a physical immediately,' I told her. She said, 'Yes.' Then, very carefully, she asked if Athabaskan boys passed through initiation rites.

"I told her I didn't think they did, but I would check with Mrs. Reliance. She did not understand the question. I explained what initiation rites and vision quest meant.

"'No,' she told me.

"But later she remembered something. Some people go through a medicine struggle, she told me. The medicine powers come to someone: he can refuse them, for accepting power means accepting a life of sorrow. But the struggle can be fierce, and sometimes it overwhelms him, and he kills himself to escape suffering."

For nearly two decades, in various parts of the state, there had been near-epidemics of suicides among young Native people; usually, alcohol was said to be involved. Malfa had been observing me closely. She remarked that a small group of Athabaskan women was getting ready to undertake an investigation of the reasons for so much death. Getting ready, she said, watching my reaction, meant: being spiritually strong.

In my notebook is a yellowed clipping from the Anchorage paper, dated March 1977, probably the first notice I saw, but not the last. I did not save them; there were too many.

> Loretta E————, the project director of K————'s alcohol program, said 12 youths between the ages of 16 and 25 have committed suicide in the K———— area since last July. All were alcohol-related, she said.

I couldn't live with F's drinking and in my sadness turned to Malfa for insight. But the larger test had been F's; so Malfa implied, and so I accepted, for I believe it possible that medicine spirits, of the kind Mrs. Reliance had named, may have sought him, and that, along with all else that besieged him, he had waged battle with them, as she had described. When I remember his torment, I believe it could have been so. And if it were so, could he have known it? I speculate, for this was a man's life; but if he had known, as I suspect he could have, then he may have been trying to drown them—the spirits, masquerading as his memories, his fears—with drink. To have answered the call would have brought a life of sorrow to him; what was his alternative? F was a man of sorrows, and his world was full of suffering, silence, and secrets.

Our questions, each of ours, F's, Malfa's, mine, were these: How do you live with this? What is this with which you must live? But for each of us the questions would have been different in content, and so would the answers have been; but we did not know them then, neither questions nor answers. And for me, at least, there was a third complication, about which at that time I had no inkling: *What is the nature of your dreams?*

I believe F lived through his torment; but I do not know what the struggle may have cost him, or how he managed it, or what, finally, he accepted, and what he refused. Nor do I know what guidance and help, beyond his strong heart, was available to him; only that, while I knew him, I saw no sign of guidance I recognized, nor was I much help to him.

McGuire's

MY TRAILER SAT in the field next to McGuire's saloon, where life passed just inside the limits of secular respectability. McGuire himself had been a goldfields gambler. The only things left of him were his name, his gun, and the stories told about him. It was said he had come into the Iditarod fields as a young man and had made his fortune at cards. Old men remembered fondly how often they had lost to him in their youth. They always found him at the poker table. Bottles of whiskey and rye and bourbon stood hospitably on the bar. A customer went straight to the bar—when the Pan Am flight landed, McGuire's was the passengers' lounge—helped himself to a drink, and paid the till. No one ever failed to pay.

McGuire never appeared to notice, but he knew what was going on. People took his word. One day a passenger got off the plane, went into the bar, showed McGuire a sum of money in an unsealed packet, and asked him to hold it for a certain man, who was going to pick it up. McGuire agreed to hold the money. Some weeks later, no one recalled how many, a stranger stopped at the bar and asked if a packet had been left for him. McGuire handed over the money, intact. Both men, the one who left the money and the one who picked it up, were passing through on their way to someplace else.

When McGuire drank, a half-yearly marathon event, everyone drank with him. He opened with beer, passed on to wine, floated into whiskey, slid back into beer; he drank whatever came to hand. The saloon never closed, except for an hour or so around five in the morning, when someone swept the place out.

McGuire was a rough man, men judged, as rough as any, but he liked women and was courteous to them, and always presented Champagne to ladies whom he held in esteem. With a complicated smile, a married woman reminisced to me about her newlywed days, when she also was new in town. Once a month, on a Tuesday evening, she had called on Jack McGuire. He closed the saloon and brought out a bottle of Mumm's, and they sat beside the barrel stove, drinking the good wine and talking. He arranged to have the latest copy of *Vogue* for her.

Stories were told about the end of Jack McGuire. I heard two or three of them. "McGuire went downriver to Bethel," Joe Devlin said gruffly. "Had cancer, and knew that was it. He set his affairs in order, sent for his gun, put on a suit, and shot himself. They cremated him. Put his ashes in two-and-a-half Champagne magnums, and poured them out of an airplane over the Yukon. Jack McGuire was a gentleman, a good man, and never gave anybody any fuss."

The school custodian, a hard-working family man, told me he had Jack McGuire's gun. He was a teenager when Jack McGuire had sent to McGrath for his gun; it had been left in the care of the young man's father, who got it back as a relic and, in the end, had passed it on to his son.

Whoever got hold of McGuire's place sold it a few years later to someone else in town. Over the years it rotated among the local high rollers whenever the current owner needed cash. The regulars stopped calling it McGuire's. When I lived there, Grog Johnson owned it; they called it "Grog's," until a pilot named Curly Johansson bought him out; then they called it "Curly's." It was not easy to pick out either of them from the crowd at the bar, some of whom slept regularly in their chairs. The jukebox played country-western music, and couples danced to the slower songs. The young men drifting in and out sometimes danced with local girls, but generally they spent their time sizing each other up. They tended to face off in the shadows behind the pool table, where no one would be much disturbed.

By then, McGuire's was soaked in decades' worth of lugubrious murk; but I had a small soft spot for the place because of my father. When my father was a young man he and his brothers and sisters and their friends went to a tavern called Bug-eye McGuire's. Bug-eye McGuire knew everyone around, and every Saturday night they went to Bug-eye's to see each other and dance. "Gussie Mitchell in yet?" they would ask. "Seen Moose McNulty?" McGuire kept track. "Gussie: not yet. Moose went down to Rooney's, says to wait for him, he's coming back."

Bug-eye was of course a fine talker. He engaged anyone in debate about the state of the world. He held strong opinions on every aspect of human folly; he believed improvement was always possible, and he suggested how to go about it.

My father, having decided it was time to tell us about the old days, said, warmly, that it was a "grand place, everyone used to meet there. You'd stop by on a Sunday morning. Of course the place was shut tight as a drum, no Sunday-morning taverns in those days. But cars would be lined up and down the streets. You'd knock at a little peephole. Bug-eye'd slide it open and look out, and if he knew you, you were in. Inside, it was packed, and everyone you knew was there. We used to tell him he should hang crepe on the door, so it would look like there was a reason for all those cars."

Then America entered World War II, and most of the young men went into the service. Four years later my father came home, and the first thing he did was drive up to Bug-eye's. He walked into the tavern.

"Hi ya, Bug-eye!"

"Well, well, well, if it isn't Rover McNamara. Now, as I was sayin' the last time ye stood at this bar ..."

"That was Bug-eye McGuire," my father said, "and he was a good man to us. He'd never forget the last word he'd said to you, and of course, you couldn't get a word in edgewise."

o

DURING THE WINTERS trappers brought green skins to McGuire's and hung them on the long side wall. They were stiff and rough and silky to the touch: thick fox pelts, an occasional cross-fox; a wolf skin or two. I saw a black wolf skin once. I saw creamy, subtle lynx skins; strings of marten skins; stretched beaver skins, round as the hoop of the world. Some of their wildness was still in them. I wondered at the long distance the skins would travel to reach their destiny. Once Outside, they would be sold, dressed, plucked, sheared, drummed, glazed, stripped, sewn, dyed, and made into garments. They would be transformed, and at the end of the journey they would have nothing of the wild left in them.

o

THE SKINS ON THE WALL in McGuire's were waiting for the cash buyer. The most famous cash buyer in Alaska was Goldberg. People called him Goldberg the Fur Buyer and His Pockets Full of Money. I met him once at a potlatch in Shelter. A young woman called to me, "Come, meet the Cash Buyer." He was a large man, well along in years, with a firm handshake: the fur business operated on handshakes, honor, and private treaties. The old-time cash buyers, like Goldberg, were men from Jewish and Greek families who ran fur-trading firms in New York, London, Montreal—international cities, centers of fashion—men who had in themselves an archaic taste for commerce and mobility.

There also were local fur buyers, entrepreneurial jacks-of-all-trades who bought skins from trappers before the season ended, discounting cash against the futures price, then sold them to large collectors like Goldberg. Some trappers were crafty and bargained with more than one buyer, or took a chance and sent their skins out to an agent in Anchorage, or Seattle, or St. Louis. It was a time of new money, and more money, and some of it was passing into local hands. The money changed hands around town, but returned home swiftly. One agent, who kept a store, traded snowmachines for furs. Grog Johnson was known to buy furs with whiskey; he also took checks when money ran short, and never doubted they would be honored.

"He knows you ain't goin' anywhere," Mick Hannigan, who ran a trapline, explained reasonably.

o

ATHABASKAN PEOPLE must have believed the land was something like a father and mother to them, for it tested and nourished them and gave them the means of life. Malfa, who used gold for medicine, told me, "We thought the world was good, and everything in it was good. We thought it was useful for us. We didn't know so much would harm us.

"When we say 'useful,' we mean that in our way: what is useful is what brings us together. It lets us live."

The bounty of animals flowered in the beautiful handwork of Athabaskan women. Boots and parkas and hats and gloves, earrings and headdresses and baby straps, table covers, altar cloths, sled bags and rifle bags, eyeglass cases, cigarette cases, butane-lighter cases: a myriad of useful objects, composed of fine skins, cloth, and elaborate embroideries of beads, quills, thread; sewn by hands disciplined to take pains; refined by eyes observing all that lived around them. Women made what was needed by hand, with the passion of all artists, for the care and comfort of their families. Even the pieces they made to sell struck the eye with their clarity of form and the skill of their execution.

Those women must have made their handwork for the consolation of their hearts. The first time I stayed in Shelter I had boarded with a grandmother, a gentlewoman educated by the nuns, who advised her female relatives, "When in sorrow, woman, take up your needle."

In the trailer I kept a pair of dance boots made by an aged woman not long before her death. She came from an Upper Kuskokwim village north of McGrath, where I had given poetry in the school; I knew the teacher, who acted as the intermediary between the maker and me. A year after I ordered them, the boots were delivered. The old lady was known for the high quality of her sewing. Her family considered these boots to be among the finest she had made. Perhaps I was wrong not to wear them. I used simply to look at them, or to hold them in my hands and enjoy touching them.

These boots were made of home-tanned moosehide, with the smell of the smoke deep in them. They were high enough to cover the ankle, where each was finished with a band of unsheared beaver, the red-brown guard hairs intact; with red flannel finishing off the top. Each was closed by a three-inch zipper and, threaded through the top of the flannel, a drawstring of blue and red braided yarn, with a pompom of yarn at each end.

But the old lady did her real work in beads, in a bright, wide band covering the vamp and upper part of each boot. Her motif was the flowers that Athabaskan women love to use in their work, drawn against a solid ground of white beads, in the style that the women of her village followed. Her design was composed of buds and opened blossoms twined in a garland. She had colored the petals pink, with maroon tips, and given them large, radiant centers of light and dark blue, yellow and orange; she had shaped and colored the leaves as mature foliage. Hers were late-summer flowers in their last, rich bloom, at the moment before they fade and die.

Another woman, perhaps her daughter, had tanned the moosehide. It was hard work. I held stone scrapers that women had used for the job and listened to old women describe how they had done it.

Like many women her age, Malfa had never been taught to tan skins. In her experience, wives were pleased not to have to do that sort of work anymore. If women sewed for their family, or for the museums and the handwork markets, their husbands bought commercially tanned skins for them. Now and then they could buy home-tanned skin from a skilled person, but such a skin was very expensive. "Our husbands want to save us all that work," she said to me. "It is the way they tell us we are precious to them."

A few years later, she mentioned a course she had taken at the university. The professor knew Athabaskan people well, she agreed—his wife, a school-teacher, was Athabaskan—but she thought he had misconstrued his subject. Her point, however, was not only about the intricate connectors between animals and humans.

"He defined roles by what people did, and that was all right," she said carefully. "Then I listened to him say that young women have 'lost their role' in our culture. He said, for example, that they don't learn to tan hides anymore!" She laughed in disbelief. "I wonder what he thinks it takes to be a woman. We don't have time for that, we have too much else to do! This is the twentieth century."

A successful season allowed people to afford to live. Men like Malfa's husband ran fifty- or hundred-mile traplines on snowmachines, and on snowshoes, in temperatures well below zero. They came home with pleasure in their eyes. A younger pleasure shone in the eyes of boys learning how to trap. They talked about it; in school they wrote about how their fathers did it. They described the good snare sets, and how they noticed where animals passed by, what they ate, how the weather hit them, and a thousand other details of place to be observed and remembered on the fly. Trapping was part of the way of living: Athabaskan people, they said, had always been taught by their fathers that they had always gone trapping. Those people, adults and children, had learned important things from the animals who died for them.

Before the Russians, before the Europeans and Americans came into their country, animals had supplied Athabaskans with nearly all of what they needed to live. I saw that animals had not stopped being useful to humans: now they gave people not only their meat and skins, they also brought money, which people needed, to stay alive.

It was expensive to live off the land. A family needed to buy rifles and shells, and snowmachines or three- or four-wheelers for transportation. Unless they could afford to fish in the summer, they needed at least enough to feed their dogs in winter, as dogs were costly to keep: they needed gasoline and heating oil; clothing, food, supplies; education; travel; funeral costs; celebrations: they needed all the goods and materials that people needed and wanted for a better life. Even those people who did not have many things needed money.

o

THE TRAPPERS had not only been male: "A man couldn't live alone in that country," said Malfa, who was telling me about her early married life. She had kept house for her husband, their first house, in Flat, when it was still a thriving mining town. For more than thirty years she had known the miners and trappers in the Iditarod country.

"No one could do without a woman. The trappers made partners of the 'steeljack men,' as they called them. They shared a little cabin and divided the line. The men trapped farther out. The women got the land around the house. They would cook; but sex wasn't part of the bargain."

When the fur buyer came to town, the men bargained first, and then got drunk together. By then, she said, "they had struck the top price, and then the 'steeljack men' would sell their furs."

○

THE OLD TRAPPER-STYLE hat was in fashion. It was made of fur and had warm earflaps you tied back with strings. The animal's tail was sewn to the crown. It was a dashing hat. You likely knew where a man came from by the way he tied back his hat; and you probably thought his wife had made it for him. Women most often used marten skins, and so the hats were called three-marten hats, because they took three skins, and three tails dangled from the crown.

I bought a three-marten hat, finely stitched and lined in soft narrow-wale corduroy, from Mary Jane Austin. She had gone trapping and had done pretty well that winter; she made the hat from darker, rarer skins, to match my dress parka.

I had met Mary Jane Austin soon after I came to McGrath, when we struck up a conversation and went off to McGuire's for a beer. She had arrived not long before I had; had come, I think, from Minnesota, and was working as an aide in the grade school to make some winter money. She was about to move into a little cabin outside of town. This was just before freeze-up; she was looking forward to having her own place.

McGuire's was dim and heavy with smoke. Men and a couple of women who looked like regulars were lined up at the bar. The district comptroller sat with them; he came from Montana, where he had been a rodeo cowboy once upon a time. I nodded and smiled; he nodded, turned pink, and looked down into his beer. Mary Jane and I found two empty seats and ordered our Coors.

A friendly sort named Tommy, who seemed to have spent a lot of time at the bar, sat on my left. At a pause in the conversation he suggested that I introduce myself. They all wanted to know who the girl in the pigtails was. They already knew Mary Jane. I told him my name, and he said, "Howdy."

A man he called John D. sat next to him. Johnny was a pilot who came from an important Athabaskan family. He was a handsome man with a handsome voice pitched deep as an aged oaken barrel. He had just been fired and rehired by the bigger taxi service; his wife was leaving him; and he had been drinking for two days.

He had been drinking with Tommy. Tommy's young blonde wife, who worked in the AC store, had recently gone off on a holiday with another man whose name I didn't catch, who was shooting pool at the back of the bar. The lovers had chartered a plane. The pilot had been Johnny. Tommy and Johnny were still, gently, healing the breach. Tommy muttered "dumb" a couple of times: Johnny agreed, but pointed out morosely that they had been friends for a long time; and besides, he added, it wasn't his fault she had gone off. Tommy agreed. Johnny asked, twice, if Tommy didn't want to talk to his wife's friend, who had carefully ignored them and was at that moment chalking his cue; but Tommy declined to say anything. At its edges his face had begun to curl in pain.

Someone played a sad song on the jukebox. The bartender set up another round. Johnny had walked stiffly out the door to the outhouse, and Mary Jane was talking to the man on her right. Tommy and I traded platitudes about honesty and traveling down bumpy roads, until the talk turned to children. His face softened, and he recollected that the town was about to throw its annual Halloween party.

"I love those kids," he said simply, and thought back to something that bothered him. "Worked in Anchorage one year. Bought must have been a hundred dollars worth of trick-or-treat candy. You know how many kids came? Three." He shook his head, his eyes a bit bleary now. "People ruining it. All that razor-blade stuff."

He chuckled for a little while at the pranks kids played and told me about a good (recent) one of his own.

○

THE WEATHER TURNED COLDER; Mary Jane settled into her cabin. I traveled almost constantly around the district, or up to the university in Fairbanks. Our paths still crossed, but not often. The following winter, she bought a share in a trapline and moved in with the trapper. She did all right on the line. She learned to sew skins, and I asked her to make me the hat. The price of marten was a little deflated that season; we agreed on a reasonable cost. Her stitches were fine and even; her lining material and yarn ties were of subdued colors, and on the back of one earflap she stitched my initials in a graceful script of beads.

The trapper hadn't quite worked out, she said. Her face looked weary, not only because of the weather. After the season ended, she got off the trapline and moved on to another place.

One hot summer day my plane landed in Farewell. Among the small group on the airstrip was a familiar golden head. I moved toward it, saw her face, and called hello. She smiled broadly, and I realized I had missed that smile. She had come to the settlement to pick up her mail. For a few minutes we traded news, and then it was time to go, and I scrambled into the plane. She was happier now, she said.

The Repetition of Their Days

FROM HUNGRY, Mary and Tom Charles sent me two fat red salmon, packed in bundles of the tall grass that grew on the riverbanks. In late summer people scythed the grass and used it to absorb fish blood. After breakup, after the last snow had gone, they burned off the straw; within a day of the first rain, green shoots were poking through the stubble. The grass grew broad-leafed and tough. In August, by the time the reds came that far up the Stony, the men cut the high summer growth and laid it down on the beach under the tables where the families cut fish.

I was away from home the day the gift arrived. The pilot left it with my neighbor, who stored the unopened box on her porch in a refrigerator that stopped working. I got back a week later; the fish were already stinking. I gave them to Mick Hannigan, who fed them to his dogs.

It was too bad about the fish; I liked them, and red salmon didn't spawn in the Kuskokwim. There was an empty seat on a chartered plane going to Hungry, I heard; and I could have it. It was the last week in August: the days were warm; the nights were cool enough for a parka. I gathered up my parka and a sleeping bag and a small pack. The plane was waiting, its freight loaded; most of it was grocery orders from the McGrath store.

For about an hour we flew south over the Kuskokwim Mountains and into the Stony River country, behind where the Alaska Range curved inland from the coast. The shapes of the ridges were pleasing, and familiar, resembling the hills around Village Below. I wondered if the Dena'ina who had gone south from Hungry Village into the Kijik country had thought the same. The mountains were green with Alpine tundra, or thick with birch and alder. It was moose country, the pilot noted, though a few caribou also ranged in the higher areas.

In Hungry lived a family of people I had come to know in the past year, the brothers Fyodor and Efrem and their sisters Alice and Emma. They were Dena'ina, and I had known their relatives in Village Below: the old woman of the fierce eye was their sister, F's mother had been their niece. A number of their grown children remained near them. The daughters had married white men, and the young families had built new homes across the river from the old settlement. Of all of them, I was closest to the Charleses. Tom taught school; Mary was Efrem's daughter.

And so, I came walking over the hill from the village and down the trail to the house where the seven Charleses lived. Nothing stirred but wood smoke drifting away into the trees. They had built the cabin into a steep bank on a small, swift creek, just upstream from where the creek joined the river: its new tin roof flashed in the sun. Directly below, at the edge of the water, stood the smokehouse; and off toward the trees a summer tent had been rigged up out of mosquito netting, where the children could laze about and read. Seven sled dogs lay by their houses at the edge of the woods. One of them rattled his chain and looked toward me, questioning, as I approached.

The two youngest children were up on the roof of the smokehouse. They *hallooed* through the quiet woods! Mary appeared, smiling, at the door, and Tom waved from the riverbank. I was in time for lunch.

Afterward, Mary and I settled into comfortable chairs with our tea. Efrem, her father, had come to visit: he and Tom sat in the sun talking about a fly-wheel wood splitter Tom had seen at the Alaska State Fair. Tom Junior, with his dirty, impish face, was tootling away on a recorder and trying to catch my eye. Mary, to distract him, suggested he wash his face and hands. He stopped tootling and looked at her, innocence itself: "Why? Don't you like dirt? What's wrong with it?" Rebecca, who was about eight, came in and curled up under her mother's arm.

"She's my grandma," Mary said fondly. "When she was a little, little girl my grandma died. They had the forty days' give-every-thing-away, you know, and my auntie was handing out everything. Rebecca stood up on a table and said, 'I'm Grandma! You stop giving all my things away and give some to me!' My auntie just dropped everything, she was scared. That's why she likes Rebecca so much." Rebecca said, "I was just little then, I don't remember." A sweet, sly smile slipped around her mouth.

o

THE AFTERNOON had declined to a hush. Mary was sewing, and the children, including the two oldest girls, finished their chores outdoors. Efrem had gone home.

"He used to find moose when everyone was hungry and had no luck," Tom said gently of his father-in-law. We were sitting on the front steps, watching the creek tumble by. "He could feed the whole village. Now he's just about the only one who can't make out a grocery order."

Tom was small and quick, and had kept his Down East accent even after a dozen years in the bush. He had met Mary and her three young children when he worked in the cinnabar mine at Red Devil; they had married not long afterward and had had two more children. He was still confused at times by the convoluted relationships in her family. Outsiders could not help but be confused, he thought; everything was subtle, subtle.

Chida and Chada had run the village until their very old age. Now they were gone, and things were falling apart. Fyodor, with his wrinkled face and cunning grin, was known for playing the fool in the white man's world: he hustled up to the mail plane and introduced himself and asked all the young women from the school district to marry him, he needed a new wife. Visiting lobbyists and corporation men knew he was partial to whiskey, and they had bought his support, or his vote, more than once.

Efrem was a silent man, not given to public talk; but lately he and Fyodor had been arguing with one another, and their aging sisters took positions, further dividing them, or remained neutral. He stayed in a tiny cabin half-buried in the ground, living without a wife, as he had lived since Mary's mother passed away, when Mary was very young. After Chida went, when Rebecca was little, he had begun to lose heart. A summer ago, two of his favorite nephews, who lived at the mouth of the Stony, drowned. He had put off making his annual visit to their family. His sadness would not go away.

"We're going to move," Tom said after a while. "At the end of the month." He named a village farther north; he would be the only teacher there.

Surprised, I asked why.

"Family politics. It's too much for us, and the older girls want to try something new."

Most of the young cousins, the schoolchildren, had asked to go along with them.

"Everybody thinks we're going to a better place," Tom said. "They ask to come along: I say 'Yes; you don't have to give money or anything.' This lets them think it over, then decide to stay. But they can always say, 'I decided not to go.' Keeps the local balance."

o

MARY'S GRANDPARENTS, Chada and Chida, had brought her up. Her *chida*, who came from a Yukon tribe, had first taken her out to the woods. Whenever they had gone to pick berries, the old lady had instructed the little girl about birds and animals.

"My grandma could understand them," Mary said, as we sat together after dinner. "Especially camprobber. She taught me how to hear him."

"He spoke English?"

"I'm not sure," she said, considering. "I can't explain it. Maybe owl, though, speaks any language.

"Camprobber always announced visitors. He would land on a bush outside our door and tell his tale. I would say to Tom that someone was coming, and someone always came. He learned not to laugh when this happened.

"When we lived downriver, near the mine, camprobber kept visiting, announcing. But no one came. I got worried that something was going to happen. One day I heard him again and I went upstairs to lie down. Then Tom came home and told me about that air crash." The crash had happened in Village Below, a few years before I was there. Mary's aunt and the aunt's son-in-law were killed; the son-in-law, a white man, was the pilot. Just after take-

off, before the shocked eyes of the watching village, the plane had plunged
into the ice. In memorium, the wreck had been left untouched; it stood, rust-
ing, a scrap-heap monument, its nose buried in the snow.

"I listened," she said, "and just lay there for a long, long time. I didn't speak,
I just stared at the ceiling. The kids thought something was wrong with me."

Her grandfather had offered to teach her animal songs so that she could
call the animals and ask them favors. She had refused him.

"I wasn't a good enough person to have that power," she said. "My dad
was a good person, until lately. He drinks more than he should. He gets angry
sometimes.

"When I was young, my cousins always teased me, because I stayed with
my grandma. Maybe they thought she liked me better than she liked them.
My mama was gone, and I didn't have anybody else. My dad worked hard; I
didn't complain. But then I got older, and I got angry. I snapped back at them,
and complained about them. It's better not to have the power of the animals
when you feel like that."

"Be wary of power," Tom had suggested. "It was bum how they used it
here. Efrem threw away what he had of it, and he's happier now. People are
afraid, and that's why Christianity looks good to them."

o

IN THE MORNING everyone rose in a leisurely way. Mary fried hotcakes and
boiled whitefish for breakfast. The fish was for Efrem, who had come up from
the village in his boat, and who preferred Native food. Tom had promised:
"When you come, we'll take you out for a boat ride." After breakfast we set
out: four adults and the youngest ones, Tom Junior and Rebecca, in a leaky
aluminum boat, heading down the creek and up the river for The Gorge.

Earlier in the summer, Sara, their teenaged girl, had navigated the family
boat through that difficult canyon (none of the village boys had done it yet,
said Tom cheerfully); along the way she had dropped a moose at two hundred yards. Because the village always needed meat, he had taught her how to
poach, on the theory that an underaged girl would not be prosecuted for taking a moose out of season.

The summer had been rainy, the water high; but the rivers now were dropping fast. Berries were scarce everywhere. The bears were hungry, people said.
The week before, pilots had reported seeing sixteen black bears along the
bank near one village on the Yukon. In McGrath, people warned that bears
were coming near the dump. Everyone was more careful; no one walked out
without a gun. On an outside wall of Tom and Mary's house two new black-
bear skins were stretched to dry.

We passed the fish camp where Efrem's sister Alice had fished with her
sons that summer. Their tents were still up, although no one was camped
there.

A golden eagle soared over the hills.

Tom pointed to a Russian church and graveyard, a few grave markers near the ridge of the hill. There had been a village once. It was unclear why the people had left: a flood after breakup? Tom did not know.

Up on a high bank sat a fish camp, stark against the sky. The fish box and cutting table stood down near the shoreline. A fish-wheel had been drawn up on the bar. Mary said her father claimed the place; Tom had helped built the smokehouse. Emma and her husband Alec Ivan had used it that summer.

Tom waved toward the spot where Sara had shot her moose.

It took a long time to go upriver. Efrem sat easily at the "kicker," his back firm and upright. When he was a boy and young man, no one had used boats with kickers: his relatives had walked through the country, or had built canvas or bark canoes; they had speared fish and bear and had hunted game with bows and arrows. His sister in Village Below had told me how she, too, had hunted that way with her brothers.

Tom had said of Efrem that, as he traveled through the day he was ready: he had that quality of alertness, of acute attention given to his surroundings, that fathers taught their sons was needed for the hunt. Sons, Tom suspected, did not often know what being ready required of them. The older man set up his day: he checked its possibilities, and set useless information to one side. Young people, without the long years of discipline behind them, watched him, and thought he passed through time in a leisurely way; they saw him seem to saunter along, or to lie back against the wall, dreaming, and called him relaxed, spontaneous. They were wrong, Tom said earnestly: the man's discipline was not only muscular; it was spiritual.

Tom had practiced his lecture on his young brother from back East, who had spent part of the summer with them: Tom thought he had nonsensical ideas about life in the bush. Mary had told me about that brother; she thought he was lazy.

She had said that her father still saw well, if not so far as he used to; he was slower, but still quick to spot an important thing. He read the river and steered around rocks and snags. His face was immobile: his dark eyes moved, without seeming to move.

o

ABOVE THE PLACE on Tin Creek where Sara had shot her moose, we entered The Gorge. All at once the banks soared above us and shaded the light. The boat bounced on the choppy current and carried us between slate and shale walls sloping, jagged, into the river: the water had eaten them in and out, in and out. Efrem maneuvered closed to their sharp edges, following the channel.

One bluff stood out from those around it. The children, delighted, shouted: "Where Nick found the hawk!"

Nick was their handsome older cousin. On Sara's birthday, a group of the cousins had gone on a boat ride up to The Gorge; Nick, daring, had scaled the cliff and carried down a fledgling fish hawk for Sara. At home she fed it meat and dried fish. One night around midnight she had heard it call, and had gone outside. She had watched the hawk circle; swoop to the edge of the water; skim off.

The hawk was gone. The children had teased her, saying she had spoiled it. Maybe it learned to hunt, Nick had said, to comfort her.

I never saw slate walls like those anywhere else in that country. They rose twenty and thirty feet above the water; and sent forth protection, as mountains do. They were a test of rock, a face that appeared immobile, until the watcher looked back, across time, and saw the seams graven in it. I saw green growth clinging to edges; owls' nests; *the hawk*; the fast lime water. Mary remarked that the walls were changing, that the shale broke off easily. Tom told his son to pay attention, he would have to navigate before very much longer. Efrem kept us off the rocks.

Above The Gorge, he and Tom glanced at one another. He spoke; Tom nodded once. He cut the boat cross-channel to the point of an island, and we tied up noiselessly.

Now everyone whispered, and Efrem, Tom, and Mary each carried a .30-.30. We split into pairs. Mary and I moved off to the left; Tom and Tom Junior, Efrem and Rebecca were going to try to drive a moose our way.

"Holler like hell!" Efrem instructed.

Mary and I cut through willows and birches. I saw plenty of moose sign, and she pointed to recent tracks. We had to cross a silty little stream. Mary stepped into quicksand and, surprised, managed to scamper across it. She grinned, and imagined the moose's surprise when he stepped into that stuff.

We came upon some old, cut willows spread neatly on the bank: someone had butchered a moose. (We learned that Tom and Alec Ivan, Emma's husband, had done it, months before.) We saw no fresh sign and heard no sound from the others.

"Keep looking," Mary said, and I moved downstream, cutting in through the brush. I saw plenty of old sign, but nothing fresh. Where the brush grew down to the water was an old track, where a moose had once crossed.

I circled back to the noisy stream. We traded places.

Almost at once Mary moved her head, waving me back, and whispered that she had just found a fresh print, a caribou's. It was so fresh she figured I had missed him by minutes; he may even have crossed the stream behind me. I stood still. She considered the next move.

When she was a little girl, she said softly, her dad and her grandpa had brought her here. She had never seen a moose, it was all new to her. "I looked hard at a stump, like the ones kids used to play airplane on: it was walking toward me! I shouted to my grandpa, 'That stump's moving!' He shot it. My first moose." She smiled.

A bump; then another. Both of us started: a shot? Too muffled; what, then? Two planes came into sight, Supercubs. She watched them closely as they flew by. Hunters, she supposed, coming from Anchorage through Merrill Pass; spotters. Moose season would open the next week.

A clacking sound, stone struck on stone: Efrem and Rebecca (with her stones) appeared. Tom and Tom Junior walked out of the brush across from them. The adults compared notes. Mary described the fresh track, and the men moved out to check, circling back into the trees, this time inside a shorter radius. Mary and I again were the lookouts. We found nothing more, no animals; no other sign than the caribou's print.

We regrouped. Indelicately, Tom remarked that he could taste the meat in his mouth. His father-in-law said nothing and turned back to the boat.

In the file, Tom walked ahead of me. He murmured, an aside, that we had missed our only chance, and we probably would not sight game. Efrem, who heard without seeming to listen, said mildly, "We could try another place." Tom looked surprised, and blushed.

Upriver, Efrem guided the boat to a spot below some rapids. We landed on a gravel bar, and made a fire for tea. Tom and Mary recalled a party of Swedes who had tried running the rapids that summer and been forced to portage most of the stretch. Downstream, later, people found some of their floating gear.

Efrem and Tom took rifles and set off up the beach, and soon passed out of sight. Within minutes a couple of empty gas cans, lashed together, came bobbing down the river toward our camp. A shout, a scramble; Mary snagged them. The children danced around the find and made up a song. Mary thought her father must have come across the cans and had not cared to pack them out.

As Tom Junior and Rebecca played on the beach, she told me a little more about their coming move: they were going to leave Hungry before the autumn set in. She was for it, if only to let the older girls have more experience among other people; they needed to meet boys who were not their cousins. She smiled, a little sadly, and remarked that this would be their last ride to The Gorge for a while.

While the children built a cabin out of driftwood, I climbed a hill above the bank. I was careful to stay within sight of Mary on the beach; and she kept her rifle handy. I found a few, very few, blueberries. When Efrem and Tom appeared, I scrambled down, and reached them just as they were drinking the last of their tea. The fire had been covered and the gear packed up. We gathered in the boat, and Tom shoved off. Efrem turned the boat downstream and we headed home.

○

ALL DAY THE SKY had been heavy with the clouds of a weather front that extended almost as far as the eye could travel. Suddenly, splendor broke through the gray cover and shards of light glinted off the rippling water. Shadows of the late day lengthened across the river. It was as if the boat had brought us this far in a dream-moment, and, without our knowing time had passed, signs of autumn had appeared between our going up and our coming down. Already, cottonwoods glowed as if lit from within. On the alders shimmered a few golden leaves. The green-browns of the brush had deepened; now, near evening, a breath of crisp air against the skin anticipated snow: soon, on the mountains. I looked back at the mountains above The Gorge. Clouds were closing down on their summits. That was how the snow would come: there would be a frost, and then another frost; ravens; low clouds lying on the mountains. One dawn, very soon, the first white line would be drawn across the peaks.

When Efrem's fish camp came into sight, he landed the boat and walked uphill ahead of us to look the place over. For a long minute his silhouette was small and dark against the sky. Then it was moving again; and we followed.

The camp held the peace of recent habitation. The remains of human movement—a tent frame, a pole-bed frame, a small piece of tin tacked up as a bedside table, a fire pit—lightened the huge country around us and told us tales of activity. Someone had been lying on the bed. Perhaps he had lain under a canvas roof, reading by candlelight on a cool night, with warm embers glowing in the pit. Nearby was a little cabin shingled with spruce bark: a story of warm days, people cutting fish down by the water, a daughter boiling spaghetti over the outdoor cook-fire near the doorway. Over there stood a big double-smokehouse, the sun fuzzing the gaps in its planked sides, the interior cool and dim. The stoves had been set back against the walls, fish-skin boots folded and hung over rafters, sheets of Visqueen folded and piled high off the floor. The throaty smells of alder smoke and fish oil smoldered in the wooden boards.

Outside, four stakes stood driven into the ground, for measuring dryfish into bundles of forty. A wash basin had been turned over to drain. A few tin cans lay about; a pile of Pampers and a faded box had not been burned. Mary was irked by the trash left behind.

Tom walked farther uphill to examine the tipi poles: during the summer his two boys had camped there. Rebecca and Tom Junior uncovered a length of antler and took turns playing caribou, holding the antler against their head, tossing it as they charged around in a circle. Mary decided to carry it home and saw it up for a buckle. Her father moved deliberately around the camp, checking equipment, testing the lock on the cabin door, settling small things back into place.

The sun began to dip. We pushed off again; there was still the chance of a moose.

A distance below the camp we neared another island. Tom and Efrem nodded to one another: Efrem touched the boat ashore and put Tom off in the brush, then drove us fast around the point to the other side. Mary, the children, and I waited on the beach; Efrem sat in the boat, watching, holding the motor on low idle. It sounded like a soft warning growl. He sat at ease, hunched over his gun. His head turned slowly as he studied the stream. When the children made more noise than necessary, he ignored them and left it to Mary to quiet them. Behind us, the brush was still.

Tom reappeared on the bank. Within moments we were back in the boat; Efrem had gunned the motor; and we were landing again, when a shout went up: "A porcupine!"

The children jumped out and went splashing ashore after the animal. Up a hill it ran, the children running close behind it, and then came the rustle of bodies thrashing about in the brush. "I got it! I got it!" Tom Junior cried.

At once his father stood beside him calmly reminding both children not to get in the way of the lashing tail. The porcupine stirred: Tom prodded it with a heavy stick and turned it over. Tom Junior held the axe as if it were a club and—*thud*—hit the stunned animal between the eyes.

Tom Junior and Rebecca bent their heads together, figuring out how to drag the *ninny* downhill. Tom nudged me and said, "Want to see my favorite place?"

He turned on to a path into the brush and trotted up a hill covered with muskeg. I followed more slowly, stepping from tussock to tussock to avoid the damp low spots. The rustle of water filled the air. We climbed over the top of a bank and made a half-circle along its lip, until we came upon a small waterfall in a pretty mountain stream. The air was cool; autumn was further along in the higher elevation. The stream tumbled away over stones.

Tom scrambled down the rock face and crouched on a ledge, looking out over the country, wrapped in his thoughts. I lifted my head, and caught my breath: across the canyon, a wall of purple mountains; beyond it, wall upon wall of blue-green mountains, falling away to the horizon like a long, rolling ocean.

The sun was dropping. Quickly we got underway. Rebecca and Tom Junior had curled up, little eaglets, in a nest of down coats, where they giggled and talked to each other as the boat carried us steadily down the river. There was one last flurry of excitement: a shout of "Porcupine!," a fast beaching, and it was Rebecca's turn to take the animal; a fat one.

"Umm," she said, "I LOVE porcupine." She and her brother compared kills for a while, and decided the next one would be mine. But there was no next one; and darkness settled down on us as we reached the cabin.

At home, the two older girls had cooked dinner. We were hungry and chilly and had wet feet, and were glad for the ease of the table. Efrem ate heartily; he had taken little food all day. The good meal was boiled fish, dryfish and dry meat, and rice, stirred with green peppers I had brought to Mary. Afterward the adults talked for a little while, then headed to bed.

By the light of a lard lamp, a lump of Crisco stuck in a small tin, with a piece of string for a wick, I read "Bach's Concerto No. 1 in C Minor," by the Turkish poet Nazim Hikmet.

. . . .

> *The repetition of my days*
> *that are alike,*
> *that are not alike.*

> *The repetition of the weave in the weaving,*
> *the repetition in the starry sky,*
> *and the repetition of "I love" in all languages.*
> *The repetition of the tree in the leaves*
> *and of the pain of living, which ends in an instant*
> *and on every deathbed. . . .*

I slept deeply. The quiet was broken only by the rustle of the cat, who daintily, thoroughly, ate a piece of dryfish. I stirred, and a sweet memory returned, of the end of the day on the water.

Just before we entered Mary's creek, not far below the cabin, I had looked up and seen a hawk against the limpid evening sky. It circled and swooped toward the bank. No one else saw it.

Traps

BY LATE AUGUST the mosquitoes were gone and we caught the faint wet smell of early snow in the mountains. After the idyll in Hungry, I was back in McGrath. New teachers were arriving in the villages. The district office suddenly was busy again. Daylight ebbed; the school year was about to begin.

In that country everything is connected; but not everything exists with the same intention. McGrath was one kind of place, and Hungry was another. Think of them as rhomboid and spherical; think of them now intersecting. What kind of extravagant geometric figure do they make? What do I see in the crystalline light? In the long darkness?

The school district had a great deal of money. Alaska was still excited by the oil boom. The state, rich with money, poured oil royalties into the public sector, inflating the bureaucracies. Middle-class white people with college educations moved into shabby river towns like McGrath and Bethel and Galena. They were building the new public life by writing manuals, arranging files, describing jobs, and organizing them into categories. New offices advertised for persons qualified by education and training and, sometimes, by rural background, words that carried an undercurrent of "Native" or "non-Native." Level upon level, Alaskans were constructing their modern hierarchies. You could watch, even participate in, the rationalization of authority; it was Weberian.

At that time, the settlement act was being worked out. In 1971, Congress had settled about forty million acres and nearly one hundred million dollars on two tiers of corporations. The corporations, established by the act, were owned by Native people; that is, they were owned by individual Native shareholders. All Alaska Natives born before December 21, 1971, were qualified to hold these shares. (Babies born afterward became, for some time, a new class of people, whom the villagers came to call the "afterborn.") The corporations were given twenty years in which to organize and grow profitable, before other investors could buy the shares, and thus acquire the assets they stood for, as the logic of capitalism requires. At a blow, Alaska Native people had come face to face with the power of capital, and were confronted by its engines: corporate finance and the market. They had had to comprehend what it meant to own their land by deed, to turn into capitalists, in order to keep and manage their remaining lands. They had to make sense of capitalism, as the Eastern European nations have had to do since 1989, and in somewhat similar ways.

Everything is connected. In the villages of our district the people needed whatever the schools could give their children that would help them prepare for the future. But they, adults and students, already had to manage in the suddenly altered present. What was happening to them? Why? They needed the skill and nerve to ask questions.

What could the public schools give them? What was an education for the new order of their world?

Picture the teachers. One by one, they go out to the bush filled, often, with a sense of benign, enlightening mission. A long plane ride cuts them off from their former world, and they find themselves in a strange country, one they had always thought (without realizing it) was their own. And there they are put in charge of children's lives.

Suppose a village is like the body. Suppose the organ of its life is the heart: not just the pumping heart, circulating life-blood, but the heart of feeling, of vivid reason that grows from shared emotion and the vital life of the senses; and from that heart grows the imagination. Suppose a village is a body, breathing. The body wants, instinctively and more than anything, to live.

Now, suppose a bureaucracy—let us say, that of a smaller school district, with a dozen administrators and thirty-odd teachers for an area the size of Ohio—is like a brain; or, better, like a computer, which is the projection of a certain kind of intelligence: a very simple computer, which adds and subtracts but is not capable of complex operations. It does what it is told to do, is happy when it has routines to follow. Its agents know what they are supposed to do, because they've got a program (one of several, competing programs) to follow. They want to make sure that their whole organization can follow the program: it has been approved.

Now, recognize that, of necessity, teachers don't feel like parts of a computer. A teacher is an individual. He can teach arithmetic very well to fourth-graders. She needs to provide for her old age. His wife left him, and he drinks alone in his trailer. She thinks Native children are disadvantaged and wants to help them. He loves children, and is engaged to an Athabaskan girl. She has taught in three Eskimo villages and wants to become the first female superintendent in the state. He's lived here for ten years and despises Natives. But these teachers all belong to the district, which is a quasigovernmental organization, although they never think of it that way.

No matter what we thought, however, or how much we resisted the idea, we all belonged to something.

Now I belonged to the district. I denied it, and I went to Shelter to pretend it was not so, and went to Malfa for a life away from offices, a life of the heart. Malfa Ivanov was not the district, and was not McGrath, she was my friend and my mother. She listened to my troubled dreams. Yet I entered her world cautiously; yet, with relief. I was an outsider, but hardly an observer. I was a seeker, I suppose. The deadening idiom of bureaucracy was spreading through the country and carried with it its pragmatic logic and its devotion to routine, as if there were nothing larger than the organization and its functions, and its impersonal desires.

○

PERHAPS I MAY remember what happened from another point of view. I consider: A man forms his ideals—from what material of the heart? How then does he live them out in the world?

Can one living person know these things about another? Don't these questions hover around us when we try to make what sense we can of our lives?

○

IN LIBERAL CIRCLES our district was considered progressive, perhaps the most progressive in the state. This was because of the superintendent.

He had come to McGrath from a port town on the Kuskokwim delta. There, he had been the principal of a Yup'ik elementary school. In his tenure he had made a practice of listening to parents and asking their advice. He was spoken about for this; it was a novel practice. When he came to McGrath, he declared that he was working now for the school board, and said that parent committees had to be given a voice in the new schools: it was the law. He told his staff that he thought they could—must—organize a new curriculum around subjects that were necessary for life in the villages.

The superintendent believed in students, in their possibility. He held that schools ought to give them a chance to change their lives for the better.

Much of one's worldly education is about other people's ideas and beliefs, which one might not share; nonetheless, it is advisable to know how they think, and why they think that they act as they do. In that light, I would call the superintendent a politician, in one real sense of the word. More than anything, he acknowledged the existence of the community and respected the fact of the polity. Above all, he respected its status quo.

"Everything is political," he would say. I used to object when he said it. But, patiently, he explained the system to me, for it justified him in his position.

His job was to oversee the schools in the eight Native villages with Athabaskan and Yup'ik populations, and McGrath, which was a white town. In each village he had taken care to measure the social standing of every family, and the respect given its head. He kept his office door open. It was true that any person could speak to him at any time. He listened; but he knew the status within the family of each person to whom he listened. He measured that family's relationship to its village representative on the district board, and compared the standing of that member to the others on the board. By these calculations he estimated public opinion.

I argued that this was a good way to ignore the substance of any issue.

"Everything is political," he replied, with a twisted smile.

And yet, he did not want to be the big man. He didn't want to tell people what to do. Responsibility and authority went together for him. They were the power that achievement offered the powerless, although he never used that word. He believed that local control, as the phrase went, was a fact, and knew he could not succeed without the agreement of the board. He thought that his political skill lay in pointing out the logic of any situation, not in forcing the members' decision. In public, he was patient with this democratic process. I think he had decided that Native people were still learning all the requirements of schools. And yet, he was nervously attuned to those who held the reins of actual power.

Was he certain of anything else? He was considered indecisive, because he side-stepped controversy, and he was cowed by professors from the university. He was amazed at how much money the district had to disburse. (One day he showed me a check from the state: "A million dollars!" he whispered.) I suppose he was even unsettled by me; he found it remarkable that I spoke to him as forthrightly as I did.

He also was insecure with Athabaskans and confided to me that he didn't understand their manners. He could not tell what they thought. He had felt at ease with Yup'ik people, he was used to them. Later, when things got rougher, he quietly looked into the possibility of going back to the Kuskokwim delta. (I turned down his shadow offer of a job, because I had no experience among Yup'iks and doubted I would be useful. He told me I was too honest, as though I had admitted some sort of weakness, or lacked ambition.)

He was as lonely a man as I knew, and as repressed. Behind his glasses, his pale eyes sank into a face that had no flesh on it. When he smiled, the smile looked like a wince; the eyes looked pained, as if he had once been punished for smiling, and had learned something awful from that. His awkward body was like a stick-puppet's, held together by wires. I feel there was a great tenderness in him; like that around a bruise.

He was the descendant of German Lutherans and came from the Midwest. "I was born on the wrong side of the tracks," he said once. His voice was as taut as a wire.

Why did he reveal this to me? Because I asked him why a person would become a school administrator. I said I thought education was a questionable field of study in the university. I argued that was a course of training where emotions and prejudices were cast in unspeakable jargon, and masqueraded as ideas, and where meager statistics were used as verified facts; and all done to support the status quo: the "old boys" in charge. I pointed out that schools in the bush were doing very little that was good for the kids and said I thought this was terribly wrong. And I thought the educationists were wrong. I had seen so many children in the bush being harmed by that system, with its careerism and its devotion to mediocrity, and I could not reconcile any of this with my love of learning.

"*I* studied. *I* studied hard, you know. It gave me my chance," he said. His was the kind of pride that is masked as humility. "I have risen by becoming an educator." He said this with dignity, to overcome my lack of respect, but then cried: "Schools have to give students a chance!" He was as passionate as I, in his strained way, and as intense: "Schools exist so students can learn to change! These people have to be able to change!"

A chance. Change. He said the words over and over, like a formula, or a prayer for redemption. I think his faith in the possibility of redemption lived in the center of his heart, and drove him to endure his unhappy life in that wretched town.

The subject of our unending conversations was education; but their theme was how to share power, or, at least, distribute authority, and how to assume responsibility. He believed that, somehow, schools and parents could cooperate with each other. And he believed in change, for how else could the students face the ferocity of our modern economy? I think he saw no irony in his position. He must have known, however, that the word *change* was hated in the villages. There it was taken to mean how white men told the native people to alter their way of life.

○

THERE USED TO BE active Catholic and Episcopalian missions along the Yukon, their territories divided by ecclesiastical treaty. The Catholic missions were founded in the 1880s by priests of the Society of Jesus sent north from the Victoria Province, who built chapels and established small schools, and invited an order of French-Canadian nuns to organize orphanages to house the children they found they had to care for.

One of their missions was built in a boundary place called In the Shelter of the Hill. Malfa, who was brought up in the orphanage there and who told me a small part of all that she knew of its history, said that Shelter ought to take as its symbol the bell and the drum, one beside the other. The bell was the Church, which once had regulated its people's days; the drum, the Native drum, even when it was made to be silent, had beat out the rhythm of their lives.

From the last decades of the nineteenth century until well into the twentieth, wave after wave of epidemics had left many hundreds of children without parents, and without families. Four generations of children, often the youngest, had been sent away by boat on their long voyage to the priests. Yup'ik children had come from the settlements downriver and from the Kuskokwim settlements; Athabaskan children had arrived from the Koyukuk River, and the upriver Yukon villages, and from the Copper River country of the Ahtna, and from the Tanana, and the upper Kuskokwim; and Aleut children, among them the tiny Malfa and her infant brother and two sisters, had journeyed north from the lower Alaska Peninsula.

Those children were raised to work hard. They learned that they were poor, but, they were told, with hard work they could hope to do well for themselves. They were taught reading, grammar, arithmetic, catechism, penmanship, fine hand work (for the girls), and (for the boys) the manual arts. Their teachers, as far as I could determine, were very good; they were very, very stern; often, they were physically cruel. As was the common practice among whites, the children were forbidden to speak their native languages; much of the time, they were forbidden to speak at all. Their days were organized by schedules, and they slept in dormitories arranged by age groups. The order of their life was described as disciplined. But I must write plainly. Some of those children were chosen by one nun or another for especially hard "discipline." The children endured mistreatment, and never forgot their suffering; nor, I believe, had many people made their peace with it. I myself, brought up in the Church, have not made peace with their stories of it.

The boys, young men at an early age, were sent out to work on the steamboats or in the mining camps. For the maidenly girls the nuns arranged marriages, to men from Shelter or the nearby villages who were considered good providers, or who came from acceptable families. "Watch how he treats his dogs," the Sisters advised the girls: "If he treats his dogs well, he will treat his wife well."

Not long after the arrival of the Sisters, word had gone out that the new mission needed builders. A band of men skilled in carpentry had traveled to Shelter over the portage from the Kuskokwim. Those men were the Ivanov brothers, Athabaskan sons of a Russian creole trader. They were fine artisans, and they built the first church. They remained to work at the mission; they lived in the village that had grown up around it. Each of them married, and, together, they founded what grew to become an important family in the Interior.

During the same period, a Scots trader named Gordon had built a trading post about a mile upriver from the mission. He married a local woman and established his own influential family, one whose men were less friendly than the Ivanovs were to the Jesuits. Gordon's trading post flourished, and his family settlement grew up around it. During my first visit to Shelter I had boarded with the grandmother of this family, old Gordon's daughter-in-law, a widow living down in the village. Her granddaughter, who was my age, told me their history.

The mission had been built, as it happened, in the boundary area between a tribe of Yup'ik Eskimos, whose nearest village was about twenty-five miles downriver, and the Athabaskan tribes native to the area. Spread out along both upriver banks were settlements, whose people spoke at least two distinct Athabaskan languages. They were numerous, I was told, until waves of epidemics began to carry them away. In Shelter, as in every Interior village, the older people carried heavy memories of death. A robust elder told us of hav-

ing gone as a boy with the priest to a sickened village, where he had seen so
many bodies that no one was left to bury the dead. The priest had wrapped
them in blankets and lowered the tents on them. In the mission, the young
women (old women, now) had scrubbed his cassock for days to erase the
green rot from it.

Across the river had stood a large Athabaskan village, a separate place
whose people followed their own way of life. Their relations with the mission were conducted formally. I was told how women, dressed in beaded caps
and finely worked parkas, crossed the river to earn wages by sewing for the
Sisters; men in furs cut wood for pay. The mission children watched them
come and go. Seldom did any child dare to say a word to them. Old women
would tell me from wondering memory about those people ("Those ladies
sat on the floor! Not us."); and still they registered the shudder of fascina-
tion that something forbidden, yet not unknown, not quite forgotten, star-
tles in the imagination.

In Village Across had lived a powerful medicine man and his gifted wife,
whose *kashim* was for decades at the center of communal life. At least until
the 1930s spirit medicine was practiced widely. Medicine men of the area were
well known. The Jesuits preached against them, saying they practiced devilry,
and forbade them to the people who depended on the mission. A pious, elderly lady, who would not hear a word spoken against her beloved priests,
whispered to me how they had warned her to keep her sons away from their
own uncle. "They said he was a devil doctor. But my sons might have been
medicine men!" she had cried in regret, fifty years later, and had then closed
her mouth and put her hand over it.

The medicine men had fought the priests, power for power, in intense spiritual battle. Stories about this were still told, and I heard several of them, but
in Shelter they were never told if the priests might hear about them. The
priests would retaliate by shaming the tellers in front of the village for speaking badly of them.

The shaped past that is history does not go away, although it may recede
from sight. It exists within a community along a series of trails through the
lighted and hidden parts of its memories; and an outsider knows little of it.
I write in brief of what I saw, and heard, and was told; and I write of what I
believe I saw living through those people I knew. In Shelter, the Athabaskan
and Yup'ik families guarded their identities, although there was intermarriage. Lineages and adoptions were traced carefully; names were important.
The matriarchs of the families were strong-minded, pious gentlewomen,
conciliators and keepers of homes; their husbands were strong-willed, hard-
driving men. Priests and nuns had lived out their lives and died, and were
buried in the cemetery: they, too, were an inescapable part of the village, the
people who had been—not parents, but those who reared the generations.
Through Shelter ran the lines of old boundaries of suffering, of birth and
marriage and death, of family love in its twists and turns, of religious battles

and economic strivings, of power and influence. Its history was composed of families, which included orphans: but it was so composed in a complicated way for, many people felt, deeply, that the village was not united. When I stayed with old Mrs. Gordon, her granddaughter had explained this feeling to me. *Not united:* the words were hers. The mission had brought together Yup'iks and Athabaskans of separate tribes, and all those people were living near each other. It was an unnatural situation. "People want to be with their own kind," she had said, as if it were obvious. But it was not obvious to me, and I puzzled over it.

The orphanage at Shelter had been closed for thirty years. The boarding school that had grown out of it had been transferred to the Copper River country. Nothing of the mission was left. The priests had condemned the church as a fire hazard, and had mobilized the men to pull it down. Women had gone to them, their hearts breaking, but had not been able to stop the bulldozers. The steeple of their beautiful church had collapsed, and its great bell had been carried away. Those women, old ladies now, still mourned. They had loved the intense spiritual life of the mission and always longed for it.

○

THE SCENT OF early snow freshened the air when the new principal moved out to Shelter.

He was an imposing man, tall and heavy, with black, unkempt hair and a rumbling voice. I don't remember his name, or where he came from. I recall a cloudiness of spirit about him, something angry and unresolved in his manner, but it may be that I saw this afterward. He has a masters degree in cross-cultural education, the superintendent announced to us, impressed. Has he worked with Indians? or Eskimos? I asked. No, replied the superintendent, annoyed by my questions.

○

IN THEIR PRACTICAL good sense, their brisk way of taking charge, the Ivanov women reminded me of my father's sisters. The eldest was Pauline, always called Polly; she was my father's age, and a grandmother. Recently, she had come back to live in Shelter, with her second husband. They owned the village store. She was a poised and seasoned traveler and a natural hostess; she was the only woman on the district board, when the board's chief business was the construction of new schools. When the superintendent went to Shelter, she invited him and his staff, including me, to her house. She poured out wine and, after the political gossip had been enjoyed, told us ghost stories. She thought people in Shelter were superstitious, but I suspected that she half-believed the stories.

Anna Ivanov had been brought up in the mission and was married to Polly's youngest brother. Kind Anna was the school's cook. She was the heart of the school; her kitchen, its place of refuge. By late morning the warm yeast smell of baking bread wafted into the classrooms and encircled the students like arms held out to them. I used to stop by to visit her, and I always saw some youngster there and watched his dismal face grow clear as she set him to do some distracting task: Anna was bread and consolation.

And there was Malfa, whose husband was Polly's cousin. I think she may have been running for the village school committee when the trouble began, but I am not certain of this. In any case, I know she told me the disturbing news about the principal, and I know why she told it to me.

The man had a temper, and it frightened people. I had learned this from Anna. Not that she had said a word: she wouldn't risk her job by criticizing a teacher; I overheard it in her kitchen, from unhappy students, and I saw the strain on her face. Malfa took me aside and told me what was really going on. Appalled, she said that the principal smoked marijuana, and that he had shared his grass with the high-school boys and young men who hung around his trailer. Parents were alarmed by this. (I doubt she knew how many kids used drugs.) The school committee could not stop him. Some members still supported him, and he knew how to bully the others. Would the district do something about him?

I saw unhappiness in the school and heard drifts of conversation. People looked dismayed and uncertain. Schoolteachers had once held an authority equal to missionaries' and game wardens'; many of them had assumed the habit of power, and many had come to take it as their due. Polly, who was a woman among the men on the board, was discreet about what she knew; Anna was intimidated. Malfa was using me as a channel of communication to the superintendent; but I was not the only one asked to deliver the message. The village hoped he would speak to the principal. People dreaded an open confrontation.

o

THE SUPERINTENDENT did not like what he heard. Was there proof? Who had started the rumors? Wasn't Malfa running for a seat? Wasn't her opponent a Gordon? Someone might not like the principal, he said decisively, but that was no reason to get rid of him. There were no official complaints; his hands were tied.

o

MONTHS PASSED. I traveled around the district and up to Fairbanks. In McGrath, I scrambled to catch up with the paperwork and my laundry. I heard nothing from Malfa for a long time, and didn't go to Shelter again until early spring.

In the meantime, some talk floated around the office. At the district there was always an undercurrent of impatience, even resentment, an unspoken feeling that Shelter was uncooperative.

So I heard with only half an ear what had been happening. Some parents, I didn't know who, had circulated a petition to remove the principal. But the principal still had supporters, because he controlled jobs, and he had made friends, including the mayor, an unmarried Yup'ik man who lived with his mother, who taught her native Yup'ik in the school and needed the income it brought her. The supporters circulated a counter-petition.

The superintendent muttered that he was not going to be drawn into political infighting. They could not run the principal out without due process. If people had a problem with him, the school committee had to settle it, it was their responsibility.

●

BY WINTERTIME, the high-school students had begun to stay away from school.

In March I had business in Shelter. Malfa came to see me, and told me how unhappy the students were. They hated conflict, she said; it made them feel sick. Parents were asking her for advice, they didn't know what to do. They were afraid of the principal.

Anna's eyes were troubled, but she would say nothing. I understood that she felt safer if I stayed out of the kitchen.

Polly let us know that the board would take no position until the village committee agreed to act. She was impatient with the committee, whose members remained at an impasse.

In McGrath, the superintendent announced that until he heard a unified voice from the village, he could do nothing. But the students' absences worried him, because the district's subsidy from the state depended upon "average daily attendance." What were classified as "unexcused absences"—the boycott by the students—would cause a reduction in funds next fiscal year.

I suggested he ought to listen to Malfa. He called her an agitator.

Sphere and rhombus: Shelter and McGrath. They intersect. What strange geometrical figure has been fashioned?

At the district offices, the old hands, who had lived in the bush a long time, said the talk of local control was a joke: Natives always looked to an outside authority. They could never make a hard decision, they wanted a white man to solve their problems, and would not admit it. They were divided, said the old hands, they wanted a scapegoat, to take the pressure off themselves.

In Shelter, someone desecrated the little chapel where the visiting priest said Mass; this hurt the old ladies deeply. Minor vandalism occurred at the school. Litter appeared in the road and the yards looked shabby. More people were drinking again; some of the younger people were having parties every night. Emotions were frayed. No one knew what would happen, and everyone knew. They knew, and they feared it. They longed for relief.

●

EVEN THE MOST cautious parents began to tell each other how lazy the principal was. Others said they saw him come to school stoned. Scandalous statements about him circulated freely. One afternoon, someone took a shot at him.

This happened late in the day, when he was alone in the school. A group of young men had gathered in the yard. One of them called him out. When he appeared on the porch, someone else aimed a .22 in his direction and squeezed off a round.

The news came over the CB radio, our only means of communication with the village schools. The district office was electric. Administrators ran in and out. Shelter is a wild and violent place! they cried indignantly: They're drunk, and the drunks all carry guns!

The teachers in the other villages were informed of the incident by radio. Caution was advised.

For a day or two I stayed away from the office. I thought about fear, and Anna's face, and Malfa's urgent message of warning; I thought about the principal and the authority of teachers, and the authority of white men; I thought about the law.

I went to the superintendent. Listen, I said: This is what happened. People were afraid of that man. He did wrong. This grieved them, but no one knew how to stop him. You wouldn't listen when they spoke quietly. The district wouldn't get him out of there, and they didn't know how to do it in Shelter without fighting among themselves. They avoid that, public disagreement pains them.

Pay attention, I said: this was not done for nothing. That shooter was not some juvenile delinquent, or a drunk with a gun. People cannot stand the pressure. He acted out what no one would resolve.

The superintendent stared at me as though I had just come down from the moon. "How can you always be so sure of yourself?" he asked.

For weeks he debated with himself about a course of action.

In the district office, the tide of feeling began to turn against the principal. The people on the staff had not much cared for him; he had never tried to fit in with them. No one stood up for him. But they stood up for themselves. With a shiver, they realized that any one of them could be the next target, if more shots were going to be fired. With their anxiety came indecision: What do we do now? Who are these people? And came false toughness: When are they going to stop the drinking!

In the villages, particularly in Shelter, teachers were isolated. A few of them recognized what was in the air and turned to their friends for protection.

In Shelter the adults and the old people suffered. They were appalled at how the principal had had to be driven out. They were sad for their young man, who was going to have to pay for his act. They were embarrassed, because the village was being talked about all over the state. They feared what the whites might do to them. They worried about the anger of their young people; they worried about containing their own anger. They turned masked faces to the teachers.

And so, for different reasons, everyone was afraid, even those who had been angry.

The school year ended without further incident.

Shelter remained quiet. When he felt there was no more risk of provocation, the superintendent announced that the district was obligated to protect its teachers and that it would stand firm against threats. He filed charges against the young man who had fired the shot. For some bureaucratic reason he could not fire the principal; but he found a way to make it difficult for the man to stay, and he left before autumn.

Several years later, the parent committee learned (from people of another village, where he had applied for a job) that the principal's credentials were not quite what he had represented them to be. In Shelter, the hiring committee, including the superintendent, had taken him at his word, as people did then, and had never thought to check his record.

o

IT WAS ALMOST the middle of May. The river ice had gone out earlier than usual. The roads were dry, mosquitoes were active. The superintendent had still not decided what to do about the situation in Shelter. One balmy evening, I dropped by his house.

He was smoking. An empty glass sat on the coffee table. He waved toward the couch, not looking at me. I decided to sit down, and asked how he was going to remove the principal.

He rounded on me in cold fury. He tore apart the villages in the district, and Shelter in particular, and called certain people "scum." "They are like pampered children," he said: "dishonest, unable to take care of themselves." He talked for what seemed a long time.

His boarder, a man named Kenneth, came into the room. Kenneth considered himself well read, and liked to discourse on patterns of conquest in history. He was an ardent Libertarian who, unperturbed by disagreement, stood for the virtues of self-reliance, personal strength, and minimal governance. He held tenure in the district. For three years he had taught in a small village on the upper Kuskokwim, unhappily for himself and the village. Recently he had moved down to McGrath. There were no houses for rent, but the superintendent had an extra room. Kenneth had asked to use it, and the superintendent had not known how to say no. He despised Kenneth.

Kenneth turned on the short-wave radio and picked up Radio New Guinea. The three of us listened to a man read the news. Kenneth commented, "Polynesian nigger." The superintendent laughed shortly and said, "Thick-lipped announcer."

I left.

I had believed we talked to each other for the sake of a greater understanding; that we argued from principle. But the house had been contaminated, and I wished reason would explain to me what sensibility could not stomach. To myself I proposed: He isn't a vicious man, but a vicious mood has fallen on him. Would he have said those things if Kenneth, who is morally reprehensible, did not live with him? How quickly he has poisoned the air.

I considered: The desecration of the chapel, the vandalism in the school, the attack on the principal, the abusive relations we see between village people, the crime-rate: how do we live in the midst of these, without art or music, and maintain our composure?

I reflected: We are the ones who are foreign. I knew he would not agree. Bewildered, I thought: If he feels such contempt for these people, why stay here?

Perhaps I should have remembered what old Mrs. Gordon's granddaughter had told me: "People want to live with their own kind."

I could have said, "The superintendent is not my kind of person," and "Kenneth isn't my kind of person." Is that what she had meant? But we were all in this together. What were we going to do about it?

I accepted: I am the one who is foreign.

❂

THE YOUTH who shot at the principal was arrested and prosecuted. People stood with him. They expected him to go to jail. Before the trial, Malfa's husband took him out to camp.

For a day or two, the older man and the young man worked together.

At last the older man said, "It's good to be out here."

"Yeah," said the young man.

"We prefer it, we don't like to stay indoors."

"No."

"Sometimes we have to do what we don't want to do. We don't like to do it; it's hard. But sometimes we make something go wrong, and we have to make it right again."

"Yes."

"We know it will be hard for you there. We know you can do what you have to do."

The young man was observed by the court to be confused emotionally and not very bright. He was put on probation. He needed counseling by a professional, and also by an elder. He never got professional help; if he got the other, by that time, it was not enough. Four years later, in an act of hatred, he stalked a white man, whose wife was from Shelter, through the village. In an awful mix-up, he shot the wrong man—a different white man, whom he did not know—at the high school dance. He fled into the bush, but soon gave himself up to the law. He was sentenced to prison for ninety-nine years.

I was in Shelter when the killing happened. For a long time I lived with the memory of his terrible act. Now I think he was like many another young man living in a similar situation (there are many young men, and similar situations): weak-minded, inarticulate, brought up in a deeply wounded family, a prey to passion and stronger wills. How did he know what was right; what was wrong? The talk among his peers had been ugly. Like many of their age, they hated white people. His friends had been drinking, and had given him drink, as they had done the other time, for courage.

Deep in the background of that trouble, was more trouble. When the young men who stood in the schoolyard were boys, one teacher had followed them through the elementary grades. I had met him when I first went to Shelter to give poetry; he had preceded the principal as head of the old primary school. He was not promoted, and had moved on to another village. A few years after he left Shelter, he was convicted of molesting children; he seemed to be partial to boys.

All the young men in the schoolyard had been close to that teacher. All of them later got into trouble with guns and alcohol. The adults learned this after the teacher's trial. Some of them believed they understood, at last, why there had been trouble; but they spoke of it gingerly, because of the shame it carried.

As for me, I believe that desperate youth felt bad about himself, as if he were contaminated; and, in atonement, had wanted to do something good for his worried people. And so, taking the way of a young fighter, he had delivered a warning to the one who harmed them, the outsider, the ghost of his past. "He was a crack shot," someone told me. "If he didn't shoot the principal, it was on purpose."

o

THERE IS ANOTHER epilogue to this story.

A new word had come into use: "rural" Alaska. It was meant to signal that the bush, its villages and tribes, was dependent on "urban" Alaska. It was a political word, and it spoke of political and economic control from the outside.

The tribes had always marked out their spiritual and physical boundaries. Every season, they had moved from camp to camp. Their traders and warmakers had traveled across long distances, and had fought or traded with distant tribes. In their movement they had observed an old law, held in common, of the right of passage, that is spoken this way: "You are welcome to pass through our country."

There exists historical memory, put into writing (by me, among others), of this law. Thus, I was instructed that in earlier times the Athabaskan tribes had worked out protocols of warfare. One tribe might find that they needed better hunting land, and so might eye the land used by a neighboring tribe. The needful tribe could decide to open negotiations, perhaps by taking a chief's son hostage, or they could venture, armed, into the new territory and fight the tribe in place for the right to hunt there. In peaceful times, however, people were normally on the move on their seasonal rounds. At such times they were allowed to travel through their neighbors' land. They must, however, follow a marked trail. They could hunt along the way, but only within certain distances of the trail, and they were obliged to report their kill to the chief of the next village.

○

THAT SPRING, Malfa was organizing a conference of elders from the nine villages in our district. It was going to be a large event, like an old-time fur rendezvous, and I was giving her technical support, writing grant proposals, while she had been doing research among the older people. We met to compare notes. It may have been then that she described to me a variation of the old law. She told it as a story that at first I thought was about something else.

There was a new teacher in the village ("Shelter?" "Some place upriver."): he had come to Alaska for the sake of the wilderness. He made friends among the older people and told them he wanted to learn their ways. They were pleased and agreed to help him. They liked it when new people wanted to learn.

He wanted to become an outdoorsman, and he decided to begin by running a trapline. After freeze-up, when the season opened, he bought a bunch of traps and laid them out not too far from the village. He didn't have a snow-machine for traveling around.

The first time he walked out to check the line, he found his traps sprung. This puzzled him. But he was new at it and figured he hadn't placed the traps right, so he reset them; and in a day or two, he went out to check them again. Once more, they were sprung.

Then it happened a third time.

Now he was annoyed. He talked about the sprung traps around the village. He called what had happened *vandalism.*

People didn't care for that word, and were irritated by his loud mouth. They began to be less friendly to him.

What he did not know was that he had crossed someone's line.

A boy in the high school ran a small line of his own nearby. According to the old law, no one else could cross it. The village hunting lands were used more or less in common, but traplines were run by partners, who had the right of way on the line. They could pass it on to their heirs; or they could sell it; or, if they let the line lie fallow for a certain length of time, the right of way would be open to anyone who wanted to use it.

And so, the new teacher, who had assumed he was on open ground, had trespassed against a line in use.

But how could he be told? Protocol intervened. No one wanted to embarrass him. The youth who ran the line was a student—he couldn't tell his own teacher about the traps. Instead, he had acted. He had sprung the traps: a polite message to quit trespassing.

The teacher did not understand the message, or even that the sprung traps were a message; he just kept setting them. The student, confused by this, began to get angry. The teacher, charging vandalism, began to get angry. Finally, to head off a confrontation, a respected older man, knowing the teacher would never see his mistake, explained the situation to him, and advised him mildly to back off.

Malfa praised the student for his restraint. "He was not allowed to question an adult who had authority over him," she said, "particularly not a teacher. Among us, teaching has always been the responsibility of all adults. In our way, we must treat teachers with respect."

I must have looked sad, or concerned, because she tried to console me: "We see how hard it is for outsiders to know how we communicate. You know how we don't like to say something directly: to be told the obvious insults our intelligence. We like to talk around the subject, without having to name it. We like to use gestures to say what we mean. When we talk, it's like we're dancing."

I wondered why the innocent teacher had never been taught—not in his education or anthropology courses, not by the teachers' union or the state department of education, not in the district's orientation sessions—that the old laws still held in the villages.

She, however, was still torn by the ethical and social contradictions of the incident. She said: "The message was so clear. That student would have felt dishonored, he would have felt like a shouter, if he had had to utter a word."

Cold

COLD WEATHER set in by late October, as the days slipped further back into darkness. By midafternoon the sky was streaked with sunset; the paths lay in shadow. Blue lights glowed along the runway. Windows in small buildings shone yellow and orange against the night. In openings scatted among the black trees, orange fires flared out of oil drums—householders were burning paper: from what source? They don't need to save paper! In their chimneys the smell of wood smoke was sharp, as cleansing as horseradish. The first snow had fallen; snowmachines were out prowling. On the river, floes skimmed downstream and collided: *Sshsshwww*, they whispered, swirled off, and ground against the cutbank.

One night the river froze. The floes had backed up for five hundred miles, from the mouth of the river into the Alaska Range. In the morning the temperature was about zero. Experimentally, I kicked clouds of powder onto the thin overflow ice. *Klinkt, klinkt,* said the snow. In the schoolyard, giggling children whirled on the merry-go-round, their down jackets ballooning, their cheeks red as apples. A man and two children fished from the riverbank. A pile of silver fish froze quietly beside them.

I turned back through a copse of rose-gray alders and paper birches. In a yard, a lone sled dog, chained to his stake, coughed and paced in circles. Near him lay thirteen dogs, chained to their houses. As I walked past they stood up and looked at me: silent, intent.

I came upon the cemetery, a small, well-tended patch under the trees. Rows of grave markers; a few Russian crosses, Latin crosses, granite headstones with names cut in them. Plastic flowers lay neatly beneath each marker. One slate was blank. The graves were mounds under the light snow. A young man lay dead at twenty-one; an airplane had been cut into his stone, and the words

> *He was born to fly.*
> *He loved the freedom*
> *it gave him and he*
> *was good at it.*

When the noon whistle blew, the dogs keened in response, their howls rising all over town.

Within weeks the temperature had dropped twenty degrees.

It was a dreaming time. Letters sent to distant friends were tiny red sparks arcing away into the immense darkness. In a note to the *Dream Songs*, John Berryman wrote of Henry, "who has suffered an irreversible loss." I wondered: which of our losses is reversible?

A friend wrote back: "But anyone can see Baryshnikov dance. How many know anything about McGrath, Alaska?"

○

MOST PEOPLE KNEW what poetry was: Robert Service wrote poetry. Their faces lit up at his name. Once, years before, when my car had broken down again on the icy road to Kenai, a cook in a nearby roadhouse had given me a bed for the night. I had been about to turn in when she tapped at the door and handed me a leather-bound volume of the collected works. She loved his poetry, she said. He wrote about us, and he made us laugh: we didn't have to be afraid of what we heard in the night. There was a canyon over by Y——, and if you went there, you often heard voices, singing some kind of chant, but no one was around. It's real, she insisted, but who are they?

In McGrath, Louis L'Amour was the favorite author. Trappers took his books out on the line. He was respected, as Robert Service was loved, because he wrote about their lives. He got the details right—guns, equipment, animal conformations, weather—because, they thought, he had experienced them, as they had, and so they could trust him. Proudly, they recognized themselves, enlarged by fiction. These were books! they said. I read Louis L'Amour, as I had read Robert Service, to learn more about what I did not know.

○

THE CHILDREN KNEW how to make poems, as children always seem to know. You had only to conjure up a safe, quiet space to work in and the poems flowed out of them. They watched the life and death around them; nothing was hidden from them. They expressed the whole of it, full-throated. Even the smallest had an incipient sense of form, in which they could write directly, lyrically, or in terse, urgent narrative. It was an endowment of life shaped by tellers of stories, and the presence of animals, and the animate landscape.

The chairman of the school board had lived in McGrath for a long time. He spoke upper-Kuskokwim Athabaskan; his favorite author was Louis L'Amour. He had been sent to the Interior villages as a young missionary-linguist, determined to translate the Bible into their language, but had given up the project when he realized that people weren't going to read it. He and his wife had stayed on, becoming tolerant voices, offering their services for the good of the community. He wasn't sure how to accept, or defend, the presence of an itinerant poet, and had asked me, "Well, will poetry help kids make a living?"

No, I answered. I didn't say, People need poetry to live. I showed him writings the students had given me. He was a patient man who had known those children from birth, and their parents and grandparents before them, and he was surprised and moved by what he read.

"They've written things about themselves I've never heard them say out loud," he said, and grew thoughtful. "I never knew they had these feelings, or thought so hard about their lives."

Where does the need to write come from? I am thinking of a young girl, as she was then, from a village north of Shelter, who had written stories, poems, memories, private thoughts, ever since she could remember, in secret notebooks, and had read everything she could get her hands on: hungry for words; for something.

Her older brother was in love with the teacher, a good one, well educated and willing to ask the best from her students. Her first classroom in the village had been a corner of the large, drafty village hall, where a dozen teenagers sat huddled, wrapped in their coats, around the roaring barrel stove. I had come walking in with my bag of books—it was my first trip out to the Yukon—and found them working in the corner without textbooks or library, with little paper and stumps of pencils, but with determination, and the encouragement of their elders.

The young girl had watched her brother, whom she adored, struggle with a fury that wounded him, the bitter knowledge that he had learned too little in school and yet, not enough in the woods. He cheered on the friend who had dropped out of school and left home. He went to the woods to be alone; then, he went there to drink. He was quick, clever, restless. His brother shot him in the leg. Grinding his teeth, he swore that if anyone hurt him again, they might as well finish him off, because he would get over the hurt and come back with a gun.

He stopped talking, and looked sideways at me.

"Katherine, I wrote a poem once," he said softly. "I was alone, and it was cold, and the forest was so lovely I made a poem about it."

Another year passed. He and the teacher lived together, in a tumble-down cabin no one else would stay in. His sister kept writing in her notebooks. He told people he was going Outside, to study to become a pilot. The teacher still didn't know he drank. They set their wedding date. She was radiant, he was tender and proud. They married, and began to rebuild their cabin. She continued to teach.

She reminded me, a little, of myself with F. She was older than he was, and she had great hopes for him, and for herself. She knew—she thought she knew—what was at stake. And he: he was like F, in his hope and defiance. In the end, however, love did not save him, and poetry didn't save him. During the summer I lived with F, he gave up his life.

They had married, I think, at midwinter. She finished out the school year. According to Deborah Madison, who sent the news to me in Village Below, they had made plans to fly Outside, to visit her parents, probably in late summer or early fall. He still talked about becoming a pilot, and he had promised her to go into a clinic to dry out.

July was a busy month because of salmon fishing, but the village always stopped work to celebrate the Fourth. There were fireworks and parties. Someone organized an afternoon excursion on a river barge; everyone knew there would be alcohol aboard. The two of them agreed to stay home, and he promised to stay dry, but he slipped away from her at the last minute and leaped aboard as the barge shoved off. There was a lot of drinking. At some point, no one knew when, he went into the river.

A year later, the mourning ended with a give-away. It gave the widow, weakened, back to the ordinary. She had gone through those months barely alive. Many mornings she had wished not to get up, the mere effort of waking being almost too much to bear; thinking it would be all right not to waken. Somehow, she went back to teaching.

Her sister-in-law, my former student-poet, had had an abortion not long before her brother's drowning. Old ladies had screamed at her: You caused it! Soon after his death, a baby was born in the village. The people knew her brother's spirit had passed into the infant; but his widow refused to believe it. The baby, she told me, had a tumor on its head, possibly a malformation due to fetal alcohol syndrome, because its parents drank.

o

THE WINTER WAS HARD. I flew to Fairbanks for meetings at the university.

o

"WHY DOES ANYONE WRITE?" Beckett asked. Over coffee and brandy he was directing the after-dinner conversation. He was a linguist, a rising scholar, who studied the narrative styles of Athabaskan storytellers, and was interested in the forms of their stories. He had published an influential paper in which he argued that Koyukon stories tended to have a consistent structure, somewhat as follows: a beginning, two middles, and an end. He demonstrated the pattern from transcribed oral texts, then contrasted it with the "Western," schooled convention that runs: beginning, middle, end. His point was that the "second middle" appeared even in ordinary anecdotes, even among Koyukon children who were English-speakers from birth. He proposed that teachers, who of course taught the Western form, often caused difficulties for those children because, invariably, they tried to edit out the "second middle," leaving the children confused and angry. He suggested that white teachers, being unfamiliar with Athabaskan conventions, didn't "hear" that unexpected element, as one ignorant of a foreign language can't "hear" words, although the words of course make perfect sense to the native speaker.

Literary curiosity was rare among the professors with whom I dealt; but Beckett read seriously. He was particularly fond of Borges and Samuel Beckett, his namesake. Their humor matched his sense of the void.

Why does anyone write? The winter was too hard, I thought, and there was too much suffering. Then, for an intense moment, poetry was with us, and trembling, I found myself reciting the opening of "Requiem," Akhmatova's great, unremitting poem.

> In the terrible years of the Yezhov terror I spent seventeen months waiting in line outside the prison in Leningrad. One day somebody in the crowd identified me. Standing behind me was a woman, with lips blue from the cold, who had, of course, never heard me called by name before. Now she started out of the torpor common to us all and asked me in a whisper (everyone whispered there):
> "Can you describe this?"
> And I said: "I can."
> Then something like a smile passed fleetingly over what had once been her face.

"To describe," I said finally, into the silence.
Beckett paused, and politely looked away, and then looked impatient.
"I meant, why did human beings invent writing?"

o

IN THE OFFICE, I found myself staring out at the frozen river, holding my head in my hands. No moving water, no birds; nothing moving. In the trailer, there was no solace. Sleepless, I made strong coffee.

Dear H,
    The temperature stays at -45°; I'm wearing six layers of clothing and look like the Michelin man. Last night I stayed with friends out in the new development, and walked back with them very early this morning. When others are around, the darkness is bearable, even interesting; it is clear and still. Our short days are brilliant with light.
    I describe the intensity of the weather because we cannot modify it; and because I wonder if it does not modify us.
    I mean myself. I love its intensity; I'm afraid of its enormity. Winter on this land is greater and more powerful than any human project I've ever known. In its face, I'm struck dumb, or blurt out in dismay what I can't comprehend, and my alarm distracts me. I recognize that, above all, composure is required. I try to stand still and look; I want to bolt.
    Somebody else died this morning, or yesterday, a woman from Hungry. This morning came the CB message: *All visitors but the trooper, stay away.* She was the sister of a woman I know—dead. Again again again again. The other week, in Shelter, a lady I once met walked into a snowbank. She taught Athabaskan in the school. Beckett is sickened by it. He thinks her death was related to stress from some sort of linguistics workshop in

Athabaskan literacy, that she had been required to go to. I don't want to think about the implications of his statement.

I weigh every motion, every breath.

If we were speaking of power, I would propose: There were two kinds. Here was the enormity of the winter, and there, facing it, the smallness and tenacity of human projection. Since the First Beginning, since the Distant Time, all life had been organized to survive on the land. As a crude analogy, I think of a patch of jack spruce, the crazy-leaning, shallow-rooted trees you saw wherever thin, sandy layers of soil covered a deposit of permafrost. If you cut a cross-section from a trunk of one of these trees, you would see growth rings of forty or fifty years, yet the scraggle-branched trunk would be no thicker than your small-boned arm. Life clings to what nourishes it, and endures, richly and unexpectedly; it is not always beautiful to look at.

I wondered, In these conditions, what is right? What is wrong? What is good; what is evil? What role does our free will play, when the commanding winter cannot not be altered?

The second power was so small and human. Let me name one of its aspects: compulsion. It is the most troubling human project for me. I always have to ask: What wish, what large idea, or, what authority, can make one person compel another—so many others!—to act? What belief, or longing, or custom, or fear, makes one—or, so many—obey?

In the end, I hear no answer to my questions. Perhaps any answer would be oblique. I remember a Koyukon phrase that describes a superior form of anger such as a strong-minded man, a true hunter, might exhibit in the face of what oppresses him, but cannot be altered by him. The phrase means, To leave the group in silence, with no expression visible on the face or in the voice.

An elderly lady walks into a snowbank.

I bow my head, and withdraw.

And in perplexity, call back what I knew, and also what I can never know, of what may have oppressed her. I am unnerved by what I see, and I wonder at it.

o

THE ELDERLY LADY was a language teacher. The district offered a program in what was called bilingual education. In practice, *bilingual* meant something other than the standard definition. An older person chosen by the village would be invited to the school for several hours a week to instruct the children in language and customs. The district called these people "bilingual teachers"; it was a job title that, to the district, meant they were paid differently, by the hour, at a lesser rate than the certified teachers. The village people were well aware of the distinction in status and pay.

The entire "bilingual" program was a function of federal and state grants, and these were a function of national educational politics, but we lived as far away from those goings-on as it was possible to imagine. In the district, the village parent committees guarded their bilingual programs. After more than a century of suppression, their languages now could be spoken in schools, and the bilingual teachers were glad for it, and for the income, which they needed.

These elderly teachers acknowledged that repeating isolated words, or reciting the names of things, or practicing discrete phonetic sounds, as they were told to do, conveyed little of all that was necessary to speak their language well. Still, they were willing to come into classrooms and let the children hear the words, and they were pleased to tell them the old stories. Most of all, they wished to encourage the young, and to show them that their elders stood with them. In that way, the village bilingual teachers adapted the program to their own needs; and some of the fiscal bounty of the school passed into the community.

The desires of the bureaucracy grew more complicated. As these ancient oral languages had now been put into writing, it was next decided that literacy in them ought also to be taught in school. The chairman of the Iditarod board, who once had hoped to translate the Bible into an Athabaskan tongue, knew how strongly the older generation resisted that idea. Gently, he encouraged the study of writing among the younger speakers, who were more open to change. He saw the need, but did not apply pressure; the pressure came from elsewhere.

After the death of the elderly lady, Beckett phoned me in distress from Fairbanks. He was at odds with his department; for some time, it seemed, a colleague had been calling together Athabaskan speakers in our area, proposing to teach them literacy in their language. His method, fumed Beckett, was to ask these old people to give him a list of words, which he wrote down, as he was compiling a dictionary. They were then to copy the words as he spelled them, in order to teach them to children. The old people told him, "This isn't the way we know our language." They told him more than once, Beckett said, meaning that they had made a strong protest. They disliked being questioned for the sake of his dictionary; but the professor would not listen to them. He went on with his project, recording what he called dying languages. He was part of the department's undertaking, federally funded, to standardize the spelling of all extant Native languages.

All this Beckett had often told me and others who worked with Native people, explaining his disagreements with his colleagues' method. Many of us had listened, often sympathetically, but without the standing needed to intervene. For some years I had heard about well-known elders who opposed the linguists' work, just as they opposed the work of many anthropologists. They had protested, but to no avail. No Native academic scholar (of whom there were only a few) had come forward to debate this important matter. On the other hand, Beckett seemed to be trusted by his Koyukon teachers, who worked willingly with him, and this carried weight with many of us.

He told me his colleague had given a workshop in literacy to the Athabaskan teachers in our district. The elderly lady, he said, had come home from that meeting; the same night, she had walked into the snowbank.

Beckett tended to be elliptical. I was startled by what he would not say directly. I don't know what I replied.

"These workshops put terrible strains on those people," he said. He was angry and depressed, unable by argument or reason to put an end to the unhappiness he witnessed.

○

MALFA WROTE, "You can come to us soon?"

I caught a charter on the back haul from Shelter. Malfa and Frederick, her husband, met me at the air strip, and we drove out by snowmachine to their winter camp. The first Ivanov brothers had hunted in the area, and their descendants after them; now it was a retreat for the extended family, who used it as a base for the fall moose hunt, or to get away from the village. Four or five houses and their outbuildings had been constructed far enough apart to be just within shouting distance. Malfa and Frederick had built a handsome, two-storey winter house of massive spruce logs.

It was a frigid day. The air was clear and smelled of woodsmoke and dry snow. Malfa, proud of her house, all but fussing over me, led the way to the upper floor, into a warm room where tall windows looked out over a frozen lake. Beyond grew the dark, vast, snowy forest. The afternoon sky was streaked with sunset. Down in the utility room, Frederick was feeding the fire. The dense *thud, chunk, thud, chunk* of logs heaved whole into the stove, then the flat iron *clang* of the fire-door, rumbled up through the floor. "He's glad you're here," she laughed, "so he won't have to listen to me all the time. He'll let us have our visit in peace."

Frederick was a handsome, genial man of dry humor. He ran a trapline. Every morning he drove his snowmachine out to the line, and remained out till near suppertime. He was going deaf. As Malfa talked to me, I noticed him glance our way now and then with approval and a flicker of relief in his eyes.

For three days, the two of us curled up in comfortable overstuffed chairs, and talked; or she let me sit and stare out the window. She told stories. She fed me. She fried salmon, and roasted moose ribs, and brought out dryfish and pilot bread and homemade raspberry jam, and baked loaves of good bread. In the morning, the smell of cinnamon rolls perfumed the house. We drank pot after pot of coffee. I began to feel human again.

○

SHE HAD BEEN preparing for the elders conference, the old-time spring rendezvous that she had agreed to organize, by making lists of questions. "They don't have to answer what we ask them," she explained. "But they will want to teach us, and they will want to know what we have to learn." She was like an archaeologist excavating some long-buried settlement, probing the surface gently, uncovering fragile, human handwork. She was digging down into the mind of their common past, layer by layer, by hand.

She had been told a story, which she recounted to me as a little test, about the first time a man saw an airplane.

On that part of the Yukon, they had not known planes yet. One day, a big noisy thing flew up the river. An old man watched it approach from the horizon. He watched: it grew larger. He watched, he watched: it grew larger and larger. It was very noisy. It passed overhead, and he fell backward.

"Oh," I said. She looked at me quickly, to see if I had laughed.

"This is why he fell down," she said. "Even though he didn't know what it was, or whether it would help or harm him, he never took his eyes off it, and, forgetting himself, he fell down rather than look away."

◦

NOVEMBER 5, at the Ivanov camp

Malfa is at the kitchen counter making another pot of coffee. It is afternoon, about four o'clock: dark beyond the windows, and we haven't changed out of our nightclothes. A moment ago, we stared at one another and realized we've been talking since breakfast. In another moment, I'll pull myself out of this chair and prepare for the day as if it were normal. It doesn't matter if I don't hurry. I feel blessed, as though I will spend all the time in the world here.

This country is full of secrets. So much seems to lay open before us; but much is not open, and as time passes, more is covered up. A mantle of silence is spreading over us, and I cannot get out from under it.

Under the cover of silence are oceans of feeling. The story is endless; the deaths are part of the story; and even I, who don't belong here, feel them, and suffer for the losses. Malfa would recover history. She would uncover history, this blessed woman who has been so carefully prepared to do that work. Is she prepared for what she will have to learn? It can be frightful. Stories choose their teller: what if she refuses them? The stories will catch in her throat.

Silence is an art of nuance, in three dimensions. It needs, as artful speech and gesture need, an attentive listener, a knowing watcher. This silence terrifies me. It is a powerful act, as in the way a beautiful dancer can touch and draw in his audience: or as a hand with a knife can strike at one's heart.

Akhmatova's poem came into being under terror in Russia. How dared I reduce her act, her poem, the terror itself, by implying a comparison to this Alaska? There was no similarity; no, surely I was wrong to imply it. The fear under which so many of these people, here, live: this fear is, surely, different.

"Can you describe this?"
And I said, "I can."

Her country-woman, her fellow sufferer, had asked the poet to tell what
happened, and the poet had answered yes. Malfa asks that question. She
believes she is asking the elders; but she is asking herself. Will she answer
her own yes?

She is chuckling, a throaty sound. She wears a pretty, flowing gown: she
enjoys feeling its softness against her skin as she moves around the kitchen.

Who can bear to be a poet? Power politics is the currency now. Poets
have no power, and are easily destroyed.

On this frontier we are different nations, with different moral claims,
living inside our disconsoling politics. Malfa and I are private persons; an
accident of birth has made us "white" and "Native." The friendship we
are forming is shaded by history and bitter experience. I want to live outside of that history. Do I know how to live beyond it? How can we live
with it?

So much is wrong. It is wrong. It's tempting for me to slump toward
despair. I want to lay out my little bombs of words, to name directly what
is constantly obscured, covered up, denied; to speak over the euphemisms
we use to soften the blows of this life.

But love always alters the story. If we do not love, what then? If they
love some and not all, what then? How does she love her neighbor as herself? What happens if he cannot love himself?

The frontier is difficult to cross, and I don't know if I will reach the
other side: but I have to try. Many things, even opposites, are true at once:
I am learning from experience, if not from philosophy, and it confuses me.
I recount what happens, to sort through the confusion. I have to learn
more, not less. I can't forget anything. None of us can forget anything.

o

THE LAMPS WERE LIT. We had eaten. In the night sky the stars shone like ice
lanterns. The Aurora danced overhead: a great, shimmering, sinuous river of
light and color pouring across the sky. Her eyes smiled with fun, and she said
lightly, "We always run outside and whistle at it!" We flung on our coats and
dashed outside, and whistled merrily at the Aurora. We danced around the
yard like children. Against the lamplight from the windows our shadows were
tiny, lively creatures cavorting on the snow. We sang and danced to the shimmering Aurora, and it danced back at us.

o

THE ELDERLY LADY was not the Ivanovs' relative. I mentioned her passing,
to let Malfa know I knew what had happened, without saying it directly; but

I wasn't used to speaking about death and, without thinking, asked what would be done with the body. But she answered me.

"They'll do an autopsy, because she died that way," she said calmly. "A funeral home will prepare the body and send it back to her family."

"What if a person dies at home?"

"If it's a natural death, people take care of it themselves. Usually there is someone to wash the body, someone to dress it, someone to make the coffin. Our people take care of the family. For the first few days we visit the home. We bring food. If we want to make something for the dead one—slippers, a scarf, mittens—these can go in the coffin. When we want to do something for the one who died, we do it ... Oh.

"I remember a woman whose baby died."

The memory caught her so suddenly that her voice dropped into sorrow so deep that it rocked her, and her eyes saw something terrible all over again.

"Our people have gone through so much. A certain woman's baby died, and I was going to visit her. When someone has died, they clear a little space in the house for the baby. You know when you go in that you won't see things the way they usually are, and so you brace yourself for the sight of this place.

"I went into their house, bracing myself, but I didn't see the little space for the body. I looked around. There I saw the woman and her husband, down on the floor by the stove. I went over to them, to see. They had put that little baby in a blanket. It was curled in the fetal position. They were thawing it out. They sent the body to her that way.

"Now people see that woman and call her a drunk. But I will never forget the sight of her crouched on the floor over her frozen baby."

We wept silently for a while, looking out the window into the night. Then she laughed a little, and said, "But it isn't our way to make you sad and leave you that way." She made a lighthearted remark and, dutifully, I smiled, and thought of an almost-funny joke, and told it, and she laughed, and the spell lifted; and our talk went on from there.

What Are You Going to Be Like with Him?

DEC. 28

All day the power was out. I sat huddled by the stove, wrapped in woolens and coats, and read *The New Yorker.* This town is absurdly dependent on oil. My head aches from reading by candlelight. It was good to get back from Fairbanks: Christmas boxes and piles of letters were waiting in the post office. Mother and Dad sent an exquisite embroidered-satin Chinese jacket. He chose it; she wrote: "Perfect with a simple black dress." And snow pants, shoe pacs, and down parka.

The sun, just glancing at us over the horizon, rises from due south. I've had many dreams lately but can't remember them. At noon I come home, eat soup, and read Akhmatova for courage.

Dec. 31

The generators have been acting up for some time now. Three of the four have blown out, just as the mercury hits minus fifty. They can now supply power only to alternate sides of town, on alternate hours. In this little metal shell the outage means no light, no heat, no water, although the propane stove works. I have a good supply of candles.

Things are pleasant enough. It's quiet here; the eternal hum of the generators and their vibration through this trailer, which make my neck tense, won't resume for a while. I sit reading and writing at my table; cook a bit; drink tea or coffee. I'm so bundled up I look like a little fat boy. Tonight I'll go to the roadhouse to look in on the New Year's party.

A pink ice-fog is settling on us. This morning I saw the round orange sun through fog on the river. It was like surprising an animal poised on the trail. It stared back ...

The power's off again. I just bought two flashlight batteries and twelve long-burning emergency candles. A man walked across the runway with a .22; I heard a crack; he came back with a fat white ptarmigan.

The post office is closed till the power has been restored. They've ordered a new generator from Seattle and are having it transported here by chartered aircraft. I'm sure we'll pay for this.

Although frost is caked about an inch thick on the wall by my bunk, I've consoled myself with pretty sheets and curtains; but they freeze to the wall. On this oaken table I've piled paper, typewriter, a camping lantern, a coffee mug, and books: Akhmatova, Yuri Olesha, four novels by Elizabeth

Bowen; Tuchman's *A Distant Mirror*, a biography of Sacajawea, short novels by Melville; *The Spawning Run* by William Humphrey (jacket blurb: "I recommend *The Spawning Run* to anyone with even the faintest interest in anything"); Margaret Atwood's *Journals of Susannah Moodie* ("Whether the wilderness is real or not depends on who lives there"); Milosz's *Bells in Winter; On Systems Analysis*, an elegant, witty, though conservative treatise by David Berlinsky; and Gass's *On Being Blue*. I can hold out.

The moon gleams out there like a giant abalone shell. Nearly full moon, nearly new year. What new astonishments await us?

In Hungry, someone got a moose. In McGrath, a young white woman, glad a Native person had outwitted the game warden but not knowing enough to keep it secret, mentioned the hunt over the C B. The game warden, alerted, flew down to Hungry and confiscated the meat that people had needed to make it through the winter. Fyodor, their oldest man, who had so often had to play the fool in the white man's world, took the blame. No charges were pressed against him.

o

IN 1405, in *The Book of the City of Ladies*, Christine de Pizan wrote: "In brief, all women—whether noble, bourgeois, or lower-class—be well-informed in all things, and cautious in defending your honor and chastity among your enemies. . . . Oh my ladies, flee, flee from the foolish love they urge on you! Flee it, for God's sake, flee! . . . Remember, dear ladies, how these men . . . try hard, using all kinds of strange and deceptive tricks, to catch you, just as one lays traps for wild animals. Flee, flee, my ladies, and avoid their company—"

Christine's City, her refuge and beguinage, was an opening onto the long view. I have no doubt her warning was well founded in the fifteenth century, when, a young widow with young children, she ventured to support herself as a woman of letters; she was the first such woman in French literature. In her critical writings she quarreled with Jean de Meun, an author of the *Roman de la Rose*, for slandering women, and mocked him for his "tiresome pose" as seducer; then and now certain critics called her "shrill" for writing as she did in the defense of women.[23] Yet there is so often a risible quality in the literary trope of man as hunter luring defenseless women to his bed, and there overpowering and "conquering" them. It is the wit of literature, not life; and, despite the evidence before my eyes, I long wondered if the metaphor does not flatter the man but demean the hunter. For, through observation, I too had conceived an association, a poetic likeness, between women and animals, as objects of the hunter's desire.

But I had come to respect hunters, that is, men who seemed to me true hunters; not the sport hunters who, like any seducer, were avid for trophies. I knew hunters and had lived with a hunter, and had learned in a hard way what it meant to honor fresh meat and the man who brought it in; I had glimpsed how men approached the animals, and the spirits of the animals, they hunted. A man of the old training would not have said, "I'm going out to get a moose": he would not presume the animal would give itself to him. His hunt required wiliness and prayer, it required all his skill, and it required the aid of a greater thing, Luck, a strong force in his world of probabilities. A hunter, as I was told it, honored the game; he learned its stringent, holy rules, and knew from experience and instruction the power of the animals to give themselves to him, or refuse to be taken. So the old hunt was described, by old men and old women; and I believed them.

A well-traveled poet who taught for a year in Nome told me about her first encounter with the bush. "When I got there, I thought the men were hand-some. They looked at me and I felt flirtatious and playful." I smiled, remem-bering that first pleasure. "Then an older woman at the college warned me about them: when they saw a new white woman in town they called her 'fresh meat.'"

The sexual imagery, men as hunters, women as meat, was unpleasant. I wondered: If a hunter honored his prey, though he shot it, and if women were similar in that they gave or withheld themselves, as the game did, by that rea-soning: would a hunter not honor women?

An Iñupiaq woman, a poet and daughter of a shaman, told me of a won-drous spring morning after a hard winter on the coast of the Bering Sea, when she woke up overjoyed: she had heard the whales singing; they had called to her in her dream. How beautiful their songs were! She rose quickly, dressed, and ran through the streets crying, "They're coming, the whales are coming." Within days, sooner than the captains had foretold, the lookouts saw a herd of baleen whales swimming up the coast.

The Iñupiat, who hunt whales in the Arctic, say, "The whale comes to the woman." Among them, the whaling captains, who are masterful and are re-sponsible for feeding many people, take men who are their wife's relatives as their boat crew. While they are hunting (the shaman's daughter told me), the captain's wife remains at home, in stately and powerful retreat. She averts her eyes and keeps them from seeking the horizon, so that her glance will not fall between the hunters and the shore. It is the strength and composure of her behavior that allows her husband and his crew to undertake so dangerous and exciting a hunt and return alive, with their bounty. The wife, by her behavior, maintains the ancient, animate order of that world.[24]

A woman gives or withholds herself and cannot be compelled without vi-olation: this is in our nature, the Artemis in us, an indrawn breath, a pulse-beat of flight into our private space. We have many ways of knowing this.

Of whose nature do you speak?

I am describing the preparatory time before a young woman of a partic-ular lineage and education and experience knows quite who she is: that is, of whose spirit she partakes; before she knows with confidence what to do. She is intuitive: she is aware of what moves around her but cannot yet name it.

If this account were of another kind, I would say: She was mixing what ought to be kept separate. She lived amidst societies at odds with each other, and she belonged to another literary tradition: she ought not mix Iñupiaq with Athabaskan hunting relations, nor introduce either of these into the hunting practices of the white frontier. Surely she understood that the Greeks and the French had nothing to do with the animate world in which she lived. All this was true: I knew this; and knew, intellectually, that they should not be mixed, indifferently, but belonged to their own civilizations, and within these, to their classes and ranks. I understood that this world, the Interior, had articulated its proper order of what was said and what was done: it was composed of orders of belief and behavior, which acted as natural laws. Many kinds of people lived close to each other and yet followed their own ways. But the young woman whose body a whole mind inhabited had to remain wary and fast on her feet. She lived in a rough place.

Christine de Pizan's cry of alarm may have reminded me of the pulse that beats beneath the social skin of cities: yet to my sorrow the bush was where I first heard women called *whores* and *bitches* by men; and where I began to learn, had to learn, to ignore the words, to look away, to keep my voice steady. I was a traveler; this was not my country. Then, in town, at a party for artists, I heard myself called *klootch* by a Native man. The word was the old Chinook trade-jargon for an Indian woman, one of those who became the wife or companion of white men, trappers or traders, and functioned as domestic slaves for them; it was harsher, in common usage, than *squaw*. Perhaps the naming was a young man's vicious way of repaying two centuries of insult to his people; but it repaid nothing. What measure could I take of his pain, and the pain of women called *klootches*, but with the ambiguous warmth of pity? In the end, weary of constant harassment in public and private, town and the bush, I avoided the company of all men, white and Native, but the few I knew well enough to call friends. I followed the advice given us down the centuries: to defend our own honor and chastity "from our enemies," to curb ourselves and our free movement through society.

The fact of violation is common in this world, and it was common where I lived. And yet, at least intellectually, my mind remained stubbornly perturbed by the analogy of women to prey. I wondered if it were not some misjudged metaphor, drawn from terrible experience, but not from experience in an older human way of hunting. I could not forget that F, who prayed to the caribou before he shot, would never take a woman to hunting camp. From knowledge so old it had become second nature, he felt the need to keep separate from women in order to find animals. He required success in his hunt: it was incomplete, and he was unlucky, if he did not kill game. And he could not control Luck. A woman, in her essence, or the scent of her blood-trail, would get in his way: so he believed.

The purpose of the hunt was meat, that is, food, which contained its own spirit. Yet, everywhere, the hunt was itself violated, by law and intrusion and by bad faith. The intention and practice of the hunt were, everywhere, frustrated; I knew this. My knowledge was salt and bitter. I wondered: had one violation been transformed into another and, so, endlessly perpetuated? But where, then, had the violence begun? From what distant root had it sprung?

In this was mystery. It was said, *The animals come to the woman:* what did this mean? If the hunt were so ordered that prey, though killed, were not murdered;[25] that, in the ceremony of the hunt, the animal gave itself to the hunter: who then violated that primal order? What, in that world, was the order of women, and why did I recognize its violation? Playing with metaphor, I asked unanswerable questions. I longed for women, the wives and mothers of hunters, to teach me; and I was taught, but slowly, carefully. I did not always recognize the teaching when it happened. Years afterward Malfa told me: "The older women watch us, to see what we need to learn. They will come to us and say, 'It's time for you to learn this.'" She, too, would give me that signal at certain times as I matured; but for a long time, she protected me from the most difficult matters. "I didn't want you to suffer," she said.

o

Dear KW,

Some women from Hungry are stranded here. I have good relations with them, so they came to me two days ago to find a place to stay. I put them up in a house belonging to someone away on a trip. Then the store was closed, and I cooked for them. Yesterday no one was flying because of the cold, so they had to stay in McGrath, and the old ladies got drunk. There are three of them, and a young woman and a girl, and a baby girl. The older women are restless because they have no work to do, so: drinking, arguments, homesickness. There is much coming and going by the younger women: the water pipes froze, the propane connection froze, the baby needed food. The girl spends her afternoons with me, avoiding them while she can.

They amaze me, those women. I imagine if they could, they would practice parthenogenesis. They look archaic; they look like falcons; they are tiny and strong beyond belief.

The older women were laughing the other day. One of them went to the store to buy a sharpener for files and chainsaws. When she asked for it, the storekeeper (who comes from here) said, "One of them flat bastards?" Later, when they were recounting it, they giggled and laughed, and decided it would be better if a man got the sharpener.

o

ON THE OTHER HAND, Jack London wrote: "When a man journeys into a far country, he must be prepared to forget many of the things he has learned, and to acquire such customs as are inherent with existence in the new land; he must abandon the old ideals and the old gods, and oftentimes he must reverse the very codes by which his conduct has hitherto been shaped." London held that such a man had to learn an old law: "Nature did not care. To life she set one task, gave one law. To perpetuate was the task of life, its law was death."

Jack London described white men in the North, and the rough edges of his sentences matched the roughness of their gestures. If this narrative were fiction, I would imagine a way into the hearts of men such as they were, and if it were poetry, I would know their hearts. But this book is neither fiction nor poetry, and so I cannot know them. I lived among men of a certain kind; they were not only white. I gazed into their heart and, not comprehending what I saw there, fell silent.

When, afterward, I read novels about the settling of the West, or the expansion of the frontier, or the encroachment on wilderness, I recognized in them something intrinsic, also, to the habitation of Alaska. I compared them in memory to what I had seen; and, holding in mind that experience and fiction speak to each other not face to face, but at an oblique angle, I believed nonetheless a correspondence existed between them. I recalled a dark night when F was exalted and told me what it meant to be Indian. "Here's what it really means," he had shouted: "It's a challenge. I'm always competing, I'm always testing myself! At home, everything you do is a direct test to see who's the better man. I'm the best fighter, the toughest, the strongest! Ask Billy, ask anybody. Being Indian means pushing yourself as far as you can go!"

Jack London wrote about a man traveling alone in the wilderness, a newcomer about to be tested: "Nevertheless he was aware of a thrill of joy, of exultation. He was doing something, achieving something, mastering the elements. Once he laughed aloud in sheer strength of life, and with his clenched fist defied the frost. He was its master. What he did he did in spite of it. It could not stop him."

F would have measured this man—his counterpart existed everywhere in Alaska—by the scars on his hands. He would have watched the hands, and led with his left, to fool his opponent; he would have walked toward him on the balls of his feet, as a fighter walked. They had something in common, F and the nameless man who struggled to build a fire. But, a long time ago, I loved F, who knew and was part of what he came from: and I am weary of the arrogance of the frontiersman, who had to learn the hard way never to travel alone. That marks the real difference between them, and distinguishes them: my brief, astonished, complicated love for one, not the other.

Jack London read Darwin and Marx; having survived the Klondike, he read Herbert Spencer, and recognized in Spencer's theory of social Darwinism the basic law governing the rugged life he had known in the North. ("He joined the issue with his rifle reversed, and the hoary game of natural selection was played out with all the ruthlessness of its primeval environment.") From that brutally materialist philosophy, London shaped his Alaskan stories. I should have taken Jack London and his social Darwinism as more than an historical curiosity. Around the world, how many readers has he not thrilled? In Alaska, I discovered, his belief that, literally, only the fittest survive is considered realistic.

In isolated places, or during conflict, or in times of great change, the line of force between survival and domination is thin. In the Interior there were quiet men, and decent men, and those lost and gloomy, and the young ones who were still testing themselves and might not go bad. There also existed bad-hearted men. I think such men have no particular history; they exist. There is a force implacable in the world: it is not centered in heart, I see, but in pure will, and the intention of that will is domination.

In that country, the force of will was enacted by hard men. Some of them lived around McGrath; others, in the larger villages of our district. To a man, they were handsome, unkempt, brutal-eyed. When it suited them, they called themselves white, like their fathers or grandfathers, although their mothers or grandmothers were Native; theirs was a nuanced hierarchy of position and family status. The men I describe were big men in their communities: pilots, bootleggers, members of the school committees. They were heads of large families. They moved with easy authority. They could fight any other man, if they had to; they could throw money casually on the bar or the gambling table. Curly Johansson, who owned McGuire's briefly, ran the best taxi service in town; Sam Hunt ran a competing charter-and-bootlegging operation over on the Yukon, from a village north of Shelter. I flew with those men. They were rough men, thugs, but good pilots; and the wild light in their eyes was briefly, disturbingly, attractive.

They appeared where opportunity lay. In the bush, opportunity meant a chance at a better life; usually, that chance was tied to liquor, and to selling liquor. In most villages in our area, though not in McGrath, town law forbade selling alcohol; thus, there were bootleggers. ("Money talks: nobody walks," said F.) Sam Hunt flew between the Yukon and the Kuskokwim delta. He came from a family of brothers—one of them sat on the district school board—who fought one another over bootlegging territories. Once in a while, after a particularly egregious act, a shooting, for instance, with witnesses willing to testify, one of them went to jail for a while. Otherwise, when they crossed the limit, nothing stopped them, except equal force.

Equal force had begun to arrive on the rivers. State troopers were stationed first in the towns, then in larger villages. Their presence compounded the difficulty of relations between Native people, white people, and the law: the law was taken as an outside force, and the troopers were visibly armed. In a curious way, their uniformed presence, and their side-arms, heightened the sense of disturbance in the air.

The director of curriculum was a woman with pretensions to the authority she assumed a graduate degree had conferred on her; but she also always knew the latest gossip. "Did you hear?" she would cry, with a thrill, and tell us that shots had been fired in a certain village. She broke the news when Jim

Hunt, who sat on the school board, was finally arrested for bootlegging, although not for his real crime. She annoyed me and I stayed away from her; but I was wrong, and had misjudged her. She was in fact a nice woman, and the giggle in her voice and her silly ways were the means women often use to mask their instinctive terror.

In time, she learned the real stories. She found out what had happened to the daughters and wives who fled their homes; she learned about incest from Jim Hunt's beautiful daughter. She stopped giggling. Her shrill voice registered shock, then disapproval; she became the teacher reprimanding an unruly class; but she was confused and upset then, because the class—the rough men, and the decent people, who would not interfere in others men's business—teased her, or ignored her.

She learned from this and grew thoughtful; her voice steadied. She was married to a good man and had growing children; they lived in a house with an extra room. She decided to take in student boarders, girls who had to leave home to be safe and came to McGrath to go to school.

From then on, every semester she gave the extra room to a young girl from a village. She had known sorrow and betrayal (as she told me, because we finally talked) that must have left her vulnerable, and shy of the hurts of others; yet in her own way she did not withdraw from the harmed ones, but offered them what protection she could. She never spoke of it publicly.

When the wives or daughters fled, new women always took their place. This, too, was part of what does not end. They were bright, capable women, Native and sometimes white women, nurses and teachers. Was it the easy physical authority, the light in the eye, that drew them? Did they believe their lives would be less restricted? This was the frontier: no one could tell a man what to do. Did that make their new women feel protected, even strengthened in themselves? Were they unable to say no?

In the villages, women turned to other women, their relatives and trusted friends, who consoled one another, or who kept safe homes and offered refuge, when that was possible.

When I traveled, I stayed in the schools, sleeping on classroom floors, or boarded with elderly women who welcomed visitors. I avoided men if their wives were not present, but not out of fear. The risk was more delicate, and ironic, and just as intense: jealousy was always at work.

In the closed world of the Interior, sex was a powerful instrument of the will. Here lived men who violated the courtesy of women, even their own daughters, as if by a right so deeply held I could not see its end, or its beginning.

o

"URBAN" ALASKA—Anchorage, Fairbanks, Barrow, Nome, Bethel, Kodiak, Juneau, Ketchikan, Sitka—had the highest rates of alcoholism, wife-beating, and child abuse in the country. Alliances of women worked to set up crisis phone lines and shelters for battered women and their children. Often, they were aided by influential men who were of strong enough character, or held positions high enough, not to be considered weak for listening to women. In 1977, a year before I went to Village Below, I joined a group of women who campaigned, successfully, to open a safe shelter in Anchorage that no vengeful husband or lover could find. In my small service to them I learned what was known to experienced workers everywhere: the violence is not particular to any single class, or background, or upbringing, or place of origin.

During that time, the state was rewriting its criminal justice code. The group with whom I worked organized a conference about violence at home, to raise issues concerning women and children, and invited the writer Del Martin as keynote speaker; her book *Battered Wives* was among the first to demonstrate the widespread danger in which many women live. She told us about the nature and frequency of spousal abuse. Other experts then spoke, all recognizing the problem, all doubtful of an effective solution. Judges explained to us the limits of the law as protector, and the limits of its actual power to mete out justice; sociologists contributed statistics, and policemen advised us how to keep ourselves safe. From personal testimonies and from expert discussions, I learned about the common situation of many woman in my country. Reluctantly, I was compelled to recognize that I, too, might find myself at risk; that at some unexpected moment I, too, might find myself unprotected by law or custom. My sheltered assumptions about civility, the rule of manners, the ordinary safety of everyday life, were revealed to me as illusions. I disliked thinking this, and resisted it. I disliked, intensely, the emotions rising in me. I disliked the words "male-dominated," "patriarchy." I was a traveler and did not want fear as a companion. Fear damages the mind.

Therefore, without denying the fact of the violence, I—reserved it, contemplatively, set it to one side, because I could not bear to look at it directly. For the group, I performed mundane tasks, setting up account books, writing reports about the conference. For a series about the justice code, sponsored jointly by the university and the state's department of criminal justice, I interviewed on camera women who were willing to tell their stories publicly. They had been beaten or sexually assaulted, and had fled their homes. Those whom I interviewed were white. If they came from a bush town, usually they were married and often the husband was a respected man in the community, where people believed that what went on in his home was a man's own business, and the law would not interfere. Their testimony was direct, and was new to me.

The tapes had been completed and were broadcast. I could not forget the women, nor forget their fear; but the strain of production had wearied me, and, restless, looking for something, I went to the bush ...

In Anchorage, during the first year of the shelter's existence, the same year I lived in Village Below, seven hundred women and a thousand children found sanctuary behind its hidden walls.

○

Dear KW,

Before I left Paris a friend predicted: "You will see things that horrify you, and you don't want this."

Here the horror is quiet and unremarked, and it is everywhere. The rough, unlettered speech of the men, the absence of rest for the eye, the crooked lines of walls, the slapdash construction of the shabby buildings of this country wear at our human kindness, and people become scythes and rakes scraping at one another. The young girls are prey. I've just heard two new stories of girls abused, one raped by her father, the other by her mother's drunken, pitiful man. The abuse; the laughing voices condemning children to isolation and a kind of death.

This is a dead and dying place; no minds grow here. People do the worst to each other, and excuse it with drink. Everyone's desperate, wanting sex, or talk. A cup of coffee is raw comfort. What is man-made is thrown together with contempt for everything but what works: that is how the North has been built; that is what this world looks like. What world is it? I don't recognize it. This is a place where they make no kind of art, where they seem not to need its beauty; it is—I was going to say, contemptible, but it is just mean. I've grown deaf and can't hear songs, only clamor, and the damned rumble of the generator. Everything contrives to strip away our humanity, and little goes toward repairing it. We should leave this land alone, if only from fear of what, inevitably, it does to us.

I came out last night into the last moments of rain. To the west, behind its shredded edge, the sun was setting. The sky was bruised-purple, like the eye of a girl I saw last week over on the Yukon, who had been hit with a rifle butt. It was a wonder she hadn't lost the eye. The battered eye was an ugly thing, but the sky the same color was beautiful.

The sun, the sky, the mountains. When you go away, you long for these afterward.

○

I COULD NOT FORESEE how I would lose my balance, my belief in right and wrong, my respect for the world and myself. When you are in agony, often you will hurt yourself, to distract yourself from the hurt that will not stop.

There are times when a young woman will try to be tough—cynical, apparently nonchalant, amid moral and physical squalor—out of anguish. Let's say she goes into Anchorage, where there is a construction boom. The middle class, from which she, too, comes, is building its new life. She sees how comfortably people live yet how earnestly they love the wilderness; how they deplore life in the bush, its uncouth hardship and degradation; how they shake their heads at the harm done to Native people by drink. She flares up. *You live cut off from the basic realities*, she says resentfully, as if life were more real in one place than another. With contempt she thinks: *What do you know about it? You could never survive out there.*

The damned generator: it made my trailer hum. My books couldn't muffle it. My neck ached. As the winter got darker, I grew more desperate.

o

MICK HANNIGAN liked to tell stories. He joked with people, knowing how to put them at ease. He came from back East, from New York, not so far from where I grew up. Some days, he sounded almost like home, and it was good listening to him. His people were blue-collar Irish, traditional people. He had left home, and that was that; he wouldn't go back. "They broke my plate," he shrugged.

He had come to Alaska five years back, he said, he and Gort, his buddy from the Marines. They had worked for a while in Anchorage, but noticed life there wasn't so different from the Lower Forty-Eight, so they spread out a map and pointed at random. The pointed finger landed on Farewell. They went down to the travel agency to buy plane tickets for Farewell, and were told they would have to fly to McGrath; from there, they could charter. They flew to McGrath, figuring to ask a real estate agent where to find property.

There was nothing like a real estate agent in McGrath, and they never got to Farewell; instead, they acquired a trapline. Old Man Demetroff, who had outlived his whole family, was well into his eighties and could no longer run his lines. He sold the right of way for five hundred dollars to Mick and Gort. They loaded up with supplies, traps, and food, and chartered a plane out to the site. The pilot was due back in a month to pick them up, enough time, they figured, to learn something about trapping.

About two weeks later they ate the last of their food. They got a moose, good luck, because they spent two more months on the line. The pilot had left town and forgotten to tell anyone to pick them up.

After a season or two they sold the line. Gort got a job flying for Curly Johansson. Mick, who was a practical man and knew how to fix things, went to work for the school district. Before long he was elected to the town council. The councilmen told him he was doing too well by McGrath, and, haw, haw, next time he was probably going to have to draw the short straw. "Jeez, what the heck," he laughed. "I been on the damn council less than a year, and already those guys are stickin' me with the mayor's job." Like most of them, he was a regular in McGuire's.

One night I walked into McGuire's on a roar of laughter. Mick was rolling: he had just begun a bear story. By then I was so unbalanced, I laughed too.

"Best bed I ever slept in was in that cabin," he was saying. "You can make one easy—build a box frame, fill it up with sawdust, put some canvas over it. 'Course your ass hangs three feet below your head and toes. One time the canvas ripped. So I took a pair of Levi's—good pair, too—and stretched 'em across the hole. Slept real good, and the Levi's kept my ass from dragging.

"That bed, though: bear fell on it. First bear Gort and I ever saw. We was sleeping, and damned if a bear didn't crawl through the goddamn window. Right into our cabin. I said, 'You gonna shoot?' Gort says, 'I dunno, you wanna shoot?' I said, 'Somebody oughtta shoot.' So we did, *bam, bam,* the bear falls in through the window. So we push it back out through the window, and the next morning we start skinning.

"I say to Gort, 'What do we do now?' 'Skin it,' Gort says. 'Okay,' I say, what do I know, first bear I ever seen.

"First thing, Gort unzips it and we get to skinning, and we come to the paw. 'What now?' I say. Gort says, 'I dunno, cut it off I guess.' 'What about all that meat?' I say. There's a lot of meat in the paw, you know. 'I dunno,' Gort says. So we cut the paw off, what the heck. We get to the head and Gort's doing the ear. There's this little piece inside, you're supposed to just reach in there, *blip,* twist, there you've got it. Gort reaches in, gives it a little twist with the knife, damn ear comes off altogether. But what the heck, the bear's dead, he don't need the ear.

"Next thing you know, Gort's cut the nose off. 'You oughtta mount that head,' I told him. Funniest thing you ever saw. Bear's got no beak.

"Gort's mother got my bear. We was coming up the trail and I see this pile of bear shit. I've got a moose up ahead, see, that I already shot. Been packing moose back for three days. So I stop to look at this blueberry shit, next thing you know, Gort goes ahead of me and shoots the damn bear. 'Hey, that's my bear,' I tell him. He shoots again. 'Thanks anyway for giving me the second shot,' I say. I shoot him a third time, but the bear's already dead, probably. Gort's gone on ahead, see, and there's the bear asleep on this pile of moose. He's got his meat and all the sunshine he wants, and he's laying there head on his paws, sleeping away. Gort shoots him. He wakes up fast and comes running through the brush, so Gort shoots him again. My bear. His mother's got him stuffed."

I was howling. Tears were streaming down my cheeks.

"I should tell you about my first moose. Gort and I were lost. We were so far back in the hills, took us two days to find the Takotna River, we were that lost. Shot a moose. We carried it for two days. Didn't know where the hell we were, walking up and down those goddamn hills, two of us was bad enough but we had a moose with us. Finally occurred to us to put the damn thing down.

"We kept walking, finally came to a lake. You know, we walked eight hours and came right back to that damn lake. We walked and walked for two days, walk up to this lake and go right into it, chest-high into the damn lake, each of us with a quarter of moose on our head. Come out; wade in, with the moose on our head, right up to our chest. Finally occurs to me. I look around, here's two sets of tracks coming in from the other side of the lake. That's gotta be us, unless there's another party of two hunters we don't know about in the area. We was so mad we camped right there. 'Course, we came up out of the water before we camped."

I howled with laughter while Mick Hannigan told his story. This was spiritual degradation, and it was a blasphemy on the bear; and I suffered for it.

○

ALMOST IMPERCEPTIBLY, a long, slow, rolling shift occurred. I sent tiny sparks, my letters to friends, flying through the night; but the actual night was thick with brilliant stars, and the Aurora danced and leaped above us across the sky. I went outside and whistled at it.

Our House
Is Open, There
Are No Keys in
the Door

THE TEMPERATURE LINGERED below
minus thirty-five for almost six weeks. The land and the air were silent. At
ground level there was no wind. The eye moved across the low horizon of
frosted rolling hills and open flats, it noted the diagonals and low arcs of
small birds darting and the assured way a raven took command of the air.
The glottal talk of ravens scraped the ear like a rasp. They spoke intelligently.
Some of their language was coherent to me, their water call and their warning to pay attention.

The snow fell higher than the dead grass, and was heaped around the
trailer and piled over its curved roof: my small ice-cave was a mound in a
white, dead field. A tall stovepipe poked through, breathing a steady line of
smoke straight as a thermometer. In the dry, dry air the snow sifted across
my boots and evaporated when I stepped indoors.

When the extreme cold broke, the round of travel started up again. Curly
Johansson was flying me up to a village on the north fork of the Kuskokwim.
Though he was a bad man, he was a good pilot. He knew the country, and
he had taught younger men to fly. He taught them how to read the land, to
see its pattern, and recognize what connected them to it. A pilot named Peter
Frost told me how Curly had talked him through Rainy Pass, a dangerous
route through the Alaska Range, before he, Peter, ever approached the mountains. Curly had told him to look for certain rock forms, slopes, soil colors,
animal trails; had described them in sequence as they appeared from the air,
so Peter would remember and recognize them. When he flew the pass for the
first time, he said, it was as though Curly's voice talked in his ear; and as he
told me about Curly, he described the pass, feature by feature, as if he were
preparing me. It was how Curly taught Peter to fly: from his imagination,
tested by experience.

That summer, a notice had appeared in the Anchorage paper, with a photograph. Missing, it said:

> Friends of Gleeman Esau of N., who has been missing since July 22, 1975
> in the Anchorage area, request information about his whereabouts. He is
> about 5 foot 7, is partially blind and walks with a cane. He has not been
> seen or heard from since the July visit to Anchorage; persons with infor-

mation could contact the Anchorage Police Dept. or call————
collect at————.

Gleeman Esau had been missing for four and a half years. We were on our way to N. I asked Curly if he had known the man, and whether he had been found.

"I knew him," said Curly, easily. "He was a shaman. One time he told a guy that when he died, he'd come back as a raven. He died. They hadn't seen any ravens around up there for a long time. Must have been late spring, summer, when they're scarce anyway. People started seeing one very big raven, about fifteen inches high." He took his hands off the stick, and measured.

"It stayed around for a while," he said. He shot a glance at me and winked. "Nah, they won't find him."

o

Dear H,

I had a dream, the impersonal kind, when you've been allowed to glimpse a state of being beyond yourself. I remember it dimly now; but know, as I knew while I dreamed, it was terribly important. Death was in it, and love, and some kind of unknowing. I don't think the dream was an omen, though I find that, at important times, dreams have told me what the next part of living is going to be. This dream seemed to be of that sort, but only as an intimation. I wonder if a visionary dream is coming.

There is power here. Not in McGrath, but in several places where I've been. I know I'm susceptible to it, but I can barely sense what this means. I'm not skittish, I don't think, and not given to these notions about "poet-shamans."

I don't feel strong enough to meet the power. I'm not part of my church anymore. My family is far away. We've always had strong dreams; there is something in us I don't know how to describe, some kind of old force, some sort of Celtic blood-memory, perhaps; but we are all of us split by modern complications. I have no protection, I'm entirely open to what is out there. About this power I know only that it exists, and that I have some of it inside me.

I've known this since I was very young. Sometimes, working with words lets me sense it; as if some finger of the mind touches it, groping, where the eyes can't see. Then, sometimes I dream. This force. This energy.

But I don't know how to organize my understanding of it. I haven't a guide, nor strong enough ties to anyone who knows what I mean. I stammer then, and think it's too dangerous to go on on my own; yet I go on, trying to keep my balance. Maybe you should burn this.

I don't want to burden you; keeping it inside isn't a good idea, either. I don't know what else to say. I'm trying not to mix up bravery with stupidity. I have no language for this, yet; the tone is wrong.

You comforted me by saying if I ever needed a place, I might find one with you. That lets me breathe a little. Burn this; somehow I'm not sure these words should exist on paper. Could that be dangerous, to stumble and try to *say?* Has that been the unbalance we feel around the white settlements, that we disturb old things?

Some people decide to *know*, and more of them decide *not to know*, and to live peacefully. I have no peace. But when and why did I choose? It was so long ago that it happened before I knew about choice. Is there any help for it?

The letter touched on a sensation for which I had no language; an impression in the psyche, perhaps, that is present, nearly palpable, but exists before language. Uneasy, yet sure of my intuition, I mailed it, and felt naked before my friend.

Yeats wrote, "Belief makes the mind more abundant." He may have meant, Our minds are widened, they open outward, they see what our narrower, exigent intellect has no eyes for. I was not thinking of Yeats, except in this way: I knew, deeply and immediately, that—in that country—words are connected to things. At the time I believed I had been set a task: to find the accurate words for what I was given to see, and say them; but the feeling I had, the sensing of shape and force I tried to describe in the letter, was not about words. It was not about poetry; it was not poetry, at all. What was it?

My friend H. had been raised in the far North and knew, far more than I, about old powers on the land. He sent a compassionate reply: "I did a reading in New York City, old faces showed up. Little sleep. I had your last letter with me. An Inuit man came to the reading, and we stayed up late talking about your letter … do you mind? not all of it, just certain parts. He asked me what you looked like. I said somewhat like a lynx, but one that unlike others likes to swim! in fact goes out of her way to do this, though in great privacy, and if you happen upon her doing so you are very fortunate. He said it helped him to talk about Alaska."

○

THAT WINTER I read Slavic poets, Mandelstam, Milosz, because it seemed to me they knew the vastness of the North and answered it without looking away. I copied out Milosz's ironic, self-mocking, profound "Ars Poetica." It brought the poem close; I read it out loud, pretending my voice was not mine, but the real voice behind the poem. I listened uneasily, humbly, knowing the poem was truthful, only half-knowing, yet half-fearing, the nature of its truth.

. . . .
> *It's hard to guess where that pride of poets comes from,*
> *when so often they're put to shame by the disclosure of frailty.*

. . . .

People therefore preserve silent integrity,
thus earning the respect of their relatives and neighbors.

The purpose of poetry is to remind us
how difficult it is to remain just one person,
for our house is open, there are no keys in the doors,
and invisible guests come in and out at will. . . .

●

THE MONTHS ADVANCED; gradually the temperature rose: minus thirty, minus twenty. The days were cold and clear; the light returned by the minute, six or eight minutes a day. The ice cracked off the trailer's small windows, and they admitted the new light.

I stole time to keep my notebook. I lived in offices and on airplanes, as Malfa and I made our final push at the university. We had become partners in a campaign to bring the teacher-training program into the district; it was going to give her the chance to go to college. I had decided to do everything possible to make that chance come to pass; it was now the only reason to remain in McGrath.

The cold, clear weather broke. The mercury inched above zero. The days began early now; the sky looked like a slow awakening, shades of early-morning-before-coffee blue, layers of clouds stretching and yawning. I yawned and stretched, and lingered over a deep mug of coffee. Light streamed into the trailer through its little rounded clear windows.

●

IT WAS CRUST-TIME, the month of lengthening days, when the top layer of softening snow freezes again at night. Snow dropped off the trees, leaving bare branches. Ptarmigan, roosting, still wore white feathers, but snow no longer camouflaged them. From the woods at the edge of town came the cap-gun pop of a .22, as a householder took that night's supper.

I lunched at home, soup and coffee over a book. It was nearly time to leave. I was closing up when I heard shots again, two, from close range: someone must have gone after birds across the runway. I decided to take the longer route back to the office, away from the woods, and headed toward the boardwalk.

I walked past McGuire's, lost in thought, but looked up at a sound. An unusual number of people were walking toward me. To the post office, already? The mail wouldn't be sorted for another hour. They walked together, they were a crowd; their bodies moved as though pulled by a common string, walking oddly upright. Ann Close, from the district office, swam forward, out of step, and waved: *no, she's signaling me to stop.* I put on my glasses. Her mouth opens and shuts: the cold thins her words to little piping notes. She is pointing behind me, toward the post office, and I turn around to look.

Five people kneel in red snow under the hard, immense, blue sky. "Hear the shooting?" a man asks, passing me. "Guy got shot. He was asking for it."

How does a man ask to get shot? The glare hurt my eyes.

The crowd advanced. A thin, angry voice drifted toward us in bursts. The nurse and—four? four medics from the emergency squad worked efficiently on a man, who lay on a stretcher on the snow. His skin looked like waxed paper. His blood flowed brilliantly over his legs, on to the snow, up the hands and arms to the elbows of the medics. Obscenely he cursed the nurse as she tried to slide an I.V. into his arm. The medics held him down.

The man next to me muttered: "Bad stuff." Gradually, silently, the crowd detached itself, and each one of us drifted away.

I walked on to the trading post. My office was too quiet. Useless to try to work; I went to see the superintendent, who looked frail and shocked. He was eager to talk, but not very lucid. He had been on his way to lunch, taking the trail through the woods to the roadhouse, when he saw the man, whom everyone called "the drifter."

The drifter was staggering along the road and talking to himself. ("Strange," said the superintendent: "Do you think he was on drugs?") He stumbled into a snowbank—a small box dropped from his hands: papers and photographs spilled out across the snow. He crawled frantically after them, grabbing at bits and pieces, but could not hold on to them. The superintendent bent to help, and picked up some papers. The drifter, on his knees, waved him away.

"His eyes were really wild," the superintendent said. He blamed himself for not having gone to the mental health counselor. "I should have found help for that poor man," he fretted.

"He had a weapon," I said.

The superintendent looked shocked all over again. "I never considered that," he said faintly.

I went to see the mental health counselor and asked her what she knew. He was a drifter, she said, and he had been waiting for something like this to happen.

I looked around for someone who always knew what was going on. Enos Chandler was coming out of the store. He had lived in McGrath for decades. I asked if he had ever known a shooting. "Can't recall a one," he said shortly, "nothing like this." I asked if there had ever been a murder in McGrath. "No," he said, and glared at me as if I were a reporter.

Shootings happened often in the bush, more often than I wanted to know. People gathered to party, something went wrong: an argument broke out, a .30-.30 appeared; someone died; witnesses were silent. A woman might shoot her husband for beating her. A drunk might get shot banging on someone's door.

The superintendent had asked the teachers to evaluate their students' plans for the future. The teacher whose husband drowned still lived in the village, near her in-laws, and still taught in the one-room school. She laughed at the superintendent's directive. "For those kids, the unforeseeable future is not what's on their minds," she said, "it's whether a gun is going to go off when people are partying. One teenager in my class, who would love to go to college sometime, sleeps in the loft in her parents' house. A rifle went off downstairs: the bullet passed through the floor close to her bed. She doesn't sleep well now.

"'What plans have your students made for the next two years?'—the district must be insane. Two years from now? These kids are wondering if they're going to live through the night."

A current, sardonic joke: the penalty for poaching a moose was stiffer than for killing a human.

Malfa thought a shooting was never a simple matter. "There is always a story," she had said. "When it occurs among our people, who have grown up together, then any death is a double loss. People mourn twice, for the dead man, and for his killer, who is a relative, too, or a friend. He might be the kind of man who goes crazy when he drinks, or because the trapping season has been bad, or because in some other way the pressures of life have begun to smother him. People have watched him grow up, too. They may have seen early that something would go bad for him, but they've lived with it; and they will bury him, too."

But the drifter was an Outsider, the kind people called an end-of-the-roader, the sort, common on the frontier, who couldn't manage to fit in anywhere else, and had drifted North and washed up like flotsam in some bush town. No one knew where the drifter came from, or if he had relatives. He had moved around, and had a reputation for anger and fighting. One village had given him a "blue ticket," paying his one-way passage out of town. Somehow he wound up in McGrath. A woman came to live with him; the word went around that he beat her. What help she found, or if she found it, was never made public.

In Anchorage, a judge had put him on probation for knife-fighting. He had had to surrender his weapons. By that time, a trooper was stationed in McGrath, and the town council had hired a safety officer. The two lawmen kept a close eye on the drifter. Their surveillance embittered him. He had a few cronies, some of the younger men and the two or three newcomers, who drank in McGuire's and muttered to one another that he was being harassed.

A few weeks before the shooting, he had gone into town and had come back, it was said, with a knife-cut on his thigh. His eyes were wilder. I heard in passing that the woman had moved out and left McGrath.

Ann Close, who had seen it, described the shooting. She had gone to the post office to buy stamps, and had just stepped out the door, when she saw the trooper: his gun was drawn, and he and the safety officer were slowly walking backward. She looked to see what they were retreating from, and saw the drifter. He was lurching toward them, holding a long hunting knife as if he meant to stab someone. The lawmen instructed him to put the knife down, and then to back away from it. He called out, "Shoot me! Shoot me!"

She decided that was no place for her to be and hurried past my trailer, going toward the boardwalk. Behind her, the trooper and the safety officer, who normally went unarmed, were still stepping backward in the snow, asking the drifter to put down his knife, and he was still stumbling toward them, asking them to shoot him. She must have reached the boardwalk when she heard the first shot. She turned, and saw the drifter grab his leg.

He limped, but kept walking. (His strength amazed her.) He still held the knife as if he meant to use it. The trooper took aim, fired again, and hit the other leg. The drifter fell down.

It came back to me that the trooper had been standing near the medics while they worked on the injured man. I had watched his face: he looked young, clean-cut, professional, near tears. Ann said she had felt bad for him. He had sounded horrified—"Put it down, please put it down!" He hadn't wanted to shoot.

Later the trooper's friends told people that he felt sick about the shooting and was going to stay quiet for a few days. I didn't see him around town for some time.

As for the drifter: after the superintendent had stopped to help him pick up his lost papers, someone else had spotted him with the knife, and had reported it to the trooper. The trooper had called in the safety officer, and they had gone together to see what the matter was.

All afternoon, people moved more slowly than usual. Distress and unease shifted around the town. Faces were sober, as if life had snapped into focus. I felt wide-eyed and dry. I stopped in at the office of the town manager, who was the husband of the curriculum director. We had some business to discuss; but both of us were thinking of other things. He mentioned having been an American officer in Vietnam, then blurted out that he had despised the ARVN, because they were incompetent, and had hated them because they were cowards.

My office was in the old trading post, a dilapidated building only partly renovated. Absently, I remarked that I had seen red-brown splotches on the floor of the bathroom, probably the drifter's blood.

I didn't know where he was sleeping, but doubted the place had plumbing. For weeks I had suspected he sneaked into the trading post at night. He might as well keep clean, I thought. Then, someone had mentioned the knife-wound on his leg. I was vaguely sickened—who could do anything for him? He trailed signs of some furtive, unkempt existence being scratched out at the edge of normality in that town. He was a carrier of its disorder, and a messenger of its coming loss.

Idly, I wondered how long the red stains would remain in the snow, or if they would be scraped up—. My mind stopped abruptly.

The town stayed quiet; the roads were empty. The wind died, and the trees across the river stood still. I telephoned H., back East, longing to hear a familiar voice; but there was no answer.

The next morning, no red smudges were left on the snow. People looked like themselves again. Within a day or two, the weather shifted. The air softened, and the snow began to melt. Mud appeared on the roads. I went down to the river to watch Don Tweed and Grog Johnson drive a D-9 Cat across the ice.

In the offices, people were back at their routines. I finished my business with the city manager. Malfa's great gathering of the elders was going to take place in Shelter; thirty-odd people from the Kuskokwim villages had been invited. He offered help with the logistics on the McGrath side.

The superintendent looked as he always did, as though he hadn't slept well. The mental health counselor flew off on her rounds to the northern villages; the nurse held her regular clinic in town. Ann Close told her story a few times more, then tired of it.

Some of the younger men and the newcomers, louder than usual in McGuire's, argued the drifter wasn't a bad guy, and the trooper never should have used his gun. They resented the ordinance that said he was the only man allowed to carry a side-arm in town.

Ancient Mariners

JOE DEVLIN had covered the field around my trailer with truckloads of dirt, burying the wild grass, the flowers, and the chamomile; graded it; then added two ugly house trailers to his slum-like little development. What kind of soul would do this? He didn't need the money, God knew.

"Got to improve the property," he said.

The university had agreed to our negotiating terms and was going to set up a field center, probably in Shelter, for training teachers in the district; my part in that struggle was over. The timing was good: my contract with the district was about to expire. I thought I would go to Fairbanks for a few weeks, then head East from there; otherwise, I had no plans.

Malfa was making final preparations for the elders conference, on which she had labored for months. She had mobilized Shelter to feed and house dozens of guests from the villages, and some important white people from town. I had made phone calls, written letters, filled out grant applications; money and promises of service were rolling in. Away from McGrath a sub-dued bustle, a current of glad anticipation, was stirring people up. Malfa and I saw each other more often; but I had not yet told her I was going to leave.

Dear H.,

It's late; this was the last night of the elders conference. I'm writing this in my sleeping bag, using a flashlight: I'm camping in a classroom with three women scholars and writers who were invited for the occasion.

Last night Shelter held an old-time dance. You'd have enjoyed it, I think. You might have thought you were back in your part of the North. The old people were zesty and full of life. You'd have seen old John Elder throw away his cane (he is ninety) and dance a two-step with a pretty young woman from town. You would have seen his stately wife, Mrs. Belle Elder, who told us, "Long time ago, they told us stories, so we could learn how to become people." I watched Old Man Demetroff, still going strong, bring out his harmonica and sing Indian songs. The hill behind his home-stead is fenced with the crosses of wives and children he has buried. Grandma Mrs. Ivanov told us about being a widow with six children, driving nine dogs out to trap and get wood: "We never know how to use driftwood, we always went way out for standing timber. And now they use driftwood," she marveled, "and it's just as good!"

Couples danced, or sat among their friends and relatives, smiling, talk-ing. They were happy. I wondered if the old men were not seeing the woman all over again as the lovely young girls they had been. Grandma

Mrs. Ivanov declared, "I was just tiny, small waist; but I was strong!" She giggled, as she does when she's delighted. She was raised here, in the old mission. The French nuns taught the young girls to make lace undergarments. They made her a beautiful corset for her wedding, but, she confided, she threw it away after the ceremony. Oh, she was beautiful: *la grande*, the nuns called her. She married the son of the eldest Ivanov brother, himself one of five sons of a Russian creole, who had come over to help build the mission: she had fallen in love with his blue eyes. This would have been around 1915, I suppose. In summertime, they used to dance on a barge on the river, under gas lamps. They had a Victrola with a needle that someone had to keep sharp with a stone. Her young husband was dashing and strong; they said he and his partner devised a greeting for important visitors entering the village: they leaped back and forth over the visitors' sleds, carrying lighted torches in their hands. When they went out to winter camp, their wives and children wrapped in furs in the sled baskets, they lashed oil lanterns to the rail to light their way. What drivers they must have been.

For the last three days people have been meeting long-lost relatives. Shelter has opened its homes to these elders and their traveling companions. The families brought pot-luck feasts to the school gymnasium, where the conference took place—plenty of dryfish and beaver meat, plenty of everything. The real events happened away from the gym, of course, in the houses, over tea and food, where people were reunited. Some of these people haven't seen each other since they were children in the mission, thirty or forty years ago. They've all been crying and laughing, and joy still glows on their faces.

Malfa's health turned bad before the conference began (rheumatoid arthritis; a flare-up), and everyone in town has pitched in to take up the slack. She is happy at the sense of unity people feel, as though they have agreed to overlook their differences. She took me to drink tea with some women, who were speaking about a man whose half-sister lived in Shelter. Once more I noticed how carefully they speak, in order not to put anyone on the spot; but I gathered something from their allusions. When these women were young, the man they spoke of was the big man in a Yup'ik village not far downriver. The priests used to go down and see him every so often, but the children never knew why. "He used to take men's wives when the men were gone, something like that," said one of the women noncommittally. Another woman said that people thought he was Yup'ik, but his mother came from Village Across, on the other side of the river from the mission, "and so she was Indian." "He was a big man, light haired," someone else said. "Maybe his father was white, and so he was Indian, but he acted Eskimo."

I asked, then, how people decided who they were. "Because people remain where they belong," they said.

There are about a dozen white guests, besides me and the teachers. The reporter from *The New York Times,* who arrived without a sleeping bag or towel, made the village people nervous. They watched him take notes, and didn't look pleased. But we had invited him; so Malfa took him aside and had a word with him about how people were afraid that what he wrote could do them harm. I caught a glimpse of them conferring. He is about a foot taller than she is, and had bent over to hear her, while she looked very serious as she talked. Her earnest plea must have startled him; Malfa said he was cold to her. I suppose he had no idea he was being watched, or why; but he may have suspected something was being concealed, or the "news" was being "managed," because he found a way to talk to an old uncle (Malfa's husband's uncle, an interesting man), who had a bottle and who gave him what sounded like mildly spiteful gossip, so that he could "balance" his article. Malfa has no idea she might be "managing" the news. She told him the people were trying to make themselves known in their own terms to the outsiders: who, I noticed, don't quite know what to make of it all.

I tried to envision the scene through the eyes of the outsiders. Does the village look shabby to them? Do the people look poor? What do they think of these old faces, with their expressions courteously masked? This isn't the usual Native public event they are used to in town, no people in gorgeous traditional dress, no expert dancers performing, no one selling hand work. The villagers look humble and unassuming, like people who have come through a disaster and are just beginning to recover from the shock of it. Do the outsiders know that those two old men haven't seen each other in twenty-five years; or that these three ladies grew up together in the mission, and haven't been back since they left to marry? What do they make of that small, timid couple, in their drab clothes, who cling to each other as they walk across the gym floor looking for people they know? Nothing's on display; it's all feeling, memory, hope, sadness. The welling-up of emotion is hard for us to accept, I think; it makes us uncomfortable, because we don't know what to do with ourselves then. We don't like being pressed to feel what others feel, and so we pull back from it; or else, feeling false or guilty ourselves, we sentimentalize it. But hearts here don't have those guards on them, and they can't figure out why we're so "cold"—as the *Times* man was, or seemed to be. As for me, I'm somewhere in-between. Maybe a little teary-eyed; want to keep it private; can't.

At the potlatch, the last night of feasting and speeches, Malfa took the floor to thank the elders and the people who had helped put on the gathering, and then said, in front of everyone, "Mothers are supposed to dress their lovely daughters in beads." With tears in her eyes she came to my seat, thrust a small packet in my hand, and turned away. In the packet was a pair of handsome earrings of beads and quills, made by a young woman in Shelter, a Gordon daughter-in-law, whose work she knew I admired.

It was time to go; but I was not sorry to leave. I could no longer live as I had, with so many moral contradictions. But my heart tightened when I said good-bye to Malfa. Literally: the bonds of motherhood yanked hard, squeezing me so that I gasped, and in dismay felt her pulling me back; but with all my heart I desired to go; I wished to leave that hard country.

○

WHAT DOES LEAVING ALASKA MEAN? I knew a woman who had tried seven times to leave. Once she got as far as San Francisco, and even kept a place there for a while. It didn't work: she came back. Some people, if they had lived in the state more than a few years, looked wistful when I mentioned going. Others, just arrived, showed me pity; but their spirit had not yet been tried by the winter.

"There are two reasons to be here if you're white," a man said, reflectively, one night in McGuire's. He had lived in the bush for a long time and was careful of what he said; and he knew something that embittered him: "If you're looking for something you haven't found; or if you've stopped looking, and don't have any reason to go anywhere else." *Here* was Alaska; anywhere else was Outside. People moved around; but if they left the state, the ones who remained felt they had been abandoned, judged wanting, and they resented this.

○

SOMETIMES, travelers are the most lost when they come home again.

In 1975, in Paris, in spring, in the late morning, I walked over to the church of St.-Sulpice to look at a painting by Delacroix; but the church was locked, and the painting was being cleaned. Before descending the steps I paused to look at the lovely Place, and noticed a man standing still, uneasily, among the pedestrians. He wasn't American, probably not German, not provincial French; he was urbane but out of place. He was going to speak to me.

I walked down the steps, turning away from him, knowing I would not evade him. The light was washed with gold and green and a little breeze stirred the leaves of the plane trees. The look on his face was intense; but he merely asked directions, and I supplied them. He spoke British English with a French accent. We went to a cafe.

I stopped for him because of his eyes. They were dark or pale: I couldn't tell. They were spinning in their sockets, they nearly jumped from his face. I could not look away. He was an Ancient Mariner, and would constrain a Wedding Guest to hear his tale.

He was an anthropologist, back from long years abroad. He laughed a little: he had got lost in this *quartier*, where he had lived as a student. He turned wistful.

"I lived in India, and would have remained there," he said. "I was happy and had many, many friends; I taught, and my students were talented. But we dream of Paris. A position opened at N. My choices: live out my life in India, where I was happy; or, return to Paris. This cold city. I look around me and no longer recognize what I see.

"I thought I would not receive such an offer again, you see. In India I could speak only English. I have left what made me happy because I can no longer exist without my language."

I mentioned Mauss, and my reading project at the Musée de l'Homme. He responded with enthusiasm; his own professor had been Mauss's pupil— *Look, here is his address, give him my name, this will introduce you.* He wrote the particulars on a page torn from a notebook. We shook hands, and parted. I can recall nothing about him but his shocked, haunted eyes.

The writer Barry Lopez said, later, that people coming out of Alaska look haunted. Their eyes are shocked, they have seen something they can't describe. I thought of the anthropologist; perhaps I thought of myself.

To leave Alaska was to leave an impossible lover: you can't go on together, but you are restless, unhappy without him. Life elsewhere was a bit drab, a bit small, a bit too ordinary. What do you love so much? a person would ask. I would reply, The men are lost; the winters are hard on you; Native people are sick and dying; the oil companies are too powerful; white people are greedy and sick … I named twenty reasons why Alaska was awful. But that's not it, I stuttered: It's, it's …

"Something knows," said a Koyukon man: "The whole country knows." If I sensed its intelligence, I didn't know what it meant to tell me. I no longer knew what anything meant. Like the anthropologist, I was shocked into incoherence. What was left to me was only what I had seen, heard, touched, smelled: sensation, a procession of images, a handful of hermetic poems.

I had entered a long story and lived there for a time. It has no conclusion. It offers no resolution, and this exhausted me. Alaska taught me that life is contradiction, at the extreme, at the heart. Alaska was frontier settled roughly on homeland; and it was the holiness of Denali, the wonder of the night sky. It was Joe Devlin, and F, the big man, and the hard men, it was cursed Emma, and the old woman of the fierce eye, the Charleses and their eaglet children, it was the game warden and the trooper and the furtive drifter and his disorder, and the curriculum director who protected girls, and it was Malfa, who was my mother.

○

NATIVE PEOPLE have often told Outsiders that they belong to their land. They describe the kinship in many ways. They speak of hunting, trapping, and fishing locations; berry-picking and egg-gathering locations; campsites; *kashim* sites; medicine plant sites; the places where people were born, and where they died, and where they are buried; where a certain animal was taken; where someone was killed; where a medicine man was killed; where big animals den; where humans and animals share territory, and where they avoid each other's company; unlucky spots, to be avoided; boundaries between territories used by families, clans, villages, or outsiders; house sites; where spirits of the dead might linger.

Some years ago, archaeologists excavated a house site in the permafrost of the North Slope, dating, they guessed, from the fifteenth century. Bodies perfectly preserved were found in the house, presumably of the family who had made it. A young woman from the nearest village, a close friend of Malfa, was hired as translator. Not long afterward, she began dreaming. In her dreams, the people of that ancient family, speaking Iñupiaq, let it be known that they did not wish to be disturbed. Fearing ridicule, she was reluctant to mention her dream to the archaeologists and found another way to relate the dream-message. The excavation continued, of course, but she stopped working with the diggers.

In that country Native people know themselves as belonging, as being related, to their place. They know this by the archaic logic of association, which does not reduce their relatives to biological categories of kinship, or deed-based laws of ownership, but recognizes the force of both human and metaphysical ties. As Malfa said, "My boundaries are my relatives." She meant it literally and figuratively, and in her phrase was figured more than I could once have imagined. Similarly, a woman had said, "People stay where they belong." And old Mrs. Gordon's granddaughter had told me, "People want to be with their own kind." In their statements, experience became language. If I consider a poetics of the relationships among them, I must understand the trope of association by contiguity, the figure of like touching like. It is more than simile, and it is not metaphor; it lies within the realm of metonym, which is distinct from metaphor. It is philosophically—although not from experience—a difficult figure for one like myself to comprehend, because it is a figure of identity and describes from experience the link between two same, although distinct, kinds of creature.

When the figure becomes distorted and experience is denied, when relations are harmed and the link is broken, the mind is profoundly disturbed. It wants unity, which is beautiful to it and which it loves, and will try to make itself whole again.

This is knowledge of another order, paying attention to what things do in that country where everything is related. When you find yourself among such people, in such a place, you may well find also that knowledge of a specific kind belongs there, and perhaps not anywhere else. It may not be translated, or carried over; and what you take away may be important to you, but irrelevant to the real story.

As for me, I had wanted to reconcile story and truth, and had not succeeded. I had left Europe, its wars and decadence, and gone north, leaving behind a classical story whose plot was death and inevitable loss; but that story had come back around to meet me. Said the old Athabaskans, Everything that exists has its own spirit, which must respected. Perhaps they had meant, It must be faced, studied, and acknowledged.

Which of our losses is reversible?

◊

I WAS WRONG, OF COURSE. The story wasn't over ("Pay attention to what things do . . ."). Something wasn't finished with me; in spite of myself, I was going to be pulled North again.

◊

JUST BEFORE I LEFT MCGRATH, I fell in love with a painter; but that is not what this epilogue is about, although it is true that love always alters the story. Long before I met him I had admired his ravishing, painterly portraits of animals. It was as if he had called the animals, and they had come to him. "Every animal has his own face," he said. This fable is about animals.

I joined him in Fairbanks, where we spent a month in a cabin outside of town. This was just after break-up. It was already warm. The place sat on a ridge, at the end of a long, dusty road. From the porch we looked out over the greening valley.

A deep-throated, three-sided gong hung from the rafter, and when the wind stirred, the gong seemed to call us to prayer. The skulls of small animals hung from the same rafter. A wolverine skull grinned voraciously, its jaws open. I thought, He is hunting me.

◊

THE STORY IS ABOUT LOVE and contradiction. Late that summer, when the silver salmon were running, we went to Kodiak, where the painter had grown up. His widowed grandmother was Aleut, born near the village of Malfa's mother; her husband had been a Russian bear hunter. He had been a rough man, she told me. She loved her grandson very much: "Take good care of my boy," she begged. She must have guessed why I could not, but she hoped for us, letting me hope; and I loved her for it.

"Time to go fishing," the painter called. He had a subsistence permit, issued to Native people and some white people, allowing them to take a household's winter supply of fish. He always gave most of the catch to his grandmother, and she shared it with his mother, who also was widowed.

He put his skiff in the water, and we motored through the harbor to an outside channel that he thought would be provident. We dropped the net and sat back, waiting for the first run to strike.

When silver salmon strike the net, they hit hard, with brilliance and flash! The water churns and splashes up loudly, the cork line bobs and dips, the drama excites the eye.

We were bobbing on a green-brown, translucent current in the blue water of the harbor. Just below the surface, close to the skiff, a humpie swam, a kind of salmon often fed to dogs. The net corks dipped sharply, tugged from below. The painter swore and wished he had brought a rifle. A seal was tearing the meshes: he wriggled through the opening, and rose swiftly toward the fish. The fish glided by, unaware of its hunter.

A rush of wings, a dark, heavy shape, a sea-eagle dropped out of the sky and swiped the salmon from the water, from under the seal's nose; climbed ponderously back into his orbit; and flew away.

The seal popped above the surface, wide-eyed. Nearby, some puffins clattered into the air, disturbed by the fuss.

Life.

That year, or the year before, the number of walrus in the western coastal waters surged, so that the animals pressed out from the shallow green Bering Sea into the North Pacific. Walrus are shovelers and use their tusks to rake the bottom for shellfish. They were so hungry, and the water was so deep, that they ate ducks. This was unprecedented, and the federal government opened a hunt. Normally, walrus were protected under the Marine Mammal Act, so that the use of their ivory was reserved for Native people who carved, painted, or otherwise used it for art or ceremony; and who, once their mark had been put upon it, were allowed to sell it. Buyers desired tusks and the *oosik*, the penis bone. When the season on walrus was opened, Native hunters were allowed to take the heads and organs, and let the vast fat bodies, which had always been food for the coastal people, fall back into the sea.

This fable is about animals, and a desecration that human love could not absolve. The painter had gone hunting for walrus with his brother, who owned a fishing boat. For several days, he told me, dolphins had been following their boat. At last the brothers caught a walrus and hauled the heavy body aboard. Hacking the head off was slow, bloody work. The two brothers kept the skull with the tusks attached to it, and the *oosik*, and shoved the rest overboard. As the body fell into the water, the dolphins turned away and disappeared.

Coda:
The Gift

One might say that Catholicism notices things,
the particular.

—Robert Lowell

Belief makes the mind more abundant.

—William Butler Yeats

The Gift

A NEWCOMER drifted into McGrath, a white man, tall and good-looking, probably in his late twenties. Somewhere along the line he had learned to build elegant dogsleds, and he collected odd mementos—tin buttons, animal skulls, old bottles unearthed in tumbledown cabins: relics of pioneer encounters with nature. One day he crossed my path in some out-of-the-way spot and halted. Shyly, sweetly, he held out a small leather pouch. "I made this for you," he said and walked away quickly. In the pouch were a necklace and earrings made of little bones.

The bones were perfectly shaped, creamy: miniatures of bones. He had strung them on dental floss, the new sinew in the bush, and glued them to gold-toned fixtures. Touched but puzzled, I went to see him and asked whose remnants these were.

They were wolverine toe-bones, he said. He had trapped the animal north of Anchorage, where he had built his best sleds.

Many Athabaskan women wore beads and quills worked beautifully into jewelry; doing this, they showed their respect for themselves and delight in the pleasure of adornment. I myself wore beads and quills, most often the long earrings that were the fine handwork of a young woman in Shelter, a Gordon daughter-in-law. She and I had become friends, and I watched her when she worked skins or beaded. She had the ability the old people called *putting something special in it.* That something infused a quality that to an observant eye identified her work as Athabaskan. I could not seem to learn it: when I practiced beading with her I made a bad imitation; we both knew it, although she was too polite to say so.

The bone necklace, the earrings made of tiny bones were like that: imitations. He knew how to make handsome sleds, after his own design; but he had not mastered the use of the bones and, because of it, his jewelry looked clumsy. Although I had been charmed, I was embarrassed for him, though I was sorry, too, to feel that way.

A feeling neither aesthetic nor romantic also came to me: an uneasy sense that it was not correct for him or me to use this animal. I had never seen Athabaskan women wear wolverine skins and took that absence as a marker, for there was nothing accidental or arbitrary in the things women used, or did not use, in their handwork. Any part of the animal, even if used for decoration, invoked a quality particular to it. I did not know much about wolverine then: even so, when I tried on the pieces I was physically uncomfortable. I took them off and slid them back into the pouch and, not knowing what to do with them, yet feeling they ought to be handled with care, tucked them into a box of odds and ends.

Around that time I went to Shelter on school business and happened to talk to a teacher who was a friend of Malfa. It was trapping season. A wolverine had been taken. "It's their most powerful animal," the teacher told me, meaning spiritually powerful, "and they potlatch it when they catch one."

The world *potlatch* was used by Athabaskans for different kinds of celebrations. I asked what it meant in Shelter, where the Catholic church was strong. She described it as a ceremony to honor the animal. Before the hunter skinned it, his wife spread a blanket in the entry of the house, or, more formally, in the place in the room where a guest of honor sat. There the husband arranged the animal's body, and there left it overnight with a small piece of moose fat or dried salmon in its mouth: so its body was honored, and so it was fed, to thank its spirit for having given itself to the hunter.

About a year later I found the small leather pouch again. What a poor thing the pieces in it looked; yet, the look on his face had been open and manly, and shy too: sweet homage paid a woman amid the sexual carnage of that country.

Yet I couldn't bear to keep the ugly things; and yet, from some obscure prick of conscience, couldn't bring myself to throw them away; until, tired of indecision, I threw away the fake gold. I cut the string and scraped off the glue; pushed the smooth, small bones into a pile, and rolled them into the pouch; and hid the pouch in the box of stuff. More time passed; I moved, then left Alaska. The pouch settled into deeper into the box, where the bones remained safe, and with me; and I forgot about them.

o

FOR THE SAKE OF ITS BEAUTY, or power, or, perhaps, from spiritual pride, any seeker may long for a revelation that will rumble the earth; and instead, find that if one is granted it may only confuse her, being ambiguous, even banal. She might feel foolish, and not speak of it to anyone; she might decide to ignore it altogether. Or, if she is of a certain cast of mind, she will not; then she must accept what follows and study its nature.

I had left Alaska, more or less for good, I thought, and had settled into a house on a hillside in the Blue Ridge of Virginia. It must have been about January of that year, 1983, a mild winter. For some time I had been writing an intellectual history of the ideas of Marcel Mauss, turning on his theory of magic, an old project begun in Paris and taken up again after a long absence. The North was far away, and I had returned again in spirit to the old world of France. Those countries stood at far remove from one another and equidistant from me, and poetry was wholly invisible.

Reading Mauss, however, had led me back, indirectly, to the Interior. Now I could read him properly, bringing experience into play, testing it against the ideas he had professed, testing them in turn against my observations; and because of that, and because time had passed, Alaska, remembered, came vividly back to life.

The long conversation between teachers and learners is subtle, delicate, unending. In the North I had been an avid child in a new world—I laugh aloud, remembering the joy of it, that great open space, the cosmos of the night sky, land that seemed so newly formed we might have arrived just after Creation: the chance to live in that difficult, profound country as a free, thinking woman (that diffident, out-of-place girl). As a guest of the land, longing for its grace, I had averted my eyes from what disturbed or frightened them, had schooled myself to withhold judgment until I knew circumstance; I trusted people, and believed we act in good faith and do our best. All the experiences of grief and anger and fear had, without my noticing it, gone into my deeper memory, which resides in the muscles, and had tightened the body and caused it to move out of step. Nor is this contradictory: the writer's alert consciousness, the watchful eye, the interior voice, had recorded the life around my invisible self (the eye that is the "I"), but had not discovered its narrative shape. This was good: I was protecting myself, regaining strength after long hardship. I believed then, as I do still, that I had been helped by careful teachers; and that I was required to comprehend what they had meant to teach.

I had been reading European anthropologists, both the theorists then prominent and the earlier workers, estimable men who had gone out in the nineteenth century "into the field"—that is, people's homes—that often was territory colonized by their father- or motherlands. What I had learned in the North too often made little sense within their explanatory schemes. Rather, as I began to "make sense" of what I had seen and been shown, the anthropological writings proved evasive and clumsy, except for those of Mauss.

There is a passage in which Mauss, working from primary sources, describes the laws of association, that is, the poetics, which inform the logic of the sacred. It is a logic of contiguity, recognizing similarity, absorbing and transforming all contradiction; desiring unity. He observes that magicians and, similarly, priests had always comprehended that some concrete (not abstract or idealized; not metaphorical) quality underlay the associations—the links, the likenesses—they uncovered. They had understood that the laws of association that governed their art *represent things* that *act only on other things*— persons, objects, spirits—by virtue of a *shared nature*. By "nature" Mauss did not mean mere formal resemblance between one thing and another, but rather the (qualitatively different) notion of *shared substance*. As Malfa had said, "My relatives are my boundaries." She, echoing Mauss's priests and magicians, through a shared, archaic consciousness, had spoken in metonym, in which like acts upon like, each touching the other.

Reading concordances written by European magicians during the late Middle Ages and early Renaissance, Mauss had discerned what he took to be a central principle of their logic: central, that is, because they themselves had understood the principle that way:

"One is the whole, and if the whole does not contain the whole, the whole is not formed." ... What is in everything is the world. For, they tell us often, the world is conceived as a unique animal, whose parts, however distinct, are bounded between them in a necessary manner. All is assembled there, everything touches.

This passage jolted me, it caused a spark in the mind.

I could not speak coherently about Alaska. It was as far away as Paris, as distant as the past; a country of dreams unimaginable in the East, where they spoke another language, where cold was never so cold as it had been in the North.

Yet, when I tried to tell about Alaska, I found myself speaking in liturgical images. *The land is like an altar.* I would stammer: *I've been allowed to walk on the altar.* Until at last, something began to move, and flow like water, and I knew with utter certainty: *The whole land is sacred.* It is as holy as the altar on which the bread and wine are consecrated and become the body and blood of Christ, where the body of Christ is the One that is the Whole, where I was never allowed to walk. I've been on the altar *where what is sacred is what exists. What is in everything is the world,* said the magicians' concordances. *I was walking down the road in Village Below. The air was still; sharply so, as though something listened. A faint throbbing rose through my boot soles, from under the earth. The land is like a drum.* The whole land was a skin-drum, and its people danced upon it. The whole land is sacred. And the sacred is all that was around me, those I knew, all that I touched, saw, ate, everywhere I stepped.

○

THE SMALL black leather pouch had turned up. It sat on my desk. It was a reminder of the wild, tangible; for—here was poetry, that this prose scarcely evokes—I had begun to feel in my body the connection of the things of the world.

That sensation: I am not certain I can describe it. It was like warm breath on the skin; it was a pricked-skin feeling, tactile alertness, as if I could see behind things. The world appeared to me, and I saw it: I saw the invisible become visible. The spaces between the trees in the woods at the edge of the yard were filled: I could see the very air between them: the ether; as something breathed.

For days I had been abstracted, deep in concentration; but on that day the weather was changing, turning gray and misty. A flock of crows circled—*Yaw! Yaw! Yaw! Yaw!*—above the treetops. I stared idly from the window, thinking of nothing in particular. From one moment to the next the insight—the spark in the mind—for which I had been searching came to me; it was complicated, but limpid in its wholeness, and I was going to be able to give it form.

The leather pouch lay close at hand, and I felt safe. I turned from window to typewriter: at the corner of my left eye a dark object, a blur of wing, sketched a movement, but at another window, not the one from which I had watched the crows. I heard a raven's water-call—Alaskan sound. Old creaky voice: odd. For a moment I was surprised—not greatly surprised; aware that something seemed odd. Crows don't flock with ravens.

Something was odd: the sound I heard was very *odd*, and I *recognized* it. Trembling, I picked up the pouch. *Oh*, said the voice in the mind: *I know what I heard: but why did I hear that?* I laid the pouch gently on the desk. I was unafraid and grew very calm; turned inward, and began to write.

There are always coincidences in an account like this, wheels turning upon wheels, arcs tangent. They are called luck; or grace. They are the motif that fits the parts into a seamless whole. If I told stories well, I could make this one seamless; but mine is a lesser account. I wanted to reconcile story and truth, but can only describe what happened.

○

WHEN THE WORK WAS FINISHED I knew I had to return to Alaska. I needed help; I could not interpret that moment, I could not describe it even to myself. Something had shifted—the psyche disturbed. I wanted to sit with an old woman who would explain it to me.

But Malfa appeared. Why were we both in Fairbanks? What were we doing at the university? An elevator door opened: there she stood, splendid in a handsome fur-trimmed *kuspuk* and her hair caught up in a fine, beaded comb. We seized each other and went off to drink bad coffee and talked away the afternoon. I had been gone for three years; they seemed like hours. Cautiously, then eagerly, we exchanged the news of our recent lives. Hour by hour, imperceptibly, as I opened myself to her, she became my mother again.

For I trusted her more than myself. She came from people who had lived in a long spiritual relationship with their land, which in its intricacies of power had been kept veiled from the rude gaze of outsiders; and I did not wish to pull back the veil: but something odd had happened, and I could not help myself, I had to know what it was. Stammering—the words came hard; I had no natural language for this; this was not poetry—I told her how I had been given the bones, and had heard the raven's voice, and had felt protected by some quality that was—that seemed—living about the bones.

Perhaps I hoped she could dismiss it all; could say, *Don't mix poetry with the unknown powers.*

Her face grew still. She did not laugh or turn away and her tender eyes held steady. Gently she explored my state of mind, asking careful questions. She must, I think, have been testing my mental balance and, I am sure, my sincerity. For some time she considered my answers.

"You cannot see if you are not supposed to see," she said, finally. "Things that are dangerous can be refused."

This was the delicate moment, the pivot, the tip into the future. I could not give my burden over to her: she gave it back into my keeping and my free will; but she stood with me. *Refused. Refuse it.* In the years to come I would hear this often from her but, for a long time, hardly knew what she meant. She had taken me seriously, and taken what I had said literally: and so, at last (although somewhat, still, to my own disbelief), did I. I searched my memory of the experience. Something had touched me, and I had felt it: something beyond myself. It had felt like a nod, a sort of encouragement, I told her; then, confident: No, it had sounded like a grunt of approval from some old person I had not known was listening.

"That sounds like a good experience," she decided. "How do you feel?"

Stronger now, I said; happy and calm.

A question had been troubling me, a matter of moral etiquette. What should I do with the bones? They did not belong to me: should I keep them? My mind had cleared, I told her (I was almost light-headed with relief): one day when I was out in the woods, I would know where to step off the trail and bury them.

"Yes," she said. "Animals in the wild aren't buried, you know."

Then I would lay them down.

"That animal is powerful, and sometimes there are spirit helpers. If you feel good and aren't afraid, I think it's all right."

○

I LIVED INTENSELY in a state of unknowing. It was at first a gentle thing, never frightening, but a sharpening of attention, a deep focus on that for which I had no words; an intent listening, a watching. I was responsible for the bones, but how to behave toward them and where to lay them down were not evident to me. It was not acceptable to ask Native people who did not know me to speak of so intimate a matter. Occasionally, however, some non-Native friends offered insights. For instance, I was told that if an Athabaskan friend gave you meat he never left the bones in it: the bones were put out in the woods for the animal's spirit to find, to return in a new body.

Such remarks were rare and needed; for the remains of a Catholic conscience, which examines skeptically one's motive at every move, beset me. Often I was uneasy, believing yet wishing not to believe. I wondered if I were trespassing, but could not make myself leave. In the long winter darkness I wondered, often, if I were losing my mind.

Surely this experience touches upon, and also is part of, an ancient widespread human experience. Nearly a year later the first intensity lifted. That was both relief and letdown: I was left in-between, neither in the air nor on the ground; I felt terribly serious, slightly goofy.

The year that followed passed in a fingersnap and was crowded with event. As I write I can see that passage clearly; all was confusion then. I traveled through the bush from school to school; I moved without judgment, absorbed in the movement. I slept in airports, teachers' lounges, local hotels, or on couches in friends' small cabins. The daily business of life obscured the deeper progress of the story in which I lived, and if intuitively I did not take its passage as random—I knew that something ordered and coherent was happening, on a level of consciousness superior to my own—the days were hectic and banal. I had fun and lost my head in love. Men were very attentive, and I was available to their appeal. Even so, I grew testy over ordinary things and hardly knew where the feeling came from.

As often and for as long as I could I cast myself upon friends, non-Native and Native, who recognized that in the bush existed something we did not understand. I talked, I wept, I complained about everything. They listened patiently, advised when they could; and politely concealed their exasperation. I tried to convince myself that I was being Literary, telling myself stories, that I had an overactive imagination and was given to self-drama; that I was making it up: but I would never accept that suggestion from anyone else. I tested everything. I *saw* and *saw* and *saw*; as if the land had pulled back its mask and revealed its inner face. I dreamed of stern, demanding, but not unkind spirits, who required fortitude of me; that is, of everyone.

Nothing made sense. I wrote everything down, otherwise I could not remember it; then I ignored it, because it was confusing. I never doubted the fact of the visitation, only that I could be patient enough to see it through in its own terms.

o

IN THE EARLY SUMMER of 1984 I went to Shelter again, to Malfa. After the winter ice broke up she and her husband always traveled the rivers, hauling supplies and freight by barge to the Interior villages. They were going to make the first run of the season. She said decisively, "We'll take you with us."

For days we traveled up the slow, clear Koyukuk. Malfa watched me and, as we neared a certain village, announced: "We can visit Mrs. Reliance."

Mrs. Reliance was well known in the Interior. Her Koyukon family was an old one. Her grandfather had been a respected medicine man; she was known among white people for telling his traditional stories again, and for allowing them to be translated and published.

Tactfully, Malfa asked me about my time of the month. Off schedule, I had just come into my moon. She knew that I carried, like a sacramental, the pouch with the bones in it. With a sense of relief it crossed my mind that I could leave them beside this peaceful river, in the woods near Mrs. Reliance's village.

The village was calm and pretty, with log cabins built amid clumps of new-leaved birches and well-tended paths laid with river gravel. Songbirds sang in the trees. The women who came down to greet the boat were Malfa's old friends. They welcomed her with pleasure, and handed her gifts of food. Among themselves they spoke their Athabaskan tongue; it sounded fluted, musical, like the birds.

Malfa took me with her on her round of formal visits, until at last we came to the big log house of Mrs. Reliance, who welcomed her old friend warmly and offered us tea. Formally, Malfa introduced me as her daughter, to signal that I was in her care. Carefully, as writers of all sorts were deeply mistrusted, she explained that I was a poet, and spoke well of the biography of an elder known to both of them that I had recently finished. Mrs. Reliance accepted the information without comment. The two women exchanged their news. I sat beside Malfa as gently, skillfully she moved the conversation toward her purpose. When the moment came, she gave me an opening and slipped away.

Mrs. Reliance looked at me pleasantly, a small query in the tilt of her head.

Who was I, before the old knowledge of this woman? I took a deep breath and told her about the man's gift. I described the misty day, the movement at the window, the raven's water-call, the prickly flush, and the clarity that had come on me when I lifted the pouch; the inner certainty, the *yes*, that had followed.

I write and rewrite, until the words are clear and accurate, until they describe exactly, or as exactly as I can make them; but speaking was difficult, and I was aware that I spoke in a rush. At the end I asked her if I could leave the bones nearby, in the woods, because it seemed to me they might be safe there.

"What is 'poet'?" she asked.

"A shaper of words."

She thought for a while. How long had I had the bones? Where had they come from, and who had given them to me? She asked me to describe them exactly.

Again she was silent; then she told me two stories that I remember imperfectly now. In each of them, a man found something—an old arrowhead in a fish's stomach; a rock shaped like a bear's paw—and had dreamed on them. It seemed that each man had used those objects to ask for power: instead, misfortune had followed. One man had developed a double personality; the other had lost children and grandchildren.

"We don't know if this is why," she said, "but it could be."

I was discouraged; the bones grew heavy in my pocket; and I was distracted by my predicament. Why had she told me her obscure stories? I wanted only words, not power; not medicine.

It was strange, she said: in their stories her people called this animal *doyon*: chief. He never came to women; they could not even use his skin except for a little bit from the stomach, and only on parkees, where it did not matter. When their daughter was still a baby her husband had hung up the skin of a doyon inside the house. The baby would not stop crying until her husband decided he had better remove it.

"He would not accept those," she said of the bones. "I know if I asked Grandma, she would not. We don't know who might find them, or what would happen with our people. This way it is orphan. It didn't come from here."

She explained that a word, even one spoken in ignorance, might insult the animal, who in revenge could hurt the person who had spoken. Her people spoke their own language among themselves: he could understand them.

She said again, firmly, that no one in the village would accept such a gift: the medicine people had known for a long time, since before the First World War, that their powers were failing. Not that the spirits were failing: but that no one could bear the burden of hearing and interpreting them.

"Maybe you should try to find out where it came from. If that man is not in McGrath, you could leave it there, since that is where you got the gift."

I had not known what was proper, I apologized; I had not grown up among people who knew how to behave this way toward animals.

"You could burn it, or bury it. Burn moose fat, and thank it for being kind to you, and say you never meant any harm.—But, as I think about it, I wonder. Maybe you should bury it in plastic. Don't destroy it. It might keep talking to you. If it wants to come back, you'll know where to find it."

For an awful instant I saw my free life gone, given over into archaic service to this orphan animal's bones, that I carried from some pious habit, the consequences of which had suddenly become tiresome. I felt rude and awkward, and wished I had never come to her. "I guess I was asking improperly," I murmured, thanked her, and left.

o

MALFA LIT A CIGARETTE, listened, then, her mind full of thought, asked if I had told Mrs. Reliance the name of the animal's spirit. Only to her, I had called him Old Husband. My face felt warm again; but she was serious.

"A power has been trying to come back for a long time," she explained. "Even the young people who refuse it can suffer terribly."

I worried that by bringing the bones into the village, I may have placed those people in some danger. She shook her head.

"You are in your strongest time now, with your period, and the bones are in your care."

"What protected me?" I asked her. "What sent my period just then?"

"Women have a very strong power of their own, which is innate," she said. "It cannot be controlled, except through proper behavior. Hutłaanee, what they say for 'taboo,' isn't just negative: it's to keep the power from getting in the way of the men."

"If women have their own power," I said, "and animals have their spirits; and if medicine people can be either men or women: then, what do men have that is their own?"

"They are the providers," she said, surprised I had to ask.

o

A DISTURBANCE OF THE PSYCHE: an opening in the mind, into which pours something unknown, unexpected. What is its nature? It is a delicate matter to tell only part of the story; but the whole story, in its intricate detail, is very long. I've reduced it to an essence, knowing every thought, every incident may also open out and unfold into a story of its own; and that all is connected to, is grounded in, the close-meshed network of old and new stories, personal histories and mythopoeae, that cover the cold North. Mine is the smallest of those stories, told briefly here, with the hope that others may find it of interest and benefit; for when we speak of such matters, are we not telling ourselves how we may be at home in this place?

o

MY STARTLED QUESTION about powers, especially the power of women, was a personal one. I understood that a spirit had made itself known to me, and that I had accepted an offer of relationship; but what sort of relationship? The two women seemed to think it a medicine call, of a kind their people were not prepared to answer. I listened to them, for they had advised me from their particular, scrupulous knowledge. I was only a struggling poet. The literature to which I was devoted was rich with the writings of religious and nature poets, and with visionary fictions testifying to the immanence of the spirit in the world: but the practice of medicine, its exacting, indigenous rituals and enormous power *to make things happen* were beyond my understanding, and were not my desire. I was more Jesuit than anthropologist about this: I accepted the ontological reality of medicine, and believed—because I had heard the stories—that in former days, priests and medicine men had fought genuine battle for the care of souls. That the priests had triumphed was evident; equally, that an old power was trying to return, I had no reason to disbelieve.

But mine was another calling, and I saw that none of us—not Mrs. Reliance, not Malfa, not me—knew a precedent for it. What knowledge was mine, and what was appropriate to me? I did not know the proper behavior, the protocol of the sacred, which the wolverine-spirit might require of me. My intentions were kind. I was concerned that my ignorance might put others at risk. I did not even know what language my animal spoke, or what words might offend it.

I did not imagine myself to be at risk. I was filled with awe and surprise, the lilt of a highly developed curiosity, deepened to a sense of mystery whose veil now covered my face.

How grateful I was to Malfa. Her knowledge had been tested; she offered it judiciously, and I could trust it and use it for my own. Women have a very strong power of their own, which is innate, she had said. It cannot be controlled, except through proper behavior. I was a young woman, carrying a bag of bones whose resting place I had to find: in Malfa's teaching lay the clue to the strength I felt rising in myself. What they say for taboo isn't just negative.

The word she used, *hutlaanee*, was Koyukon, which was Mrs. Reliance's language, an Athabaskan tongue; I had often heard it used. Its root is *hutłaa*, the word for menses: similarly, *taboo*, the word we use for forbidden behavior, came from the Tongan word for menses. Captain Cook had brought the word back to England in 1777 and it passed into our tongue to mean consecrated; set apart; forbidden for use, especially forbidden to women. Within that application lies the Judeo-Christian connotation of womanhood as unclean and morally inferior (to men); or, as Catholic teaching has held since St. Paul, and the Desert Fathers, and as I was taught in my youth: a near-occasion of sin; a vexed subject, theologically and socially.

But its native meaning was less narrow. It spoke not of an absence, loss of goodness or purity, but abundance, a metaphysical enlargement, from which I was not excluded. Native people of the Pacific and Alaska freely mention their feelings of kinship with one another. They know the world in similar ways; and the similarity between them may exist even in etymological form. Just as taboo and *hutłaanee* come from a similar root, so is the derivation similar in Iñupiaq, the language of the people of the North Slope. Their word *agliganaq* refers to the laws of behavior toward the supernatural: the rules applied to personal relations between men and women; and to their treatment of fur-bearing animals. The same connection, of game-rules and taboo to menses, exists in Yup'ik, and, as I suppose, in other Athabaskan tongues.[26]

Thus it came to me that within the center of my nature, from the innate, archaic power of the blood-taboo, lived the authority with which my imagination composed and was composing the rules of the game. Within my own ancient, impersonal, feminine nature existed the protocol by which I would act: the devotion and reverence, the mercy and pity, the sense of duty in which I carried the bones of a fur-bearing animal, although I was neither wife nor mother nor was I allied to a hunter, as was expected in that country.

o

ACCORDING TO Catholic teaching, that which earliest formed my intellect, animals have no souls. *Soul*, fateful word in the New World. Its historical and theological echoes are very loud; perhaps they have deafened us. For example I turn to the great and horrifying disputation of 1550 in Valladolid, between Bartolomé de las Casas, Dominican missionary and defender of the Indians of the Spanish colonies, and Juan Gínes de Sepúlveda, chaplain to Charles V of Spain: who meant to prove, by rational argument, whether or not the Indians of the Spanish colonies possessed soul and intellect.

I still read Las Casas with admiration and sadness, for how often in the literature of travelers, those who find it in themselves to leave home and wander, to meet the various people of the earth, how often do we not find some subtle, or desperate, argument by which to prove that Others are human, as we ourselves are? For we know how often it has been denied. Yet after all, in Las Casas' treatise there existed a detail of Christian moral theology that had to attract my particular attention. There he argued, mightily and with love, in order to redeem the Indians from their enemies, that "the Creator of every being has not so despised these peoples of the New World that He willed them to lack reason and made them *like brute animals, so that they should be called barbarians, wild men and brutes. ...*"[27] His analogy of savages to brute, soulless animals, incapable of redemption, was typical of the learning of his time and civilization; his great work was to portray the Indians of the New World as possessing souls: thus, as being human. My point of exception is small; yet it marks a fateful barrier between old and new beliefs.

A spirit had come to me in the bones of an animal. In the North it is the old belief of Athabaskans that everything that lives has its own spirit, and that that spirit must be respected. It is the principle that underlies all life, reaching back to the dawn of human consciousness; it is revealed in the earliest stories, the explanatory myths of Creation. How did one like myself, who had not been taught this belief, who had been taught that only humans are endowed with souls: how did she accept it, and imagine such a world, in its minute particulars? I was not from that country. In need, I turned to others for help.

I found then that I had to begin all over again. The emotional intelligence of people who had guided me, of Malfa who was my mother, had been of a reach beyond my own. I undertook a task of the spirit: to register nuances of plain words; to trust myself to give form to feelings, when I would rather turn away from them; to find right words for images that had no words.

That work is very close to the work of poetry, and also it is part of the work of poetry; but it occurs in a realm of belief that is more finely articulated than I could have foreseen. Catholicism had prepared me for it in this way, at least: through the Mystery at its center; its formation of the intellect as the handmaiden of intuition; its ceremonies, their beauty; and its belief in the possibility of grace.

o

BUT THE WOLVERINE is a greedy, malicious, evil-natured animal, and Mrs. Reliance's warning that he was dangerous for women and would retaliate if insulted was not to be disregarded. The old Athabaskan stories tell this over and over. Nothing good is said about him; he is, and must be recognized for his nature.

The anthropologist Richard K. Nelson, who knew Mrs. Reliance and reported her teachings accurately, wrote of the retaliatory nature of certain powerful animals, including wolverine:

> Not all spirits are possessed of equal power. Some animal species have very potent spirits called *biyeega hoolaanh*, which are easily provoked and highly vindictive. These dangerous spirits can bring serious harm to anyone who offends them, taking away luck in hunting or trapping and sometimes

causing illness, disability, or even death. Animals possessed of such spirits include the brown bear, black bear, wolverine, lynx, wolf, and otter.
The beaver and marmot have similarly powerful spirits but are not so
vengeful.[28]

To the Dena'ina Athabaskans, among whom I lived before I met Malfa,
wolverine was *yes hughn'u*. The word refers to the varied colors of his skin, and
describes how he moves: he is a strong, powerful animal, shifting around inside his skin almost like a cat; he is "rough and tough," always on the move.
But more familiarly, he was called *idashla*, "little friend," meaning "(bad one)
for a friend." Their stories about him are grim, particularly in his treatment
of women: wolverine does no good to women.

But, looking back, I cannot tell exactly when I learned this. The accumulation of my knowledge was slow and circular, and inconclusive, because the
story in which I lived was not finished.

From curiosity, perhaps, or caution I fell into the habit of carrying the
small bag of bones in my pocket. On occasion, the bones seemed to move:
not literally: metaphysically. At such times, perhaps two or three times, I
found myself in the company of priests or ex-priests, Jesuits. Then, agitation
amid the bones, restlessness, unease; power meeting power: mutual hostility
in the air. For I noticed signs of agitation, also, in those priests and former
priests, who also were highly placed men. I moved away from such encounters. They were fascinating, disturbing, whiffs of danger: small glimpses into
a realm of power I had no wish to enter. I took them seriously. It was I who
carried the bones; and if in that country of stories I knew I lived in a story,
the story was no fiction, not a novel, seldom poetry. For *I* was the visible one,
the outward sign. The agitation swirled around *me.*

I used to laugh then: my shoulders were broad and could carry weight. On
them I balanced everything: all possibility; all that I knew, and also did not
know. I was going forward and could not look back until the story was over,
and I was released by it.

Only then did I recognize that behind that strange experience had always
breathed the sweet, secret circumstance of the gift: the man's intention, his
boyish love, that had come to me with the bones. In Athabaskan stories, the
wolverine's spirit was vindictive and evoked fear, subdued for survival into the
grimmer form of respect; but the white man, who had so clumsily worked
the bones, was innocent of fear.

Here was paradox, a literary jest, an irony of the sacred; a form, shall I say,
of poetic justice? I had received a gift, and had taken it literally, object and
word; and had accepted its consequences, though they perturbed me; but
much remained hidden, until I came to learn how the word lived in this our
language. Gift, the word and deed, comes to us, in part, from the Old English
forgi(e)fan: to give up, to leave off (anger), to forgive.

○

AS THE DECADE of the eighties took shape, oil prices dropped. The economy that the old-timers called boom-and-bust was going bad. New people, the whites who had come north toward the end of the boom, once again moved away. As the money dwindled, the people who stayed grew fearful. The normal violence in the towns and bush, the abuse of women and children, the suicides, the unexplained deaths, increased rapidly. The economy of oil had bluntly imposed itself across the North and was beyond the reach of national governance. The Alaskan tribes felt the changes and took them hard, and drew their boundaries in upon themselves. Even Malfa, feeling ambivalent, encouraged me to be silent.

In those years many people, often unknown to each other, dreamed heavily. One summer in mid-decade, in my literature class at the university, young Native men and women spoke hesitantly yet urgently to me of dreams. They described a state of leaden sleep, from which one cannot awaken; one dreams, yet the dream is as clear as daylight, as if the dreamer were awake. Disturbed, they compared their dreams, and asked me how to interpret them.

White women, friends, artists, poets, dreamed of animals. We described our dreams to one another: bear, wolverine, wolf: animals of power, looking at us, speaking, asking some act of us, in words we could not quite hear. There also were white men, I knew, who saw what they did not understand; many of them were frightened. To whom could they speak of such things?

The animals are crying, a woman told me, describing her dream.

Older Native women were cautious about speaking to me, unless they knew, as Malfa knew, why I cared to learn. Rather, often I heard: "We don't know."

A polite rebuff or a fearful response, but also a mark of empirical thinking, practiced by people who counted as knowledge only what they might verify from experience. Since the First Beginning, since the Distant Time, the animal protocols had been tested and considered. In the last century, newer powers had come on the land: the monotheism of the missionaries, the far reach of the law, developments seemed to leave non-Natives, the people like me, immune to their old spiritual sanctions. It seemed, I was told, sadly or in wonder, that we were not punished for violating the rules of the game.

But I began to think: We live now, in a new time. What do the animals make of us, who come North into their country so easily? What do we want? What can they tell us?

Troubled, wondering, I turned again to Mrs. Reliance, whom I saw now and then in town. I told her about these dreams that fascinated and disturbed me.

"But Katherine, you don't understand," she said, in pity and consolation. "The animals are trying to come to the women."

○

MY CIRCUMSTANCES CHANGED. I moved back East and did not return to Alaska for more than a year, till early April 1989.

The day I flew north was cloudless. From Seattle onward the great coastal range of snow-covered mountains shone bright and hard in the April sun. Several hours into the flight the pilot announced that below us lay Prince William Sound, where a few weeks before a commercial oil tanker had struck a reef and poured eleven million gallons of crude oil into the living waters. We were at 35,000 feet; passengers seated on the right could observe where the tanker had run aground. The pilot's voice was measured, even thoughtful. Trying to assimilate those separate facts, I looked down through the clear air and followed the line of the coast to Valdez Arm.

The lovely fjord that is the Arm was from that height a long narrow file of entry into the port. At its mouth six tankers fanned out in a wide semi-circle, ranked to go in. They were very long ships: next to them the great mountains, the St. Elias range, looked—docile. A distance away, but in sight from the plane, tugs were drawing the *Exxon Valdez* off Bligh Reef. In the slant of the sun I couldn't make out the oil slick. The pilot reported its charted movement, and named the bays and ports along the coast toward which it was predicted to be heading.

Anchorage was a raw and rowdy place; but that city lay grieving and strangely still, as if shocked into silence by the disaster. In the previous year, friends told me, so many people, even white people, had taken their lives that the newspapers no longer reported them, for the public good. Exxon was spreading money along the coastline. In the villages around Prince William Sound, food was running low, as all available planes and fishing boats, which normally carried supplies, had been chartered for use in the clean-up. With the first wash of money came the first cover-up of despair, the new round of drinking and fighting and wife-beating and child abuse; as usual, but more severe than usual.

And the lost animals. After the spill, the media ran sympathetic pictures of dead and dying otters. It was said that the Aleuts call otters Half-Man, because their spirits pass into otters after death. I wondered: To whom could those human spirits go now?

o

TOWARD THE END of my visit I stayed alone in a house north of Anchorage. I had brought the bones in their small leather pouch. On the last day, for no reason, I remembered the man who once had sweetly courted me: he had trapped the wolverine near a town not far up the highway. On a hunch I decided to drive there.

After about half an hour, I suppose, the road crested, and descended a long slope into a small wooded valley. As I passed a certain spot, not remarkable, a muscle under my heart twitched slightly, as if I had had a small electric shock. *Pay attention.* I drove through the valley, felt nothing, turned around, and drove back to the same stretch of road; I drove it three or four times, testing, until my heart, I thought it was, was composed.

The place was a few miles from a small Athabaskan settlement, but not within its boundaries. I pulled off the road and parked on the gravel shoulder. Across the way, houses appeared here and there among the trees. *White people.* I felt easy; surely no one would be at risk. I turned and went into the forest, which was calmly busy and took no special notice of me. The air was fresh, spruce-sharp; but I was nearly weeping. The voice in the mind was bemused. I walked among the trees; the ground was boggy and covered with dried needles. I was going on intuition and, perhaps, desire. The stump of a fallen tree, and a hollow in the stump, stood out from its surrounds. *Here.* I shook the small, perfect, white bones into my hand and tipped them carefully into the hollow; set the black leather pouch in the stump-top; and turned away. And as I turned, there came a leap in the vitals, the small shock again: an impulse, as of a shadow-form, that had so long resided inside and outside of myself. In the same thrilling instant the shadow parted from me and, released at last, bounded away into the forest: light, young, eager; at home.

○

IN A COMFORTABLE HOUSE, in a comfortable study, I sit and think and look out on a domesticated landscape in Virginia, and find comfort in it, if never the awe and elation of the North where once I lived; but my mind is large and I can believe that here I may be blind: that another poet, some dreaming woman or man, may see here what I cannot. I am content not to be in the North. In 1976 I had come into Alaska; three years later, in a sad Interior town, a man had given me his gift; and for ten years afterward I had carried the bones until, on my last journey North, I had known, finally, where to lay them down. The path I followed had led me far beyond the person I was, or had thought I was, when I set out. I had wanted to learn truth, and I had wanted to learn to tell a story. The wheel has turned: I've finished what I was called to do there; it remains only to tell the story of what happened, when I learned a way to see the country.

A squirrel runs from branch to high branch across the canopy of maples, as if the air were a woodland creek and the limbs of trees the stepping-stones across it: a small, usual movement, fleet and airy as a poem can be; and it pleases me to compare that dart of movement to the logic of a poem, which links things like and unlike by tracing the arcs of movement between them. Invisible trails above our heads.

In Alaska, during the dreaming years, when animals were coming to the women, I woke one morning into the wondering sense that a veil had been drawn back and an important instruction given during the night.

In the dream, I was about to read a paper before a group of Alaskan an-thropologists. In fact I had given such a talk, a poet's reading of a fine Atha-baskan story that described in mythopoetic figures the compact between hu-mans and animals, by which each kind lived in mutual respect, need, trickery, and delight.[29] In the dream (unlike at the actual meeting) I was seated among the audience rather than above them on a dais. In the dream, although only there, Native people, too, sat as participants. The topic of the meeting was "Subsistence," as whites called it, referring to the intricate culture of hunting relations between humans and animals in that animate country, which Native people called "Our way of life." In the dream, the dreamer—the I—knew all this in a moment.

I saw myself stand among the seated people and read my paper. As I finished, feeling young and terribly earnest, a voice behind me called: *Kathy.* It was a man's voice, Athabaskan, calling me by a childhood name. From the corner of my eye I saw him: seated behind me and to the right, still dressed in his work-stained clothes, accompanied by his wife, who sat silent and com-posed beside him. "Kathy," he went on: "you've got it wrong. It's not that *your* spirit, *your* way of knowing, goes out toward what lives: but that the spirit of the animals and plants *rushes toward you.*"

○

THE WORLD HAS CHANGED. Great powers are at play; every possible human behavior has come out of the dark and once more into the open. We are as-tonished and distressed. The world divides, as Alaska divided, into small and smaller groups of *us.* Fear grows; uncertainty feeds it, and smothers our cour-age. We stammer. We don't know what can happen next.

I lived in a world where, for all its confusion, humans and animals speak to each other. Alaska is a great land, fragile and deeply sensitive to the terri-ble disturbances done to its body. The manifestation of its spirits compelled me to maintain a respectful watch and reminded me to listen carefully to my dreams. The animals are terribly lonely. They miss their old relations with humans. They try to establish relations with us through dreams, but we can-not hear them clearly enough. Perhaps we don't talk the same language, as we are not hunting people. They are trying to learn our language.

I observe that the experience of the holy is open to anyone. It is a gift of grace, or luck, as it is called in the North; and having received this gift—a vi-sion, a message from a bird, a sign from an animal, a dream—we must try to understand what we've been given, for it is not necessarily benign. But the North sits under a weight of imposed silence. "Let the old knowledge die with the old people," say so many Alaska Natives: "It's too dangerous; they told us not to stir it up." Surely they are right, for themselves; and their de-sires should be honored.

But the stories of our dreams and visions might help us all to enlarge the relationships we seek with one another; for when this earthly gift comes to us, we are obliged to pass the news of it on to our neighbors and ask for their help in understanding what has happened. The experience of the holy is, intensely, singular: but its form, its expression, the art by which we share it, is ancient, social, and religious. Alaska is in us. We are given voices, we have marvelous languages: we are able to sing; we can praise. We can give warning. We can speak truth.

Notes

Out on an Edge

1. R. P. Porter (compiler), *Report on population and resources of Alaska at the eleventh census: 1890* (Washington: 1893), pp. 94–95. Quoted in James W. VanStone and Joan B. Townsend, *Kijik: An Historic Tanaina Indian Settlement,* Fieldiana: Anthropology, vol. 59 (Chicago: Field Museum of Natural History, January 16, 1970), pp. 16–17.

2. Cornelius Osgood, *The Ethnography of the Tanaina* (New Haven: Yale University Publications in Anthropology, no. 16, reprinted by Human Relations Area Files Press, 1976), p. 194.

3. In 1981, Professor Ernest Burch, of the Smithsonian Institution, a respected anthropologist and student of Iñupiat history, in a speech presented to the thirty-second Alaska Science Conference in Fairbanks, described how he had learned to trust and believe narratives told him by respected Native historians—he used the word "historians" deliberately—about warfare between "Eskimo nations" in the early part of the nineteenth century. At some length he explained also how and why his "preconceptions" about Native narrative history had "blinded" him to the credibility and accuracy of his Native "informants." It was, or should have been, an important paper, as Professor Burch was one among the handful of scholars of Alaskan Native life with a national reputation. By being specific about his methodological "errors," by questioning their assumptions, Professor Burch could have shaken the foundations of Alaskan studies. But he did not go so far. "Twenty years ago," he said, "my view was that all narrative history which challenged my notions of common sense should be regarded as false until confirmed as true.... In 1981 I would restate my position as follows: narrative history that is provided by people whom the Natives consider competent historians should be regarded as true until proven false, no matter how extraordinary what they say may first appear.... Despite my embarrassment and frustration for [*sic*] having committed them, I have been confessing my errors for some time now in the hope that others may benefit from my experience. So far, I regret to report, this effort has been a miserable failure. Many of my colleagues still do not believe what Natives have to say about their own histories." (Ernest S. Burch, Jr., "Studies of Native History as a Contribution to Alaska's Future," unpublished paper, 1981, Drawer D, Harrisburg, Pa., 17108.)

This speech had not been given when I went to the bush. Even if it had, and if his reconsiderations had been more generally shared, there remained the belief that studying Native history was beneficial for "Alaska's future." A scholar's disinterest was nowhere evident. Nor was there any question, or self-questioning, of the right to investigate Native life from a superior position.

The Mouse Mother

4. Athabaskan elders are—or were, when I lived there—particular about their stories and who possesses the right to tell them. Each village tends to its own repertoire, keeping it separate from others'. Often, a traveler will hear in one village a story that, to her ear, sounds similar to one she has heard in another. If she comments on the resemblance, the teller will (almost always) draw a sharp distinction and explain why the story belongs to *this place, our own people,* and to no other. The experience reveals

the intimate connections people make between their language, their place, and their way of knowing.

But an interested reader needs such particulars. He or she can then find Dena'ina stories, including one similar to the story of the Mouse Mother told me by the students, in the collection gathered and written by Bill Vaudrin, *Tanaina Tales* (Norman: University of Oklahoma Press, 1969). Bill Vaudrin was Native American, from Outside, and had taught at the University of Alaska. In 1976 he died on the highway north of Anchorage, when on a snowy night his car hit a moose. He was missed by many people, including F, who had handled dogs for him. Vaudrin knew the area around "Village Below" well. He was spoken of with affection and respect and was considered trustworthy.

It may interest the reader further to know that in this children's story, as in the stories Vaudrin gathered, recurs a Dena'ina motif, the number three. In Native American cosmology, the number four is a fundamental number and a ritual motif worthy of respect, although too often in popular culture it is used as cliché, and is among the clichés applied to American Indians. However, it does not appear universally or automatically in Native American cosmologies. In Alaska, scholars have noted that certain tribal peoples did not observe their word as ordered in fours. For instance, the anthropologist William McLaughlin found that among the Aleuts (of the Aleutian Islands), the number five was the number represented most often in women's stories and knowledge, while the number four was associated with the male order. (N.B.: Native people of the Alaska Peninsula call themselves and their language "Aleut." Linguists and anthropologists argue that technically these people are of Yup'ik stock, and that their language is called Suqpiaq. "True" Aleuts are considered by them to be the peoples of the Aleutian Islands, speaking the Aleut language, which is linguistically distinct from Yup'ik.) The anthropologist Lydia Black mentioned to me that in her Dena'ina studies, she found that the number three is associated with men, and four with women.

I wondered if the number three might have been introduced into the stories as a syncretist adaptation by Dena'ina storytellers to the Christian trinity, following missionaries' work, or whether it might even recall and echo some pattern of the Ancients, such as the Pythagorean triad. In Vaudrin's Dena'ina stories, in those told me in Village Below, and in the stories written by Peter Kalifornsky, the number three recurs noticeably. (My experience among Dena'ina women, in this regard, was limited.) I asked Mr. Kalifornsky to explain the number three to me. He obliged, having considered the question for some time.

He said, "Anything they did was three, it was always three times. That three seems to go in cycles all through the stories. Why three?" He described what he meant by recalling to me two stories, and pointing out their ritual patterns. The stories were "Gambling Story" (p. 129), and "Mouse Story" (below). (These stories, and Mr. Kalifornsky's commentaries, are adapted from my unpublished manuscript, *From the First Beginning: When the Animals Were Talking*.) These stories are about belief. They belong to the cycle called The First Beginning and were given to a Dreamer, a man who prayed to dream for the truth. At that time, humans and animals talked to each other. The animals were under the protection of the Giants, especially the two called The Mother and Father (or Guardian, or Boss) of the Animals, who lived deep in the mountains of the Alaska Range.

In "Mouse Story," as in "Gambling Story," ritual acts recur in threes: turning with and against the sun, spinning the sticks, using down feathers. The pattern of three is associated with reversals, as Peter Kalifornsky called them. They are a corrective: they curb excess and restore balance and harmony to the world. He figured this movement with an image from the natural world: "These reversals, and what's behind the stories: as the world revolves, or the moon turns upside down in its cycles."

In Dena'ina, every word carries meaning; every detail is significant. The lexical and ritual meanings, and their patterns of meaning, reverberate from story to story, down through the ages. (See also note 13, below.)

Mouse Story

Long ago, the Dena'inas lived this way. They built fish traps and jigging racks; they fished with dip nets, preparing for winter.

One man was lazy, though. One day, not thinking at all of winter, he went walking. In the brush he noticed a little mouse with a fish egg in its mouth. It was struggling, and he gently lifted it over the windfall in its path.

Then winter came to the Dena'inas, and sickness struck them. Bad weather came to them. Their winter supplies ran out. Sickness struck them.

One day, not feeling hopeful, the young man who had lifted the mouse over the windfall set out for the foothills. After walking and walking, he came to a great shelter where there was life. Smoke was rising from the smokehole. There was no door, but from the inside a voice called, "Yes, we were expecting you. Turn three times the way the sun goes round, stoop down, and come in."

Three times he turned the way the sun goes round, and as he stooped a doorway opened. Inside, near the fire in the center of the room, sat a very big old lady. "My husband is coming back," she said. "Sit here. We were expecting you." She fed him. "I know why you are doing this," she told him. "We know who you are. When my husband gets back, he will explain."

Not long after this, it began to hail, and the earth shook. "Yes, my husband is coming back," she said. And a giant man came into the house.

"Hello," he said. "I know why you are doing this. Your relatives are all hungry. Sickness had struck them. You are coming around here to save your relatives. Good, I will help you," he said. "You too have helped me."

Then, a pinch at a time, he put onto a small skin all kinds of fine little fish eggs and meats and dryfish. Pinch after pinch he put down, and he wrapped them up in the skin. It didn't come to much of a pack. He put down feathers inside.

"When you arrive, lay this down and let it lie in the village scent. Turn three times the way the sun goes round, and sprinkle these down feathers over it. Then turn once against the sun, and touch it, and it will grow into a large pile. And then you will go back and tell your relatives to go with you to carry it to the village. You will save your relatives with it. Before it is finished, all of them will regain their strength. They will return to the forest, and there they will kill game. You will be saved," he said.

And, as the story goes, he said to the young man: "When everyone was preparing for winter, no one took pity on the little mouse. You were a lazy man. You were out walking about. You came to me and you picked me up and lifted me, with the little fish egg in my mouth, over the windfall. You helped me then. That is why it has turned out this way." He said: "My name is 'Mouse's Relative'; but it really is Gujun. Gujun is related to all of the animals."

They Cover Up Too Much

5. Peter Kalifornsky explained this etymology to me. His Dena'ina is similar to, but not quite the same as, the tongue of Village Below. I note this distinction for the sake of accuracy.

6. About five years later, I met this anthropologist, who told me the purpose of her trip through the Kijik country, where earlier she had done archaeological re-

search: she needed to collect "hard" evidence that the "traditional culture" still existed. She and a number of her colleagues were trying to prove that the American economy and popular culture were not necessarily replacing "tradition," as was being publicly argued by the tourism and sports-hunting lobbies, with some encouragement from the state and federal governments.

The work of those anthropologists had to be done quickly: the federal government planned a vast expansion of national wilderness lands, and therefore required environmental, socioeconomic, and cultural impact statements. Experts hired by the state and federal governments, and also by the tourist and sportsmen's lobbies, proposed that "traditional Native cultures" (as these had been defined by academic archaeologists and physical anthropologists) were "dying"; and that legal protection of Native ways, especially Native hunting, would no longer be necessary once the present older generations had passed away. (Both the government and the sports and tourism industries had a strong interest in limiting Native hunting, in favor of their constituencies' use of the lands in question.)

In the working-out of this serious political issue, the methods, not to say rigor, of whatever might have been called scholarship about Alaska Native matters was hopelessly compromised. Reading from the background of my own studies and experience, I found no more than a handful of scholarly investigators whose work I could consider reliable for theoretical underpinnings or for accurate representations; these were scholars I knew personally or whose Native teachers were known to me. In Alaska, every public issue was, and remains, at heart about the control of land. Academic studies were, and are, used as partisan weapons in ideological and commercial arguments.

Fishing Is for Women: We Are Hunters

7. In the dream I knew that the dream itself was a marker, a sign, an indicator, but of what I did not know.

In Jung's writings on alchemy are several comments on the motif of the ladder in alchemical dreaming and the process of spiritual transformation. It represents, he says, stages of the alchemical process, its rites of initiation. "As listed above, the steps and ladders theme points to the process of psychic transformation, with all its ups and downs." (C. G. Jung, *Psychology and Alchemy*, trans. R. F. C. Hull [Princeton: Bollingen Series XX, Princeton University Press, second edition, 1968], pp. 57n, 62.)

Mircea Eliade, in his beautiful book on shamanism, collects several instances of spiritual techniques in which holy people have ascended from "earth" to "heaven"—to the place of origin—with ladders; and he refers to sources that annotate many other instances. He writes: "We have seen countless examples of shamanic ascent to the sky by means of a ladder. The same means is also employed to facilitate the gods' descent to earth or to ensure the ascent of the dead man's soul." This motif exists, he says, among, for example, tribes in the Indian Archipelago; the Dusun; some Malay tribes; the Mangar, a Nepalese tribe. The ancient Egyptians wrote in their funerary texts "the expression *asken pet* (asken = step) to show that the ladder furnished them by Ra is a real ladder." "A ladder (*klimax*) with seven rungs is documented in the Mithraic mysteries." It is a common cosmological symbol in "Oriental conceptions"; it stands for "the 'Center of the World' that is implicitly present in all ascents to heaven," for example, the ladder of Jacob; similarly, Mohammed saw "a ladder rising from the temple in Jerusalem." The ladder motif is documented in Christian mystical tradition, and in alchemical tradition. And, the "myth of ascent to the sky by a ladder is also known in Africa, Oceania, and North America."

He adds: "A volume would be required for an adequate exposition of these mythical motifs and their ritual implications. We will merely point out that the various roads are equally available to mythical heroes and to shamans (sorcerers, medicine men, etc.) and certain privileged persons among the dead." (Mircea Eliade, *Shamanism: Archaic Techniques of Ecstasy,* trans. Willard R. Trask [Princeton: Bollingen Series LXXVI, Princeton University Press, 1964], pp. 487 ff.)

What Are You Going to Be Like with Him?

8. *Hutłaanee:* The etymology of this Koyukon word is found in Kathleen Mautner, "The Role of Koyukon Athabaskan Women in Subsistence," in *Tracks in the Wildland,* Richard K. Nelson, Kathleen H. Mautner, G. Ray Bane (Fairbanks: Anthropology and Historic Preservation, Cooperative Park Studies Unit, University of Alaska, 1982), pp. 190–92.

Agliganaq: "Eskimo rules," comes from *aglinigaqtuni,* meaning "to menstruate"; it also means "to begin to grow full or big." N. J. Gubser, *Comparative Study of the Intellectual Culture of the Nunamiut Eskimos at Anaktuvuk Pass,* Alaska, 1961 (unpublished monograph), p. 220. Anaktuvuk Pass is the actual name of the village; it is inhabited by Nunamiut, who are caribou-eating Iñupiat.

9. I have listened to and read many Athabaskan traditional stories; but I was told only one story in which a man killed another man from his own village. In that story, which was in fact the record of an incident that happened within the last hundred years, a starving man killed his hunting partner for the tiny bit of dryfish the poor man carried. An old man told me that story, and he was horrified at the killing. He spoke of it in a hushed voice filled with grief, so that his listener would understand how terrible it was.

And yet, the old woman of the fierce eye was certain a murder had taken place recently in the village, and that it had been covered up. Under the old law, I surmise, the murderer would have been forced into exile, and his family would have gone with him rather than live with his shame. The people of Village Below were living between the old and the new laws; that indeterminate state often left them with a sense of confusion and dread.

F's story was a hero-tale, or a variation on a hero-tale. That the blind storyteller later gave me his own telling, similar to F's in certain details, yet a different story, told me that some older people were concerned that I learn at least part of their history accurately. As the outsider, I accepted his instruction, if with some confusion. Because of the blind man's standing in the village, I take his story as canonical; but I wonder if it is the complete story.

As for F's version, it was part of my life and education in his village. In the intensity of his telling, in the ring of his voice, I heard truth that may have been a different sort than the old man's.

10. The storyteller is no longer living. His story remains with his family, in the form he left it. Before I moved away, I returned the tape to him. I have edited the opening lines, which tell the name and specific location of the village.

11. According to Professor Burch, the existence of warfare must be accepted as it was reported by those who spoke with the authority of their people. Professor Burch's speech detailing his own methodological errors had not been given at the time I was in Village Below, and I, at least, had seen little monographic evidence that Native "informants" were, by the social scientists who consulted them, considered scholars of and reflexive commentators on their own cultures. More specifically (I witnessed instances of this; Burch recounts his own disbelief and mentions his colleagues'), Natives who were used as "informants" were usually not believed when they presented knowledge following their own classical or speculative conventions (see note 3, above).

According to Our Nature

12. This section, and the English versions of the stories, are taken from an unpublished manuscript written by me with the collaboration of Mr. Kalifornsky, called *From the First Beginning: When the Animals Were Talking.* The first part is composed of his stories, in English; the second part consists of our conversations about the stories, organized to complement the first part. A description of his theory and method of writing, and of my method of working out the English versions of his stories, occurs in "'Then Came the Time Crow Sang For Them': Some Ideas about Writing and Meaning in the Work of Peter Kalifornsky," in *New Voices in Native American Literary Criticism,* ed. Arnold Krupat (Washington, D.C.: Smithsonian Institution Press, 1993).

"Gambling Game" in my English version also appears as "Gambling Story (Dena'ina Indian)," in *Northern Tales,* selected and edited by Howard Norman (New York: Pantheon Books, 1990), and in *Alaska Quarterly Review,* vol. 4, nos. 3 + 4, 1986.

13. The eternal return of life in a new body, or reincarnation, as Mr. Kalifornsky called it, is an early Athabaskan belief and underlies their oldest stories; it is in tune with their literally conservative description of the world, in which every element had meaning. "In that Gambling Story," Mr. Kalifornsky said, "it's a human life cycle: live, die, come back. So, there's a combination along the line there."

The word *shaman* was the old man's, which he pronounced in the French manner and used to translate *el'egen;* the usual term, *medicine man,* is generally used among the tribes farther north from the Dena'ina, while *shaman* is used by the Yup'ik and Iñupiat. *El'egen* comes from words meaning "formlessness" ("play," and "giving form to"). As Mr. Kalifornsky described the *el'egen,* he had the power of transformation, and could send out his spirit to inhabit a familiar, usually an animal; he also had great facility in using his mind to transmit wishes (for good or ill) and thought.

In "Gambling Story," the one called Believer had no power of his own, but believed in the power that might be called, approximately, the great unknown power; a force that—uncharacteristically—has no image in Dena'ina. This may indicate its magnitude, and also, an acknowledgment of the complexity of the supernatural. It seems to me also to indicate that the Dena'ina classified the supernatural into a hierarchy, based on potency. The word for the great unknown power, *k'echel'tanen,* derives from the word for "speck of dust," a classic Dena'ina metonym, born (I infer) from fear and awe. (Mr. Kalifornsky distinguished it from the word *naq'eltani,* for "something powerful," and *nak'ech' eltani,* used for the Christian God, which he insisted came into use after the arrival of the Russian priests. The latter word means "the one above us who is like us"—that is, who has the same image as we do. Mr. Kalifornsky was quite sure the words are not related, and that they refer to distinct, separate powers. I observed that the word for "great unknown power" does not describe a being, or figure it, as is the usual way with Athabaskan naming words; rather, as if to underscore its awesome quality, it is referred to only by euphemism.)

When I was there, some Dena'ina still played the gambling game, *ch'in lahe.* It is similar to a game played by Native peoples of the Northwest coast; and is the province of canny old men, who still sing *di ya du hu,* the chant of the old Dena'ina, as they wager on their own acuity, against their opponent's. There are many gambling songs, according to Mr. Kalifornsky; when the players run out of songs, they sing *di ya du hu* (sung, dee yah doh hoh) to refresh themselves and gather strength for the arduous contest.

Athabaskan song makers have described how their songs begin in sound, the murmurings of emotion. They are lyrical in the first meaning of the word. Often, the refrain, the part of the song that gives the rhythm, is the repetition of syllables, of sounds, as *di ya du hu* is a refrain. Mr. Kalifornsky, who was himself given a great song in a dream, but did not call himself a songmaker, proposed how a Dena'ina thinker might link the syllables to actual words, to reveal an associative meaning: "It [*di ya du hu*] is used for the end of any song during potlatches. Everything needs to have some refrain or ending there. If they sing a love song, they finish it with *di ya du hu*, cheery and happy. They sing it and dance, to do away with bad things."

He suggested, experimentally, that the syllables *du hu* "related to *hunduh,* 'for nothing,'" a common way of speaking of anything useless, meaningless. And so, "This little song twists us around. It's built on 'for nothing,' but they're working for something."

On the basis of one of his earliest stories, I believe this chant—in its particular rhythm—is, or was, fundamental to Dena'ina identity; it was part of them, somewhat as, perhaps, the first four notes of Beethoven's Fifth Symphony are part of many Europeans.

Endurance

14. The stories of the Whale Hunter were told to me by Peter Kalifornsky. The stories, and his comments about them, are in *From the First Beginning, op. cit.*

15. Walter Burkert, *Greek Religion,* trans. John Raffan (Cambridge: Harvard University Press, 1985), pp. 174–75.

16. Judy Duhose, quoted in *Athabaskan News,* vol. 3, no. 3., October 1983.

17. Richard K. Nelson, *Make Prayers to the Raven: A Koyukon View of the Northern Forest* (Chicago: University of Chicago Press, 1983), pp. 30, 241.

18. The relation between *dnelnish* and the Dena'ina stories, particularly Crow Story, is discussed in Katherine McNamara, "'Then Came the Time Crow Sang For Them': Some Ideas about Writing and Meaning in the Work of Peter Kalifornsky," in *New Voices in Native American Literary Criticism, op. cit.*

19. Nelson, *Make Prayers,* p. 22.

Hungry, Holy

20. Prophesying, *seeing,* was not rare, but it was considered a difficult burden to bear. Peter Kalifornsky told me that, in modern times, anyone—an ordinary man or woman—could relieve a vision or a dream that foretold the future. The seer told his dream to the assembled men of power: the shaman, the man who read the sky, the dreamer, the doctor, the man whose word came true. These people discussed the dream or vision, to see if it matched known experience. The shaman tested it for the scent of another human, to see if it had been sent in ill-will. If the vision or dream matched nothing that was known at the time, the people stored it in their memory, said Mr. Kalifornsky, "just like putting it in a book."

The Dena'ina storyteller Shem Pete told of a prophecy that came true in part, but has not yet been completed. It is similar in certain respects to what 'Efrem's' mother told 'Tom Charles,' but—I emphasize—I don't say it is the same prophecy, or that it was made by the same person. Prophetic stories have been well known and widely discussed among Native people for several decades.

Shem Pete was born in Tsat'ukegh, or Susitna Station, on Cook Inlet, in about 1898; he passed away in the 1980s. The prophecy he told in this speech was recorded in a longer version in 1975, and is in the archive of the Alaska Native Language Center, University of Alaska, Fairbanks. Mr. Pete was said to be the last Dena'ina potlatch song leader. Simeon Chickalusion, who is mentioned below as the last traditional chief of Tyonek, was related to Peter Kalifornsky, on the latter's mother's side. Tyonek is on the west coast of Cook Inlet, at the foot of the Alaska Range.

Shem Pete said:

"I came from Susitna Station. That's where I born, and my father was a chief. He had a brother. He was a big medicine man in Susitna. There were a lot of people all over there. And he told them Susitna Station people, 'And pretty soon all you people gonna die and not even one going to be alive around here.' I never seen him. 'You people all gonna die,' he said. They pret' near clubbed him.

"They told him, 'We was over six hundred people here.' A lot of people. A lot of village. Out at Alexander Creek, and Susitna Station on the island there, I don't know how many hundred. And on the west side of the Susitna [River] another big village, about a mile long, just lined up the cabins. A lot of Indians still alive yet.

"He said, 'The way I look at it is I'm a medicine man, don't forget my word. Someday it may help you. I'm gonna be gone too. And pretty soon measles maybe gonna come. And this your skin gonna be stretched all over your body, see.' He don't know that was the measles. 'Your body gonna be crippled all over,' he said. 'Some of them gonna make them blind. Quite a few gonna die of that sickness, and after that pretty soon you people gonna hear about a fight down in the states someplace. And that sickness come from down south. And that gonna kill lots of people. You people used to walk around on the trail, are just gonna lie down and you people don't know how to die. You people gonna die though.' So now when the flu coming (1918) I see thirty-five people one week we lose. That was just the beginning.

"And he told them, those people, 'Don't eat too much white man grub. Use your own grub. Put up lots of fish. Put up meat. Pretty soon, I don't know, after the flu, I see the airplane, *grgrgrgrgr*, and I see the train, *whoooowhooo whoooo, whoowhoowhooooo*. I hear that too. On the ground, the bare ground got a wheel. Just like a boat go, go fast. Then thereafter a little while *whowhowhoooooo-whoowhooooo*.' He copy that. He hear that.

"'So that Susitna Station gonna be nothing left like it is today. You'll all be gone, not even one.' I didn't see him. They would say, *'Nononono.'* There was over six hundred people here. There were kids born, about fifteen, twenty kids born. 'How many we lose a year you think?' He said, 'Two, three.' Average is about three persons die each year. 'Yahyah, about fifteen, twenty kids. We just increasing right along. We can't die at all.' He told us, 'I see nothing left from that sickness come. You people just like burn the grass down. Gonna be killing all, everybody. Now remember, who got a little money gonna buy some matches, buy ammunition. Buy axe, buy file. Pretty soon something gonna be happen. Listen careful,' he said.

"'There gonna be white man gonna be just like this sand,' he picked it up in his hand, the sand. 'You fellows gonna be not living one place. Few here, few there, all over just scattered along like little berries between them white people. You all the native not gonna be staying one place. Be here, there, all over Alaska. So I think, what the white man gonna eat off? They can't live on the berries. They don't know how to hunt. It's gonna be tough for the white man. Listen to me. And all the white men they gonna see something happen. *Grgrgrgrgr* airplane gonna be just like mosquitoes. So they all gonna get into the airplane. They gonna pick it up and take them all back to the States.

"'And listen, put up lots of fish. And put the matches away. Put the ammunition away. Put up a file and an axe. You people, how many gonna be left here? Go up to Rainy Pass country.' He told them, 'Don't stay too long. Soon as the white man gone, you just take off and take a little fish. When you get there, lots of caribou, lots of game, lots of sheep. And you people go so far you can go. And after I go away, you people gonna live quite a long time. So listen to me, now you gonna see that Susitna gonna be not even one left,' he told them.

"Well, it's true. What now, not even one Indian left of all the young people in the Susitna. There's nothing. There's nobody left. So just few ones that were left, in the 1930s Chief Chickalusion of Tyonek picks us up, about dozen of us altogether. He put them in the dories and take 'em down to Tyonek. Now the young Susitna people increasing. Lots of Susitna Indians down in Tyonek. Tyonek Indians only about five or six left. Those Susitna Indians take it over now. Lots of Susitna people down in Tyonek."

Shem Pete ended by saying he hoped this story is true, that the white men will leave. He said he tells it to the young Natives who listen, so that they could hear the word. He doesn't want this story lost.

From *Exploration in Alaska: The Captain Cook Commemorative Lectures* (Anchorage: Cook Inlet Historical Society, 1980), pp. 196–97. I read this long after my stay in Village Below.

21. Richard Dauenhauer, *Riddle and Poetry Handbook,* Alaska Native Education Board, 1976. The book contains a fine bibliography, including Julius Jetté's "Riddles of the Ten'a Indians," *Anthropos* 8 (1913) 181–201; 630–651.

A Man's Life

22. From this definition, given by the census, Turner offered his interesting, complex explanation of American development from "the existence of an area of free land, its continuous recession, and the advance of American settlement westward...." His essay entitled "The Significance of the Frontier in American History" is worth re-reading. If one still finds much to agree with in his brilliant thesis, nonetheless, my own experience of the recurrence of "the American development" in its modern instance in Alaska, i.e.: a "return to primitive conditions[,]" was sobering. The essay was read, according to Ray Billington, at the World's Congress of Historians held in Chicago in 1893, in connection with the World's Columbian Exposition. It began:

"In a recent bulletin of the Superintendent of the Census for 1890 appear these significant words: 'Up to and including 1880 the country had a frontier of settlement, but at present the unsettled area has been so broken into isolated bodies of settlement that there can hardly be said to be a frontier line. In the discussion of its extent, its westward movement, etc., it can not, therefore, any longer have a place in the census reports.' This brief official statement marks the closing of a great historic movement. Up to our own day American history has been in a large degree the history of the colonization of the Great West. The existence of an area of free land, its continuous recession, and the advance of the American settlement westward, explain American development.

"Behind institutions, behind constitutional forms and modifications, lie the vital forces that call these organs into life and shape them to meet changing conditions. The peculiarity of American institutions is, the fact that they have been compelled to adapt themselves to the changes of an expanding people—to the changes involved in crossing a continent, in winning a wilderness, and in developing at each area of this progress out of the primitive economic and political conditions of the frontier into the complexity of city life."

He wrote, further: "The American development has exhibited not merely advance along a single line, *but return to primitive conditions on a continually advancing frontier line,* and a new development for that area. *American social development has been continually beginning over again on the frontier. This perennial rebirth, this fluidity of American life, this expansion westward with its new opportunities, its continuous touch with the simplicity of primitive society, furnish forces dominating the American character."*

(Frederick Jackson Turner, "The Significance of the Frontier in American History," *Frontier and Section: Selected Essays of Frederick Jackson Turner,* Intr. and notes, Ray Allen Billington [Englewood Cliffs, N.J.: Prentice-Hall, 1961], pp. 27, 38; emphasis added.)

What Are You Going to Be Like with Him?

23. Christine de Pizan, *The Book of the City of Ladies,* trans. Earl Jeffrey Richards; foreword, Marina Warner (New York: Persea Books, 1982), p. 256. See also Charity Cannon Willard, *Christine de Pizan: Her Life and Works* (New York: Persea Books, 1984), pp. 73 ff.

24. Barbara Bodenhorn, "'I'm not the great hunter; my wife is': Iñupiaq and anthropological models of gender," *Études/Inuit Studies* 14(1–2): 55–74, 1990. Bodenhorn's very interesting, reliable paper on relations between men and women in several Iñupiat villages on the North Slope does point out that male-female relations are gendered; that is, the woman's fullest role, and the basis of her authority, is as wife. The fact and idea of marriage are central to Iñupiat society and set the context for women's roles and positions.

25. Peter Kalifornsky explained the distinction. Murder, a horrifying act, was committed against one human, by another human. The act of hunting an animal, properly done, was more appropriately considered ceremonial, for it was believed that the hunter was guided, or hindered, not merely by his skill, but also by Luck, or the watching and intervention of animal spirits. Accordingly, the animal he sought gave, or withheld, itself, following an elaborate cycle of right behavior and belief in which man and prey were complementary actors.

The Gift

26. The sources of the etymologies are given in note 8, above. The anthropologist Kathleen Mautner, who was taught Koyukon beliefs by "Mrs. Reliance" and other women of her village, wrote:

"The ... more important types of taboos [*hutłaanees*] relate to the power women have to bring good or back luck in subsistence [i.e., hunting-KM] activities. Some of these taboos concern the direct effect of women on men, but most of them are followed to show respect for the animals with which women interact in their environment. Women can cause bad hunting luck by merely stepping over a man's feet or, more seriously, by not treating animals correctly.

"The Koyukon believe that all animals have spirits and that these must be treated respectfully....

"The reason that women possess a special power to bring good or bad hunting luck is that from the onset of puberty through menopause they are menstruating, and it is believed that the menses has its own powerful spirit. Because of this attribute, women can feminize men and cause them bad hunting luck....

"It is believed that the menses (*hutłaa*) has its own spirit that contains the essence of femininity. Thus, the woman at this time is easily prone to the bad luck that can be caused when animal spirits are not treated correctly....

"There were also some traditional practices which indicate that the *hutłaa* (menstrual matter) could bring good luck. It contained a special power against evil spirits because it represented the life-giving, procreative force. Women saved menstrual rags and used them as a remedy to prevent disease in children. Mothers who had lost several children would make harnesses of menstrual drawers for their other children to protect them from sickness and death."

(Kathleen Mautner, "The Role of Koyukon Athabaskan Women in Subsistence," in *Tracks in the Wildland*, Richard K. Nelson, et al., *op. cit.*, pp. 190–92.)

Mautner described various behaviors proscribed to women in relation to different animals, according to their various spiritual powers. About wolverine, she wrote:

"Traditionally, when a man caught a wolverine in his trap, a ceremony was held in the village. The animal was dressed up and placed on the floor and a potlatch was held in its honor. Only old women could attend but they could not eat any food. If a young woman attended, the wolverine spirit would bring bad trapping luck, sickness, or death to her family. Although this ceremony is no longer held today, the trapper still presents the wolverine with a gift of fat and good food; he then burns its carcass out in the woods with more food.

"Women should not trap or skin a wolverine. They must not say its name *niltseel* but must refer to it as *tlonyee* or *hubaaghayee*, both of which mean 'clothing trim.' Violators will have mean children and will cause bad trapping luck." (Mautner, *op. cit.*, pp. 194–95.)

Mautner (somewhat reluctantly, I think) followed the traditional anthropological view of taboo as negative, with its hint of the traditional epithets "dirty," or "unclean." Certainly, she described these beliefs and practices chiefly in relation to the men's hunt. Malfa's view was not this sort of "negative," however. She (and later, Mrs. Reliance) gave me no sense that *hutɬaa*, the menstrual matter, was in any way a weakness or uncleanness. They were joyous about it: it was about giving life. They knew it as a woman's time of strength and true power. They were quite clear that the woman's power could not be altered or diminished, only managed by behavior. Both women talked at some length about how they had hunted for food, particularly during those times when their husbands held seasonal wage jobs and could not hunt. Mrs. Reliance said that she had been "raised like a man." She enjoyed hunting; Malfa did not.

Ann Fienup-Riordan does not trace the etymology in Yup'ik; but she describes concisely the necessity of proper behavior on the part of a menstruating girl: "If a girl observes the taboos she can actually draw the game animals, while if she breaks them she is dangerous to both herself and the hunter. A girl must never come face to face with a hunter or he will 'get her bad air.' In the spring when it is the time of the seals, the menstruating girls are said to have the boats behind them. As a wife, if she looks up or goes outside while her husband is off hunting, she will see him as an animal or dead man, and he will not return. Where he is at the moment of her transgression determines where he will be forever after. Taboo breach by a woman collapses the distinction between the world of seals and the world of men, just as appropriate action on her part can maintain it." (Ann Fienup-Riordan, *The Nelson Island Eskimo: Social Structure and Ritual Distribution* [Anchorage: Alaska Pacific University Press, 1983], p. 216.)

27. Quoted in Lewis Hanke, *All Mankind Is One: A Study of the Disputation Between Bartolomé de las Casas and Juan Ginés de Sepúlveda in 1550 on the Intellectual and Religious Capacity of the Indians* (DeKalb: Northern Illinois University Press, 1974), p. 82, emphasis added. It is well to remember that it became necessary to make it illegal for Spanish occupiers of the Indies and South America to call Indians "dogs."

See also the Introduction by Anthony Pagden to Bartolomé de las Casas, *A Short Account of the Destruction of the Indies*, ed. and trans. Nigel Griffin (London & New York: Penguin Books, 1992). See also *The Tears of the Indians: Being An Historical and true Account of the Cruel Massacres by the Spaniards in the Islands of the West Indies, Mexico, Peru, Etc., An Eyewitness Account written by Bartolomé de las Casas*, translated into English by John Phillips and published in London in 1656; Introduction by Colin Steele (New York: Oriole Editions, 19 W. 44th Street, NY 10036, 1972). John Phillips, writer and translator, was a nephew of John Milton, the poet, and served in the government of Cromwell. His translation usefully stirred up anti-Spanish feelings, in favor of the Lord Protector's policies, particularly in regard to Ireland.

28. Nelson, *op cit.*, note 17, above.

29. The actual paper turned (as did the paper in the dream) upon a story written by Peter Kalifornsky. I went to visit Mr. Kalifornsky because of the following story, which I first read in an uninspired translation. Nonetheless, the story caught my attention: not only because it was turned on a primal theme that would naturally appeal to a poet—the myth of the origin of stories; the implication of rhythm and song in human life—but also because of the lovely way the complexity of the relations between humans and animals were told. Every creature had its part in the round of life. I asked Mr. Kalifornsky if I read this correctly. "Yes," he replied, with enthusiasm, "there is a compact between humans and animals." Because of my question about the meaning behind this story, he invited me to come back and work with him. What follows is my version, approved by him, of his interlinear translation.

Crow Story

Long ago the Dena'ina did not have songs and stories. Then came the time that Crow sang for them. Till then, as they worked together and traveled, *di ya du hu* kept them in time.

And so, Crow was flying along the beach. Where a creek flowed out lay an old, rotten fish. Crow looked up the bank and spotted a village. He turned into a good-looking man and went to visit the people.

Only women were at home. "Where are the men?" he asked. "They're in the woods, hunting," the women said. "Have a bite to eat with us," they said.

"I never eat with strangers," he told them (he lived on fish washed up on the beach). He asked for the loan of a dipnet, and back down to the creek he went.

A cottonwood driftlog lay on the beach. He plucked an eye from his head and set it on the log. "If you see people, shout *Yu hu!*" he told it, and tied a bandage around his head. He went down to his fish and began to eat.

The eye called, "Yu hu."

He ran to it. No one was there. He smacked the eye and set it back down. "If you see anyone, shout *Yu hu!*" he told it.

Once again, no one was there.

A third time the eye called, *"Yu hu!"* But Crow stayed with the fish.

But soon he heard people talking. He walked up to meet them.

"What are you doing?" they asked him.

"Fishing. But no fish here. Only only old ones lying around—some bird picked at them."

"What hurt your head?"

"Sand in my eye."

"Let's see," one of them said. "It might be bad."

"Oh no!" he said. "When I'm hurt I heal it myself."

They spotted the eye lying on the driftlog. "Ah. That looks like an eye," they said.

"No! Don't touch it! You'll do something wrong. It looks out for your good luck," he said. "I know what to do," he told them.

He picked up the eye. He tossed it into the air three times. Three times he sang:

"We found a wonder!

Ch'i'ushi chi'i'un!
Ch'i'ushi chi'i'un!
Ch'i'ushi chi'i'un!"
He pulled the bandage from his head. The eye dropped back into its socket.
And again he sang:
"Ya la ya la ah hi ah hi hi yu!"
Now he turned back into Crow. Three times he crowed, *"Gyugh!"*
And he flew away.

○

THEN *di ya du hu* became a song, with the Crow songs, and they sang them and danced to do away with bad things.

Then they sent a runner to the next village, to tell the neighbors what they had learned.

Now the neighbors were on the trail, coming to visit and celebrate the songs. It grew dark, and they wanted to camp. The runner, cutting wood, began to say, "Lend me an axe." His words became a song.

"Du gu li
Sh ghu ni hish
Y ha li
Yli ma che ha
A ya ha a li
Lend me an axe.
It will be fine!
We will have fire!
We will have game!"

Now they had four songs.

The young runner had worn through his moccasin. An old woman, always prepared for emergencies, took a piece of skin and cut it. She poked holes along its edge and threaded a skin thong through them. He stepped onto the skin, and she tied the thong around his ankle. After the Dena'inas had their new song, he had a new moccasin.

The people built a fire and had a celebration. They talked about this Crow and sang his song. Crow turned himself into a handsome young man and came to visit them, but did not speak.

"He doesn't speak our language," they said. "Welcome him anyhow."

He listened to their stories about clever, foolish Crow; then, when they weren't looking, he slipped away.

"He's gone!" they said.

Sometime later, Crow visited his friend Camprobber and told him the story. "I went to visit the Campfire People," he said. "They tell stories about me, full of jokes and good times. When they go hunting I wish them good luck. Then they make a kill, and all of us Crows have a good dinner party!"

(From Katherine McNamara, "'Then Came the Time Crow Sang For Them': Some Ideas about Writing and Meaning in the Work of Peter Kalifornsky," *op. cit.*; and *From the First Beginning*, vol. I [unpublished ms.].)

Acknowledgments

A GREAT MANY people helped me with this book, offering friendship, instruction, advice, knowledge, encouragement, and love. Many of them read it critically, whole or in part; all of them surely kept me relatively sane during the years of writing and the years afterward. In Alaska: my dear Martha Demientieff, Ann Fienup-Riordan, the late Dena'ina writer Peter Kalifornsky, and the old, good friend who prefers to be unnamed. Elsewhere: the late, deeply missed Gila Bercovitch, Cornelia Bessie, Barbara Bodenhorn, Patricia Bulitt, Kathy Callaway, Benjamin Cheever, Susan Garrett, Edith Grossman, Linda Hogan, Barry Lopez, Jack Miles, Fae Myenne Ng, Reynolds Price, Thomas Pynchon, the late Mary TallMountain, Abigail Thomas, Anne Twitty. My gratitude is unending.

The work is dedicated to the memory of Lee Goerner, editor and publisher, who was my husband.

Katherine McNamara
New York, 1988–Charlottesville, 2000